THE
BURNT
BOOK

THE BURNT BOOK

Reading the Talmud

Marc-Alain
Ouaknin

Translated by
Llewellyn Brown

PRINCETON UNIVERSITY PRESS

PRINCETON, NEW JERSEY

First published in France as *Le Livre brûlé: Lire le Talmud*
copyright © LIEU COMMUN, 1986
Translation © Marc-Alain Ouaknin and the ALEPH Center in Paris
Published 1995 by Princeton University Press, 41 William Street,
Princeton, New Jersey 08540
In the United Kingdom: Princeton University Press, Chichester,
West Sussex
All Rights Reserved

Library of Congress Cataloging-in-Publication Data

Ouaknin, Marc-Alain.
[Livre brûlé.   English]
The burnt book : reading the Talmud / Marc-Alain Ouaknin :
translated from the French by Llewellyn Brown.
p.   cm.
Includes bibliographical references and index.
ISBN 0-691-03729-9
1. Talmud—Commentaries.   2. Naḥman, of Bratslav, 1772-1811.
3. Talmud—Hermeneutics.   I. Title.
BM504.O92   1995
296.1'206—dc20   94-39674   CIP

This publication was made possible in part by a grant from the
ALEPH Center in Paris

This book has been composed in Sabon Typeface

Princeton University Press books are printed
on acid-free paper and meet the guidelines
for permanence and durability of the Committee
on Production Guidelines for Book Longevity
of the Council on Library Resources

Printed in the United States of America

10 9 8 7 6 5 4 3 2 1

To my mother
To my father, my master
the great rabbi Jacques Ouaknin

For Dory,
Gaddiël-Yonathan,
Sivane-Mikhal,
Shamgar-Maor
Nin-Gal Néta Shlomtsion

To Sarah, David, and Richard Cohen,
who gave this project wings so that it might cross the Atlantic

It is forbidden to be old.
     RABBI NAHMAN OF BRATSLAV

May never the voice of the child
In him be silent, may it fall
Like a gift from heaven giving to
Parched words the burst of its
Laughter, the salt of its tears, its all-
Powerful savagery.
     LOUIS-RENÉ DES FORÊTS, *Ostinato*

Once again it is the enigma, the enigma of strangeness, of childhood—childhood that knows more because no answer satisfies it, uttering aloud—the ravishing voice, ravished to the silence that ever restrains itself there—the *non serviam*, the glorious refusal in the acquiescence of extreme distress.

Being unwilling, unable to conclude, I hand over, for the moment, to a Hasidic master (who always refused to be a Master), Rabbi Nahman of Bratslav.

"*It is forbidden to be old!*"

What we can discern at first: forbidden to renounce renewing oneself, to be satisfied with an answer that would no longer challenge the question—finally (but it is endless) writing only to efface the written or, more exactly, writing it through its very effacing, maintaining exhaustion and inexhaustible together: the disappearance that never wearies.

Thus, he came to write the secret Book only to burn it, becoming famous as the author of the "Burnt Book."

     MAURICE BLANCHOT, extract from "Anacrouse," a fragment of *Une Voix venue d'ailleurs* (Dijon: Ulysse, Fin de Siècle), 1992

Contents

"THE GOOD LORD did not create religion; he created the world."

For Franz Rosenzweig,[1] this sentence means that religion is not some separate reality, superimposed on our everyday world. Quite the contrary, it means that the primary essence of religion is in our very way of being, which amounts to saying: God created religion. In this sense, the term "religion" is "noble"; it has nothing in common with the unctuous, mystic, pious, homiletic, "clerical" meaning of the term.

And yet this sentence provides the epigraph for the thought expounded in this book, restoring its banal and everyday meaning to the word "religion." Thus the statement "The good Lord did not create religion; he created the world" is the starting point we have chosen for a critique of religion.

It is a critique, not only of religion, but also of politics. Politics, in the sense of the established power assuming the right to perpetrate acts of violence, whatever they may be, and justifying this violence by means of the Law that, even if it is civil, is merely another image of religious phenomena. This critique seeks not to eliminate but to reduce the political; it is a matter of reducing the state to a minimum, of limiting politics to make room for another, nonviolent discourse.

Some may object that it is only too easy to criticize politics and religion if they are already endowed with negative (or, rather, pejorative) meanings or connotations. These meanings, however, are part of their essential properties! One has only to look around oneself and consider the rise of political and religious fanaticism that perpetrates violence and takes control—by means of this violence—in the very heart of democratic countries.

Yet this is not a textbook of political science, giving a series of examples of negative situations that could then be taken apart, analyzed, and criticized. This has already been done[2] and will be again.

Our purpose is rather more limited, more specialized and indirect: this book deals with Judaism and the Talmud. To understand what follows, it is important to understand the project involved; the same book, exactly the same, with another project would be a different book.

Why *The Burnt Book*?

The subtitle indicates that it is to do with the Talmud. But let us try to avoid such ready-made reactions!

This "Burnt Book" is not the history of the various measures aimed

at petrifying Jewish tradition; the latter are a product of ordinary political violence and reveal the usual methods of repression. So it is nothing
to do with the fact that the Talmud, after a court case lasting two years,
was confiscated and, on 6 June 1242, twenty-four cartloads of Talmudic manuscripts were burnt in Paris at Place de la Grève, now Place
de l'Hôtel de Ville. That was under the reign of Saint Louis! It is nothing to do, either, with the fact that all copies of the Talmud were confiscated by Inquisitorial decree and burnt in Rome, on 9 September 1553
. . . Nothing to do, either, with 21 March 1564 when Pope Pius V
went back on the various interdicts of his predecessors, adding that the
Talmud could be used if the word *Talmud* was not written in full on
any of the copies . . . Nothing to do either with . . .

No, this is not another version of the *Vale of Tears*.[3]

First of all, the "Burnt Book" is the title of the book by Rabbi Nahman
of Bratslav, a Hasidic Master of the late eighteenth century who decided, one winter day in the year 1808, to burn one of his books, which
he later named the "Burnt Book." Of this book, only the title remains
and the tradition that tells us of the necessity of burning holy books . . .
This constitutes the third part of this book.

The "Burnt Book" is also the setting used in the sixteenth chapter of the
Shabbat tractate for the following question: "What is a book?" The
Talmud imagines a fire that breaks out on *Shabbat* (the seventh day of
the week), a holy day during which no one is allowed to light or even
extinguish a fire. What should be done about the books? They are burning, we must save them . . . To what extent is a book deemed worthy of
being saved? Strange questions that the Talmud takes seriously. This is
a part of the first "Opening" of the *second book*, entitled: "What Is a
Book?"

The "Burnt Book" is also a reflection on the "Text" that, in the *Yoma*
tractate 54a, appears in the form of a veil that both masks and reveals
meanings, faces and bodies, words and letters, a twinkling world, "visible and invisible": that is the second "Opening" of the *second book*.

Finally, the "Burnt Book" is our rereading of the history of the Talmud, of Talmudic interpretation, where we try to show that the "book"
(which is not a book) comes into being through its withdrawal, through
its effacing, its burning, which, simultaneously, it "signifies"; that is the
first book of this work, which is both a history of the texts and an
introduction, based on the internal thinking of the Talmud. We have
tried to respect, in the first part, a style and a sensitivity that, since they
remain very close to the texts, may seem to display a certain degree of

naïveté (but only in appearance; perhaps "naïveté" is just another word for "faithfulness"?); we shall be setting out the historical and methodological background, with the intention of illustrating a certain way of viewing the listening to the Talmudic texts, as we explain them.

The three parts of this book can be described as follows:

    1. Historical and methodological references
    2. Talmudic openings
    3. The "Burnt Book": an aspect of the thinking of Rabbi Nahman of Bratslav

That gives us the structure of the book and the themes studied. Let us try now to define as precisely as possible the questioning set out here or, if one prefers, the specific project we evoked above.

Here are two propositions:

    1. "The central question of Judaism is that of interpretation, and the Talmud is situated at the intersection of conflicting interpretations."
    2. "In every society, it is a text (Law or Revelation, *nomos* or *Torah*), a spoken and written code of communication between men (and the divinity) that is at the origin of the space of the city and of consciousness. The text founds society by providing a form of mediation between men. It forms both its intimate texture and its surrounding environment."[4]

The question that this book will be discussing issues from the confrontation of these two propositions and the attempt to combine them.

Given the founding role of the text, what is the place of the individual and of subjectivity within the textual society?

But is not the organization of society—politics—founded on the Law of the text, simply "the annihilation of the subject, where a ready-made discourse—propaganda, whatever it may be—takes the place of the subject, transforming subjectivity into a prefabricated subjectivity,"[5] and therefore an illusion?

Is not the human being, who, according to Jewish tradition, draws all his ontological dignity from the ability to speak, reduced to a "*spoken being*" by the dogmatic discourse of institutions?

These questions are possible only within a certain worldview, from a precise standpoint involving the anthropological and philosophical definitions of man. Faced with the question "What is man?" the Talmudic Masters reply that he is a "what?" a "what is it?" It is an enigmatic answer that one must not hasten to understand, for fear of destroying its effect. We could say that the Talmudic Masters develop a philosophy of the subject where the personality of each person is at the center of their reflection. Each person must try to bring out what is unique in himself, in which he himself is the bearer of a question, his own, which makes of him a specific and differentiated "what is it?"

In that respect, the Talmudic Masters are heirs of the prophetic revolution that took place at the time of Jeremiah: the change of attitude, which occurred in the sixth century B.C.E. and which consisted in a shift from the collective to the singular. Whereas the "classical prophets had, above all, insisted on the salvation of the people, as such, and on its collective identity, with Jeremiah there was a deepening of the personal and human aspects, and emphasizing of these aspects within the social and natural order."[6] This deepening was not the invention of selfishness but the understanding of man as a separate and unique being. This separation was not the negation of society founded on relationships. On the contrary, it was its very possibility. In this philosophical context, the text of the Law was to play a double role; on the one hand, it was to make social existence and intersubjective relationships possible and, on the other hand, to prepare for the emergence of the individual as a specific being on the basis of interpretation.

Here are two contradictory and apparently irreconcilable demands: a single law for both members of the relationship and their diverging—or opposite—interpretations of this same law. We do not claim to have solved this problem; we hope, however, to have succeeded in defining it more closely, in exploring its implications, its epistemological and metaphysical premises. In the process, several fundamental notions are treated: time, history, truth . . . Suffice it to say that we have tried to clear the way . . .

The Burnt Book takes the form of a defense of subjectivity founded on the ability to restore a "speaking word," in spite of the existence of texts, politics, and religion.

We have attempted to enumerate and explain the means that make the transition from the "Book" to speech possible. In this Preface, we are obliged to retract the first sentence of our book as it may lead to some confusion; we wrote, "In the beginning was the Book." The Book is, of course, at the beginning; but only at the beginning . . . After the beginning, there is the work of deconstructing the book, the movement from the Written to the Oral Law . . .

The history of the Book is the history of its effacing, and man is "condemned" to interpret. And the Jewish people is not the people of the Book!

It is a special effacing that is not necessarily the effacing of the text since—paradoxically—it takes place through the adding of the spoken word, of additional texts. We may say that there is effacing of the control of the discourse, of the violence perpetrated by the discourse. This effacing is not silent, since words are required to silence the discourse.

And perhaps it is a matter of many other things as well . . . It most certainly is. This book should then be read as an introduction to the Talmud where we answer the simple question "What is the Talmud?" It is an oft-quoted but rarely read and understood text. A historical and methodological introduction is followed by two examples, two Talmudic texts that we have presented in Hebrew with a translation and commentary. These two "openings" are not to be read but to be worked on, studied, meditated, put aside, taken up again and again . . . In other words, the reader must try out his own interpretations, his own reflections, before forging ahead in the maze of our particular interpretations.

After this introduction and these examples, a journey will lead us to the thought of an original Master who left us the enigma of the "Burnt Book."

Apart from the Talmudic Masters, we have made references to several other writers in this book—often contemporaries.

Is it really necessary to go into a debate on interpretation? Did the authors referred to really have the intentions we ascribe to them? Who can tell?

The only criterion for judging an interpretation is its richness, its fruitfulness. Anything that gives matter for thought honors the person who proffers it . . .

Notes

1. Quoted by Emmanuel Lévinas in *Difficile liberté* (Paris: Albin Michel, 1976), p. 242.

2. Cf., among others, Régis Debray, *Critique de la raison politique* (Paris: Gallimard, 1981); Bernard-Henri Lévy, *Le Testament de Dieu* (Paris: Grasset, 1979).

3. *La Vallée des pleurs (Emek Habakha)*, a history of the sufferings of Israel, by Joseph Hacohen (Avignon, 1557); French translation by Julien Sée (Paris, 1881).

4. Shmuel Trigano, *La Demeure oubliée* (Paris: Lieu Commun, 1984), p. 363.

5. Pierre Legendre, *L'Inestimable objet de la transmission* (Paris: Fayard, 1985).

6. Armand Abécassis, "Le *Midrash* entre le *mythos* et le *logos*," *Les Études philosophiques*, no. 2 (1984): 198.

Acknowledgments ───────────────────

A BOOK is an adventure in which numerous persons participate who, by their presence and their readiness to listen, by their questions, objections, and encouragements, make the work of thinking and writing possible.

The research for this book, undertaken in the context of the ALEPH Center, a center for Jewish research and study, has been presented and deepened in the form of various lectures, talks, conferences, and workshops . . .

May all those who have welcomed these meditations in their faltering beginnings with understanding and friendship find here the expression of my appreciation and my gratefulness . . . And first of all, my father, my master, the great rabbi Jacques Ouaknin, for his precious teachings, and my mother Éliane-Sophie, for her ever-invigorating encouragements.

This work owes a great deal to the frequenting of the texts of contemporary philosophers and writers, all of whom are cited in the notes and bibliography. It owes even more to the remarks and criticisms of those who received me with kindness and understanding and who read a part or the whole of the manuscript: A. Abécassis, A. Derczanski, E. Jabès, P. Kaufmann, E. Lévinas, C. Malamoud.

I could not conclude without expressing my indebtedness to all my masters who have taught me and communicated their passion for the Talmud, in particular Rav Itshaq Weil, Rav Meïr Wreschner, Rav M. Gabbay, Rabbi Rahamim Monsonégo, Rav A. Gurvich, Rav Chajkin, and Rabbi Gilles Bernheim.

I particularly wish to thank Michèle and Claude Kaminsky, directors of the Cours Spinoza, as well as Monique and Gérard Sander who, year after year, through both their talents and their warm and generous friendship, have created and provided a venue for these researches and teachings.

May all those who have succeeded in conferring on study a familial and friendly character by warmly welcoming classes and conferences find here the expression of my most cordial thanks: Maurice and Danièle Biderman, Claude Bochurberg, Thérèse and Michel Edel, Arlette and Jacques Garih, Mary and Lazare Kaplan, Chantal and Léo Zauberman, Noëlle and Georges Meyer, Roland Meyer, Jeanne and Aldo Naouri, Nicole and Sydney Ohana, Sylvie and Georges Pragier, Simone and David Susskind (CCLJ) and Pérèle Wilgowicz, Liza and Robi Lifchitz, Sabine Mamou and Julio Maruri.

And may all those who, throughout these last years, have made this research possible by their affection and generosity find in these lines the expression of my friendship and gratitude: my friends Mimi and Max Benhamou, Mrs. Odette Chertok, Mr. and Mrs. Dana, Claudie and Raymond Danziger, Arlette and Jacques Garih, Simone Harari, Max, David and Bernard Jessner, Bernard Touret, Murielle, Rysia and Jacques Zehmour, Alain Ziegler.

A book is also a team, people who share the same passion. Thanks to all my publishers for their ever-considerate and smiling reception that has enabled this book to be realized.

Special thanks are due to Sarah, Richard, and David Cohen of Britt International Publications, whose dedication and enthusiasm have enabled this book to appear in English.

Thanks also to Llewellyn Brown who has succeeded in rendering, in this other language, the full scope of the first text.

This book would never have existed without the warm and kindly enthusiasm of Jean-Luc Allouche, who gave me this extraordinary chance to enter into the world of writing.

Last, but certainly not least, my especial thanks go to Sylvia Metz who, year after year, ever cheerful and patient, has constantly striven so that this book might take on new forms. May she find here the expression of my deepest gratitude for her generosity and devotion.

BOOK ONE

Talmudic Landmarks

IN THE BEGINNING was the Book . . . The Book preceding all books: the Revelation preceding all revelations. Israel is the people of the Book, because "if there is a world where, seeking truth and guidelines for life, what one encounters is not the world but a book, the mystery and the commandment of a book, it is in Judaism that, at the beginning of everything, the power of the word and exegesis is asserted, where everything starts with a text and comes back to it, a unique book, in which unfolds a prodigious series of books, not only a universal library but something even vaster and more enigmatic that replaces the universe."[1]

"The Volume of the Book as living space!"[2] declares Lévinas. The library: we shall be coming back to it again and again. It is not a question of a library that, situated afterward—after the book—may, but not necessarily, refer to other texts, other authors, as this is often a deceptive, apparently demonstrative reference that aims to be objective, to confirm speech or knowledge.

Revelation and the Book are two totally contemporaneous terms. Revelation begins with the Book. The Book is Revelation. To enter the Book in the way one enters History that is in the process of being written is to hear Speech as it is being revealed—right here and now.

In the chapters that follow, several fundamental landmarks are provided which give us entry into the books of the library.

Notes

1. Maurice Blanchot, *L'Entretien infini* (Paris: Gallimard, 1969), p. 575.
2. Emmanuel Lévinas, *L'Au-delà du verset* (Paris: Éditions de Minuit, 1982), p. 159.

I

Revelation and Transmission

God has spoken once; twice have I heard this.
  Ps. 62:12.

Written Law, Oral Law

The event of Revelation is the gift of the Torah: *Matane Torah*. But the Torah is plural.

> "These are the *Torot* that YHVH made between him and the children of Israel in Mount Sinai by the hand of Moses" (Lev. 26:46). The *Sifra* comments this verse as follows: "Why is *Torot* in the plural and not in the singular? To teach us that two *Torahs* were given to Israel: one written and the other oral."[1]

This point is crucial: Judaism—a "biblical" religion—does not have only one canonical book. Besides the *Tanakh* (the Hebrew part of the Bible, the "First Testament") there is also another book: the Talmud. Only the Bible read in the light of the Talmud can guide the reader in a Jewish reading of Scripture.

The Written Law: The *Tanakh*

The Written Law, or *Torah shebikhtav*, is what is commonly known as the Bible. The Bible is a key word, so we must decide what we mean by this term.

Originally, the word Bible is plural. The Greek expression it comes from, *ta biblia*, means "the books." The Bible takes the form of a collection of works whose content differs according to the various traditions. People speak of a Jewish Bible, a Catholic or Protestant Bible. The shortest Bible is the Jewish one, and it was only after very lively debates that the Jewish canon was established, somewhere around the second century c.e.[2]

The Jewish Bible is divided into three main parts:

—The five books of Moses, or the Pentateuch, in English; the *Humash*, in Hebrew[3]

—The prophets; in Hebrew: *Neviim*[4]
—The Hagiographa,[5] or Writings; in Hebrew: *Ketuvim*

It is interesting to note that the word "Bible" has no equivalent in Hebrew: we use the word *Tanakh*, made up from the initials of the words *Torah, Neviim, Ketuvim* (TaNaKh).
So, the Written Law is the *Tanakh*.

The Torah is made up of:

—Genesis: *Bereshit* (The beginning)
—Exodus: *Shemot* (Names)
—Leviticus: *Vayikra* (He called)
—Numbers: *Bamidbar* (In the desert)
—Deuteronomy: *Devarim* (The words)

(The Hebrew names of the five books correspond to the first words of the first verse of each book.)

The *Neviim* consist of:

(*The first prophets.*)
—Joshua: *Yehoshua*
—Judges: *Shoftim*
—Samuel: *Shmuel* (two books)
—Kings: *Melakhim* (two books)

(*The three major prophets.*)
—Isaiah: *Yeshayahu*
—Jeremiah: *Yirmeyahu*
—Ezechiel: *Yeheskiel*

(*The twelve "minor" prophets.*)
—Hosea: *Hoshea*
—Joel: *Yoel*
—Amos: *Amos*
—Obadiah: *Ovadiah*
—Jonah: *Yonah*
—Micah: *Mikhah*
—Nahum: *Nahum*
—Habakkuk: *Habakuk*
—Zephaniah: *Tsephaniah*
—Haggai: *Hagay*
—Zechariah: *Zehkariah*
—Malachi: *Malakhi*

The *Ketuvim* include:

—Psalms: *Tehilim*
—Proverbs: *Mishlei*
—Job: *Yov*

(*The Five Scrolls.*)
—The Song of Solomon: *Shir Hashirim*
—Ruth: *Rut*
—Lamentations: *Eikhah*
—Ecclesiastes: *Kohelet*
—Esther: *Esther*

—Daniel: *Daniel*
—Ezra: *Ezra*
—Nehemiah: *Nehemiah*
—Chronicles (two books): *Divrei hayamim*

The total number of books is thirty-six. However, tradition counts only twenty-four books. The twelve "minor" prophets (the *Tre-assar*) are considered as a single book divided into twelve parts. In Hebrew, twenty-four is called *Kad*, a mnemonic meaning "jug."

The Hebrew Bible closes with the return from exile in Babylon in 516 B.C.E. (after the first destruction of the Temple in 586 B.C.E. and the seventy-year exile in Babylon).

The Oral Law

We need not go into all the historical details of Tradition; our task is to understand how the men of this Tradition viewed their own history. Therefore, we will not be giving a description of the history of the Tradition but the tradition of the history of the Tradition. The references we shall be using are taken from within this tradition: Talmudic, Midrashic, and rabbinical references.

It may be useful, at this point, to insist on the contemporaneous nature of the Written and the Oral Laws.

We can read in the *Midrash*:

Rabbi Joshua Ben Korha said: "Moses stayed forty days on the mount. During the day he read the written text (*mikra*) and, during the night, he studied the oral commentary (*mishnah*). . . . Moses stayed forty days on the mount, seated before the Lord, bless his name, as a disciple is seated before his master. He read the Written Law during the day and the Oral Law during the night . . . ."

Ben Betera said: "Moses stayed forty days on the mount. He interpreted (*doresh*) the words of the Torah and examined its letters."[6]

The two Laws are contemporaneous . . . And yet, for many authors, there is something paradoxical about the chronological order of these two *Torot*:

> Here is one of the paradoxes of Judaism: the oral Torah, the interpretation of the written Torah, is older than the latter! At the moment of the Revelation, the oral Torah was virtually included in the written Torah; by means of logical deductions, man can reconstitute it in its original structure. . . . The seniority of the oral Torah is indicated by signs, evidences in the written Torah. . . . The oral Torah recounts that certain *mitzvot* (commandments) were observed by the Hebrews before being formulated in the written Torah. The patriarchs observed the instructions of the Torah before they were even given on Sinai. In the midst of Egyptian slavery, the Hebrews had already observed the *Shabbat*, studied and fulfilled the teachings of the Torah (cf. *Yoma*, 28b).[7]

As a matter of fact, the Oral Law, written prior to the Revelation, is different from the actual Oral Law given to Moses, in that the latter was rewritten in order to be passed on. Rewriting in view of a faultless and specific transmission: the writing and wording is also Revelation. What is the Oral Law? Why must the text be passed on at the same time as the commentaries? Is it not understandable as it is?

The aims of the *Torah she-be-al Peh*[8] were originally set out in five categories:

1. phonetics
2. spelling
3. syntax
4. method
5. semantics

1. *Since Hebrew is a consonantal language*, no vowel that would provide for a more precise reading should appear. Any given word should lend itself to several different interpretations, according to the way it can be pronounced, and it should take on a different meaning each time. The first commentary takes place as one reads: how are these words to be pronounced?

2. *Hebrew has no vowels*, and yet five consonants assist in reading (*matres lectionis*). They may be present ("complete") or absent (The word is "defective"). Oral tradition has the duty to pass on these essential details.

3. *Moreover, the biblical text has no punctuation*: no commas or periods. Where does a sentence begin and end? That too must be explained, passed on, and used to aid memorization. In the same way, the layout obeys strict rules, the knowledge of which must be passed on by the oral tradition.

4. "Rabbi Abbahu said: Could then Moses have learned the whole Torah? Of the Torah it says: *The measure thereof is longer than the earth, and broader than the sea* (Job 11:9); could then Moses have learned it all in forty days? No; but it was only the principles (*Klalim*) thereof that God taught Moses."[9]

According to this text, the keys or rules of interpretation were given to Moses on Mount Sinai, then handed down by the Oral Law from generation to generation, without interruption, until they came to the Sages of the Talmud. These rules were codified, at the time of the Talmud, successively by Hillel the Elder, Nahum of Gimzo, Rabbi Akiva, and Rabbi Ishmael.[10]

Right from the Revelation of the Written Law, the Sages possessed an authentic methodological tool that allowed them to go beyond the written text, "beyond the verse." In its revelation, the Law contains the resources necessary for its development. The text is written in such a way that it implies the necessity of being interpreted, unfolded. The text's complexity is eminently calculated and worked out in a will to seize the reader's attention: an "invitation to research and deciphering, to *Midrash*, which is already a participation, on the reader's part, in Revelation, in Scripture."[11]

5. *Once the text is legible*, owing to a correct spelling, pronunciation, and syntax, there remains the explaining of the meaning of the words. Naturally, those for whom the Written Law was intended speak Hebrew. But since Revelation is the revelation of a law, it is set out in a much more technical language that necessitates numerous explanations. The explanation that Moses gave concerning these words does not amount to a "translation." He explained in great detail all the circumstances surrounding each law: details and circumstances that are not all contained in the text of the Bible.

Modes of (the First) Transmission

According to the Talmud,[12] the transmission of the Written and Oral Laws was carried out in the following way:

Our Rabbis learned: What was the procedure of the instruction in the Oral Law? Moses learned from the mouth of the Omnipotent. Then Aaron[13] en-

tered and sat opposite Moses (according to Rashi, the disciple should always
be face-to-face with his master and able to see him). Moses then taught him
the Written Law, i.e., the exact wording of the text, then the oral commentaries. Aaron then moved aside and sat down on Moses' left. Thereupon
Aaron's sons, Eleazar and Ithamar, entered. Aaron arose and sat on Moses'
left.[14] The two sons sat opposite Moses and Aaron, and Moses repeated the
same lesson for the first time. Then the seventy Elders entered. Aaron and his
two sons arose; Aaron sat on Moses' right. One of the sons sat to the right of
his father, the other to the left of Moses. The Elders, opposite Moses, heard
the lesson that he repeated for the second time. When the Elders moved aside,
the representatives of the people entered. The Elders sat on either side of
Moses, Aaron, and his sons (we can suppose that there were thirty-five on
each side). The representatives, opposite Moses, heard the teaching that he
repeated for the third time. It thus followed that Aaron heard the lesson four
times, his sons heard it three times, the Elders twice, and the people's representatives once.

At this stage Moses departed and Aaron taught them his lesson: so his sons
had heard it four times, the Elders three times, and the representatives twice.
And so on, until everyone had heard the lesson four times. Then, the representatives returned and, in turn, taught the people.

The text of the Written Law was then written down on parchment[15] and
the Oral Law committed to memory by painstaking repetition.[16]

The Thirteen Copies of the Written Law

Before dying, Moses gathered the people of Israel together and said:
"Everyone who has learned and forgotten should come: I shall explain
to him; everyone who has learned and doubts the exactness of his
knowledge should come: I shall clarify. . . ."[17]

Before dying, Moses wrote with his own hand thirteen copies of the
"Five Books": he then handed a copy to each of the twelve tribes and
one to the Levites, to be placed in the Holy Ark (which already contained the fragments of the first and second Tables of the Law).

Two Modes of Writing

The Talmudic Masters held long discussions to find out what Moses
had written and how he wrote it. A. Y. Heschel, in his very important
work *Torah min hashamayim beasklapariah shel hadorot*,[18] sets out in
extraordinary detail all the arguments of the different opinions. Here
are the main ones: did Moses hear and write down the Torah in one

sitting? Did Moses write the whole of the Torah, including the account of his own death?

Did Moses pass on everything he heard?

The comment that can be made concerns the diversity of the names for the Book. We find:

—*Sefer Hatorah*:[19] the book of the Torah
—*Sefer Torat Mosheh*:[20] the book of (the) Torah of Moses
—*Sefer Torat Hashem*:[21] the book of (the) Torah of God
—*Sefer Torat Hashem beyad Mosheh*:[22] The book of (the) Torah of God in the hand of Moses
—*Sefer Mosheh*:[23] the book of Moses
—*Sefer Torat HaElohim*:[24] the book of (the) Torah of Elohim
—*Sefer Torat Hashem Elohim*:[25] the book of (the) Torah of God Elohim
—*Sefer Hashem*:[26] the book of God

These expressions invite us to attribute the Book to God, on the one hand, and to Moses, on the other. But is it the same book?

According to several masters, Moses heard the word of God and copied it down: that is the case for all the historical events, the stories, and the laws.[27]

This method, called *hakhtava* (dictation), contrasts with the method called *haataka* (copying), according to which Moses was "like a scribe copying a preexisting book (*sefer kadmon*) that was before him, written by the 'hand of God' and of which the parchment was of white fire and the writing, of black fire: 'black fire on white fire.' "[28]

However, whatever the principle of writing, the text was revealed.

A Perfect Text

The masters tell us:

Another *Baraita* taught: "Because he has despised the word of YHVH" (Num. 15:31)—this refers to he who maintains that the Torah is not from Heaven. And even if he asserts that the whole Torah is from Heaven, excepting a particular verse, which he maintains was not uttered by God but by Moses himself, he is included "because he has despised the word of YHVH." And even if he admits that the whole Torah is from Heaven, excepting a single point (*dikduk*), a particular *ad majus* (*kal vahomer*) deduction or a certain analogy (*gezerah shavah*), he is still included "because he has despised the word of YHVH.[29]

Maimonides[30] considers this respect for the whole of the text as one of the thirteen foundations of Judaism:

The eighth foundation is the belief in the divine origin of the text of the Torah;[31] that is to say: the whole of the Torah that we now possess—in its present version, given through Moses our Master—is entirely from the mouth of the *Gevurah*,[32] that is to say that it came wholly from God by a means that we call metaphorically speech (*Dibbur*).

We do not know how it came about! But "speech" came to Moses. He was like a scribe; it was read out to him and he wrote down all the historical events (*Me'orot hayamim*), the narratives (*sipurim*), and the laws (*mitzvot*). . . .

There is no difference (when it comes to the divine origin and its importance) between the verses: "And the sons of Ham: Cush, and Misraim, and Phut and Canaan";[33] "And Baal-hanan the son of Achbor died, and Hadar reigned in his stead; and the name of his city was Pau; and his wife's name was Mehetabel, the daughter of Matred, the daughter of Mezahab";[34] "And Timna was concubine to. . ."[35] and the verses "I am YHVH your God. . .";[36] "Hear, O Israel: YHVH our God is one YHVH."[37] There is no difference, because everything is from God and the Torah is a whole, the "Torah of a perfect God," pure and holy truth. And he who maintains that the verses like the ones just quoted and the narratives (*sipurim*) emanate from the mind of Moses is considered as a heretic (*kofer*) by our Masters and Prophets. . . . In each one of the words of the Torah, there are wise councils (*Hokhmot*) and mysteries (*Plaim*) for he who is able to understand.

Not only must the sentence be respected in its entirety, but also each word, each letter, each coronet.[38] The early masters were called *sofrim*, not "scribes" but "numberers," because they counted all the letters of the Torah.[39]

Tears of Ink: True Knowledge

We read in the Talmud:[40]

Mar has said: Joshua wrote the book that bears his name and the last eight verses of the Pentateuch. This statement is in agreement with the *Baraita*, which says that eight verses in the Talmud were written by Joshua, as it has been taught: It is written, "So Moses the servant of the Lord died there."[41] Now is it possible that Moses was alive[42] and wrote the words, "Moses died there"?

The truth is, however, that up to this point Moses wrote, from this point Joshua wrote. This is the opinion of Rabbi Judah, or, according to the others, of Rabbi Nehemiah.

Said Rabbi Simeon to him: Can we imagine the *Sefer Torah* being short of one word, and is it not written, "Take this book of the Law!"[43] No; what we must say is that up to this point the Holy One, blessed be He, dictated and

Moses repeated and wrote, and from this point God dictated and Moses wrote with tears.[44]

The fact that Joshua may have written the last eight verses of the Torah is mentioned once again in the Talmud,[45] concerning a verse from the book of Joshua: "And Joshua wrote these words in the book of the law of *Elohim*."[46]

On a first reading, we understand that Joshua introduced some words into the book of the law of Elohim, i.e., in the Pentateuch. "Which verses did Joshua write? Rabbi Judah and Rabbi Nehemiah have diverging opinions on the subject: one says, 'eight verses' and the other says, 'the cities of refuge.'" Rashi comments this discussion as follows: the eight verses, that is to say, from "So Moses the servant of the Lord died there" to "in the sight of all Israel," because the book of the Torah was defective (*hasser*) and Joshua completed it. "The cities of refuge": that is to say that Joshua included in his book a passage that was already in the book of Moses. And so we have two totally contradictory opinions since, according to the first one, it is the writing of Moses that is included in the writings of Joshua, and according to the second one, it is a writing of Joshua that is included in the writings of Moses.

Apart from the critical aspect of these references, we come across the problem of "opening" and the "transmission of opening"—which is perhaps one of the fundamental teachings of Judaism. Joshua represents the figure of the disciple and, as such, the Master (Moses) had to make way for him, had to withdraw from before him.

It is the tears that symbolize the withdrawal from the totality: *Demah*, whose letters, arranged in a different order, mean knowledge (*mada*). The Master understands—even if it is hard for him—that he must leave and this absence begins with the impossibility of writing with visible ink. It is the disciple who finishes the book of the Master. But who is the Master? And who the Disciple?

The Talmud[47] says, of the verse "Enough for you"[48] (*Rav lakh*): "Do not read *Rav* in the sense of 'a lot,' of 'too much,' but as 'Master.'" God said to Moses: transmission occurs because now *you have a Master*; and who is it? It is Joshua."[49] The mingled writings represent the first stage in a conception of "opening."

In spite of the insistence on the perfection of the text, there is present, in the minds of the Talmudic Masters, in their critical attitude that never questions the complete nature of the text, the will to refuse all enclosure.

In Praise of Forgetting

The *Midrash* and the Talmud contain some very beautiful texts dealing with the episode of the death of Moses. One of the essential problems

of these texts consists in the issue of transmission. What is handed on?
How does it happen? Who hands it on? Here are two important texts:
the first, taken from the *Midrash Tanhuma*, shows us Moses on the
verge of dying, asking God for the chance not to die. God replies:

> "This is how I have decided, and it is a universal law: each generation has
> its interpreters, each generation has its economic guides, each generation has
> its political leaders. Until now, you have had your share of service before Me:
> now, your time is over and it is your disciple Joshua's turn to serve Me."
> Moses said: "Lord of the world, if I am dying because of Joshua, I shall go
> and be his disciple." And God replied: "Do as you desire!"
>
> Moses arose early and went to Joshua's door. Joshua was seated, interpret-
> ing the Torah. Moses was standing but Joshua did not see him. The children
> of Israel went to Moses' door to study the Torah and asked: "Where is Moses
> our Master?" They were told: "He arose early and went to Joshua's." They
> went and found him, as they had been told, at Joshua's door. Joshua was
> seated and Moses standing. They said to Joshua: "What is going on? Why are
> you seated and why is Moses standing?" No sooner had he looked up and
> seen Moses than he rent his garments, wept, and cried, saying: "Master, Mas-
> ter! Father, Father! Master!" The children of Israel said to Moses: "Moses,
> our Master, teach us the Torah." He said: "I do not have permission." They
> said to him: "Do not leave us!" A voice came from heaven saying: "Learn
> from Joshua. Agree to sit down and learn from Joshua." Joshua sat in the
> head position, Moses at his right, and the children of Aaron at his left.
> Joshua, seated, interpreted the law before Moses.
>
> Rabbi Samuel bar Nahmani said in the name of Rabbi Jonathan: "The
> moment Joshua said 'Blessed be He who chooses amongst the righteous,' the
> methodological and pedagogical rules of wisdom were taken from Moses and
> given to Joshua. And then Moses no longer understood what Joshua was
> interpreting. After the lesson, the children of Israel said to Moses: 'Give us
> the conclusion of the Torah.' He replied: 'I do not know what to tell you!'
> And Moses stumbled and fell. Then Moses said to God: 'Until now I asked
> for my life, but now my soul is given to you.' "[50]

The second text comes from the Talmud:

> Rav Judah reported in the name of Samuel: Three thousand traditional
> laws were forgotten during the period of mourning for Moses. They said to
> Joshua: "Ask"; he replied: It is not in heaven (*lo bashamayim hi*). . . .
>
> Rav Judah reported in the name of Rav: When Moses departed this world
> for the Garden of Eden he said to Joshua: "Ask me concerning all the doubts
> you have." He replied to him: "My Master, have I ever left you for one hour
> and gone elsewhere? Did you not write concerning me in the Torah: 'But his
> servant Joshua the son of Nun departed not out of the Tabernacle?' " (Exod.

33:11). Immediately the strength of Moses weakened and Joshua forgot three hundred laws and there arose in his mind seven hundred doubts concerning laws.[51]

Another text tells us the following:

> It has been taught: A thousand and seven hundred *kal vahomer* (conclusion from major to minor) and *gezerah shavah* (analogies based on verbal congruities) and specifications of the Scribes were forgotten during the period of mourning for Moses. Said Rabbi Abbahu: Nevertheless Othniel the son of Kenaz restored these forgotten teachings as a result of his dialectics (*pilpul*), as it says: "And Othniel the son of Kenaz, the brother of Caleb, took it" (*Kiryath Sefer*: "the city of the book").[52]

These forgettings, these erasings of knowledge, must be considered as something positive and necessary. No, Joshua, you cannot know everything! Absolute knowledge is not possible. The disciple is not he who learns everything that the master has said; he is the one who knows how to lend himself to the disappearance of the master in order to continue his path, to go even further.

Knowledge is not given; it has to be conquered.

Othniel seized: *vayilkad* is a military term; moreover, it is the conquest of a town that is evoked here. The Talmudic Masters interpret this town as being a "Book of lost laws."

There is no such thing as passive receiving of Tradition. He who receives, the disciple, is always—must always be—the scene of a creation. To receive is to create, to innovate! "The petrification of acquired knowledge—the freezing of spiritual things—allowing itself to be placed like an inert content in the mind and to be handed on, frozen, from one generation to another, is not real transmission. . . ."[53] Handing on is "resumption, life, invention and renewal, a mode without which revealed thinking, that is to say, thinking which is authentically thought, is not possible."[54]

"Man Is Born into Trouble . . ."

This verse from Job[55] (*ki ha-adam leamal yulad*) is commented in the Talmud[56] by Rabbi Eleazer. The word *amal* calls for several translations: "pain," "toil," "work." Rabbi Eleazer shows that the work is a work of the "mouth," the study of the Torah. So the verse can be translated as follows: "Man is born into the study of the Torah." "Maharsha"—Rabbi Samuel Edels, a classical commentation of the Talmud—continues this interpretation, explaining that study has a dual dimension and, as such, constitutes a dynamic of transmission.

One possibility offered by traditional exegesis consists in taking the letters of a word and turning them into the initials of several other words: words within words, so to speak. The word *leamal* could be read (it is one of a multitude of possible readings) *lillemod al menat lelamed*, which means learning in order to teach. The importance of this attitude is attested by this teaching of Rabbi Meir:[57] "Who does this verse apply to: 'Because he has despised the word of YHVH . . .'?[58] To he who learns without teaching others." "So transmission contains a teaching that becomes apparent in the very receptivity of learning and that continues it: real learning consists in receiving the lesson so profoundly that it is transformed into a necessity of being dispensed to the other person; the lesson of truth cannot be limited to the mind of one man, it bursts out toward others."[59]

We in Turn Must . . .

Moses did not transmit everything![60] The Master must refrain from passing everything on in order to leave a space for the disciple. In the last four books of the Pentateuch this verse constantly appears: "And YHVH said to Moses: Speak to the children of Israel, *leemor* (in these words)." Emmanuel Lévinas recounts that his master "claimed to be able to give 120 different interpretations of this phrase, whose literal meaning is, however, totally clear."[61]

Lévinas continues: "He disclosed only one of them to me. I tried to guess a second. The one he disclosed consisted in translating *leemor*[62] by 'in order not to say.' Which meant: 'Speak to the children of Israel in order not to say.' The unsaid is necessary for listening to remain thinking; or speech must also be an unsaid so that truth (or the word of God) does not consume those who listen, or the word of God must be able to enter, without causing danger for men, into the tongue and the language of men."

It is the disciple who constitutes the reality of the Master. If the disciple continues the word of the Master, there is transmission and mastery. The disciple has to forge ahead and penetrate the silence prepared by the Master. So Lévinas is compelled to continue: "In my own reading of this verse, *leemor* means 'in order to speak': "Speak to the children of Israel in order that they might speak'; teach them profoundly enough so that they begin to speak, so that they hear to the point where they start speaking."

So, teaching is Speech that creates speech.

But the Master carries away with him the secret of the 118 other meanings of the term *leemor* that remain to be rediscovered. We in turn must . . .

The 613 Mitzvot

The Torah is made up of two categories of texts that are completely interwoven. On the one hand, we have the historical texts: the history of the patriarchs and the matriarchs; the account of the creation of the world; the episodes concerning the life of the Hebrews in Egypt and in the desert, etc. These narrative texts constitute the category called *Haggadah* (story). On the other hand, there are the purely legislative or instructive texts, which explain what one must and must not do; this second category is called *Halakhah* (law). It is interesting to notice that the *Halakhah* appears well before the actual Gift of the Torah,[63] i.e., before the text of the "Ten Words" written on the tables of stone. We could mention, for example, the commandment of circumcision given to Abraham;[64] the man who marries his widowed and childless sister-in-law;[65] the prohibition of eating the sciatic nerve;[66] the Sabbath rest;[67] the seven days of marriage and mourning;[68] the paying of tithe.[69]

It is necessary, at this point, to describe in more detail the term *Mitzvah* (plural: *Mitzvot*). From the root *tzav*, order, it is a commandment, a ruling. Oral tradition has given us the number of 613 *Mitzvot*, all contained in the Pentateuch, subdivided into 248 positive *Mitzvot* and 365 negative *Mitzvot*.

A positive *Mitzvah* is called *Mitzvat asseh* or *Tsivui*.

A negative *Mitzvah* is called *Mitzvat lo taasseh* or *Azharah*.

The *Mitzvot* are generally concerned with four areas.:[70]

—opinion (*Deot*)
—action (*Maassim*)
—ethical behavior (*Midot*)
—speech (*Dibbur*)

Early on, the *Mitzvot* were counted, but their detailed naming began to appear only at the time of the *Geonim* and the *Tossafists*. Three works are particularly worth mentioning:

1. The *Sefer hamitzvot*[71] (The book of the commandments of Maimonides, which describes the 248 *Mitzvot asseh*, then the 365 *Mitzvot lo taasseh*). This description is preceded by 14 rules necessary for understanding how the 613 *Mitzvot* are drawn from the text of the Torah.

2. The *Sefer Ha-Mitzvot Ha-Gadol* (The great book of commandments) by Moses ben Jacob of Coucy (ca. 1250).

3. The *Sefer Ha-Hinnukh* (The book of education) by Rabbi Aaron Halevy (before 1310). In this work, the description follows the chronological order of the appearance of the *Mitzvot* in the text of the Torah.

The Torah, the Body and Time; the Name and Memory

The main Talmudic text concerning the 613 *Mitzvot* introduces a relationship between the body and time: "Rabbi Simlai teaches that 613 commandments were taught to Moses (on Sinai), 365 negative commandments corresponding to the number of days in the solar year, and 248 positive commandments: as many as there are members in the human body." Rabbi Hanina said: "Which verse teaches us that? 'Moses commanded us a law, even the inheritance of the congregation of Jacob.'[72] The numerical value of the word Torah is 611. If one adds the two first commandments of the "Ten Words" spoken at Sinai that we heard from the very mouth of God, that makes 613."[73]

For this verse, "It is my Name forever and my memorial-title from generation to generation"[74] (*zeh shemi leolam vezeh zikhri ledor dor*), the *Zohar*[75] introduces the numbers 248 and 365 in the following manner: "My Name" (*shemi*) has a numerical value of 350; if the first two letters of the Tetragram *Yod-heh*, whose numerical value is 15, are added together, we obtain 365.

"My memorial-title" (*zikhri*) has a numerical value of 237; if the last two letters of the Tetragram, *Vav-heh*, whose numerical value is 11, are added together, we obtain 248. Indisputable calculations! However, we should not limit our thinking to simple relations between figures and letters; we must go even further . . .

The Two Fundamental Aims of the Oral Law

In his introduction to the *Mishnah*, Maimonides insists on a very important idea: "There has never been any moment of History from which thought and creation, innovation in meaning (*Hidush*) have been absent. The wise men of each era consider the words of their predecessors as fundamental principles (*Ikar*), learning them and innovating from them."[76] Hence, the Oral Law has been amplified from generation to generation. Innovation (*Hidush*) follows two different aims.

The first aim has to do with explanation and apologetics. In this case, the *Hidush*—the speech of commentary—adds nothing to the established corpus of the laws. The only role of the arguments put forward is to explain and justify, that is to say, to use one's reasoning—logical reasoning—in order to come back to the law that is already given in advance and posited as a pure a priori. This aim belongs more to the domain of study than to that of practical application. Apologetic or explanatory *Hidush* is dissociated from the concrete world. We could cite this text from the Talmud: "It has been taught: 'There never was a condemned city, and never will be.' Why then was this law written? That you may study it and receive reward. There never was a leprous house to need destruction, and never will be. Then why was its law written? That you may study it and receive reward. There never was a 'stubborn and rebellious son,' and never will be. Why then was the law written? That you may study it and receive reward."[77] *Explanatory Hidush* concerns the theoretical aspect first, and then the practical. *Apologetic Hidush* seeks out the allusions and the arguments to understand in what way an oral law is related to the text of the Written Law. *Apologetic Hidush* tries to find the relation between the oral and the written: it creates this relation. The Law—written or oral—in its applied form is in no way changed by the existence of this relation.

The second aim concerns amplification. If the logical procedure of the first aim is demonstrative, that of the second is deductive. By means of the methodological rules revealed on Sinai, called *Midot shehatorah nidreshet bahen*, the masters of each generation create new laws. In this case, everything is done with the practical implementation in mind. These new laws are added to the juridical corpus of laws that already exist in the written text. These are rabbinical laws called *Mitzvot derabanan*, which are distinct from the laws of the Torah. These *derabanan* laws were not revealed at Sinai and so are not part of the 613 *Mitzvot*.

In this second case, it is not a matter of returning to an already existing law to understand or create a relation between the written and the Oral Torah, but of actually inventing, producing new laws.

On this account, the invention and creativity that the masters have to display is equally great, both in the demonstration and in the deduction.

The Existence of Discussion: *Mahloket*

Mahloket refers to the polemical discussion that takes place between two masters about the same subject. It is possible because the law is *Halakhah*: the etymological meaning of this term being "walking," "step." *Mahloket* appears because the law is not a product but production.

Hence, in both categories described in the previous section, *Mahloket* is possible. In the first case, it does not affect the law, which is already given, but the relation that links the Oral Law—handed down—to the text of the Written Law.

In the second case, *Mahloket* may concern the law itself, because, through two logical arguments of equal strength or through a single logical argument, one can arrive at different laws.

In any case, *Mahloket* is not the product of a failure in the transmission but a creative power conferred on the interpreters of the text.

The Five Categories of Laws

What we have just explained allows us to divide the oral laws into five categories:[78]

1. *The first category* concerns the commentaries (*Perushim*) received by Moses of which there are already traces, allusions (*remez*) in the text of the written Torah, and that can be found by means of rules of interpretation (*midot*); about these laws, there is no discussion (*Mahloket*).

2. *The second category* includes all the laws and commentaries received by Moses, but of which there is no trace in Scripture and no logical way of finding them. These are laws that tradition calls *Halakhah lemosheh misinai*, meaning laws that go back to Moses at Sinai; here again, there is no *Mahloket*.

3. *The third category* is made up of all the laws that have been created by deduction and about which there has been no *Mahloket*. It is a positive controversy that, we can never stress it enough, is not due to logical weakness or forgetfulness. And Maimonides adds that we must not think that, in these discussions, one person is right and the other wrong.[79]

4. *The fourth category* consists of all the decrees instituted by the Prophets and the Masters of each generation to protect the integrity of the already existing law. Here, one might say, there is no logical but rather a preventive deduction: these laws are barriers, hedges, which are usually called *Gezerot*. There are frequently *Mahloket* about these *Gezerot*: one Master finds the prevention justified, the other does not!

However, the moment a preventive law has been accepted by the community, it cannot be annulled, even if the circumstance that gave rise to it has disappeared.[80]

5. *The fifth category* is made up of institutions called *Takanot* and customs: *Minhagim*. They are not deduced from existing laws and do not have the same "preventive" or "protective" character as the laws of the fourth category. These are social institutions that are applied in either civil or religious law, and that aim to improve the social relations of everyday life. (These laws are indicated in the Talmudic texts by the expression *Hitkin . . . , Tikenu*.)

Toraic and Rabbinical Law

From the previous description, it appears possible to distinguish two main categories of laws. The first, made up of the laws of the first three above-mentioned categories, includes the actual Toraic laws that constitute the corpus of 613 *Mitzvot*. These laws are called *min hatorah* or *mideorayeta*,[81] that is to say: "from the Torah."

The second category, which combines the laws of the last two above-mentioned categories, includes the rabbinical laws, much more numerous than the Toraic laws forming the greater part of the legal corpus of Hebrew law. The rabbinical laws are called *miderabanan* or *derabanan*,[82] that is to say: "of the Rabbis."

The Two Manners of Expounding the Oral Law

The texts of the Oral Law that are available today—the ones that have been transcribed—reveal two ways of expounding and, thereby, of teaching the Oral Law.

The first consists of teaching the Oral Law as an explanation of the biblical text. "It is written, 'In the beginning God created the heavens and the earth . . .': that means . . . Rabbi 'X' comments as follows . . . On the other hand, Rabbi 'Y' comments as follows . . . ," etc. This method of direct exegesis is called *Midrash*: we shall come back to it in more detail.

The second manner consists of teaching and expounding the Oral Law independently of its scriptural basis. This method of indirect exegesis is called *Mishnah*.

Notes

1. *Sifra Behukotai.* The *Sifra* is the *Midrash halakhah* on Leviticus, (cf. below: "The Midrash Halakhah").

2. Cf., for example, *Mishnah Yadaim*, chap. 3.

3. *Penta* means five in Greek. *Humash* comes from *Hamesh*, which also means five.

4. *Navi* = prophet. *Neviim* is the plural.

5. From the Greek *hagios*, "sacred," and *graphein*, "to write."

6. *Pirkei de Rabbi Eliezer*, chap. 46.

7. A. Safran, *La Cabale* (Paris: Payot, 1983), p. 73.

8. We are talking here about the Oral Law in its first form, which is not yet the actual Talmud. We can also distinguish three categories of "Oral Law": (1) prerevelation (oral); (2) pre-Talmudic (oral); (3) Talmudic (written).

9. *Midrash Rabbah*, Exod. 41:6.

10. See below: "Talmudic Hermeneutics," p. 70.

11. E. Lévinas, *L'Au-delà du verset* (Paris: Éditions de Minuit, 1982), p. 162.

12. *Eruvin* 54b; cf. also Maimonides, Introduction to the Mishnah (Mossad Harav Kook ed., in Hebrew), p. 10.

13. Brother of Moses and high priest.

14. A disciple may not sit on his master's left if he is alone with him.

15. That confirms the opinion of Rabbi Johanan according to whom the written Torah was put together fragment by fragment: *Torah megillah nitnah*.

16. Rabbi Eliezer deducts from this structure of teaching that the master should repeat at least four times the same thing.

17. *Sifri Devarim* 1, 5; cf. also *Temurah* 16a (Verdier ed.), p. 1333.

18. A. Y. Heschel, *The Torah from Heaven* . . . (in Hebrew) (New York: Soncino Press, 1965), chaps. 14 and ff. of the second volume.

19. Josh. 1:8 and 18:34; 2 Kings 22:8; Neh. 8:3; 2 Chron. 34:15.

20. Josh. 8:31 and 23:6; 2 Kings 14:6; Neh. 8:1.

21. 2 Chron. 17:9.

22. 2 Chron. 34:14.

23. Neh. 13:1; 2 Chron. 25:4 and 35:12.

24. Josh. 24:26; Neh. 8:18.

25. Neh. 9:3.

26. Isa. 34:16.

27. It is Rabbi Meir's opinion in the *Sifre Beraka, pisqa* 357, and Rabbi Shimone's *Bava Batra* 15a and *Menahot* 30a (cf. also Rashi). It is also the opinion of Maimonides, cf. *Introduction to the Chapter Helek*, "Eighth Foundation" (Mossad Harav Kook ed., in Hebrew), p. 144.

28. Quoted by Nahmanides in his *Introduction au Pentateuque*; cf. also *Devarim Rabbah*, chap. 3, 12.

29. *Sanhedrin* 99a.

30. Maimonides, *Introduction to the Mishnah*.

31. *Torah min hashamayim*.

32. Of God.

33. Gen. 10:6.

34. Gen. 36:39. Maimonides quotes only "the name of his wife Meheytabel."

35. Gen. 36:12.

36. Deut. 5:6.

37. Deut. 6:4.

38. Maimonides, *Mishneh Torah*, "teshuva" 3, 8.

39. *Kiddushin* 30a.

40. *Bava Batra* 15a.

41. Deut. 34:5.

42. The classical edition reads "dead"; here we are following the reading of the *dikdukei sofrim*.

43. Deut. 31:26. In the *Sifri*, Rabbi Meir, in a parallel text, quotes the verse Deut. 31:9: "And Moses wrote this Torah."

44. "Ritba" in the *Ayin Jacob* reads this text at the literal level. The whole Torah was written with ink and this passage about death with tears. "Maharal" understands thus: he wept when he wrote this passage.

45. *Makkot* 11a.

46. Josh. 24:26.

47. *Sotah* 13b.

48. Deut. 3:26. The verses 23 to 29 are very important because they contain the problem of passing on, of transmission . . . and the risk of transgression. Moses asks God to let him pass over the Jordan into the Promised Land. But, at this moment, he hands his powers on to Joshua.

49. Cf. the following paragraph: "In Praise of Forgetting."

50. *Midrash Tanhumah*, "Vaethanan" 6. To be compared with *Menahot* 29b. Cf. also *Sotah* 13b (Verdier ed.), p. 766.

51. *Temurah* 16a.

52. Ibid.

53. Lévinas, *L'Au-delà du verset*, p. 99.

54. Ibid.

55. Job 5:7.

56. *Sanhedrin* 99b.

57. *Sanhedrin* 99a.

58. Num. 15:31.

59. Lévinas, *L'Au-delà du verset*, p. 99.

60. Cf. Heschel, *The Torah from Heaven* . . . (in Hebrew), last paragraph of vol. 2.

61. Lévinas, *L'Au-delà du verset*.

62. The word *le'emor* can be broken into *lo emor*, the *aleph* being repeated.

63. Exod. 20.

64. Gen. 17.

65. Gen. 38:5.

66. Gen. 32:33.

67. Exod. 16:23.

68. Gen. 29:27 and 50:10.

69. Gen. 14:18–20.

70. Maimonides, *Sefer ha-Mitzvot* (Mossad Harav Kook ed., in Hebrew), p. 30.

71. Ibid.

72. Deut. 33:4.

73. *Makkot* 23a and 23b.

74. Exod. 3:15.

75. Behar 110b.

76. Maimonides, *Hakdamah lamishnah* (Mossad Harav Kook ed., in Hebrew), p. 28.

77. *Sanhedrin* 71a.

78. Cf. Maimonides, *Hakdamah lamishnah* (Mossad Harav Kook ed., in Hebrew), p. 37.

79. Ibid., p. 39.

80. Ibid., p. 40.

81. It is the prevailing expression in Aramaic.

82. Maimonides, *Hakdamah lamishnah* (Mossad Harav Kook ed., in Hebrew), p. 37.

II _____

Transcription

Transcription of the Oral Law: The Talmud

For centuries, the interdiction of transcribing the "oral teaching," the *Torah she-be-al peh*, was considered a fundamental law: "He who writes down *Halakhot* is as one who commits the Torah to flames."[1] "He who transcribes the *Haggadah* loses his share in the world to come."[2]

Later, the masters of the tradition decided to put the oral teaching into writing. They justified this action by interpreting a verse from the Psalms[3] as: "There comes a time when you can abolish the Torah in order to found it." It is better to repeal a part of the Law than to allow the whole of the Law to be forgotten.[4]

The transcription of the Oral Law constitutes the Talmud. The history of the writing down of the Talmud is very complex, too complex for us to describe it in detail here. But here is the essence of what should be known in order to start a Talmudic study without encountering too many pitfalls.

The Talmud

The Talmud is the heart of Hebrew thought. Everything that is said in Judaism takes root in this monumental work that was developed in its present form over a period of more than seven centuries: from the second century B.C.E. up to the middle of the sixth century.

The Talmud is made up of two distinct parts: the *Mishnah* and the *Gemara*. The former represents the actual text and the latter is its commentary.

The *Mishnah*

Mishnah refers to a collection of decisions and traditional laws embracing all aspects of civil and religious legislation. This code, which several generations of masters called *Tannaim* worked on, was given its final form by Rabbi Judah ha-Nasi, around the second century C.E. It is divided into six parts (or orders), which are in turn subdivided into tractates, chapters, and paragraphs. The part is called *Seder*, the tractate *Masekhet*, the chapter *Perek*; the smallest paragraph of the collection bears, like the collection itself, the name *Mishnah*.

In all, there are 63 *Mishnah* tractates, which contain a total of 524 chapters.

The Six Orders of the *Mishnah*: The "Shas"

The six orders of the *Mishnah* correspond to six themes:

1. *The earth*: order entitled *Zera'im*, literally "Of the sowing"
2. *Time*: order entitled *Mo'ed*, literally "Times of appointments"
3. *The feminine*: order entitled *Nashim*, literally "Of women"
4. *Society*: order entitled *Nezikin*, literally "Of damages"
5. *The sacred*: order entitled *Kodashim*, literally "Of sacrifices"
6. *Death*: order entitled *Taharot*, literally "Of pure things"

Maimonides gives a mnemonic acronym, made up of each of the Hebrew names, which gives us : Z e M a N e N a K a T. Two words that can signify "to take time."

In Hebrew, the six parts are called *Shishah Sidrei*, abbreviated as *"Shas,"* a term that is often used to refer to the whole of the Talmud.

The Sixty-Three Tractates of the *Mishnah*

Even if it is possible to summarize the six themes of the *Mishnah* as we have done, it is important to describe, if only briefly, the exact subject of each tractate in a sort of thematic index.

Zera'im, "Sowing"

1. *Berakhot*, "blessings." Rules concerning the liturgy.
2. *Pe'ah*, "corners." Questions raised by the laws dealing with the "Corners of fields" (Lev. 19:9).
3. *Demai*, "doubtful." About seeds, etc., acquired by someone suspected of not having paid tithe to the priests.
4. *Kilayim*, "mixes." About crossing seeds, animals, etc., prohibited by Lev. 19:9.
5. *Shevi'it*, "seventh." Law about the sabbatical year (Exod. 33:11; Lev. 25:2f.; Deut 15f.).
6. *Terumot*, "gifts for the priests." Law about offerings (Num. 18:21f.).
7. *Ma'aserot*, "tithes." Law about the tithe for the Levites (Num. 18:8f.).

8. *Ma'aser Sheni*, "second tithe." Rules based on Deut. 14:22.

9. *Hallah*, "dough." The portion of dough to be given to the priests, according to Num. 15:21.

10. *Bikkurim*, "firstfruits." The firstfruits to be offered at the Temple (Deut. 26:1f.).

11. *Orla*, "uncircumcision." Law about fruits of trees during the four first years after their planting (Lev. 19:23).

Mo'ed, "Festivals"

1. *Shabbat*, "sabbath." Work forbidden during the Shabbat.

2. *Eruvin*, "putting into community." Notion of community: the territorial limit not to be crossed on the Shabbat; how it can be extended.

3. *Pesahim*, "Passover." Observance of the Passover festival.

4. *Shekalim*, "shekels." The annual tax for the Temple treasury (Exod. 30:12f.).

5. *Yoma*, "the Day." Rituals on the day of Atonement (*Kippur*) (Lev. 16).

6. *Sukkah* "booth." Observance of the feast of Tabernacles (Lev. 23:34f.).

7. *Beitzah*, "egg," or *Yom tov*, "solemnity." Work forbidden and work permitted during a festival.

8. *Rosh ha-Shanah*, "New Year." Observance of the festival that marks the beginning of a new year.

9. *Ta'anit*, "fast." On public fasting.

10. *Megillah*, "scroll." The public reading of the book of Esther on the day of the festival of Purim.

11. *Mo'ed Katan*, "small festival." Days between the festival of Passover and the feast of Tabernacles.

12. *Hagigah*, "festival sacrifices." Sacrifices offered during the three annual pilgrimages (Deut. 16:16f.).

Nashim, "Women"

1. *Yevamot*, "Levirate marriage." About the law concerning marriage with a childless sister-in-law (Deut. 25:5f.). Degrees of kinship that exclude the possibility of marriage (Lev. 18).

2. *Ketubbot*, "matrimonial documents." Laws concerning the dowry and the marriage contract.

3. *Nedarim*, "vows." How they are made and annulled, particularly those concerning women (Num. 30:3).

4. *Nazir*, "Naziriteship." On the vow of a Nazirite (Num. 6).

5. *Sotah*, "supposed adultery." About the woman suspected of adultery (Num. 5:12).

6. *Guittin*, "divorces." Laws annulling marriage (Deut. 24:1f.).

7. *Kiddushin*, "sanctification." Matrimonial status.

Nezikin, "Damages"

1. *Bava Kamma*, "the first door." Damages to goods, injuries to persons.
2. *Bava Metzia*, "the middle door." Land, lease, sale, renting, lost property.
3. *Bava Batra*, "the last door." Real estate. Inheritance.
4. *Sanhedrin*, "tribunals." Tribunals. Juridical procedure. The death penalty.
5. *Makkot*, "blows." Penalties punishing false witnesses. Cities of refuge (Num. 35:10f.). Crimes incurring flogging.
6. *Shevu'ot*, "oaths." Private oaths. Oaths in court.
7. *'Eduyyot*, "accounts." All the accounts of rabbis concerning the decisions of the ancient authorities.
8. *Avodah Zarah*, idolatry." Pagan rites and worship.
9. *Pirkei Avot*, "chapters of the fathers." Moral tractate consisting of a compilation of the favorite maxims of the *Tannaim*. Appendix: "The Chapter of Rabbi Meir on the Acquisition of the Torah."
10. *Horayot*, "rulings." Sins committed unknowingly after receiving erroneous advice from the religious authorities.

Kodashim, "Holy Things"

1. *Zevahim*, "sacrifices." On the sacrificial system of the Temple.
2. *Menahot*, "meal offerings." On offerings of flour and drinks (Lev. 2).
3. *Hullin*, "unholy things." On the slaughtering of animals. On food mixing milk and meat foods.
4. *Bekhorot*, "firstlings." On the firstborn of men and animals (Exod. 13:12f.; Num. 18:15f.).
5. *Arakhin*, "vows of valuation." On the estimated value of persons and things vowed to the Temple (Lev. 27).
6. *Temurah*, "substitution." Tractate on the exchange of animals offered in sacrifice (Lev. 27:10–33).
7. *Keritot*, "extirpation." On sins incurring the "cutting off" (cf. Exod. 12:15).
8. *Me'ila*, "encroachment." On the sacrilege involving the property of the Temple.
9. *Tamid*, "daily sacrifices" (Num. 28:3–4). Description of the daily ritual of the Temple.
10. *Middot*, "measurements." On the architecture of the Temple.
11. *Kinnim*, "birds' nests." On the offering of birds (Lev. 1:14, 5:7, 12:8).

Toharot, "Pure Things"

1. *Kelim*, "utensils." On the impurity of containers (Lev. 11:33f.).
2. *Ohalot*, "tents." On impurity occasioned by death (Num. 19:14f.).
3. *Nega'im*, "wounds." Laws concerning leprosy (Lev. 13f.).

4. *Parah*, "cow." Rules concerning the Red Heifer (Num. 19).

5. *Tohorot*, "pure things." A euphemism referring to impurities in general, which last until sunset (Lev. 11:24f.).

6. *Mikva'ot*, "baths." Law on ritual ablution (Lev. 15:11f.).

7. *Niddah*, "impurity resulting from menstrual indisposal." About laws figuring in Lev. 12, 15:19f.

8. *Makhshirin*, "preparations." On the impurity of liquids.

9. *Zavim*, "persons affected by a discharge." On the impurity thus occasioned (Lev. 15:2f.).

10. *Tevul Yom*, "immersing for a day." On the state of someone who undergoes immersion, but whose purification is not complete until sunset.

11. *Yadayim*, "hands." The impurity of hands and their purification.

12. *Uktzin*, "stalks." Details concerning the impurity of foods.

Some modern scholars* believe that there is a seventh order bearing the name of *Seder Hokhmah*: Wisdom. It would have dealt with ethics, rules of behavior for daily life, and would have contained counsels of wise men that are not laws. The *Avot* tractate would, in this case, be a vestige of this seventh order.

Baraita and *Tosefta*

Rabbi Judah ha-Nasi did not include in the *Mishnah* all the decisions of the Doctors who preceded him. A number of them were not included, either because they duplicated those already published or because they did not have sufficient authority in his opinion. Most of them were collected a little later under the title *Baraitot*—"which are outside"—in the order of the *Mishnah* itself and with the same divisions and subdivisions. These *Braitot* gave birth to a new book, the *Tosefta*, or "supplement."

We owe the *Tosefta* to the Babylonian schools and its authors Rabbi Hiyya and Rabbi Oshiya; it shares the same external characteristics as the *Mishnah*, the same language, the same style. And yet anecdotes have a more important place here. Moreover, there is no *Tosefta* for the tractates *Avot, Tamid, Middot, Kinnim*.

Written in a Hebrew strongly influenced by the Chaldean language and including a number of Latin and, particularly, Greek words, the *Mishnah* and the *Tosefta* use a simple, concise, but often elliptical style; they avoid digressions, and the rare anecdotes one encounters here and there have the purpose of shedding light on the various opinions by means of a fact.

---

* A. Steinsaltz for example; *Hatalmud lakol* (The Talmud for everyone), in Hebrew.

The *Gemara*

The *Gemara* is the continuous commentary that follows the *Mishnah* in all its divisions and subdivisions. In fact, we possess two different commentaries for the same text of the *Mishnah*: the first, developed by the masters of the schools situated in Israel, which will later constitute the *Gemara* of Jerusalem; the second, fruit of the research of the masters of the schools situated in Babylonia, which will form the *Gemara* of Babylon.

The Talmud

The word Talmud, from the root *lamed*, refers precisely to the whole of the *Mishnah* followed by its commentary, the *Gemara*. Given the fact that there are two distinct *Gemarot*, we also have two different Talmuds: that of Jerusalem and that of Babylonia.

The Jerusalem Talmud

The Jerusalem Talmud is the product of the schools established in Israel: the academies of Sepphoris, Tiberias, Caesarea, and Lydda (Lod); it was written down at Tiberias around the year 380. Of the two Talmuds, it is the more ancient. The commentary is not as long as in the Babylonian version. For this reason, it was somewhat neglected by the doctors and copyists of the Middle Ages. It has come down to us in bad condition, not without having lost a number of pages through the years. We have only one manuscript copy, which was used to make the first edition. It was printed for the first time, without commentary, in Venice in 1523.

The Babylonian Talmud: Opening and Incompletion

The Babylonian Talmud, the second writing up of the *Gemara*, comes from the schools of Babylonia, from the academies of Sura, Nehardea, and Pumbedita. The Babylonian *Gemara* was written down by Rav Ashi (376–427) and his disciple Ravina (ca. 400), then completed by Rav Yose around the year 500. The Babylonian commentary is clearer and much more complete than that of Jerusalem.

The relation between the two parts of the Talmud is most significant.

It is double and complex: the *Gemara* and the *Mishnah* both aim at fixing an elusive oral doctrine, transcribing ideas emanating from the collective creativity of the Sages, but without altering their ability to evolve. It is a constant of their style that it shows the precautions taken to safeguard the developmental power inherent in the law. They record the norm that constitutes the authority while maintaining the scope for further research. *The written text must remain a matrix for future decisions*; the dynamic aspect of belief must not be interrupted.

The relation between the two parts of the Talmud then becomes clear: on one hand, the *Gemara* gives additional precision to the *Mishnah* in that it allows one, either to determine the meaning, or to come to conclusions on details that are like circumstantial "decisions" (*halakhot*). But on the other hand, the *Gemara* remains closer to the liveliness of the oral discussions, which it tends to reproduce. If it follows historically the *Mishnah*, and completes it (*gamar*: complete, finish), we can nonetheless suggest that it precedes it, from a dialogical point of view. In fact, the writers, considering that the sedimentation undertaken by Rabbi Judah was often obscure and allusive, rewrote the discussions in order to show up the deliberative nature of a certain number of conclusions.

That is why the *Gemara* seems more like a commentary. In one sense, its precise and radical discussions are intended to precede the final setting out of the *Mishnah*, which is in effect the codification, the concentrated verdict of the former. The deep relationship between the two parts of the Talmud is as much of an explanatory origin as of exegetical amplification.

> It is striking to notice the length of the commentary, compared to the text. A *Mishnah* of five or six lines has twenty or thirty pages of explanation, but in this wordy development, one should not look for the logical order of a grand lecture. In vain would one seek the overall layout of a clear plan where all the parts of the *Gemara* could find their place. The modern scholar, being used to method and order, would feel extremely out of place. The *Gemara* often gives us the impression of being an infinite sea of discussions, digressions, stories, legends where the *Mishnah*, which requires explaining, is completely drowned. On reading these pages where the most disparate items seem to come together naturally, where everything mingles and jostles in the splendor of a wild disorder, it is as if one were watching an immense dream which knew no law other than that of the association of ideas. Even in the discussions that are the most carefully defined this disorder seems to be given free rein.[5]

And yet nothing is left to chance; everything is calculated and precise.

The *Mishnah* is not considered as the final text; it quotes several diverging, contradictory opinions, without deciding in favor of one or the other. The questions are left in abeyance. The commentary of the *Gemara* returns to them, finishing off the commented discussions, pronouncing a final decision on the contested points, establishing light and order everywhere (in the apparent disorder we have just described). The *Gemara* concerns itself first of all with the laws considered as definitive: it seeks their origins and chooses among the different explanations proposed, until it finds one that no longer raises any objections. Often it shows that the decision put forward by the *Mishnah* is incomplete, obscure, contradictory, and that it is not applicable in all cases. An older *Mishnah*, or one of the same age, is then put up against the *Mishnah* in question, that is to say, one which can boast as much authority but which says exactly the opposite. Whence the immense variety of hypotheses; the discussions gain in length and depth until the complete elucidation of the text is arrived at.

The Language of the *Gemara*

If the basic language of the *Mishnah* is Hebrew, the same cannot be said of the *Gemara*, whose language is closer to the popular idiom, somewhat like a more or less corrupt form of Aramaic. However, we can find there Hebrew from all ages and even, sometimes, almost classical Hebrew, according to the age of the text quoted. A single page of the Talmud contains three or four layers of languages or, rather, a single language at three or four stages of degeneration. It is not rare to see the writer of the Talmud quote, in Aramaic, the opinion of a fourth-century rabbi and confirm it by quoting an opinion, identical, word for word, from a doctor of the second century, but this time written in Hebrew. As a rule, of the texts copied in the Talmud, one can say that the degree of purity of the language is proof of its ancientness.

The Edition of the Babylonian Talmud

There is no shortage of manuscripts, even if they are often in fragment. The first complete edition dates from 1520–1523 (Venice); it is the Bomberg edition. The text is printed with two commentaries: that of Rashi and that of the *Tosafot*. The pagination of this first edition was respected in the editions that followed. In all, the Talmud, including the *Mishnah-Gemara* and commentaries, has 2,947 leaves, which means about 6,000 pages. A leaf (*daf*) is made up of two pages. In references the name of the tractate and the *daf* number are given. The first side is indicated by *Aleph* (a), and the back by *Beit* (b).

The Talmudic Corpus

We have defined the Talmud as being made up of the *Mishnah-Gemara*. In fact, ever since it first appeared in print, the term "Talmud" has had a larger meaning: it means *Mishnah-Gemara-Rashi-Tosafot*. Ever since the first complete edition (Bomberg, Venice, 1520–1523), it is accompanied by two commentaries, those of Rashi and the Tosafists. Since then, the latter two are a part of the Talmud: so when we say "Talmud," we are saying, at the same time, "*Talmud-Rashi-Tosafot*." We call "Talmudic corpus" the Talmudic text flanked by its two faithful companions.

The Commentary of Rashi

The commentary of Rashi is the commentary par excellence. It is practically impossible to understand the Talmud without it. Rashi is an acronym for Rabbi Solomon ben Isaac. Born at Troyes in 1040, he died in 1105. Of his works, two items are essential: a commentary on the Bible and another on the Talmud, written in very clear Hebrew. In many cases where he could not find an adequate explanation for a word in Hebrew, he gave a translation in the French of his time. His commentary is written in an extremely concise manner, without superfluous words to enrich his style. The conciseness of Rashi is legendary: "In Rashi's time, every drop of ink was a precious stone." His commentary follows the sentences of the Talmud step-by-step. He explains difficult words, adds words necessary for the understanding of an idea, gives basic references that are found in other texts or tractates. Rashi is a neutral commentator; he does not take sides. He does not settle any of the discussions and comments the ideas of each side with equal clarity. According to Abraham Heschel, "Rashi was the principal architect of the intellectual emancipation of the people. Without the commentaries, the Jewish texts, and particularly the Talmud, are accessible to only a few select scholars. The ancient commentaries interpreted only isolated passages and limited themselves to a single tractate of the Talmud. Rashi's commentary explains practically every word of the enormous text with singular simplicity. It untangles all the twists and bends of the complex Talmudic dialectic. It is a faithful companion at the student's service, whichever part of the text he chooses to tackle. Humbly, discreetly, it takes the student by the hand and, in as few words as possible, gives him a maximum amount of knowledge. A short sentence, sometimes even a single word, sheds light on what seemed to be impenetrable darkness. There are no long abstract dissertations on matters of principles, methodology, or jurisprudence, but what one would hope to find is given: the meaning of a term is clarified, the consequences of a statement are extracted, the leading idea of a tricky argument is underscored." It has also given us a tightly argued criticism of the text and a clear and corrected version; these are the well-known *Hakhi Garsinan* ("thus must one read"). Right up to the present day, Rashi remains the greatest commentator of the Talmud.

The Commentary of the *Tosafot*

The commentaries of the *Tosafot* (or Tosafists) can be found on the external margin of a page of the Talmud, the internal margin being reserved for the commentary of Rashi. The word *Tosafot* means "additions." The Tosafists, or *Baalei ha-Tosfot*, lived during the twelfth and thirteenth centuries in France, Germany, and England. It is the work of a group of masters largely of the family of Rashi, who, himself, had no sons. His numerous daughters married his disciples, who contributed to the enrichment of his work. The style of the *Tosafot* is completely different from that of Rashi. It does not consist of a continuous commentary. They locate difficult points in the text, compare them with other passages, and show up the contradictions, which they then try to resolve. Often, the *Tosafot* teach Rashi a thing or two: they argue and show where Rashi's commentary presents difficulties. Some tractates had not been entirely commented by Rashi: so the *Tosafot* filled in the gap. His son-in-law, for example, Rabbi Judah ben Nathan ("Riban"), completed the *Makkot* tractate starting from folio 19b. His grandson, Rabbi Samuel ben Meir ("Rashbam"), continued the commentary on *Bava Batra* starting from page 29a, and he also commented the last chapter of *Pesahim*, even though Rashi had already explained it. Yet others: his son-in-law Rabbi Meir ben Samuel, his grandson Isaac ben Meir ("Ribam"), as well as Rabbi Jacob ben Meir, known as "Rabbenu Tam." We also come across a nephew of R. Tam, R. Isaac ben Samuel of Dampierre ("Ri Hazaken"). Other authorities frequently mentioned in the *Tosafot* are R. Judah ben Isaac of Paris, called Sire Léon (twelfth century), R. Perez ben Elijah of Corbeil (thirteenth century).

Like the Talmud, the *Tosafot* form a collective work of the masters of twelfth- and thirteenth-century France and Germany. Some commentaries have come down to us with the names of their authors, but many are anonymous. The *Tosafot* did not write books; however, we do have two anthologies from the different schools of Tosafists, that of Sens and that of Touques. The *Tosafot* that can be read in the edition of the

Talmud are those from the anthology of Touques, assembled by Rabbi Eliezer of Touques (end of the thirteenth century). Apart from these anthologies, numerous manuscripts remain unpublished to this day.

The Talmudic Page

"The written, printed page, like any linguistic practice, brings into action a theory of language and a historicity of discourse. . . . Each page is a scene: that of its practice of discourse, the practice of rationality, of a theory of language. Whether the page be dense or sparse, the scene is ancient. In the Talmud, the circularity of the commentary around a text that itself is repetition (*Mishnah*) of a text which is both present and absent represents transmission itself."[6]

The Talmudic page, since the first edition of 1523, takes the form of three columns. In the middle, the text of the *Gemara* and the *Mishnah*.[7] In the inner column (next to the central axis of the book) can be found the commentary of Rashi, in what is known as "Rashi characters," whereas the central text is written in square Hebrew characters. In the outside margin, the column of the commentaries of the *Tosafot* is also printed in "Rashi characters." But further still in the margins, there are yet other commentaries, often taking the form of simple references: a sort of intertextual concordance. We can find, for example, the *Ayin Mishpat-Ner Mitzva* of Rabbi Joshua Boaz: concordance between the passages of the Talmud and the texts of *Halakhah* by Maimonides, by R. Joseph Caro, by Moses of Coucy, etc. By the same author and also in the margins, we find the parallel texts in the Talmud: *Masoret hashas* as well as the references of biblical verses quoted in the Talmudic text (*Torah or*).

Halakhah and *Aggadah*

Like the biblical text, the text of the Talmud is made up of two categories of texts that are completely interwoven. The first category is that of *Halakhah* and the second, *Aggadah*.

Halakhah

Halakhah is the legal part of the Talmud, covering both the religious and the civil aspects of law. *Halakhah* gives Jewish life the orientation of action and law. *Halakhah* consists not only of laws made up by the Doctors but also of all the discussions that led up to the founding of

מאימתי

מאימתי קורין את שמע בערבין.. משעה שהכהנים נכנסים

First page of the *Berakhot* tractate (the *Mishnah* appears here in white on
black)

ע	ע		י	י		א	א
פ	פ		כ	כ		ב	ב
ף	ף		ר	ר		ג	ג
צ	צ		ל	ל		ד	ד
ץ	ץ		מ	מ		ה	ה
ק	ק		ס	ם		ו	ו
ר	ר		נ	נ		ז	ז
ש	ש		ו	ז		ח	ח
ת	ת		ס	ס		ט	ט

Characters known as "Rashi" characters

these laws. We can now understand the term *Halakhah* in its etymological
sense: "progression" (from the verb *halakh*: to walk). *Halakhah* represents
the development or the progress of the mind leading to the conclusions of
a law. This interpretation of the word *Halakhah* is confirmed by the fact
that a "halakhic" Talmudic passage is called *Sugya*, in Aramaic, a literal
translation of *Halakhah*. *Halakhah* is not only the conclusion, the law, but
also the whole "verbal intercourse" that leads up to it.

Aggadah

It is difficult to define *Aggadah*. The most accurate answer to the question "What is *Aggadah*?" would be: "It is everything that is not *Halakhah!*" Everything that, in the Talmud, does not belong to the legal discussion and does not concern the explanation of *Halakhah*. It covers not only the homilies, the preaching and edifying exegesis of the Bible, things that speak to the heart in order to move, to the mind in order to persuade; but we can also find real or legendary history (accounts of the destruction of the Temple) as well as notions about the most varied sciences (mathematics, astronomy, physics, medicine, natural history, botany). We can also find discussions on dream symbols and their interpretation, different ideas about the end of time, the messianic era, the resurrection of the dead, etc. If we have recourse to etymology, we find that *Aggadah* is Saying in a broad sense, Saying par excellence.

Unity and Tension of Halakhah *and* Aggadah

The classical distinction and division of Talmudic texts into *Halakhah* and *Aggadah* should be reconsidered. It would be wrong to confine and divide the texts into these two strict categories. If we can say that the "halakhic" texts concern behavior, that they give practical laws, describe behavior, a certain "action of being"[8]—and if we can also put forward the idea that the "aggadic" texts take the form of apologues, parables, that they represent the theological and philosophical part of tradition—it is also important to insist on the necessity of seeking the "halakhic project" of a text of the *Aggadah* as well as the "aggadic project" of a text of *Halakhah*.

The seeking of the "aggadic" project of a text of *Halakhah*—seeking the "inter-diction"—consists in shedding light on the thought that founds the prescriptions.

In the same way, the "halakhic" or "aggadic" project of a text of *Aggadah* means the will to say something else, to go beyond the saying by unfolding a sort of "inter-diction" in the vicinity, or not, of an interdiction.

The "inter-diction"[9] (*inter-dit*) and the "between-saying" (*entre-dire*) never—or rather, should never—compose a peripheral discourse but constitute speech that has its roots in the text and that continues to inhabit the text: a constant back-and-forth movement between the text and this "other text" that it generates. The "other text" is not an orphan: there is a veritable genealogy of saying.[10]

Classification of the *Aggadot*

There are two basic categories of *Aggadot*: those called *biuriim* and those called *limudiim*.

We shall be using, here, the terminology of Rabbi M. H. Luzzatto, given in his *Maamar al aggadot* (Remarks on the *Aggadot*).

The Aggadot Biuriim

These are all the Talmudic texts that comment a verse of the Bible. *Biuriim* comes from *levaer*, which means to explain; we can translate this as exegetical *Aggadot*.

The Aggadot Limudiim

These are all the "aggadic" texts that do not call upon the commentary of verses: *limudiim*, or teachings. They shape the thought of the reader. These texts, which are numerous, take the form of anecdotes from the biographies of one or several masters. But this is only in appearance. The *Aggadah* must never be reduced to a simple anecdote: "The *Aggadah* is not a source of a wealth of Israelite folklore. Nothing is less naive than these apologues" (Lévinas). These texts are not to be "read" but to be mediated; not to be "skimmed" through but to be opened, in a perpetual "Talmudic opening."

Midrash

We have seen ("The Two Manners of Expounding the Oral Law") that the direct exegetical method is called *Midrash*. The whole of *Midrash* is made up of different collections that are completely independent of the Talmud, even though numerous texts could often be read together or may even coincide perfectly. The reason for this is simple: the authors of the *Mishnah* and the *Gemara* were the same as those of the *Midrash*.

Once again we find the distinction between *Halakhah* and *Aggadah*. But here, this distinction is clearly marked, so we can notice the existence of two different collections: the *Midrash Halakhah* and the *Midrash Aggadah*.

Midrash Halakhah

If the explanation of the Bible offers a teaching concerning the laws, the result is a *Midrash Halakhah*. The most important collections are the *Mekhilta*, the *Sifra*, and the *Sifrei*.

The *Mekhilta* is a work originating in the school of Rabbi Ishmael. The word *Mekhilta* means collection (from the root "to contain"); it is a commentary in nine sections that deals with verses from the book of Exodus, from chapters 12 to 23 and from chapter 31.

The *Sifra* is the *Midrash Halakhah* of Leviticus. In fact, it has two names: *Sifra*, in Babylonia, and *Torat Kohanim* in Israel. The Talmud refers to it explicitly several times. It too is made up of nine parts; each part is divided into sections, and the sections into chapters. It is called *Sifra de-Vei Rav* (*Sifra* of the "house" of Rav).

The *Sifrei Bamidbar* is a *Midrash Halakhah* on the book of Numbers. It comes from the school of Rabbi Ishmael. There is also a *Sifrei* from the school of Rabbi Akiva, which bears the name *Sifrei Zuta* (The little *Sifrei*).

As for the *Sifrei Devarim*, "aggadic" for the most part, it is nonetheless a part of the *Midrash Halakhah*. It is composed of two parts: the first corresponds to the first part of the book of Deuteronomy and is the work of the school of Rabbi Ishmael; the second corresponds to the second part of the same book and comes from the school of Rabbi Akiva. It should be noticed that the second part was also commented by Rabbi Ishmael and bears the name of *Mekhilta* of Deuteronomy (there are a few fragments of it in the *Genizah* of Cairo).

The authors of the *Midrash Halakhah* are *Tannaim* (authors of the *Mishnah*), such as Rabbi Ishmael and Rabbi Akiva. Later on, the *Amoraim* took up the *Midrash* and completed it. Frequently, one finds parts of the *Midrash Halakhah* either in the *Mishnah* or in the *Gemara*.

Summary

	School of Rabbi Ishmael	School of Rabbi Akiva
Exodus	*Mekhilta* of R. Ishmael	*Mekhilta* of R. Simeon bar Yohai
Leviticus		*Sifra* or *Torat Kohanim*
Numbers	*Sifrei Bamidbar*	*Sifrei Zuta*
Deuteronomy	*Mekhilta Ledevarim*	*Sifrei Devarim*
	Sifrei Devarim	

Midrash Aggadah

In cases where the explanation of the biblical text gives rise to a teaching that does not directly concern the law, it is a *Midrash Aggadah*. These *Midrashim* were produced at a later date than the *Midrash Halakhah*. The production covers a period extending from 400 to 1500 C.E. for the later *Midrashim*. We can distinguish five periods:

1. 400 to 640: Genesis *Rabbah*, Leviticus *Rabbah*, Esther *Rabbah*, *Pesikta deRab Kahana*, Song of Songs *Rabbah*, Ruth *Rabbah*.

2. 640 to 900: Ecclesiastes *Rabbah*, Deuteronomy *Rabbah*, *Midrash Tanhuma*, Numbers *Rabbah II*, *Pesikta Rabati*, Exodus *Rabbah I* and *II*, *Midrash* Psalms *I*.

3. 100 to 1100: *Midrash* on the Song of Songs, *Midrash Aba-Gurion*, Esther *Rabbah II*, *Midrash* Psalms *II*.

4. 1100 to 1200: *Midrash Lekah Tov*, Genesis *Rabati*, Numbers *Rabbah*.

5. 1200 to 1550: this last period consists mainly of the production of "Midrashic" anthologies. We can find the *Yalkut Shimoni*, the *Midrash Hagadol* (of Yemenite origin), and the *Ein Yaakov*.

In its classical Vilna edition, the *Ein Yaakov* is accompanied by numerous commentaries: mainly those of Rashi and the "Maharsha." The best known of these *Midreshei Aggadot* is the *Midrash Rabbah*. A glance at the chronology tells us that the writing of the *Midrash Rabbah* series was accomplished in a very regular and progressive fashion. Only the *Midrashim* on Genesis and Leviticus were written down during the Talmudic period.

Notes

1. *Temurah* 14b.
2. Jerusalem Talmud, *Shabbat* 16, 1.
3. Ps. 119:126.
4. *Temurah* 14b and *Gittin* 60a.
5. Arsène Darmesteter, "Le Talmud," in "Aspects du génie d'Israël," *Cahiers du sud*, 1950, p. 13–44.
6. H. Meschonnic, *Critique du rythme* (Paris: Éditions Verdier, 1982), p. 303.
7. A great number of pages do not include the *Mishnah*.
8. We can call them prescriptive texts.
9. We use this word to denote the positive *Mitzvah* as well as the negative. Prohibition connotes prescription, the "limit" in general.
10. On the *Halakhah-Aggadah* relation, cf. also some very beautiful pages: A. Y. Heschel, *Dieu en quête de l'homme* (Paris: Seuil, 1968), pp. 337–66; and a famous text, "*Halakhah veaggadah*," by H. N. Bialik (in Hebrew). Cf. also B. Dupuy, "Unité et tension de la *Halakha* et de la *Aggada*," in *Mélanges à la mémoire de M. H. Prévost* (Paris: PUF, 1982).

III

The Talmudic Masters: The Schools

THE AUTHORS quoted by the *Mishnah* and the *Baraita* belong to three different periods.

The *Soferim*

The word *sofer* (*soferim* in the plural) means scribe. It refers to scholars who came after Ezra during a period of about two hundred years. Numerous extensions to the Mosaic law are attributed to them: these are the *Takanot Soferim* and the *Divrei Soferim*. The *Soferim* are also collectively called "the people of the Great Synagogue" (*Anshei Knesset Hagedolah*). According to tradition, this synod had 120 members. No name has come down to us except that of Ezra, the founder of the aforesaid assembly, and Simeon the Just (the high priest Simon I, 310–292 B.C.E., of whom it has been said that he was one of the last members of the Great Synagogue). Antigonus of Sukho, a disciple of Simeon the Just, ensured the transition between the period of the *Soferim* and that of the *Zugot*.

The *Zugot*

The term *zugot* means pairs. It refers to a duumvirate (government of two people). *Zugot* is the name given to the directing masters from Yose ben Joezer to Hillel. Of these pairs that "governed" and legislated at the same time, one was president of the Sanhedrin or *Nasi* and the other was vice president or *Av Beit Din*. The names of these pairs are mentioned in the first chapter of the *Avot* tractate:

—Yose ben Joezer and Yose ben Johanan, at the time of the wars of independance of the Maccabees
—Joshua ben Perahyah and Mattai the Arbelite, at the time of John Hyrcanus
—Judah ben Tabbai and Simeon ben Shetah, at the time of Alexander Yannai and Queen Salome Alexandra (who was Simeon ben Shetah's sister)
—Shemaiah and Avtalyon, at the time of Hyrcanus II
—Hillel and Shammai, at the time of King Herod

The *Tannaim*

The period of the *Tannaim* began with the disciples of Hillel and Shammai. This period lasted about 210 years (from 10 to 220 C.E.). It is at this time that the masters who receive the ordination begin to be called *Rabbi* and the presidents of the Sanhedrin *Rabban*. The word *tanna* means to repeat: he is a "repeater" of the words learned from his masters. Repetition was, in fact, the method of study and of passing on tradition. It is said to be by modesty that the masters were given this name, for, in actual fact, the period of the *Tannaim* was more a time of creation than of repetition. However, the term *tanna* does not appear in the *Mishnah*; the masters that we call *Rabbi* were called *Hakhanim* (sages). It is in the *Gemara* that the word *tanna* appears for the first time. In fact, it is the first word of the *Gemara* of the first tractate of the Talmud (*Berakhot* 2a). The period of the *Tannaim* is usually divided into five or six generations. The chronological charts that we give here cite only the names of the principal masters of each generation.

First generation: some authors have it starting in 10 C.E., others in the year 40. However, all the authors agree on the date of the closing of this first generation: the year 80. The principal masters are the school of Shammai and that of Hillel, Rabban Gamaliel the Elder, Rabbi Simeon ben Gamaliel, and Rabbi Johanan ben Zakkai, founder and director of the Academy of Jabneh.

Second generation: from 80 to 120 or from 80 to 110 C.E. The principal masters are Rabban Gamaliel II, Rabbi Zadok, Rabbi Eliezer and Rabbi Joshua, Rabbi Eleazar ben Azariah and Rabbi Yehuda ben Betera.

Third generation: from 120 to 139 or from 110 to 135 C.E. The masters are Rabbi Tarfon, Rabbi Ishmael, Rabbi Akiva, Rabbi Yose ha-Gelili.

Fourth generation: from 139 to 165 or from 135 to 170 C.E. The great men of this generation are Rabbi Meir, Rabbi Judah (bar Ilai), Rabbi Simeon bar Yohai, Rabbi Eleazar, Rabbi Simeon ben Gamaliel (grandson of the master of the same name of the first generation).

Fifth generation: from 165 to 200 or from 170 to 200 C.E. We find here Rabbi Judah ha-Nasi (also known as "Rabbi"—"the Master"), Symmachus, Rabbi Simeon ben Eleazar.

Sixth generation: the contemporaries and the disciples of Rabbi Judah ha-Nasi belong to this generation. They are not mentioned in the *Mishnah*, but in the *Tosefta* and the *Baraita*. They form the transition period between *Tannaim* and *Amoraim*. This period goes from 200 to 220 C.E.; Rabbi Hiyya and Rabbi Abba are the best-known masters.

The Masters of the *Gemara*: *Amoraim* and *Savoraim*

We can distinguish between two generations.

The Amoraim

The authors of the *Gemara* are the *Amoraim*: the interpreters. The root of this term is the verb *emor*, to say. Their authority is lesser than that of the *Tannaim*, and consequently they cannot contradict them. The *Amoraim* belong to two large geographical centers: Babylonia and the land of Israel. The *Amoraim* of *Eretz Israel*, ordained by the *Nasi*, usually bear the title of *Rabbi*, whereas those of Babylonia only have the title of *Rav* or *Mar*. The period of the *Amoraim* starts with the death of Rabbi Judah ha-Nasi and goes up to the writing of the Babylonian Talmud, i.e., from the beginning of the third century to the end of the fifth century. This period is divided by some authors into six, by others into seven or even eight generations, according to the end of the activity of the most important master of the era. The number of *Amoraim* mentioned in the Talmud reaches the hundreds. Here are the most important.

THE FIRST GENERATION OF *AMORAIM*

—*In Eretz Israel* (219–279): Rabbi Hanina bar Hama (180–260); Rabbi Johanan (199–279); Rabbi Simeon ben Lakish (Resh Lakish); Rabbi Joshua ben Levi; Rabbi Aphes; Levi bar Sisi; Hiskiya; Rabbi Simlai
—*In Babylonia* (219–257); Rav (175–247); Samuel (180–257); Mar Ukba (the Exilarch)

THE SECOND GENERATION

—*In Eretz Israel* (279–320): Rabbi Eleazar ben Pedath; Rabbi Ammi; Rabbi Assi; Rabbi Hiyya bar Abba; Rabbi Simeon bar Abba; Rabbi Abbahu; Rabbi Zeira
—*In Babylonia* (257–320): Rav Huna (212–297); Rav Judah bar Ezekiel (199–299); Rav Hisda; Rav Sheshet; Rav Nahman bar Jacob; Rabbah bar Hana; Ula bar Ishmael

THE THIRD GENERATION

—*In Eretz Israel* (320–359): Rabbi Jeremiah; Rabbi Jonah; Rabbi Yose bar Zabda

—*In Babylonia* (320–359): Rabbah bar Huna; Rabba bar Nahamani or Rabba (270–330); Rav Joseph (nicknamed Sinai) (?–333); Abbaye (280–338); Rava (299–359); Rav Nahman bar Isaac; Rav Papa (?–375)

THE FOURTH GENERATION OF BABYLONIAN *AMORAIM* (375–427)

—*Academy of Sura*: Rav Ashi
—*Academy of Pumbedita*: Rav Zevid (337–385); Rav Dimi (385–388); Rafram bar Papa (388–394); Rav Kahana bar Talifa (394–411); Mar Zutra (411–414); Rav Aha bar Rabbah (414–419); Rav Geviha of Bei-Katil (419–433)
—*Academy of Nehardea*: Ameimar (390–422)

THE FIFTH GENERATION OF BABYLONIAN *AMORAIM* (427–468)

—*Academy of Sura*: Mar Yeimar (433–443); Rav Idi bar Avin (432–452); Mar bar Rav Ashi (455–468); Rav Aha Midifti
—*Academy of Pumbedita*: Rafram II (433–443); Rav Rehumei (443–456); Rav Samma bar Rabbah (456–471)

THE SIXTH GENERATION OF BABYLONIAN *AMORAIM* (468–500)

—*Academy of Sura*: Rava Tosfa'ah (468–474); Ravina bar Huna (488–499), last *Amora* of Sura
—*Academy of Pumbedita*: Rav Joseph (475–520), last *Amora* of Pumbedita

The Savoraim

After the death of Ravina, considered the last of the *Amoraim*, begins the period of the *Savoraim*: the "thinkers." These are the masters of the first half of the sixth century. Their authority was not sufficient to allow them to contradict the decision of the *Amoraim*. They brought the last touches to the Talmud, to the discussions that had not been resolved and on which they give their opinion, etc. Rav Joseph is considered as the last of the *Amorim* and the first of the *Savoraim*.

The Talmudic Academies

There were numerous Talmudic academies at the time of the *Tannaim*; in the land of Israel there were academies in the following towns: Pequiin (founded by Joshua ben Hananiah before the destruction of the

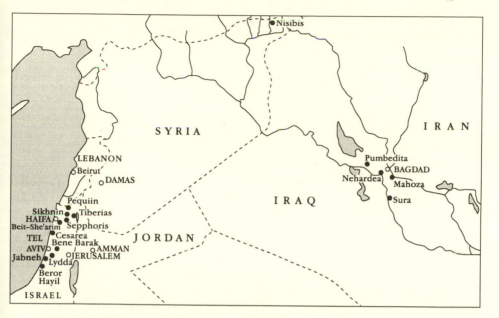

Principal Talmudic Academies of Eretz-Israel and Babylonia

Temple), Tiberias (founded by Rabbi Meir), Sepphoris (founded by R. Yose bar Halafta), Beit She'arim (founded by R. Johanan ben Nuri), Caesarea, Bene-Berak (founded by R. Akiva), Lod (founded by R. Eliezer), Jabneh (founded by R. Johanan ben Zakkai), Jerusalem, Beror Hayil (founded by Rabbi Johanan ben Zakkai), Usha (founded by R. Simeon ben Gamaliel), Tekoa (founded by R. Simeon bar Yohai), Sikhnin (founded by R. Hananiah ben Teradion). Elsewhere, we find such schools at Nisibis in Mesopotamia, founded by R. Judah ben Bathyra, and at Rome, founded by R. Mathiah.

At the time of the *Amoraim*, only the following academies remained: those of the towns of Lod, directed by R. Joshua ben Levi, Sepphoris, directed by R. Hananiah bar Hama, and Tiberias, directed by Rabbis Johanan, Ammi, and Asi. In Babylonia, new schools flourished in the towns of Utsal (founded by Rav), Nehardea (founded by Samuel), Pumbedita (founded by Rav Judah), and Mahoza (founded by Rava).

IV

The Post-Talmudic Period

The *Geonim*

During the five centuries that followed the ending of the Talmud, the Babylonian academies remained at the head of Jewish life. The Jews from all countries of the world consulted, on contentious points, the *Geonim*—the name given to the directors of the academies of Sura and Pumbedita, principal centers of Talmudic studies in Babylonia. They continued studying the teachings of the Talmud in the tradition of the *Amoraim*. In their most influential period, students from numerous countries came to listen to their teaching. As soon as they struck an ambiguous or obscure passage of the Talmud, a difficulty in the interpretation of the law, a problem concerning belief, they sent *sheelot* (questions) to Babylonia. The rulings, conclusions, or interpretations, the *teshuvot* (*responsa*) of these eminent masters, were considered judicial precedents. However, their literary activity concerning the commentary of the Talmud remained limited; in fact, nothing has come down to us of what was contained in the *responsa*, in which the *Geonim* explained to those who asked them the meaning of difficult words, curious expressions, and sometimes even complete subjects (*sugyot*) that posed a problem. These *responsa* are the first commentaries of the Talmud; the later *Geonim* started writing the commentaries on whole tractates, but, once again, these were generally only annotations, explanations of difficult words and, here and there, obscure expressions. The greater part of this literature is juridical (*psakim*: legal rulings, practical conclusions based on an in-depth study of Talmudic subjects).

Two Great Centers

The period of the *Geonim* ends in the eleventh century; the Babylonian center had already lost much of its importance. In this century there were already two important Jewish centers; the first was the Muslim world—North Africa and Spain; the second was the European center—mainly Italy, France, and Germany. In many respects, the Afro-Spanish center was, from the point of view of Jewish culture, the continuation of Babylonian Judaism, because, as in Babylonia, this Judaism was dominated by the Muslim Empire. People spoke Arabic, were subjected to the same cultural influences, and maintained strong links with the last Babylonian *Geonim*. Thousands of *responsa* came from Babylonia to Africa, along with some collections of texts. The Jews of North Africa and Spain modeled their conduct on the norms given by the Babylonian masters in the areas of courts of law, approaches to studying, and Judaism. But, on the other hand, the European center could be considered as attached to the land of Israel; the link passed through the geographical line of Eretz Israel-Greece-Italy-France-Germany. Numerous texts of prayers, fundamental ideas of Judaism came from Eretz Israel. Here, there was no influence from an outside culture for the simple reason that none existed . . . In North Africa and in Spain, Arabic culture was at its peak in every field: philosophy, science, poetry, linguistics, etc. In Europe, the culture was that of the "Dark" Ages. In fact, the European Jews were at a level above that of the surrounding culture; spiritual and intellectual life had yet to be developed. These two great Jewish centers gave birth to two parallel trends, two lifestyles, two ways of viewing the world, and also two different types of Talmudic commentaries.

Rishonim and Aharonim

In the history of Talmudic literature, and in particular "halakhic" literature, time is divided into periods corresponding to a hierarchy in the authority of the masters. The closer a master is to the Revelation of Sinai, the greater his authority. The Talmud itself states this principle (Babylonian Talmud, *Shabbat* 112b): "If the first masters (*Rishonim*) were as angels, we are as men, and if the *Rishonim* were men, then we are as donkeys." The period of the *Rishonim* (meaning "the first ones") begins at the end of the period of the *Geonim* and ends toward the middle of the fifteenth century. The two last representatives are "Ribash" of Barcelona (1326–1408) for the Spanish school and Rabbi Isserlein (1390–1460) for Germany. The period of the *Rishonim* ends with the expulsion of the Jews from Spain in 1492. After 1492, the Spanish school disappears as a geographical center but continues to prosper as a method: this continuation gives us the line of great "halakhic" codifiers. The Jews, fleeing from Spain, spread throughout the world; the great Jewish centers were then established in Holland, in Germany, and particularly in Poland, which gave the history of Jewish thought its greatest Talmudists. After the period of the *Rishonim* ("the first ones") began that of the *Aharonim* ("those who follow"), which continues up to the present day.

Different Trends in the Study of the Talmud

The Spanish School: The Synthetic Approach

The sages of Spain and North Africa[1] descend in a direct line from the Babylonian *Geonim*. The greater part of their literary creation is of a legal nature, and their approach is a synthetic one. The first of the great commentators is Rabbenu Hananel ben Hushiel (?–1056) from the town of Kairuan (North Africa). His writing is characterized by an extreme concision and consists in a summary and an overview of each Talmudic *sugya*, giving the essential ideas of the content. At the same time and in the same town lived Rav Nissim Gaon, another commentator. The thrust of his style of commentary was, as we have said, the "halakhic" decision, a practical approach, the will to arrive at a general synthesis of the Talmudic content. We could also mention others from this Spanish school: Rabbi Meir Abulafia (1170–1244), Nahmanides of Gerona (1194–1270), Rabbi Salomon ben Adret of Barcelona (1235–1310). But the great literary event was constituted by the work of Maimonides (1135–1204), the *Mishneh Torah*, which characterized what we have called the synthetic approach: "Maimonides created the first encyclopedic code, both clear and concise, covering the whole of the field of the law; it is a masterly construction, unsurpassable in the depth of its decisions and deductions, brilliant in its briefness and clarity, which leaves out everything that is pure argumentation and dialectical discussion."[2]

The European School: The Analytical Approach

If the Afro-Spanish school is characterized by the synthetic approach, the European school and the French school in particular, that of Rashi and the *Tosafot*, are distinguished by their analytical approach. There is no attempt at codification, no encyclopedia but, rather, a close analysis of the Talmudic text.

Between France and Spain: "Meiri" (1249–1316)

Between these two trends, we encounter an exceptional case: a commentary that uses both the synthetic and the analytic approaches. This case is that of "Meiri" (1249–1316), Rabbi Menahem ben Solomon, author of *Beit ha-Behirah*. His commentary includes both a philological and textual analysis, like those of the French masters, and legal conclusions and decisions in the manner of Maimonides. It is interesting to notice that this meeting of two intellectual trends may possibly be the result of a geographical confluence. "Meiri," who spent all his days at Perpignan, was situated at the very crossroads of France and Spain.

Notes

1. Cf. "Two Great Centers."
2. A. Y. Heschel, *Les Bâtisseurs du temps* (Paris: Éditions de Minuit, 1969), p. 32.

V

Jurisprudence Derived from the Talmud

ONCE the Babylonian Talmud was considered as the main source of all "halakhic" decisions, it became urgent to bring all the laws together in a systematic manner and to create works that would be easy to consult in order to settle disputes and govern the conduct of all Jews.

Here are the main works of this strictly "halakhic" literature.

First Attempts

The first attempts at systematizing were made in the period of the *Geonim*. Rabbi Yehudai, Gaon of Sura (eighth century), wrote a text entitled *Halakhot Ketanot*, which means "The Minor Laws." Rabbi Simeon of Kahina (ninth century) wrote another book: *Halakhot Gedolot* (The major laws). These two works, which were later combined in a single volume, under the second title, were overshadowed by the "halakhic" works that followed.

"Rif": Rabbi Isaac ben Jacob Alfasi (1013–1103)

Rabbi Isaac Alfasi, also known as "Rif" (initials of his title and his name) wrote a sort of "digest" of the Talmud. Retaining the division, the language, and the style of the Talmud, he leaves out the "aggadic" part and the whole part dealing with the laws no longer in force since the destruction of the Temple. He summarizes the long Talmudic discussions and resolves the *Halakhah*, expounding his own decision when the Talmud does not take sides and leaves the debate open.

"Rif"'s commentary, printed with a layout similar to that of the Talmud, appears at the end of each tractate in the "Vilna" edition (the model for all contemporary editions) accompanied by Rashi's commentary referring to the passages quoted (in the inner margin) as well as the commentary of Rabbi Nissim ben Reuben ("Ran") or Rabbi Joseph Habiba "Nimomukei Yosef" (in the outer margin). And in the margin of the margin, the commentaries of Rabbi Zechariah ha-Levi and Rabbi Mordecai ben Hillel.

"Rosh": Rabbenu Asher ben Jehiel (Ca. 1250–1327)

A German rabbi, having settled in Spain, he taught at Toledo and died in 1327. Like "Rif," he wrote a synopsis, introducing decisions from more recent authorities. His commentary also appears at the end of each tractate. His son, Rabbi Jacob ben Asher, added a summary of this synopsis bearing the name of *Kitzur Piskei ha-Rosh*: summary of the decisions of "Rosh."

The *Mishneh Torah* of Maimonides

The *Mishneh Torah*, "The Repetition of the Law," written by Maimonides (1135–1204), is the most systematic and most important synthesis of the two Talmuds. Only the conclusions of the discussions are described. Maimonides sometimes adds the decision of post-Talmudic authorities such as the *Geonim*. This enormous work is written in classical Hebrew, very close to that of the *Mishnah*, and is of an extraordinary beauty and purity: the style is perfect; the ideas are of a masterly clarity. The division into fourteen books was the reason for the subtitle of the work: *Sefer ha-Yad* (The handbook: Yad = *yod-dalet*, meaning "fourteen" and "hand"). It was later called *Yad ha-Hazakah* (The strong hand). It is divided into chapters and *halakhot*. A modern edition in twenty volumes has been compiled by Mossad Harav Kook, with a practical critical apparatus. During a very long period it was edited along with numerous commentaries. Here is the list:

1. *Hasagot Rabad*: critical remarks by Rabbi Abraham ben David of Posquières ("Rabad"), a contemporary and antagonist of Maimonides
2. *Migdal Oz*: by Rabbi Shem Tov ibn Gaon defending Maimonides against the censure and criticisms of "Rabad" (beginning of the fourteenth century)
3. *Haggahot Maimoniyyot*: annotations by Rabbi Meir ha-Kohen of Narbonne (fourteenth century)
4. *Maggid Mishneh*: commentaries by Don Vidal Yom Tov of Tolosa (fourteenth century) that, in general, note the Talmudic sources of Maimonides
5. *Kesef Mishneh*: commentaries in the style of the previous commentator, by Rabbi Joseph Caro, author of *Shulhan Arukh* (sixteenth century)
6. *Lehem Mishneh*: by Rabbi Abraham of Botton, Safen (sixteenth century)
7. *Mishneh la-Melekh*: by Rabbi Judah Rosanes, rabbi at Constantinople, died in 1727

אמר רב הונא היה מהלך בשבתא ופגע באמת המים...

ומדאמרי ואי לוי ליה סחיותה ולא אמרינן גו מצוה...

רש"י

סליק להו ואלו קשרים

כל כתבי הקדש ...

סליק להו ואלו קשרים

כל כתבי הקדש...

מלחמה ה׳

דמאור הבקן

A page of the "Rif"

פרק ארבעה ועשרים

קרבן נתנאל

A page of the "Rosh"

פרק ואלו קשרים

דף קכב

חכמת שלמה

ואלו קשרים פרק חמשה עשר

דף קכב ע״א בגמ׳

מהרש״א

ואלו קשרים פרק חמשה עשר

דף קכב ע״א בגמ׳

דף קכג ע״א

דף קכג ע״ב

A page of the "Maharsha"

Sefer Mitzvot Gadol ("SeMaG")

Written by the Tosafist Rabbi Moses of Coucy (France, thirteenth century), divided into two parts: one dealing with the positive laws, the other with the negative laws; set out according to the 613 *Mitzvot*.

Sefer Mitzvot Katan ("Semak")

A similar work, smaller in scope, also called *Amudei Golah*, written by R. Isaac of Corbeil (died in 1280).

The *"Tur"* or *Arba'ah Turim* by Jacob ben Asher

The son of "Rosh," Rabbi Jacob ben Asher (1269–1343), reorganized the *Halakhah*, completing a synthesis of the work of Maimonides and of his father's commentary. He retained only the practical *halakhot* that were still valid for his time; so he ignored all the laws referring to the Temple and to the sacrifices, and certain laws concerning the land of Israel no longer relevant because of the Exile. He also included post-Talmudic laws and customs.

The work of R.J.B. Asher is composed of four parts:

1. *Orah Hayyim* (liturgical laws): prayer, Shabbat, festivals
2. *Even ha-Ezer* (laws on marriage): divorce, etc.
3. *Hoshen Mishpat* (civil laws): business law, property
4. *Yorei De'ah* (ritual laws): killing animals, circumcision

Each part is called a *Tur* (row), whence the name *Arba'ah Turim* (Four rows).

The *Shulhan Arukh* by Rabbi Joseph Caro (1488–1575)

Rabbi Joseph Caro was not unknown when he published the *Shulhan Arukh* (The upright table). He was already the author of an important commentary on Maimonides' *Mishneh Torah*, entitled *Kesef Mishneh*, and one on the *Arba'ah Turim*, entitled *Beit Yosef*. In fact, the *Shulhan Arukh* is a large synthesis of the three previous works, maintaining the division of the *Turim*. It has become everyman's "halakhic" reference book. At the end of each paragraph one can find the additions (*Hagahot*), which sometimes contradict the decisions of Rabbi Joseph Caro, but which often complete them. These "additions" are the work of

Rabbi Moses Isserles (1522–1573). When there is a debate between R. J. Caro and R. M. Isserles, the *Sephardim* (Jews originating from Spain and North Africa) follow the decisions of the former and the *Ashkenazim* (Jews originating from Germany and eastern Europe) accept the authority of the latter.

In the current edition, the commentaries are printed on the same page around the text of R. J. Caro. The commentators all belong to the seventeenth century:

—*Be'er ha-Golah*, by R. Moses Rivkes of Amsterdam
—*Turei Zahav*, by R. David B. Samuel ha-Levi
—*Siftei Kohen*, by R. Shabbetai Meir ha-Kohen
—*Magen Avraham*, by R. Abraham Gombiner
—*Beit Samuel*, by R. Samuel B. Uri of Furth
—*Helkat Mehokek*, by R. Moses of Brisk

VI

Interpretation

The Art of Understanding

Having explained the transmission of the Written and Oral Law, the transcription of this Law (the Talmud), its content, its presentation, and having introduced its masters, its commentaries, we will now look more closely at a few methodological principles.

How should the Talmud and the *Midrash* be approached? In what manner and what spirit?

What are the rules of interpretation that aid in understanding and giving the text its real scope? We are now going to attempt to answer these questions.

We can, in a somewhat simplified but nonetheless exact manner, distinguish two approaches to the Talmud: the historical and the existential.

The Historical Approach

The historical method considers the past as belonging totally to history. The past is intelligible only after the knowledgeable and critical mediation of the historian. In this case the texts acquire a mythical dimension and are considered as a "surviving mythogenic fabric" that the scholar attempts to decipher. He seeks to find, reconstitute, and understand the life of the Hebrews in the desert, the life of the Jews at the time of the Talmud, etc. He shows us how the Jewish language, clothing, habitats were borrowed from the Greek or Roman world; the philologist will find grist for his mill in deciphering words with Persian, Greek, or Latin sounds, which will then allow him to shed light on the similarities or differences in customs, attitudes, and myths.

In spite of this will and this effort to get to know texts and traditions, the historian keeps his distance: in other words, he ensures that the past remains the past and the present the present. The historical method consists in objectivizing tradition and methodically eliminating any influence that the present may exert on the understanding of the historian.

The historian-interpreter tackles the object of study with one very precise rule in mind: "Only he who refuses to become involved will be able to understand."

To whom are the texts of Tradition addressed? For the historian the answer is simple: to every one except himself. Following this way of interpreting the methodology of human sciences, one can say that the interpreter imagines an addressee for every text, whether the text refers to him explicitly or not. It is impossible for the historian to conceive himself as the person to whom the text is addressed, to submit himself to the demands of the text.

The historian bases his work on the following hypotheses: he must put himself in the spirit of the era, think with its concepts, with its representations, and not according to his own time, in order to attain historical objectivity. All this means that the temporal distance is a barrier to understanding: objective understanding. Or else, paradoxically, this temporal distance is the very thing that makes the historical situation of interpretation possible. Objective understanding can be attained only on the basis of a certain degree of historical distance. However, even if this distancing of the object conditions a certain objectivity and a certain positivity of research, a negative aspect of the historical method then appears that rests in fact on the tacit hypothesis which runs as follows: a thing can be objectively knowable, in its lasting meaning, only if it belongs to a clearly defined context. In other words, when it is so dead that it is only of purely historical interest . . .

The Existential or Situational Approach[1]

"No one can refuse the light of the historian; but we believe that it is not sufficient for everything" (Lévinas, *Quatre Lectures talmudiques*). Here, no temporal distance separates the interpreter from the text. This famous text from the *Midrash* commenting Deut. 29:15 could provide the epigraph to this approach:

> "It is not with you alone that I make this covenant, as well as this plea, but with whoever is present today with us in the presence of God . . . and with whoever is not here today with us."
> All those who will be born in the future until the end of all generations were present with them at Mount Sinai. (*Pirkei de-Rabbi Eliezer*, chapter 41)[2]

The existential attitude is based on the idea that every era must understand the text in its own way. The real meaning of a text, as it addresses itself to the interpreter, does not depend on accidental factors concerning the author and his original audience. Or, at least, these conditions do not exhaust its meaning.

And so one can state that the meaning of a text—if it is a great text—not just occasionally but always escapes its author: that is why understanding is not simply a reproductive attitude but is always a productive one.

It is not just a matter of understanding better but of understanding differently. In this context, the temporal distance should be considered as a positive and productive possibility offered to the understanding. "So it is not a gaping abyss, but it can be crossed by means of the continuity of its provenance and its passing on in the light of which all tradition is offered to our gaze" (H. G. Gadamer).[3]

The existential approach is based on the personal involvement of the interpreter in the event of understanding. The interpreter is literally "inter-ested" by the text he comments and understands; the ideas of the interpreter are, from the very start, involved in revitalizing the meaning of the text; his personal background is a decisive factor. But it is not so in terms of a personal point of view that would be maintained or imposed but, rather, like an opinion or a possibility that comes into play, allowing one to apply the content of the text to oneself.

The subjective interpretation precedes the understanding itself, so that one could say, *To understand is already and ever to interpret*, or *Understanding always contains a degree of interpretation*.

In fact, it is not the text that is understood but the reader. He understands *himself*.

To understand a text is, from the start, to apply it to ourselves. But this application does not diminish the text, for we know that the text can and must always be understood differently.

The Importance of Each Person

Each person born into this world represents something new, something that did not exist before, something original and unique.

It is the duty of every person in Israel to know how to appreciate that he is unique in this world because of his particular character and that there has never been someone like him in the world, because if there had been someone like him, there would have been no reason for him to be in the world. Each man taken individually is a new creature in the world, and is called to fulfill his particularity in the world. The very first task of each man is the actualizing of his unique possibilities, without precedent and never renewed, and not the repetition of something that someone else, were he the greatest person of all, would already have accomplished. It is this idea that Rabbi Zusya expressed shortly before his death: in the other world I will not be asked, Why were you not Moses? I will be asked, Why were you not Zusya?[4]

Lévinas takes up this text by Martin Buber in the following manner:

> The personal—subjective—relation to the text, "Revelation" inasmuch as
> it appeals to what is unique in me, that is the actual meaning of the signified
> of Revelation. It is as if the multiplicity of persons—and is this not the very
> meaning of personal?—were the prerequisite for the fullness of "absolute
> truth" as if each person, by his uniqueness, ensured the revelation of a unique
> aspect of truth, and that some of its aspects would never be revealed if some
> members of humanity were missing. This suggests that the totality of truth is
> made up of the contributions of multiple persons: the uniqueness of each
> reaction bearing the secret of the text; the voice of Revelation precisely inas-
> much as it is inflected by the ear of each person, would be necessary for the
> Whole of Truth![5]

The same idea is expressed in the texts of Hasidism[6] in the following
manner: each man is a letter or a part of a letter. The Book has been
completely written when there is no longer any letter missing. Each man
must write his letter, must write himself, that is to say, create himself by
renewing a meaning: his meaning.

The Risk of Subjectivity

We have insisted on the fact that understanding and interpreting are
inextricably intertwined; it is an essential criticism that goes against the
historical approach of texts. The historian-interpreter fools himself
when he hopes to eliminate all subjective participation in understanding. For "historical thinking always contains, from the start, a mediation between these principles and personal thought. To try to avoid
one's own concepts in interpretation is not only impossible but quite
obviously absurd. To interpret is to bring one's own ideas into play."[7]

Here is a short passage from Maimonides in his introduction to the
commentary of the *Merkavah* (The fiery chariot), one of the parts of
Jewish thought where one might have thought it possible to count on
the objectiveness of knowledge, interpretation, tradition, and transmission.

> What I believe I possess myself is only a matter of circumstance and per-
> sonal opinion. I have not had any divine revelation on the subject that might
> have allowed me to know what was really meant there, nor have I learned
> from a master what I think, but it is the texts of prophetic books and the
> speeches of the doctors, as well as the speculative propositions that I possess,
> which have led me to believe that it is so. However, it may possibly be other-
> wise and something else may have been meant.[8]

The aim of this quotation is not to deny the existence of "inspiration" but rather to suggest that "there is inspiration in the very exercising of reason. The *logos* itself is prophetic!"[9]

That being the case, the commentator can become involved. With his personality, his experiences, his readings; in short: with the whole of his experience. The commentary is not a disembodied text, nor is it an orphan text.

As a result, one must be wary of the objectivist or pseudo-objectivist effort that tends to promote a way of cutting itself off, negatively, from the meaning of the text. The commentator, in spite of his refusal, inevitably intervenes much more than he says or believes himself.

Therefore, it would probably be wiser to highlight the way in which one progresses instead of aspiring to the illusory transparency of the ideal commentator. It is time to stop alleging an invisibility that would allow the commentator to discover the truth of the work . . . The commentator is not subordinate to a so-called original text, at least to the extent that he seeks to "repeat a development which in fact has never been undertaken."[10]

Even when he simply repeats, the commentator is already other. "In repetition, what is said enters into its essential difference."[11]

Talmudic Openings

If we had to find one word to describe, as accurately as possible, what commentary and interpretation should be, we would suggest the word "opening."

Why "opening"? This word does not have the meaning of the Hebrew word *Petihah* that would be its translation. In Hebrew *Petihah* means "introduction," in the sense of a history and an overall view of the work.

"Opening," here, is to be understood in the sense of the expression from the *Midrash* and the *Zohar*, "*Patah veamar*"—he opened and he said—that one encounters on the verge of Saying. "He opened and he said," he shattered the verse and he said. So there is a shattering, an opening of the word, of this *tevah* that is also a box, a volume.[12]

Interpretation implies the bursting open of literary space: the text is no longer to be considered in it linearity, but in its spatiality, its volume. Or perhaps we should say that the bursting open of the text is what will allow the passage from the line-text to the volume-text. All the elements of the text will then be subjected to this breakup, this opening: letters, words, sentences, books . . . This opening operates to the point of effacing the letters, the words, the sentences, and the books . . .

To illustrate what I mean by "opening," I wish to quote here a beautiful page by Jankélévitch from his book *Quelque part dans l'inachevé* (lit.: Somewhere in the unfinished), a title that indicates precisely where the "opening" must lead to. He does not give any precise rules for Midrashic or Talmudic hermeneutics, but we are already intuitively involved here in the process of opening.

Study[13] consists of thinking everything that is thinkable in a question, thoroughly, at all costs. You must untangle the inextricable and only ever stop when it becomes impossible to go any further; with this rigorous research in mind, words that are used as a medium for thought must be used in all possible positions, in the most varied locutions; you must turn them over, turn them around again showing up all their facets in the hope that a gleam will burst forth, feel them and sound their tone in order to perceive the secret of their meaning: do not the assonances and resonances of words have inspirational virtues? This rigor must sometimes be attained at the cost of an illegible discourse: you sometimes come very close to contradicting yourself; you just have to follow along the same line, slide down the same slope, and you leave your starting point further and further behind, and the starting point ends up by refuting the finishing point.

I try to compel myself to keep to this faultless reasoning, to this *strenge Wissenschaft*, a rigorous science, which is more like asceticism. I fell temporarily less anxious when, after having gone round in circles for a long time, sounded and kneaded words, explored their semantic resonances, analyzed their allusive powers, their powers of evocation, I verify that indeed I can no longer go any further.

Of course, to claim that one can one day arrive at the truth is a dogmatic utopia; what matters is to go through to the end of what one is able to do, to attain a faultless coherency, to bring to the surface the most hidden, the most inexpressible questions, to make of them a smooth world.[14]

The "Caress": Experiencing

But let us not be too hasty! The smooth world Jankélévitch is talking about does not allow one to *grasp* the text, to *understand* its meaning, because the presence of levels of meaning and rules of interpretation nullifies the possibility of appropriating the text, thus banishing its otherness and exteriority. In brief, interpretation—interpretations—never actually bite into the text itself. That is the guarantee of the inexhaustible richness of the text.

Signs—in this case objects, biblical verses, persons, situations, rites— work like perfect signs:

Whatever the changes may be that becoming introduces into their tangible texture, they preserve their privilege of revealing the same meanings or the new aspects of these meanings.[15]

Perfect signs, for

never does the meaning of these symbols completely dismiss the materiality of the symbols that suggest it and that always preserve an undreamed-of power to renew this meaning; never does the mind dismiss the letter that reveals it to itself. On the contrary, the mind awakens in the letter new possibilities of suggestion.[16]

As a collection of perfect signs, the Text can never be attained. One could say that it is caressed. So in spite of the analysis undertaken, it spite of the research, the bursting open, the laying bare, the text slips out of our grasp, remains inaccessible, always yet to come. It reveals itself only to withdraw immediately.[17] The text is both "visible and invisible"[18] at the same time; ambiguous, its meaning twinkles, it remains an enigma: "Transcendence owes it to itself to interrupt its own demonstration. Its voice has to be silent as soon as one listens for its message."[19]

But the Text withdraws only if we let it; the interruption of the demonstration of transcendence, the movement of necessary withdrawal depends, above all, on the interpreter, on his way of being as he reads the text, on his approach. We call this way of being the "caress":[20] the caress is a modality of the subject, where the subject in his relation with the Text goes beyond the relation, for "that which is caressed is not actually touched"[21]; "the caress is the non-coinciding proper to contact, a denuding never naked enough."[22]

The caress consists in seizing upon nothing, in soliciting what unceaselessly escapes its form toward a future never future enough, in soliciting what slips away as though it *were not yet.*[23]

In short, the caress is research. In this research the caress does not know what it is seeking. This "not knowing," this "fundamental disorder,"[24] is central to this way of being. The relation to the Text authorizing the transcendence of the voices of the Text will therefore be like "a game utterly without project or plan."[25]

Study, considered as research, allows one to experience. In this respect we can contrast the expressions "to have an experience" and actually "to experience."[26] "To have" refers to possession, to knowing, to settling back with satisfaction, to the confidence that acquisition confers; in the "having," the experience is confirmed by repetition. But since the experience is repeated and confirmed, it cannot be something that renews itself. Consequently, that which originally was unforeseen is now foreseen. "To have" an experience of the Text is to understand it, grasp it, possess it, because it is its repetition that gives it substance. But once it becomes visible, graspable, the Text takes on the shape and status of an idol. Its language becomes totalitarian: "stereotyped, remaining frozen in meanings set and imposed once and for all without consideration for situations and experiences that may have changed."[27] The idol-text is "set out and crushes because of both its weight and its unchangingness."[28]

There is no longer any question of "having" an experience with the Text. Studying no longer means knowing in advance the results of one's research. Nothing should fulfill our expectations. "Experiencing is always, at first, an experience of negativity: the thing is not such as we thought. Our knowledge and its object are both altered with the experience of another object."[29]

"To experience" means to participate in opening. The "man of experience"—in our context, the interpreter—is not only the one who has become such as a result of his experiences (already acquired), but the one who is open to experiences.

> The fullness of experience, the fullness of being of the person we call experienced, does not consist in the fact that he already knows everything and knows it better. The man of experience turns out to be radically foreign to all dogmatism.[30]

The interpreter experiences things by caressing: never seizing anything, he allows himself to be carried, negatively and infinitely, from one meaning to another, so that if one had to locate (in the Text) a center, an origin of meaning, a god that gives the meaning, one would find it only in the void, empty of language, the "blanks of writing."[31]

We can then understand why *study* is symbolized by the written form of the letter *Lamed*, the only one of the twenty-two letters of the Hebrew alphabet to go over the line, to trans-gress, to thrust itself "beyond the verse." *Lamed*, the last letter of the Torah . . .[32]

Refusing the Idol-Text; or, The Necessity of Atheism

So the Text should be elusive, impregnable, and should never take on the form of an idol. The Cabalists explain that the Text, the Torah, and God are one (*Rahamana vekudsha beirikh hu, had hu*). In refusing to lay one's hand on the Text, one also refuses to lay one's hand on the divinity. The relationship with the text and with God is paradoxical: one must move away, create a distance, if the relation with God is not going to be idolatrous. This is what Henri Atlan calls the "atheism of writing":

The primary preoccupation of biblical teaching is not the existence of God, theism as contrasted with atheism, but the fight against idolatry. In all theism there is the danger of idolatry. All theism is idolatry, since expression signifies it, thereby freezing it; except if, somehow, its discourse refutes itself and so becomes atheistic. In other words, the paradoxes of language and its meanings are such that the only discourse possible about God which is not idolatrous is an atheistic discourse. Or: in any discourse the only God that is not an idol is a God who is not God.[33]

All the masters of Jewish thought, from the prophets to the contemporary masters, have understood that . . .

The system of interpretation—besides its necessity for the phenomenon of understanding—*is founded on the will to refuse idolatry.* The Text, which is the primary relation to God, must not turn into an idol. The temptation of idolatry is strong—one need only remember the golden calf, made right after the Revelation; it is the temptation of appearances, of Presence. "The idol gives us the divine, and so does not deceive or disappoint."[34] The idol—in this case, the Text, given up to the grasp of the hand, the *manual*—reassures; the idol brings things closer:

What the idol tries to reduce is the gap and the withdrawal of the divine. . . . Filling in for the absence of the divinity, the idol brings the divine within reach, ensures its presence, and, eventually, distorts it. Its completion finishes the divine off. The idol tries to bring us closer to the divine and to put it at our disposal: because he is afraid of atheism, the worshiper lays his hand on the divine in the form of a god; but this taking in hand loses what it grasps: all that is left is a too-familiar, too tangible, too assured amulet. . . . The idol lacks the distance that identifies and authenticates the divine as such—as that which does not belong to us, but which happens to us.[35]

Pardes: The Levels of Meaning

To avoid the trap of idolatry—the illusion of possessing *the* meaning—Hebrew tradition has introduced the idea of levels of meaning.

We shall not go into all the debates about the history of religion, nor shall we undertake a comparison of Judaism and Christianity to study the borrowings and influences. It is sufficient to say that four levels of reading can be found, which are called:

—*Pshat*: the simple or literal meaning
—*Remez*: allusive meaning
—*Drash*: solicited (exegetical) meaning
—*Sod*: hidden or secret meaning

The initials of these four words form an acronym that, when pronounced, gives us *Pardes*, meaning "orchard" or "paradise." What methods and what levels of understanding does *Pardes* refer to? No traditional text describes precisely the difficult paths of *Pardes*.[36] It seems more as if we are faced with a trial-and-error procedure, each person having his own definition of the *Pshat* and the *Drash*, making no particular effort to define or to clarify them before use. This is a permanent feature, because "Talmudic rabbinical thinking loathes the metalanguage of meaning. In vain one will seek to find the expounding of a principle, and even less of a theory."[37]

In the absence of a theoretical description, here is an oft-quoted but little-studied (and even less understood) classical text dealing with the subject. It is a passage from the Talmudic tractate *Hagigah* (14b, 15b, 16a). This text is not situated in this tractate by chance. The *Hagigah* tractate is the text where the problematics of interpretation, perhaps in a more pointed fashion than elsewhere, are set out. In this tractate, we can distinguish three main lines of thought:

1. The absence of God, that is to say, his withdrawal and his invisibility[38]
2. The relation between master and disciple
3. Interpretation, its role, its possibilities, and the prohibitions involved

The title of the second chapter from which this text is taken speaks for itself: "One Does Not Interpret . . ." (*Ein dorshin . . .*).

Hagigah 14b, 15b, 16a

Our rabbis taught: Four men entered the "Garden" (Paradise), namely, Ben 'Azzai and Ben Zoma, Aher, and Rabbi Akiva. Rabbi Akiva said to them: When you arrive at the stones of pure marble, say not, Water, water! For it is said: "No liar keeps his post where I can see him" (Ps. 101:7). Ben 'Azzai cast a look and died. Of him Scripture says: "Precious in the sight of the Lord is the death of His saints" (Ps. 116:15). Ben Zoma looked and became demented. Of him Scripture says: "Eat to your satisfaction what honey you may find, but not to excess or you will bring it up again" (Prov. 25:16). Aher mutilated the shoots. Rabbi Akiva departed unhurt.

Ben Zoma was asked: Is it permitted to castrate a dog? He replied: "You are not to do this in your country" (Lev. 22:24); this means, to none that is in your land shall you do thus. Ben Zoma was further asked: May a high priest marry a maiden who has become pregnant? Do we in such a case take into consideration Samuel's statement, for Samuel said, I can have repeated sexual connections without causing bleeding; or is perhaps the case of Samuel rare? He replied: the case of Samuel is rare, but we do consider the possibility that she may have conceived in a bath. But behold Samuel said: A spermatic emission that does not shoot forth like an arrow cannot fructify! In the first instance, it had also shot forth like an arrow.

Our rabbis taught: Once Rabbi Joshua ben Hananiah was standing on a step on the Temple Mount, and Ben Zoma said to him: Whence and whither, Ben Zoma? He replied: I was gazing between the upper and the lower waters, and there is only a bare three fingers' breadth between them, for it is said: "And God's spirit hovered over the water" (Gen. 1:2)—like a dove that hovers over her young without touching them.

Thereupon Rabbi Joshua said to his disciples: Ben Zoma is still outside. See now, when was it that *"God's spirit hovered over the water"* (Gen. 1:2)? On the first day of Creation; but the division took place on the second day, for it is written: *Let there be a vault in the waters to divide the waters in two* (Gen. 1:6)! And how big is the interval? Rav Aha ben Jacob said, As a hair's breadth; and the rabbis said: As between the boards of a landing bridge. Mar Zutra, or according to others Rav Assi, said: As between two cloaks spread one over the other; and others say, as between two cups tilted one over the other.

Aher mutilated the shoots. Of him Scripture says: "Do not allow your own words to bring guilt on you" (Eccles. 5:5). What does it refer to? He saw that permission was granted to Metatron to sit and write down the merits of Israel. Said he: It is taught as a tradition that on high there is no sitting and no emulation, and no back, and no weariness. Perhaps—God forfend!—there are two divinities! Thereupon they led Metatron forth, and punished him with sixty fiery lashes, saying to him: Why didst thou not rise before him when thou didst see him? Permission was then given to him to strike out the merits of Aher. A heavenly voice sounded forth and said: "Come back, disloyal children" (Jer. 3:14)—except Aher.

Thereupon he said: Since this man has been driven forth from yonder world, let him go forth and enjoy this world. So Aher went forth into evil courses. He went forth, found a harlot, and demanded her. She said to him: Are you not Elisha ben Abuyah? But when he tore a radish out of its bed on the Sabbath and gave it to her, she said: It really is Aher.[39]

Rabbi Akiva went up unhurt and went down unhurt; and of him Scripture says: "Draw me in your footsteps, let us run" (Song 1:4).

And Rabbi Akiva too the ministering angels sought to thrust away; but the Holy One, blessed be He, said to them: Let this elder be, for he is worthy to avail himself of My glory. By what biblical exposition was he able to learn this? Rabbah ben Bar Hanah said that Rabbi Johanan said: "And he came from the myriads holy" (Deut. 33:2). He is the Sign among His myriad.

And Rabbi Abbahu said: "He is known among ten thousand" (Song 5:10). He is the Example among His myriad.

And Resh Lakish said: "The Lord of hosts is His name" (Isa. 48:2). He is the Lord among His host.

And Rabbi Hiyya ben Abba said that Rabbi Johanan said: "But YHVH was not in the wind. After the wind came an earthquake. But YHVH was not in the earthquake. After the earthquake came a fire. But YHVH was not in the fire. And after the fire came a still small voice" (1 Kings 19:11–12). And behold, the Lord passed by.

Here are some passages in extenso from the excellent article by Henri Atlan[40] that will serve as points of reference for us:

1. *Pshat*

This level is characterized by the presence of the meaning, the explanation, in the text: the *Pshat* meaning is to be found in the text itself, whether it be there explicitly, or whether it can be deduced in such a way as one can reasonably expect to find it again. The *Pshat* brings grammar and history into play. Each word is explained in itself, and the logical existence of each word in the general context of the sentence or the passage can be explained. The logic of the narration and of human possibility is respected. The *Pshat* should be clear and simple. The *Pshat* leaves a chance for discussion that accounts for the differences of opinion between the commentaries.

2. *Remez*

Here, the meaning is not totally present in the text. Allusion makes up for a lack that appears as such compared with something that is present, expressed in the text. The *Remez* interprets the fact that the text is elliptical, whether it really be so or not, but the commentary acts as if it were. At this level, we leave classical logic. The logical dimensions of time and space are not necessarily respected. And the discussion between commentaries no longer follows the lines of a logical debate. We can say that at this level we have left behind the binary logic of true and false to enter into the logic of meaning.

3. *Drash*

The characteristic of *Drash* consists in being absent from the text, and this very absence demands to be filled. The text, by an absence, *doresh*—"asks"— something. Unlike the allusive meaning that is still in the text, even if only in an allusive manner, the *Drash* expresses a meaning that is not attached to anything in the text, except for questions, in theoretically unlimited numbers, that one may ask about the context. The text itself does not even make allusion to the latter; it passes over it in silence.

The explanation of the *Drash* consists in seeking in the text, demanding from it, if necessary, something different from what it contains; "soliciting" the text, as it were. This explanation is not attached to something in the text but to something that is missing.

So the text, which may be quite adequate and without particular difficulties at the *Pshat* level, has nonetheless a lack if we start asking questions about what it does not say. The most typical case of *Drash* is where the text itself asks to be solicited, because we cannot understand it at the *Pshat* level. It is as if the text solicited us to solicit it. As Rashi often says, appearing to excuse himself for resorting to the Drash: *Hamikra hazeh omer darsheni*, "This text says: 'Interrogate me, question me, solicit me.'"

Several explanations are possible at this level; several *midrashim* coexist without contradiction: one is no more true or false than another.

4. *Sod*

The inexistence, in the explicit or implicit meanings of the text, of the meanings ascribed to it by the interpretation, is even more obvious at the fourth level of meaning, the *Sod*, the hidden meaning. Here, there is no longer a lack or an appeal of any sort from the text. So it is really a question, here, of a hidden meaning, a secret, insofar as it can be said that the best secret is the one you do not even know exists.

We find this level of commentary mainly in cabalistic literature. The main idea is that the written text of the Torah should be considered as a coded text, not only in its verses or chapters, but in all the signs of which it is made up: letters, vowels, coronets on the letters, traditional vocalization and punctuation when reading, and even, of course, the blank spaces of the parchment that separate and link the signs. Cabalistic teaching is the code that deciphers this text, and that can be seen in many ways: as an ethic based on a cosmogony, as a mythical story, as a psychology of the unconscious, or many other things, but the common denominator and the most basic principle is to be found in the rigorous formalism, built around abstract categories (called *Sefirot*) that can only really be defined by the relations which they establish with each other.

And so the interpretation of verses at the *Sod* level leads us right away to meanings that no longer have any relation other than formal to the text, such as, for example, the one that can be found by breaking up the words and combining the letters in different ways (*notarikon*)[41] or in setting up numerical equivalences more or less directly derived from the traditional numerical values ascribed to letters of the Hebrew alphabet (*gematria*).[42]

5. *Readings*

So we can see how there is a progression from the present-in-the-text to that which is increasingly absent, passing from one level to the next.

The meaning is totally present in the text at the *Pshat* level, the simple meaning. It is no longer there at the *Remez* level, that of allusion, but something of this meaning is still present in the text, although incompletely; *Remez*, allusion, comes to fill in for a lack that appears as such in comparison with something which is present, expressed in the text. At the next level, that of *Drash*, it is a lack that is not even in the text but that is added, in the form of a question about the context—an added-on lack, so to speak, a second-degree lack, which has no longer to do with the text but with the unsaid context.

Finally, at the *Sod* level, it is not even a question of a lack in the text, nor even of a lack detected in what is present but incomplete, as it was for the *Remez*, nor a lack detected in what was already absent in the text, as for the *Drash*. The *Sod*, the hidden meaning, is totally absent from the text, even in the form of a gap, a lack, some form of appeal. And so it constitutes a text in its own right, another reading of the text based on a different arrangement of the signs of the text. That is why some say that the *Sod* reconstitutes a *Pshat*.

Talmudic Hermenutics

Hermeneutics is the science of interpreting according to certain rules. This term is applied, in particular, to exegesis or the interpretation of the Scriptures. By the expression "Talmudic hermeneutics," we mean the expounding of principles and rules that the Masters of the Talmud established for the interpretation of the Written Law.

The Rules of Hillel

Hillel the Elder is the first to have given a certain number of rules of interpretation: there are seven of them. Some of these rules were probably known before Hillel, even though they were not applied systematically. These are:

1. *Kal Vahomer*: inferring from the minor to the major
2. *Gezerah shavah*: reasoning by semantic analogy
3. *Binyan av Mikatuv ehad*: generalization from a single case
4. *Binyan av Mishenei Ketuvim*: generalizing from two cases
5. *Kelal u-perat*: reasoning that takes particular and general cases into consideration
6. *Kayotze bo bemakom aher*: analogy with another text
7. *Davar alamed me'inyano*: explanation from the context

The Rules of Nahum

In addition to the seven rules of Hillel, which were generally accepted, other rules were introduced by later masters. Nahum of Gimzo thus gave us the *Ribbui* and the *Mi'ut* methods: extension and limitation. According to this method, certain particles or conjunctions from the text of the Written Law express the extension or the limitation of a law, or the content of the text. The particles that "extend" the case are *gam* (also), *et* (introducing the direct object), *af* (even). The particles that "restrict" the case are *rak* (only), *min* (of), *ela* (however).

The Rules of Rabbi Akiva

The new method of Rabbi Nahum of Gimzo was not unanimously accepted by his contemporaries. One of his opponents was Rabbi Nehunia ben ha-Kanah, who wanted to keep only the rules of Hillel. In the following generation, Rabbi Akiva summed up the method of his master Nahum and systematized it. The basic postulate of this system is *Lo diberah Torah kileshon benei adam* (The Torah does not speak the language of men). In human language, we use more or fewer words to express an idea; we find superfluous words that are there only to create a stylistic effect, or for added force, etc. This is not the case of the language of the Torah: here, not a word, not a syllable or even a letter is there by chance.

Everything is essential; each letter has a meaning and a vital importance. According to this principle, it is not only the particles which Nahum noticed that are to be interpreted, but any anomaly, any words, syllables, or letters that are not strictly necessary to the meaning of the text. Rabbi Akiva and the supporters of this method found indications for the extension of the application to the repetition of words such as in the doubling[43] of a verb and its infinitive form ("to send, you will send"; "to help, you will help," etc.). They push the analysis as far as the interpretation of the coordinating conjunction (*o*) and of the conjunction *vav*. For the restriction of elements, they call on the demonstrative pronouns (*zeh*, "that one, but not another") or else the definite article *he hayediyah*: the verse could have written "first"; "the first" restricts the law to this particular case. Or else when the personal pronoun is added to the verb (in Hebrew, the personal pronoun is included in the inflection of the verb, except in the present), so the personal pronoun becomes redundant and requires interpretation.

The Rules of Rabbi Ishmael

The ingenious system of Rabbi Akiva, although accepted with admiration by many of his contemporaries, also had its opponents. The most noteworthy is Rabbi Ishmael ben Elisha; unlike Rabbi Akiva, his motto is *Diberah Torah kileshon benei adam* (The Torah speaks the language of men). Consequently, no particular attention should be paid to unusual expressions, repetitions, etc. He accepted only deductions that could be justified by the spirit of the passage analyzed. He recognized only the seven rules of Hillel, which he set out as thirteen, subdividing some, omitting one of them, and adding one of his own. These rules are:

1. *Kal Vahomer:* the same as Hillel's first
2. *Gezerah shavah:* the same as Hillel's second
3. *Binyan av:* contraction of Hillel's third and fourth rules
4. *Kelal u-perat:* subdivision of Hillel's fifth rule

5. *Perat u-kelal:* idem

6. *Perat u-kelal u-Perat:* idem

Rules 7, 8, 9, 10, 11: modification of Hillel's fifth rule

12. *Davar alamed me'inyano:* the same as the seventh rule

13. *Shenei ketuvim amakhishim zeh et zeh:* a new rule dealing with the resolution of a contradiction between two verses.

The thirteen rules of Rabbi Ishmael were generally adopted as authoritative rules for Talmudic interpretation, but without replacing Rabbi Akiva's method, which continued to be used by many masters and even by some disciples of Rabbi Ishmael. Of the thirteen rules, only six are used often: rules 1, 2, 3, 4, 12, and 13. Of these six rules, rules 1 and 2 are without doubt the most frequently utilized.

The Rules of Rabbi Eliezer ben Rabbi Yose ha-Gelili

The thirteen rules that we have just enumerated mainly concern the field of Halakhah. Rabbi Eliezer completes these rules with others that will be used for "aggadic" exegesis. The Talmud speaks of Rabbi Eliezer as one of the great masters of "aggadic" exegesis (*Hulin* 89). However, no explicit mention is made of the thirty-two rules. A list of them appears for the first time in a tenth-century text written by Abu Walid ibn Janah. He is the first to quote them, ascribing them to Rabbi Eliezer ben Rabbi Yose. The list of these rules is also given by the *Sefer Hakritot* (thirteenth century) of Rabbi Samson of Chinon. We can also find an enumeration of the rules in the book of Judah Hadassi the Karaite: *Eshkol ha-Kofer* (1149). The new principles are elision (*derekh ketsara*), repetition, (*davar shanui*), the rules dealing with the interpretation of the context, parable (*mashal*), interpretation and putting identical numbers together (*neged*), phonetic comparsion and the study of etymologies (*ma'al*), *Gematria*, calculation of the numerical value of words and comparison with a word of the same numerical value, and, finally, a procedure called *Notarikon*, which consists of the dividing of one word into several, the combining of several words into one, and the breaking up of words in acrostics—each of the letters of one word giving another word, the initials of several words giving one word, and the final letters of several words forming one word. These last two procedures are directly inspired by methods of Greek origin. In the Talmudic *Aggadah* and in the *Midrash*, all the rules except those of Hillel and Rabbi Ishmael are usually used.

Hebrew: The Man and His Language

There are two relations to the Hebrew language. On the one hand, Hebrew is a language that adheres extremely closely to matter, space, and time; "its words, sounds, the materiality of the shape of its letters follow the contours and the rhythms of the world and creation. Hebrew is the geo-graphy (the writing of the earth) and the geo-metry (the measuring of the earth) of the created."[44]

Hebrew brings the world before our eyes, frees the world from itself in order for us to apprehend it, understand and take hold of it. For the Hebrew mind, the Hebrew language is the most immediate of realities. "The Hebrew mind knows of a profound secret, that all reality—the densest and most physical—is constituted by language, by its words, by the infinite vibrations of its voices and echoes."[45] In Hebrew tradition, language is first of all a spectacle. Revelation is, above all, seeing! "And all the people *saw* the voices . . ." (Exod. 20:18). The visible is the voices made writing.[46]

That being the case, the world is revealed, shows itself; we can grasp it because language has offered it to us. But is the world there? Is it not, in fact, a projected being, a reality that passes by in movement? Does not the world made visible run the risk like the text and through the text, of becoming an idol?

These questions imply a second function of the Hebrew language that, contrastingly, does not freeze the world and the whole of reality in the present, but that, on the contrary, forges a path toward absence; it is a function of this language, which has the ability to burst open, to pulverize itself in a thousand pieces, to work a derealization of reality "by which the proud self-assurance of all the realities of this world, the clear conscience of idolatry, fall in ruins into the emptiness of their vanity."[47]

It is important to stop here a moment to examine the Hebrew word for "Hebrew," the man and his language: *'Ivri* and *'Ivrit*.[48] The Hebrew, in his etymological meaning, is a passer-through (*la'avor*), a breaker-off (*'avera*), a transgressor (*'avera*), a passer-on, a producer and a creator (*ubar, me'uberet, ibur hahodesh*); he is also someone who takes into account that which is outside of himself (*Ba'avur she . . .*). These are all words from the root 'I, V, R.

The Hebrew tears himself away, protests, passes through . . .

The Hebrew-passer-through "not only invites us to go from one riverbank to the other [*passeur*, lit. "ferryman"], but to head everywhere where there is a passage to be achieved, while maintaining this between-two-banks that is the truth of the passing."[49] For the Hebrew, existing is becoming. The Hebrew is not something that is, but something that will be. It is a matter of creation. So, the Hebrew will be in a perpetual becoming, in a becoming that is yet to come (*à-venir*). The Hebrew is messianic! inasmuch as "messianism is not the certainty of the coming of a man who will bring history to a halt,"[50] but a way of being of every man in time. The Hebrew-messiah lives in the temporality of the yet-to-come (*à-venir; avenir*: "future"), of the ever yet-to-come. *The Hebrew is not in time; he produces time.* Time is what emerges from the "caress" between the hand that approaches and the body of the text (and of the world) that slips away. In this messianic temporality, it is "as if the world existed and did not exist at the same time, perpetually slipping away, re-creating each instant."[51] The Hebrew language, *'Ivrit*, should reflect this passing, this "in the process of being" (*en-train-d'être*)—the essence—of man and of the world . . .

The contradiction between the two functions of language cannot be resolved in an artificial synthesis or by giving more importance to one of the two terms. The Hebrew language gives and takes at the same time, fixes and dissolves, builds and destroys, states and retracts.

That is why it has been said that Hebrew is metaphorical.[52] We would prefer—from the point of view of contemporary philosophical research—to say that Hebrew is a trace.[53]

And if "the trace is not a presence but the simulacrum of a presence that dislocates itself, displaces itself, postpones itself, it properly speaking does not take place"[54] because the effacing is part of its structure, then we now have to describe all the strategic means that have been set up to make the effacing, the breaking up of Hebrew possible.

Books within Books: Black Fire on White Fire

"In the beginning was the Book!"

But is the book of the beginning the same as the one we can read in our libraries? Is there not *the* Book and, simply, *books*? Is the Torah we have identical to "God's Torah"?

Rabbi Simeon ben Lakish teaches:[55]

> The Torah that the Holy One, blessed be He, gave to Moses is a white fire, engraved on a black fire; it is of fire, graven by fire, given by fire, as it is said: "Written with his right hand, a law of fire (*Esh-dat*) for them."[56]

Nahmanides comments this text in the following manner:

> We possess an authentic tradition, according to which the whole Torah is made up of all the Names of God. So the words that we read can also be

distributed in quite another manner. The Torah written "black fire on white fire" means that the text was written without any breaks, in an uninterrupted sequence from the first to the last letter. This writing makes up a Name that can be divided into Names.[57]

The Book of the beginning is illegible and meaningless. Before the book can be read, it must be composed; the reader is actually a creator. Reading becomes an activity, a production. And so an infinity of books are constantly present in the Book. There is not one story but many stories.

The first function of the reader is to introduce breaks between the letters to form words; between certain words to produce sentences; between certain sentences to close and open paragraphs, and, finally, between paragraphs to create books.

So the first task is that of *spacing*, the application of the difference defined as "the movement by which the language, or any code, any referential system in general is constituted 'historically' as a fabric of differences."[58]

So, like Mallarmé, we may say that it is the "blanks" that "ensure the importance."

Words within Words

After "spacing," the first moment of "writing-reading" that is only one of the infinite possibilities of reading, the process of bursting open, breaking up, fracturing, narrows down, the field of research becomes more precise: the *word* becomes the material to be worked, shaped, made and unmade. If we accumulate all these terms to express the work that is carried out on the word, it is in order to reveal the scope of the phenomenon; different methods are used, each quite compatible with the others.

The Numerical Structure of Language: Gematria

The Hebrew language has a numerical structure; that is to say, each letter corresponds to a number, as shown in the following chart.

For example: the word *Adam (Aleph-Dalet-mem)* has a numerical value equal to 45 $(1 + 4 + 40)$; the word *Tardemah* (cf. Gen. 2:21), which means "sleepiness," has a numerical value of 649 $(400 + 200 + 4 + 40 + 5)$.

The numerical value of a word is called *Gematria* (probably from the Greek *geometria*).

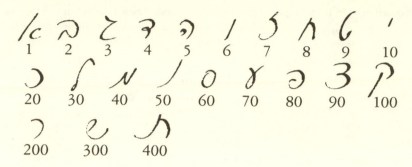

Gematria is not simply a game but a method of interpretation, an opening tool. It is neither futile nor contingent; note: "The reader is not to pay attention so much to the size of the numbers as to the words that the numerical equivalences bring together and the comparison of which always has a great many implications for philosophy. It is from this comparison that thought springs up. It constitutes a process of reflection and contemplation."[59] The *Gematria* is a way of opening one's mind to something else: a pretext, a springboard, a mode of transition. It is not enough to complete the equation, to show up the equivalences; the meaning is not in the original word, nor in the final word, but between the two. *Gematria* is not itself thinking; it is a starting point for thought.

To continue the preceding example, we could show that the word *Tardema* ("sleepiness") has the same numerical value as the word *Targum*, which means "translation." We can easily see the role of the *Gematria*: in no way is it a proof. It is there to make us think. What logical (or illogical) link is there between "sleep" and "translation"?[60]

There is also a form of *Gematria*, called *Gematria Ketanah*, that brings every letter down to a number between 1 and 10 by removing the zero(s). So 20 = 2, 200 = 2, 80 = 8, etc.

Breaking Up Words: Notarikon

The second procedure that the Talmud and the *Midrash* offer us is *Notarikon*: this method consists in decomposing the word into two or more parts. The word is cut up, split open, burst, shattered. The word becomes a sentence: "its deeper meaning emerges as the relations between the letters within the words become clear."[61]

For example, the word *Anokhi*, which starts the Decalogue (Exod. 20:2), becomes *Ana Nafshi Ketivat Yahavit.*[62] We go from the word "Me" to the sentence "I state my soul in writing."

Another example: the word *Bereshit* (Gen. 1:1), split in two, gives *Berit-esh*; here we go from the word "(in the) beginning" to the expression "covenant of fire."

The Anagrammatical Reading

A word can dilate and explode into a sentence; the opposite movement also exists. This method consists in "reading," in the etymological sense of the term.[63]

The verb *to read* had, for the ancients, the meaning of collect, pick, spy, recognize traces, take, steal, glean (it is the meaning we find in *leket* and in the *lek* of *likro*). This reading collects, gleans, here and there, a letter in this word, another in another word, etc., and so makes up a word or a name. This is the case, for example, for the name of Moses (*Mosheh*), reconstructed from the three letters M-SH-H, "harvested" in the song *Haazinu*[64] (Deut. 32).

This way of reading is particularly noted for the expressions *Rashei Tevot* and *Sofei Tevot*. In fact, it is the same idea as the acrostic,[65] with the difference that it is not a matter of lines or stanzas but of words.

Rashei Tevot means the "initials" of words that are extracted to make up a new word; for example, *Divrei Elohim Hayyim* (words of the living God). The initials extracted give us *Ehad*, which is "one" (*Aleph-Het-Dalet*).

Sofei Tevot means the "final" letters that are taken to make up a new word; for example, *Bereshit bara Elohim* (In the beginning, God created). The final letters form the word *Emet*, which is "truth" (*Aleph-Mem-Tav*).

This reading concerns either words that follow each other in the same sentence, or words scattered in the text and even in several different texts.[66]

"Gleaning-reading," which, in one way, can be called "writing-reading," is not a late invention of the *Midrash* or the Talmud.

It originates in the *Hoshen*, the breastplate of the high priest. According to a text from Exodus (39:8f.), the high priest wore a sort of square plaque in which were set twelve precious stones on which were engraved the names of the tribes of Israel (50 letters); there were also the names of the three patriarchs, Abraham, Isaac, and Jacob (13 letters), and the expression *Shivtei Yeshurun* (tribes of Israel) (10 letters). So, all the letters of the *Aleph-Beit* appeared on it. When the high priest wished to know the future, for example, the question was asked and the *Hoshen* replied (under certain conditions). The letters "lit up" and the reader combined them to form the text of the answer.[67]

Permutation and Combination: Tseruf

Another way of reading consists in switching around the letters of a word: for example, the word *Rehem*, the "womb," gives, after permutation, the word *Mahar*, which is "tomorrow,"[68] etc.; another example, the word *Ani*, "I," gives us *Ayin*, which is "nothingness."[69] Let us not forget the *At-Bash* reading, which consists in replacing the first letter of the alphabet by the last, the second by the second-to-last, etc., which is yet another way of finding the word within the word.

All these methods, we must not forget, are only tools for reflection: one must still go beyond them.

Letters within Letters

The work of interpreting goes as far as dissecting the smallest part of the language: the letter. The letters break up and signify over and beyond themselves: for example the letter *Aleph* א breaks up into one *Vav* and two *Yod*, and by a game of numerical values we can go from the unit—*Aleph*—to the Tetragram.[70] Another example: the letter *Heh* ה breaks up into a *Dalet* and a *Yod* or into a *Dalet* and a *Vav*[71] or again the letter *Zayin* splits into a *Vav* and a *Yod*, etc.

Notes

1. For the meaning of this term cf. A. Y. Heschel, *Dieu en quête de l'homme* (Paris; Seuil, 1968), p. 11.

2. Cf. *Pirkei de Rabbi Eliezer*, trans. M.-A. Ouaknin (Paris: Éditions Verdier, 1992), p. 249.

3. For all these reflections, cf. H. G. Gadamer, *Vérité et méthode* (Paris; Seuil, 1976).

4. Martin Buber, in *Darko shel Adam al-pi Torat ha-Hassidut* (in Hebrew), (Jerusalem: Mossad Bialik Editions, 1964).

5. E. Lévinas, *L'Au-delà du verset* (Paris: Éditions de Minuit, 1982), p. 163.

6. Mainly in the writings of Rabbi Zadok ha-Kohen of Lublin. Here there is an allusion to the 613th *Mitzvah* of the Torah: each man and each woman must write a book, his book; cf. *Shulhan Arukh*, "Yoreh De'ah," p. 270.

7. Gadamer, *Vérité et méthode*, p. 245.

8. Maimonides, *Guide des égarés*, pt. 3: "Preliminary Observations," transl. S. Munk (Paris: Éditions Verdier, 1979), p. 480.

9. Lévinas, *L'Au-delà du verset*, p. 141.

10. Roger Laporte, "Quatre Lectures pour Jacques Derrida," in *Écarts* (Paris: Fayard, 1973), pp. 209–10.

11. Maurice Blanchot, *L'Entretien infini* (Paris: Gallimard, 1969), p. 501.

12. Rabbi Isaiah Horowitz, *"Shlah"* on *Parashah Noah.*

13. We have slightly modified the text, substituting the word "study" for the word "philosophy."

14. Vladimir Jankélévitch, *Quelque part dans l'inachevé* (Paris: Gallimard, 1978), pp. 18–19.

15. E. Lévinas, *Quatre Lectures talmudiques* (Paris: Éditions du Minuit, 1968), pp. 20–21.

16. Ibid.

17. Rav David ha-Kohen, Kol Hanevuah (Massad Harav Kook ed., in Hebrew), p. 223.

18. *Yoma 54.*

19. E. Lévinas, *Otherwise Than Being or Beyond Essence*, trans. Alphonso Lingis (The Hague: Nijhoff, 1981), p. 152.

20. Here, we are following E. Lévinas's idea of "caress" developed in all his works from *Le Temps et l'Autre* (Time and the Other) to *Otherwise Than Being.* It is an essential mode of being that fits perfectly into a phenomenology of the hand where the problematics of the book, the "manual," are situated.

21. *Le Temps et l'Autre* (Paris: Fata Morgana, 1979), p. 82.

22. *Otherwise Than Being*, p. 90.

23. E. Lévinas, *Totality and Infinity: An Essay on Exteriority*, trans. Alphonso Lingis (Pittsburgh: Duquesne University Press, 1988), pp. 257–58f.

24. Ibid.

25. *Le Temps et l'Autre.*

26. H. G. Gadamer, *Vérité et méthode* (Paris: Seuil, 1976), pp. 198f.

27. H. Atlan, "Niveaux de signification et athéisme de l'écriture," in *La Bible au présent* (Paris: Gallimard, 1982), "Idées," p. 86.

28. Ibid.

29. Gadamer, *Vérité et méthode.*

30. Ibid.

31. Atlan, "Niveaux de signification," p. 86.

32. Deut. 34:12.

33. Atlan, "Niveaux de signification."

34. J.-L. Marion, *L'Idole et la distance* (Paris: Grasset, 1977), p. 24.

35. Ibid., pp. 24–25.

36. For a preliminary approach: Gershom Scholem, *La Kabbale et sa symbolique* (Paris: Payot, 1980), pp. 69f.

37. J. Genot-Bismuth, "De l'Idée juive du sens," in *Hommage à G. Vajda* (Louvain, 1980), pp. 105, 116.

38. Cf. below, "Visible and Invisible."

39. *Aher* in Hebrew means "the other."

40. Atlan, "Niveaux de signification."

41. See below, "Words within Words."

42. Ibid.

43. Somewhat like the "Attic" doubling in Greek.

44. S. Trigano, *Le Récit de la disparue* (Paris: Gallimard, 1977), p. 310.

45. S. Trigano, Preface to *L'Épître des sept voiles*, by Aboulafia (Paris: Éditions de l'Éclat, 1985), p. 16.

46. E. Lévinas, "Exégèse et culture," *Cahiers du Nouveau commence*, no. 55 (1983): 90.

47. Trigano, *Le Récit de la disparue*, p. 322.

48. We refer the reader to the classical texts by André Neher, *L'Existence juive, solitude et affrontements* (Paris: Seuil, 1962), pp. 132f., and Maurice Blanchot, *L'Entretien infini* (Paris: Gallimard, 1969), pp. 180f.

49. Blanchot, *L'Entretien infini*, p. 184.

50. E. Lévinas, *Difficile liberté* (Paris: Albin Michel, 1963), p. 120.

51. Trigano, *Le Récit de la disparue*, p. 327.

52. Ibid., p. 319.

53. We refer in particular to the works of E. Lévinas, "La Trace de l'Autre," in *En découvrant l'existence avec Husserl et Heidegger* (Paris: Vrin 1974), pp. 187f.; Jacques Derrida, *Marges de la philosophie* (Paris: Éditions de Minuit, 1972), pp. 25f.; *De la Grammatologie* (Paris: Éditions de Minuit, 1967), pp. 96f. and also L. Finas et al., *Écarts: quatre essais à propos de Jacques Derrida* (Paris: Fayard, 1973).

It should be pointed out that it is not only language as a signifier that is a "trace"; "the trace affects the totality of the sign in both of its aspects. The signified is originally and essentially a trace" (*Grammatologie*, p. 107–8). This remark allows us to speak again of an adequacy of language with the world: adequacy of a "trace-language" with a "trace-world."

54. J. Derrida, *Margins of Philosophy*, trans. Alan Bass (Chicago: University of Chicago Press, 1982), p. 24.

55. *Yalkut Shimoni*, "*Terumah*," *Remez* 365; *Shir Hashirim Rabba* 5; *Yerushalmi Sotah* 8, 3 and Y. *Shekalim* 10.

56. Deut. 33:2.

57. Nahmanides, *Introduction to the Pentateuch* (Mossad Harav Kook ed., 1959, in Hebrew), p. 6.

58. E. Jabès, *Du désert au livre* (Paris: Belfond, 1980), pp. 130f.

59. Trigano, "Le Livre au coeur de l'être" Preface to *L'Épiître des sept voiles*, by Aboulafia, p. 17. For the *Gematria*, see in this book, for example, pp. 75f.

60. See, on this point, *Likkutei Moharan*, by Rabbi Nahman of Bratslav, vol. 1, reflection no. 19.

61. Trigano, *Le Récit de la disparue*, p. 317.

62. *Shabbat* 105a.

63. On this subject, see Heidegger, *Essais* (Paris: Gallimard, 1958), p. 252, and also J. Kristeva, *Sémeiotikè* (Paris: Seuil, 1969), "Points," p. 120.

64. Moses is the author of the song *Ha'azinu*; his name is not mentioned explicitly. It is, however, implied. If we take the first letters of verses 1, 2, 3, 4, the sum of their numerical value is equal to 40, that is to say, to *Mem*. The first letter of verse 5 is *Shin Heh*, which gives us *Mosheh*. *Heh* is an "abnormal" letter, which, for some, constitutes a word. For others, it is with this letter that the text written by Moses ends. See A. Heschel, *Torah min Hashamayim . . .* (New York: Soncino, 1965), 2:398.

65. According to the definition of the *Robert* dictionary: "poem of stanza of

which the first letters of each line, when read vertically, give a name (author, person it is dedicated to) or a key word." We take the anagram in the sense of Saussure: "sounds or letters composing a proper noun that can be found scattered throughout a poem as a whole." Cf. *Dictionnaire encyclopédique des sciences du language* (Paris: Seuil, 1972) "Points," by O. Ducrot and T. Todorov, p. 245.

66. *Ta'anit* 2b. See below concerning the word *Mayim*.

67. *Yoma* 73a and b; Maimonides, *Hilkhot kelei hamikdash, Halakhah* 7 of chap. 10; Rabbi Nahman of Bratslav, *Likkutei Moharan*, vol. 1 no. 281.

68. On this example: Trigano, *Le Récit de la disparue*, p. 25 and passim.

69. For example, Safran, *La Cabbale* (Paris: Payot, 1979), pp. 311f.

70. *Aleph* decomposed into *vav-yod-yod* = 26 = Tetragram. See Rabbi Nahman of Bratslav, *Likkutei Moharan*, 66, 2.

71. See "Maharal" of Prague on *Menahot* 29b.

VII

Dialogues

The Talmudic Project

What is the Talmudic project?

Like every great text, the Talmud conceals its project between rather than within the lines. For this reason, it is clear that the Talmud cannot be approached from a thematic standpoint. In the Talmud, the "problem" should not be identified with the individual questions that serve as a starting point, nor with the dominant and permanent motifs of its questioning. There is an additional difficulty: the "problem" is usually not put into words, even though it influences all the individual questions. It is always there, never expounded, behind all the individual thoughts, as their driving force.[1]

Emmanuel Lévinas expresses this idea, not without a degree of humor: "It is certain that, in discussing whether one can or cannot eat 'an egg laid on a feast day'[2] or the compensation due for damages caused by a 'raging bull,'[3] the masters of the Talmud are not discussing the egg, nor the bull, but, without seeming to, are challenging fundamental ideas."[4] The mistake made by contemporary Talmudists is to refuse to trace back from the problems of rituals (which are, of course, most important for the durability of Judaism) to the long-forgotten philosophical problems, to trace back from the "theme" to the "problem."

The themes and the problems are numerous, even if the latter are rarely brought to light.

However, over and above all the themes and problems of the Talmud, there is the question of "opening," of life and meaning. It is a somewhat political question, since it is the place where liberty takes root and it provides the most striking expression of the refusal of closure. In short, the Talmud is the "anti-ideological" discourse par excellence.

What would, in fact, give us an anti-ideological "ideology" (paradoxically) is strategically borne by two fundamental principles, principles of dialogue: *Mahloket* and *Gezerah shavah*.

Mahloket, or the Necessity of Dialogue

> A sword for loners, they lose their wits!
> (Jer. 50:36)

First, let us notice the contrast between the monastery and the *ye-shivah*:

> Novices squatting, heads shaven, looking like athletes of undividedness. Everything—posture, gait, percussion, dress, synchronism—conspires to the ordered production of a single body, the brotherhood liberating each individual from his own identity by a sensorial discipline. And so, the rhythmic reading of the *sutra* should be carried out by the ears. The voice of the group speaks through the mouth of each person, with its scansion, individual intonations, and meditation culminating in a threnody, the abolition of the individual ego, a path toward impersonality to prepare for *nirvana*.[5]

Disorder, hubbub, vehement gesticulation, incessant comings and goings—that is how the *Beit Hamidrash* appears: the school that serves as a synagogue and also, on many occasions, as a dining room. The students of the Talmud do not have the tranquillity of the monks. Silence is not the rule; on the tables—rarely in line—piled up any which way, along with the *Gemarot*, a profusion of books of the Torah, of Maimonides, of the *Shulhan Arukh*; open books piled up on top of each other.

The students—seated, standing, a knee on a bench or a chair—are bent over the texts of the Talmud; next to each other, but usually facing each other, they read aloud, rocking to and fro, or from left to right, punctuating the difficult passages or arguments with large gestures of the thumb, frantically striking the books or the table, or even the shoulder of a colleague, feverishly leafing through the pages of commentaries quickly taken out and replaced on the shelves of the huge bookcase that covers all four walls. The protagonists of this "war of meaning" try to understand, interpret, and explain. Rarely in agreement, fortunately, about the meaning of the passage being studied, they will consult the master, who explains, takes a stand on the ideas put forward, and calms for a moment the impassioned battle of the students. On another table, a little farther off, one student has fallen asleep, arms crossed on his copy of the Talmud; next to him, another sips coffee and smokes a cigarette, assuming a thoughtful air: concentration is necessary for the rest of the study. Everything bustles! The *Beit Hamidrash* is a place continually buzzing with activity where, day and night, voices echo to the infinite hum of study.[6]

If we have described the Talmudic house of study, it is because it accurately displays the spirit of Talmudic thought. It is perhaps here that we can best understand the political dimension and function of the world of the Talmud, its anti-ideological character.

To provide a brief typology, we could contrast the "unidimensional" world with the "bidimensional" world.

The Talmudic world is bidimensional, and that is why it is profoundly anti-ideological. The Talmudist—the "real" one—never says,
"We"; nor he does he have the right to say, "The Talmud says. . . ."

He can say: "There is an opinion in the Talmud that says . . . but
there is also another opinion that says just the opposite. . . ."[7]

The first thing the reader of the Talmud notices is the importance of
dialogue in the working through of thought. Rare are the subjects that
are not challenged, so much so that when one speaks of "a" notion, one
says *Mahloket ploni veploni*, which means "discussion between so (one
master) and so (another master)."[8] Talmudic thought is often set out as
a debate between Hillel and Shammai, Rav and Samuel, Rav Huna and
Rav Hisda, Abbaye and Rava, Rabbi Johanan and Resh Lakish, etc.

In *Mahloket*, reconciliation is not sought. If the term "dialectic" can
be used—and it is often used to describe Talmudic thinking—we would
have to talk of an "open dialectic," since no synthesis, no third term,
cancels out the contradiction. "Everything does not subside in the
'Same,' in the identity of the identical and the nonidentical."[9] *Mahloket*
is a way of saying and of thinking the refusal of synthesis and systems:
it is an antidogmatism that, alone, makes a living truth possible.

The Talmud says of Talmudic discussions: "The words of one and
the words of the other are words of the living God."[10]

This sentence should be understood as conditional: "*If* there are
words of one *and* words of the other, *then* they are words of the living
God, and, as a result, are living words." The role of the *Mahloket* is to
undermine satisfaction, to undermine "knowledge where thought is always shown as true to type."[11]

Moreover, *Mahloket* leads us along the path of nonconceptual
thought. In conceptual thought, "diversity is brought together in the
presence of representation; accepting synchrony, it confirms its aptitude
to enter into the unity of a type or a form: everything can be thought
together; it is a Thinking of Presence,"[12] a thinking of "Everything-is-
present-here-and-now."

Mahloket shows, precisely, that everything cannot be resolved in the
"Same," everything does not lend itself to synchrony and synthesis; perception is not simply "com-prehension," "graspability."

Mahloket breaks open the immanent structure of synthetic and lim-
itative thought; it stirs up the tranquillity of a truth that is one, a truth
that goes off to sleep and forgets for want of being thought out.

Mahloket is the only chance for the event of thinking to unfold in a
"thinking thought."

Mahloket combats against "pre–thought-out thinking," against the
death of thinking, and, as "Maharal" of Prague says, against death.[13]

In the word *Mahloket* we can read *M-ḥlk-t*, which means that the duality refuses to give the word "death" (*met*) the chance to constitute itself. The logical structure of *Mahloket* is that of the "book."[14] Writing and effacing (trace), saying and unsaying.[15]

Once a Master proffers a thought, his interlocutor shakes him from his position, from his positivity: it is an incessant destabilization, an athetical thinking that resists synchronization, making way for a sojourn in infinity.[16]

"Transcendent" and "Immanent" Dialectics

To define *Mahloket*, we used the expression "open dialectic," which means that the mind opens itself up to the recognition of the otherness of another mind: it implies the transcendence of the subject as the acceptance of leaving the world, the constituting of the Other before me. Here are three points that define this notion of "open dialectic";

—First, study and thinking are possible only in an experience of dialogue.
—Second, dialogue is not simply an exchange of ideas, but "questions and answers" (*she'elot-u-teshuvot*).
—Finally, the questioning and the answer do not develop within the same sphere of thought.

Then, we can contrast two ways of experiencing the dialogue, two types of dialectic.[17] We shall speak of a "transcendent dialectic" and an "immanent dialectic."

Talmudic *Mahloket* is a "transcendent dialectic," since the Other-man of the dialogue is not a mere stylistic device; the interlocutor is not there to show up the speaker to advantage. In order to understand what Talmudic dialogue consists of, we can contrast it with what it is not: we can mention Plato and the "Platonic" dialogues. "The reference to Plato is only negatively enlightening. It enables us to eliminate all pretentions of dialogue. The Socratic dialogue is not an authentic dialogue in that it belongs entirely to the postulation of the unity of Reason as the scene of truth; even if this scene is, in one way, yet to be discovered, it is nonetheless already there. Truth as Truth is 'One' and is attained by reminiscence. Consequently, the dialogue becomes a ruse of the *logos*, and the duality of characters and the voices that are heard are only a path toward the One. The dialogue is purely didactic, an embellished and eminently skillful form of discourse."[18]

In that respect the Platonic dialogue is an "immanent dialectic." The interlocutor, in many cases, contents himself with saying: "Yes . . .!" "No . . .," "That's right . . .," "I think so too . . .," etc. It is the central character of the dialogue who gives the questions and answers.[19]

"Everything takes place inside a single consciousness: it is an internal discourse where thought splits, easily, while seeming to ask itself questions and answer, but where, in the end, everything comes back together."[20] In the "immanent dialectic," thought remains the same; "it goes from one term to the opposite term that calls for it, but the dialectic where it takes place is not a dialogue or, at least, it is the dialogue one soul has with itself, proceeding by questions and answers, an internal discourse in which the mind, while thinking, remains nonetheless single and alone, in spite of its procedure and its coming and going where it can challenge itself."[21]

The Master of the Talmud, at a given moment of his research, knows that he knows; so his study through dialogue is not intended to comfort him in his preconceived ideas. On the contrary, he seeks to be shaken up, to be disturbed, to suffer setbacks, to be overwhelmed.[22]

Learning is not the acquiring of knowledge that is already there, present from time immemorial in the student's mind; learning is not "reminiscence" and teaching is not "maieutics."

The Preeminence of the Questioning Word

Mahloket, the first principle of dialogue of the Talmud, is profoundly linked to a certain conception of hermeneutics and truth.

The fact that a single text can offer innumerable interpretations implies that there is no "right" interpretation. This leads us to leave behind the binary logic of true and false[23] (of Greek logic), to enter into what we shall call the "logic of meaning."

As Nietzsche expresses very well: "There are all sorts of eyes . . . and consequently there are all sorts of truths, and consequently, there is no truth."[24]

To really enter Talmudic thought, each time a certainty is asserted one should seek the opposite assertion that it is related to. In this way, Talmudic thought never stops opposing itself, yet without ever contenting itself with satisfying this opposition.

With this form of thought goes a speech whose modality keeps open the requirement for a dynamic approach. This is, to our mind, the "questioning word," the question.

The question is movement. In the mere grammatical structure of the question we already feel this opening of the questioning word: there is the request for something else; incomplete, the word that questions recognizes that it is only a part. Thus the question is essentially partial; it is the setting where speech offers itself as ever incomplete. . . .

The question, if it is the unfinished word, bases itself on incompletion. It is not incomplete as a question; on the contrary it is speech that the fact of declaring itself incomplete fulfills. The question puts the sufficient assertion back into the void; it enriches it with this preexisting void. Through the question, we give ourselves the thing and also the void that allows us to not have it yet or to have it in the form of desire for thought.[25]

Talmudic thought is the thinking of the question, and it is no mere chance that the very first word of the Talmud is a question: *Meematai* (From what time?).

Rabbi Nahman of Bratslav explains[26] that the interrelational space of *Mahloket* issues from the *hallal hapanui*, necessary for creation. God withdraws; he leaves an "empty space" (*hallal hapanui*) that is essentially the original space of all questions, because it contains the question of questions: the Enigma! God withdraws: so he is absent! But can something exist cut off from the vitality that the divinity breathes into it? No! So God is present. *Yesh-ve-ayin*, "Being and nothingness" coexist. When two masters discuss together, the relation originates in this paradox: that is what is called the *Bina*. It is not a matter of intellectual capacity or quality, but of a relational attitude, of dialogue, that must be maintained.

What is there between the two masters who confront each other?

A nothingness more essential than the Nothingness itself, the emptiness of the in-between, an interval that is ever deepened and, as it deepens, swells up, the nothing as work and movement.[27]

"All my life I have grown up *between* the masters."[28] According to Rabbi Nahman, this maxim means: I have grown up "between" (*beyn*), that is to say, in the space of nothingness, in the empty space that separates and joins the masters in the situation of *Mahloket*.[29]

To maintain the paradoxical relationship at stake in the *Mahloket*, the question should not await the answer: "The answer is fatal for the question."[30] Through the question, things are taken and transformed into possibilities, uplifted "dramatically to their possibility, beyond their being."[31]

To answer would be to allow that which was reaching beyond to subside into being. The answer suppresses the "opening," the richness of possibility; whereas the role of the question is to open up. The question "heralds a type of relationship characterized by opening and free movement."[32]

Within the context of the hermeneutic problem, the question has pride of place and takes on the meaning of "calling into question." Hermeneutics, that is to say, the art of interpreting and not of repeating, implies the fundamental suspending of our own prejudices.

All suspension of judgment, even and especially that of prejudices, has, from a logical point of view, the structure of a question. The essence of the question is to open up and to leave open possibilities . . .

The opening of that which is asked lies in the undetermined character of the answer. The thing asked should remain in abeyance . . . suspended so that the "cons" balance the "pros." A question exhausts its meaning only by going through this suspending that makes it an open question. "Every genuine question calls for this opening."[33]

The Question: Talmud and Philosophy

Mahloket has led us to the "question" and "opening" and, in the process, in the course of the preceding developments, we have outlined the social, political, and philosophical implications of the first principle of dialogue.

Before closing the chapter on *Mahloket* and questioning, I offer several remarks on the eminently philosophical character of the Talmudic attitude,[34] inasmuch as it is a questioning attitude.

The Talmud, like all philosophy, begins with astonishment.[35] Why be astonished and of what? Philosophical and Talmudic astonishment are not concerned with an "astonishing object." It is not a matter of "being astonished" (*être étonné*), but more precisely of "wondering" (*s'étonner*). Philosophical and Talmudic astonishment is not a reaction provoked by the world; it is a deliberate, voluntary, totally active, and creative act all at once. The origin of this astonishment is not in the world but in man.

Astonishment should concern everything that surrounds us: time, space, things, fellow men, animals, plants, tools, etc., and ourselves.

Paradoxically, the question is not aimed only at the Unknown, mysterious and invisible worlds that are far off and remotely accessible, "worlds behind the scenes," but at the "close" and "neighboring," everything that is nearby and that we encounter "first off."

Why?

> Because what we encounter "first off" is not that which is close but that which is ever usual. (Now) the usual has this property of having a frightening power of making us unused to living in the essential and often so decisively that it never allows us to live there anymore.[36]

All personal existence is the assuming of a prepersonal tradition. Yet the meaning of this tradition—in spite of its effective transmission—is lost and is always forgotten: "Man in the world always moves about on the ground of an unanalyzed and long since impenetrable traditionality."[37]

Man is essentially a "traditional being";[38] that is to say, he succumbs to a tradition that he grasps only more or less explicitly. This tradition unburdens him of the concern of directing his life himself, asking a radical question and making a decisive choice. . . . Tradition, which thus imposes its supremacy, far from making what it "hands on" accessible, usually contributes, on the contrary, to its covering up. It degrades its content, turning it into something obvious, and bars the access to the original "roots" where traditional categories and concepts were, partly at least, really thought out. It eliminates all need to understand the necessity of a return to the roots.[39]

Here is where the question, astonishment, comes in, "inasmuch as, at this moment, man witnesses the destruction of his traditions of knowledge, of his preconceived knowledge of the world and things, and as he feels the necessity of a new explanation of the world."[40] In order to revive an ossified, petrified tradition, to eliminate the excesses with which it has been strained over time, to rid itself of the alluvion that has been deposited, one must adopt a fundamentally critical attitude that one might call "destruction"[41] in order to emphasize its radicality and importance. It is a matter of a totally positive act of destruction that will allow man "to open himself up 'anew' and, so to speak, 'originally' to the world, to find himself at the dawn of a 'new day' of the world, where he and everything that is begin to appear in a 'new' light, where the world reveals itself in a 'new manner.'"[42] This idea of the newness of perception, in the understanding of the world and things, is a constant feature of Talmudic[43] and Midrashic[44] thinking, and even more explicitly in the Hasidic thought of Masters such as the author of *Sefat Emet*,[45] Rabbi Nahman of Bratslav, or even Rabbi Zadok ha-Kohan of Lublin!

It is the notion of *Hithadeshut* that is the main reference for the commentaries of Deut. 26:16: *Hayom hazeh Hashem Elokekha metzavekha la'assot*: "YHVH your God commands you to. . . ."
The *Tanhuma Midrash* inquires:

> What does "today" (*Hayom hazeh*) mean? Had the Holy One, blessed be He, ordered nothing up till now? And yet the "today" in question is situated in the fortieth year after the Revelation?[46] This is what should be understood: Moses said to Israel, The Torah should be so dear to you that each day should be, for you, the very day of the Revelation (*Keilu hayom haze kibaltem otah mehar Sinai*).

We also have another version of this *Midrash*, given by Rashi in his commentary on the verse quoted. It is in fact this version that is generally quoted by commentators:

> *Today*, that is to say that they (the commandments) were considered in your eyes as if they were new (*Yiyu beenekha kehadashim*).

The rest of this *Midrash*, more rarely quoted, is of prime importance:

> Rabbi Johanan said, He who makes the Torah (*Kol haosseh et Hatorah*) according to his truth (*laamitah*) is considered as having made himself (*Keilu hu assa atsmo*) as it is said: "In those days (*baet hahi*) God ordered me to teach you these rules and these laws so that 'you would make them' (*laassoteikhem otam . . .*)." It is not written that "you make them" (*laassot otam*), but that "you make yourself" (*laassotekhem atem*);[47] it is thus that man creates himself and makes himself (*hu assa uvara et atsmo*).

From this *Midrash* we can make several remarks about the motives and the purposes of the "questioning attitude."[48] Astonishment and questioning "have man leave the fundamental mode of accomplishment of life,[49] the neglect and metaphysical laziness where he ceases to question the world. . . ."

Astonishment and questioning—*Hokhmah/Koahmah*—throw man out of the engagement of everyday familiarity with the world, with pre-set traditional and archaic familiarity, with a world that has been debated from time immemorial, leading him to the creative penury of unknowing.[50]

Through astonishment and questioning, man is able to free himself once and for all from the domination (were it unconscious) of certain thinking habits, convictions, theories accepted without verification, opinions, prejudices, ready-made decisions, which decree what the world, things, people, knowledge, etc., are.

Until now, the function of *Hokhmah* has been represented, from a theoretical point of view, in the context of a "theory of knowing." The *Midrash* we have quoted seems to insist on the knowledge of being and doing, as well as on the relationship between being and knowing. *Kol yom kehadashim*, which we could translate as the "tradition of newness," necessitates a reactivation of meaning, after the period of "positive destruction" . . .

The term "reactivation" does not have the same meaning for us as it does for Husserl.[51] For the latter, "by this reactivation of meaning, I actively re-produce the primordial evidence; I make myself fully responsible for and conscious of the meaning that I espouse. *Reaktivierung* permits bringing to life, under the sedimentary surfaces of linguistic and cultural acquisitions, the sense arising from instituting evidence."[52]

We can say that there is, in Husserl's thought, the notion of an "essence-of-the-first-time,"[53] an inaugural signification that is always reproducible, whatever its de facto example may be.

Phenomenological questioning, which Husserl calls a "question in return" (*Rückfrage*), allows, both owing to the sediments and in spite of them, the restoration to history of its diaphanous tradition.

Reactivation, in the Husserlian sense, leads us (is supposed to lead us) to the "meaning of the first time." From the point of view of the study of texts, that means that study, through questioning, should bring us to the very first, original meaning of words. Study would then mean repetition, rediscovering: the student would then be a "raider of the lost meaning"!

Here we are right back in the world of finiteness.[54]

On the other hand, Talmudic questioning never seeks, even when it seems to, the "meaning of the first time." *Hidush*, innovation of meaning, always aims to be beyond the already-given meaning. We do not leave the usual to go back to the origin; the movement is not regressive. On the contrary, there is an imperious will to build meaning in order to construct the development of history.[55] Reactivation awakens the creative force of interpretation. It is not the meaning that is reactivated but always the power of the word, of the event, or of the thing to signify ever again and beyond.

Gezerah Shavah

The Talmud sets out a strategy of "opening," with an anti-ideological function: a fundamental guarantee for all liberties.

The two "principles of opening" are:

1. *Mahloket*, which we have just seen
2. *Gezarah shavah*, whose main themes we are about to describe

Mahloket deals with persons, *Gezarah shavah* with the text; so we can contrast a "principle of external dialogue," *Mahloket*, and a "principle of internal dialogue," *Gezarah shavah*, or a "horizontal" and a "vertical" dimension of dialogue.

Gezarah shavah is one of the thirteen rules of interpretation developed by Rabbi Ishmael. An ordinary bilingual dictionary translates this word by "analogy, comparison." French Talmudic language uses the expression "semantic analogy." Instead of these terms, we prefer that of *intertextuality*, which perfectly expresses what is at stake in this way of approaching text(s).[56]

Intertextuality means that no utterance exists outside of its relation to other utterances. A text is always in relation with another text, and the meaning of these texts is not exclusively to be found in one or the other but in the relations between the two. In other words, no text is closed.

> Every text opens on another text; all writing refers to another writing, is always cut open, gashed. . . . It is open like this, in fact, on all texts, of all time, of all genres; each text is of an infinite density.[57]

Jabès says, "One letter in common is enough for two words to know each other."[58] We would say, "One word in common is sufficient for two texts to know each other."

The principle of *Gezarah shavah* lies in the word. The word is the smallest unit of the textual structure. In the Hebrew sentence words are not subordinated to each other by grammatical or other logic; they "co-exist"[59] with each other and can, at any moment, signify outside of their contexts or be shifted into another context, while still preserving the meaning from the initial context.

In short, *Gezarah shavah* consists in listening to the intertextual echoes. As Lévinas points out, "when the Talmudist, commenting a biblical text, refers to another biblical text—even if the reference is arbitrary—one must carefully read the context of the passage mentioned. It is not the explanation of the word that counts. It is a matter of associating the biblical 'landscape' with another one in order to extract from this coupling the secret perfume of the first one."[60]

And so *Gezarah shavah* is a process that goes beyond polysemy or semantic ambiguity, because it is not simply the contextual meaning of word "x" or "y" that is shifted, but the actual context.[61] So by this dialogue of texts—we can also speak of polyphony—the single, fixed meaning no longer exists; the text no longer reveals a meaning. The meaning is not given; it must be built.

Thus, *Gezarah shavah* can help us to approach a new conception of the text (of the book).

> The text is not a linguistic phenomenon—in other words, it is not the structured meaning that takes form in a linguistic corpus seen as a flat structure; it is something that generates itself.[62]

We are now confronted with the *Pshat-Drash* pair. The text is *Pshat-Drash*. *Drash* dissolves *Pshat*, stratifies it, spatializes it, dynamizes it, opens it up into a signifying volume, frees it of its heaviness and its typographical petrification.

By means of *Gezarah shavah* as a foundation of *Drash* "the text takes the form of an echo chamber with multiple registers, where each of its elements obtains a multi-dimensionality that, referring to texts present or absent, gives them a scope which opens it up" to infinity. Apart from this energizing and productivity of the text, *Gezarah shavah* introduces a new relation to time and history.

Through *Gezarah shavah* we leave the writing-reading of the line to enter into the writing-reading of a volume. It is interesting, in this respect, to pause a moment on a passage from the *Zohar* that comments this verse from Genesis: "Here is the book of the generations of Adam. In the day that God created man, in the likeness of God made he him; male and female created he them and blessed them."[63]

So there is a "Book of generations" (*Sefer toldot Adam*). Not a book that recounts the history of the generations, but a book that is the very scene of the generation of the production of the history of the generations. This book is "the book," the archetype of all books yet to come (itself also being a "book yet to come"). What form does this book take? The answer of the *Zohar* is surprising. It is a verse from the book of Proverbs that does not speak of a book, but of a righteous man running to a strong tower: "The name of YHVH is a strong tower, the righteous man runs to it and is secure."[64] Up to this point, nothing surprising; one may be disappointed or disconcerted, nothing more . . .

But what is rare is that the *Zohar* provides an "illustration" of its remarks, rewriting the verse quoted in the form of the following diagram.

מבש   עוי   מיץ

גרג   ווה   יצד

דצב   זדו   היי

לקה   שוה   ומך

Three vertical lines—each column is divided into four lines; each line (or row) has three letters—which can be transcribed as follows.[65]

← reading direction

	9	8	7	6	5	4	3	2	1
A	ts	y	m	y	v	h'	ch	b	m
B	d	ts	y	h	v	v	gu	r	gu
C	y	y	h	v	d	z	b	ts	d
D	q	n	v	h	v	ch	h	q	l

To simplify the explanation, we have given the lines the letters A B C D, from top to bottom, and the columns the figures 1 to 9.

We remind the reader that Hebrew writing is consonantal and that it is read from right to left.

What does this rewriting mean?[66] How should it be read? The commentaries explain how we can find the original words.

Let us point out that what is important is not to rediscover them but to understand the scattering and bursting movement of the sentence and of the words and the way they are reorganized.

We witness the transition from a classical linear, horizontal and consecutive writing to a voluminal, vertical and horizontal writing forming a veritable network. Reading becomes possible only by "leaps."[67]

First sentence: vertical reading, column 1 should be read in order from top to bottom, which gives us *Migdal*; column 4 enables us to read *h'oz* and *sh* (first letter of the word *shem*, which only appears in column 7). In column 7, there is the *m* of *shem*—first divided word that necessitates a change of column (axis) and a movement from bottom to top (remember that *shem* is the "name" and the "book"); still in column 7, we can read the first three letters of the Tetragram (Y H V). The fourth letter is put off until the end of the verse.

After this first stage of vertical reading, and by "leaps" (we went from column 1 to 4 and from 4 to 7), we move on to the *second stage*: *horizontal (classical) reading*, still by "leaps."

Here, reading is like gathering, like a harvest (*leket*). We find the word *Bo*, "in it," taking A2 and A5; the word *yaruts*, "he runs," in A8, B2, B5, B8; the word *Tsadik*, "righteous," in C2, C5, C8, D2; finally, the word *venisgav*, "and is secure," in D5, D8 (for the letters *vav* and *nun*). Next, in the middle of the word, we turn to the vertical reading.

Third stage: the word *venisgav* is completed by column 3, except for D3, the last letter of the Tetragram, which was deferred. So the verse is complete, but to create the "book of generations," one must add the Tetragram (Y H V H), column 6, and the word *Tsadik* ("the righteous"), column 9.

It will be noticed that no word suffers a traditional reading. Whole words go from the horizontal to the vertical axis. Those that remain in the traditional position are burst or scattered. Here we are really confronted with a "text" that must be understood in its etymological meaning: fabric, texture, built by interweaving of vertical threads (warp) and horizontal threads (woof). Gaon of Vilna, speaking of this diagram, explicitly uses the term "woven."[68]

However, a difference will be noticed between the diagram given and the fabric. In the fabric, the woof is always continuous; the thread is passed once over, once under; the "leap" is not real but only a matter of perspective: the metaphor has its limits (unless we can suppose the existence of letters beneath the letters).

The "book of generations," as an archetype of the "text," "bursts the surface of language and allows the breaking up of the conceptual mechanics that establish a historical linearity and make us enter into the reading of a stratified history with a cut-up, recursive, dialectical temporality, which cannot be reduced to a single meaning, but is made up of types of signifying practices whose plural series is without beginning or end."[69]

Consequently, *Gezarah shavah* is not a stretched, unorthodox reading. On the contrary, it builds and composes the text, the book. By means of this mode of reading, we attain the dimensions of multiplicity and dynamic time.

That may be the meaning of the famous Talmudic and Midrashic expression *Ein mukdam umeuhar batorah*: "There is no before and after in the Torah."[70]

Notes

1. Here the fundamental distinction between "thematics" and "problematics" is set out. The mistake of "classical" Talmudic study is due to the neglecting of this distinction: because such study retains only the "theme" and forgets to seek out the "problem," the Talmud becomes a positive science. "The theme is a determined field of the world, given and known in advance. Positive science possesses the object of its research in advance. The methods may be difficult and not very accessible, but what it is dealing with, what it is concerned with, the field of its research, is necessarily that which, within itself, is clearest and most well-known, however thorough this given familiarity with the thematics of a positive science may become, in the course of the research" (E. Fink, *De la phénoménologie* [Paris: Éditions de Minuit, 1974], p. 206).

2. Allusion to the first *Mishnah* of the *Betsa* tractate, i.e., the "egg."

3. Allusion to the *Bava Kama* tractate on the damages caused by a bullock and the compensation its owner must pay!

4. *Quatre Lectures talmudiques* (Paris: Éditions de Minuit, 1968), p. 12. It is this shifting that constitutes the whole of philosophical analysis, and, as Lévinas asserts, "even if the Talmud is not a philosophy in the Greek sense of the word [but even so, we would still have to decide exactly what we mean by this expression; on this topic, cf. *L'Au-delà du verset*, pp. 42f.], it is an eminent source of those experiences in which philosophers seek inspiration" (p. 12). The philosophy of the Talmud unfolds within the tension between *Halakhah* and *Aggadah* and, in fact, there is more philosophy in the problematics of the *Halakhah* than in that of the *Aggadah*. This method of analysis is also present in the works of authors such as R. Josef Rozin, known as "Rogachover"; see also the research of the School of Brisk and Rabbi Nahman of Bratslav in his *Likkutei Halakhot*.

5. Régis Debray, *Critique de la raison politique* (Paris: Gallimard, 1981), p. 210, concerning the Buddhist ritual of a Zen Monastery of the Sota-Eihifi sect (Japan).

6. The *Beit Hamidrash* is a room that can contain eight hundred students at any one time (all expressing themselves aloud!); for the atmosphere at the *Beit Hamidrash*, cf. the film *Yentl*, which admirably re-creates the life of the study hall; the magnificent photographs of F. Brenner, *Jerusalem: Instants d'éternité* (Paris: Denoël, 1984), for example, pp. 56, 57, 59, 66, 67, 81, 88; *La Danse des fidèles*, photographs by L. Freed (Paris: Chêne, 1984), pp. 27, 28, and 30; Chaïm Potok, *L'Élu* (The chosen) (Paris: Calmann-Lévy, 1987).

7. Cf. H. Marcuse, *L'Homme unidimensionnel* (Paris: Éditions de Minuit, 1968); the chapter titles are eloquent: "The Lethargy of Criticism: A Society without an Opposition" (Introduction), "The World of a Closed Discourse" (chap. 4). Cf. also Debray, *Critique de la raison politique*, pp. 205f., the chapter "The Imperative of Adherence," which begins as follows: "Our hypothesis: everywhere a *we* sets off, there will be an 'ideology,' and when the *we* can no longer be pronounced, there is no longer an 'ideology.'" Jewish thought is not monolithic.

8. For example: *Makloket Hillel ve-Shamai* which is the most famous discussion from the Talmud, between the "schools of thought" of Hillel and Shammai.

9. E. Lévinas, *De Dieu qui vient à l'idée* (Paris: Vrin, 1982).

10. *Elu veelu divrei Elohim hayyim.*

11. Lévinas, *De Dieu qui vient à l'idée*, p. 130, pp. 215f. In fact, a great part of this book by Lévinas develops this problem.

12. Ibid.

13. Quoted by André Neher in *Le Puits de l'exil, la théologie dialectique du Maharal de Prague* (Paris: Albin Michel, 1966).

14. Which is not a "manual," since it refuses to be held by a hand, by the grasping of understanding, of "comprehending."

15. On this point, cf. E. Lévinas, *Otherwise Than Being* (The Hague: Nijhoff, 1981).

16. See *Bava Metsia* 84a, concerning the controversies between R. Johanan and Resh Lakish.

17. Lévinas, *De Dieu qui vient à l'idée*, pp. 211f.

18. F. Collin, *Maurice Blanchot et la question de l'écriture* (Paris: Gallimard, 1971), p. 95.

19. We may also notice that the titles of these dialogues are single proper nouns: Meno, Crito, Protagoras, Gorgias, etc.

20. Lévinas, *De Dieu qui vient à l'idée*, p. 215.

21. Ibid.

22. Cf., by way of counterpoint, Heidegger, *Qu'est-ce qu'une chose?* (Paris: Gallimard, 1971), pp. 81f.

23. Cf., among others, J. Kristeva, *Sémeiotikè* (Paris: Seuil, 1969), pp. 188f.

24. Quoted by K. Jaspers in *Nietzsche* (Paris: Gallimard, 1950), "Tel," p. 189. The basic thesis of Nietzsche is that every being is an interpreted being: "Nothing exists in itself, no absolute knowledge, the perspectivist illusion is inherent to existence" (p. 291).

25. M. Blanchot, *L'Entretien infini* (Paris: Gallimard, 1969), pp. 13–14. Cf., concerning this passage, Lévinas, *De Dieu qui vient à l'idée*, p. 136: "When we want to speak about the question of research and desire. . . ."

26. *Likkutei Moharan*, 1:64.

27. Blanchot, *L'Entretien infini*, p. 8, not a Hegelian synthesis, no dialectic, but a hyperdialectic. Cf. M. Merleau-Ponty, *Le Visible et l'invisible* (Paris: Gallimard, 1964), p. 175; and J. Weiss, *Studies in Braslav Hassidism* (Jerusalem, 1974), chap. 8, "The Question in Rabbi Nahman's Thought."

28. *Pirkei Avot.*

29. *Likkutei Moharan*, 1:64.

30. Blanchot, *L'Entretien infini*, p. 15.

31. Ibid., p. 14.

32. Ibid., p. 16.

33 H. G. Gadamer, *Vérité et méthode* (Paris: Seuil, 1976), p. 208.

34. On the philosophy/theology opposition, cf. also A. Y. Heschel, *Dieu en quête de l'homme* (Paris: Seuil, 1968), pp. 9f.; cf. also pp. 54 and 55.

35. On astonishment in philosophy: Plato, *Theaetetus* 115d; Aristotle, *Meta-physics* 982b, 11. Schopenhauer said: "To have a philosophical mind is to be able to be astonished by everyday events and objects. . . . The more a man is intellec-tually inferior, the less existence is mysterious for him. Everything seems to him to contain the explanation of its how and why." *Le Monde comme volonté et comme représentation* chap. 17 of the "Supplements" (Paris: PUF, 1989), pp. 852f.

36. M. Heidegger, *Qu'appelle-t-on penser?* (Paris: PUF, 1973), p. 141.

37. E. Fink, *De la phénoménologie* (Paris: Éditions de Minuit, 1974), p. 212.

38. Heidegger uses the following expression: "The being-there *is* its past," *L'Être et le temps* (Paris: Gallimard, 1964), p. 36.

39. Ibid., pp. 37–38.

40. Fink, *De la phénoménologie*, p. 203.

41. It is the term used by Heidegger, *L'Être et le temps*, p. 39 (*Destruktion* in German). Rabbi Zadok ha-Kohen of Lublin (*Peri Tsadik*, on *"Ki Tavo,"* par. 9) speaks of *Bitul*: of "abolishing."

42. Fink, *De la phénoménologie*, p. 203.

43. *Eruvin* 54b.

44. *Tanhuma* on *"Ki Tavo,"* 1.

45. Rabbi Judah Arie Lev of Gour.

46. Deut. 1:3.

47. The word *otam* being defective—without a *vav*—it can be read as *atem*, as "you."

48. Which is, in fact, the translation of *Hokhmah* ("wisdom")/*Koah-Mah* (the ability to say: "what?").

49. "Traditionalness." Quotation taken from Fink, *De la phénoménologie*, p. 212.

50. On this subject, cf. Rabbi Nahman of Bratslav, quoted by Rabbi Nathan of Nemirov in "Words" (*Sihot Haran*), no. 266 of the punctuated edition (1982) and no. 153; also *Likkutei Moharan*, 2:78.

Shortly before his death, R. Nahman of Bratslav spoke to his disciplines: "Why come to me? Now I do not know anything (*halo ani eini yodea ata klall*). When I impart a teaching to you, I understand why you come to me, but why do you come now? And yet, I do not know anything, I am totally simple and destitute. . . ." He repeated several times, sincerely, that he did not know anything. . . . Then, he began to speak and teach. This admirable statement by Rabbi Nahman, which could sum up his entire questioning attitude, should also be retained: "It is forbidden to be old . . .", *Likkutei Halakhot, "Orah Hayim," "Hilkhot Tefillin,"* 5. 7 (*Tsarikh lehathil bekhol pa'am mehadash*: "It is necessary to start over, each time . . .").

51. In the phenomenological tradition to which we have been referring since the beginning of the paragraph.

52. J. Derrida, *Edmund Husserl's "Origin of Geometry": An Introduction*, trans. John P. Leavey Jr. (Lincoln: University of Nebraska Press, 1978), p. 99.

53. Ibid., p. 48.

54. Derrida discusses in detail the text by Husserl to see if reactivation leads to "finiteness" or not. We are exaggerating the negative aspect of Husserl's approach in order to better understand the contrast with the Talmudic approach (cf. pp. 100f).

55. We read the word *zeman*, which is "time," in the following way: *ze man*, which means "it is manna" or "here is the questioning" (cf. Book Two, "First Opening").

56. "Intertextuality" is a term introduced by Julia Kristeva in her introduction to Bakhtin, then adopted by T. Todorov in his *Mikhaïl Bakhtine, le principe dialogique* (Paris: Seuil, 1981). See, in particular, *Sémeiotikè*, pp. 54, 72–76, 13f.; also O. Ducrot, T. Todorov, *Dictionnaire encyclopédique des sciences du langage* (Paris: Seuil, 1972), p. 446.

57. S. Kofman, "L'Opération de la greffe," in *Écarts* (Paris: Fayard, 1973), pp. 117–18.

58. E. Jabès, *El, or the Last Book*, trans. Rosemary Waldrop (Middletown, Conn.: Wesleyan University Press, 1986), p. 10.

59. E. Lévinas, *L'Au-delà du verset* (Paris: Éditions de Minuit, 1982), p. 161.

60. Lévinas, *Quatre Lectures talmudiques*, p. 120.

61. We refer to P. Ricoeur, "La Structure, le mot, l'événement," in *Le Conflit des interprétations* (Paris: Seuil, 1969), pp. 93f.

The reflections on the word and isotopia (term used by Greimas, cf. *Sémantique structurale* [Larousse, 1966]) are interesting for a linguistic formulation of *Gezarah shavah*; see also Roland Barthes, *Writing Degree Zero*, trans. Annette Lavers and Colin Smith (New York: Hill and Wang, 1967), p. 48, on the word: "Word here is encyclopaedic, it contains simultaneously all the acceptations . . . and is reduced to a sort of zero degree, pregnant with all past and future specifications." It is the vertical dimension of the text we have just spoken of.

62. Kristeva, *Sémeiotikè*, p. 224; also p. 53: "We define the text as a translinguistic apparatus that redistributes the order of the language, connecting a communicative speech aiming at direct information with different types of previous or contemporaneous utterances. In this way the text is a productivity, which means: (1) its relation to the language in which it is situated is redistributive (destructive and constructive); consequently it can be approached through logical rather than linguistic categories; (2) it is a permutation of texts, intertextuality: in the space of a text, several utterances, taken from other texts, cross and neutralize each other."

63. Gen. 5:1 and *Zohar Bereshit* 37b.

64. According to the texts of the Cabala, this verse is one of the names of God. Rabbi Nahman of Bratslav points out that the word "book" (*sefer*) has the same numerical value as the word "name" (*shem*): 340.

65. The *h'* transcribes the letter *Ayin*.

66. This passage is commented in detail by Gaon of Vilna (1720–1797) in *Likkutei Hagrah*, commented by Rabbi Isaac Aizik Havere ("Ria") (Warsaw, 1889), p. 366. The chapter is entitled *Shem Migdal Oz*, "The Name of the Strong Tower." The commentary shows how this diagram is constructed, its relation to the organization of the twelve tribes in the camp of Israel in the desert. The rewriting of the verse composes twelve names. So there is a relationship with the "breastplate" of the high priest (cf. Exod. 39:8f). The centrality of the figure 12 can be noticed in the verse itself, because the word *zeh* (*zayin-heh*) has a numerical value of 12 (7 + 5). The "tower" in question in this verse refers to the letter *lamed*, which in other texts is called *Migdal haporeah ba'avir*, that is to say, "the tower that flies in the airs" (cf. Rashi on *Sanhedrin* 106b and Rabbi Zadok ha-Kohen of Lublin, *Mahashavot haruts* [Pieterkov, 1912], p. 92; cf. also *Zohar Hadash Shir hashirim* 52b).

67. *Pesah* (plural: *pesahim*) that Rabbi Nahman reads as *Peh-sah*, i.e., "the mouth (*peh*) that speaks (*sah*)." Cf. *Likkutei Moharan*, 1:49,6.

68. *Likkutei Hagra*, p. 336; *veneerag beorekh uberohav*: "the verse is woven in its length and breadth." On the subject of "weaving," cf. Derrida, *La Dissémination* (Paris: Seuil, 1972).

69. Kristeva, *Sémeiotikè*, p. 15; cf. also: Derrida, *De la grammatologie* (Paris: Éditions de Minuit, 1967), pp. 105–6, cf. also pp. 127f.; cf. Starobinski, *Les Mots sous les mots*, (Paris: Gallimard, 1971), pp. 45–46; cf. also A. Leroi-Gourhan, *Le Geste et la parole* (Paris: Albin Michel, 1964), vol. 1, chap. 6, pp. 261–300, "Les Symboles du langage" (this bibliography is given by Derrida, *De la grammatologie*).

70. *Pesahim* 6b; *Yerushalmi, Shekalim*, 6; *Sanhedrin* 49b and *Kohelet Rabbah* 1.

BOOK TWO

Openings

First Opening

WHAT IS A BOOK?
OR,
THE STORY OF AN EFFACING

The "animal endowed with language" of Aristotle has never been thought out, in its ontology, to include the book, nor questioned on the status of its religious relation to the book. This relation has never merited, in the philosophical "promotions" of categories, the rank of a mode so decisive for the condition—or noncondition—of humanity, and as essential and irreducible as language itself or thought or technical activity, as if reading were only one of the incidents of the circulation of information and the book one thing among many others, revealing in the manuals—like a hammer—its affinity with the hand.

    E. Lévinas, *L'Au-delà du verset*

The philosopher speaks of phenomena and noumena. Why would he not lend his attention to the being of the book or bibliomenon?

    G. Bachelard, *L'Activité rationaliste*

NUMEROUS TEXTS of the Talmud, of the *Midrash*, of the Cabala, and of Hasidism are concerned with thinking, questioning, toward, from, about what is called a book. "Toward," "from," "about": because, quite often, the question of writing or of reading is substituted for that of the book. The question of the book has been allowed to slip away, to become one of the marginal questions, as if the reflection about the book were impossible or even forbidden. The book as such has been forgotten. As when we speak about the forgetting of a being. There is a "forgetting of the essence of the book within the book."[1] Consequently, we have to go about getting back to the book, setting off for the beginnings, the foundation of the book. This return will not be a historical inquiry; such an investigation, in spite of its undeniable interest, would teach us nothing about the foundation we are seeking.

Here is a text whose main reflection concerns the definition of the book. Of course, the definition is not given immediately, and, once again, it would have been easy, obsessed as we may be by the "theme," to leave the "problem" aside, since this text takes the form of a Talmudic ruling concerning a fire on the Shabbat . . . The Talmud asks the following question: "What should be done on the Shabbat day when a fire breaks out, given that it is forbidden to put the fire out."[2]

Chapter 16 of the *Shabbat* tractate of the Talmud is devoted to this question. One is not allowed to put the fire out, but it is permissible to save certain objects by taking them out of the blaze.[3] Among the objects to be saved from the fire, holy books have absolute priority.

So the books should be saved, but not all books . . . There are holy books and then there are the others, "real books" and "false books." So the question underlying the whole text is: "What is a book? What is a book that makes it worth saving from the fire?"

The relation between the book and the fire,[4] we shall see, is extremely important, so important that the expression "it may be saved from the fire (the book)" is, in this text, the equivalent of "it is a book." The saving reveals the book.[5]

Below, we have given the complete translation of the passage of the Talmud we shall be using for our analysis. But the complexity of the Talmudic process obliges us to limit the purely technical analysis. Consequently, we shall be "technically" commenting only the first part, following, step by step, the twists and turns of this page of the *Gemara*. Then, starting with a core passage of the *Sugya*, we shall proceed by recurrence and extension. So this first part can be read rapidly, returned to later if necessary.

If need be, one could simply not read this part. In that case, the reader will go directly to the section headed "The Two *Nunim*," after having read the translation in order to immerse himself in the Talmudic "atmosphere." The introduction of the first part, "Legible and Illegible," is only to show how "halakhic" questioning progresses; it attempts to open the largest possible number of directions, even if it means not using them all right away . . .

Notes

1. Laruelle, "Projet d'une philosophie du livre," in *Cahiers Obsidiane*, no. 5 (1982): 156.

2. Shabbat is defined mainly by the nonrealization of a certain number of actions (thirty-nine for generic cases) of construction and setting-up of space (that of the Sanctuary in particular) and by the prohibition of lighting (and extinguishing) fire (Exod. 35:3).

3. A second Shabbat rule comes in here: the prohibition of transporting from a so-called private domain to a public one, and vice versa (in Hebrew: *issur hotzaha*). It is a fundamental rule, analyzed in several chapters of the *Shabbat* tractate. In case of a fire, if the outside of the house is considered a private domain, the fact of taking the books outside does not pose any problem whatsoever. One may save all the books, without distinguishing, as does the *Mishnah*, between holy and profane books. The commentary of the *Tosefot* poses the problem and resolves it in the following manner: it is true that if the *Halakhah* of the *issur hotzaha* is taken into consideration, there is no reason to distinguish between books that can be saved and books that cannot, and so they all may be saved. However, the *Tosefot* explain, the Masters thought that it was necessary to raise a barrier (*seyag* or *geder*) and authorize only the saving of holy books. The reason for this limitation: to delimit, define a precise behavior allowing actions of panic to be channeled, and so avoiding the risk of an action of extinguishing. The origin, the motivation of the distinction, and so, the definition of books, is—we shall be constantly coming back to it—to not end up being extinguished; the proof of that is, say the *Tosefot*, that the neighbor, the one who does not own the books, not being panic-stricken (*bahul*) is allowed to take the books out without any distinction. We can say that the whole reflection of the *Mishnah*—i.e., its existence—lies in this limitation. The *geder* is a limit that separates the permitted from the permitted, situated in front of another limit that separates the permitted from the forbidden. The behavior described by the *Mishnah* and containing the definition of the book (if only in embryo) is thus set in out in a relation to transgression, the limit-action. The *Mishnah* gives the impression of being pretextual. This impression is reinforced by a remark in the Jerusalem Talmud that calls on the notion of "*melakhah sheeinah tsrikhah legufah*" ("work that is not necessary for its own object"), a notion, which, if

taken into account, would make the extinction of the fire legal. In this case, the question of the saving of the book would not even have been raised! The commentary of the *Tosefot* broadens and opens up the initial perspective in which the *Mishnah* should be analyzed. The *"halakhic project"* is coupled with an *"aggadic project."* We have noticed that it may possibly be an approach that the *Tosefot* is particularly fond of (cf. *Bava Batra* 54a, first *Tosefot*).

4. With Rabbi Nahman of Bratslav and his "burnt book" we will see this idea reversed: the *auto-da-fé* reveals the book.

5. We may add that the root *S.F.R.* means both "book" and "border" (among other meanings): cf. *Even Shoshan Dictionary* (Hebrew), 2:936–37; cf. also the beginning of *Sefer Yetsirah* (Book of Creation), which analyzes the different meanings of this root.

ואלו קשרים פרק חמשה עשר שבת קטו

עין משפט
נר מצוה

מסורת
הש״ס

רבינו חננאל

אליבא

עילמית

ובידין

הדרן עלך ואלו קשרים

כל כתבי הקדש מצילין אותן מפני הדליקה

הגהות
הב״ח

הגהות
הגר״א

גליון הש״ס

Shabbat tractate, 115a

Shabbat tractate, 115b

עין משפט
נר מצוה

כל כתבי פרק ששה עשר שבת קמז

מסורת
הש״ס

פורענות

רבינו חננאל

פילוסופא

רב נסים גאון

Shabbat tractate, 116a

Translation

Shabbat Tractate, 115a, b, and 116a

Mishnah*

A. All holy writings may be saved from the fire, whether we read them or not;

B. and even if they are written in any language (other than Hebrew), they must be buried.

C. And why do we not read these books? Because of neglect of the *Beit Hamidrash*.

Gemara

It was stated: If they are written in Targum (Aramaic) or in any other language—Rav Huna said: They must not be saved from a fire; while Rav Hisda ruled: They may be saved from a fire. On the view that it is permissible to read them, all agree that they must be saved. Rav Huna says: We may not save them, since they may not be read. Rav Hisda says: We must save them, because of the disgrace to Holy Writings.

Question against Rav Huna

We learned in the *Mishnah*: "All sacred writings may be saved from the fire, whether we read them or not," and even if they are written in any language. Surely "whether we read them" refers to the *Neviim* (Prophets), while "or not" refers to the *Ketuvim* (Writings, or Hagiographa), and even if they are written in any language," though they may not be read (publicly), yet he (the Tanna) teaches that they "may be saved," which refutes Rav Huna?

Answer

Rav Huna can answer you: Is that logical? Consider the second clause, "they must be buried": seeing that they must be saved, need burying be mentioned?

*Titles and divisions by the author.

Two Reasonings

But Rav Huna explains it in accordance with his view, while Rav Hisda explains it according to his. Rav Huna explains it in accordance with his view. "Whether we read them" (i.e., the Prophets), "or not" (i.e., the Writings). That is, only if they are written in the Holy Tongue (Hebrew), but if they are written in any other language, we may not save them, yet even so they must be buried. Rav Hisda explains it according to his view: "Whether we read them" (i.e., the Prophets), "or not" (i.e., the Writings); "even if they are written in any language," we must still save them. And this is what he states: And even their worm-eaten material *must be buried*.

Second Question against Rav Huna

An objection is raised: If they are written in Targum or in any other language, they may be saved from the fire. This refutes Rav Huna?

Answer

Rav Huna answers you: This Tanna holds; they may be read.

Third question against Rav Huna

Come and hear: If they are written in Egyptian, Median, a trans-Euphratean Aramaic, Elamitic, or Greek, though they may not be read, they may be saved from a fire. This refutes Rav Huna?

Answer

Rav Huna can answer you: It is a controversy of Tannaim. For it was taught: If they are written in Targum or in any language, they may be saved from a fire.

Anecdote

Rabbi Yose said: They may not be saved from a fire. Said Rabbi Yose: "Ma'aseh (It once happened that) my father Halafta visited Rabban

Gamaliel Berabbi at Tiberias and found him sitting at the table of Johanan ben Nizuf with the Targum of the book of Job in his hand,
which he was reading. Said he to him, "I remember that Rabban Gamaliel, your grandfather, was standing on a high eminence on the Temple
Mount, when the book of Job in a Targumic version was brought before him, whereupon he said to the builder, "Bury it under the bricks."
He (Rabban Gamaliel II) too gave orders, and they buried it."

Another Version of the Anecdote

Rabbi Yose, son of Rabbi Judah said: They overturned a tub of mortar
upon it. Said Rabbi: There are two objections to this: First, how came
mortar on the Temple Mount? Moreover, is it then permitted to destroy
them with one's own hands? For they must be put in a neglected place
to decay of their own accord. Which Tannaim differ on this question?
Shall we say the first Tanna and Rabbi Yose—but perhaps they differ in
this: one Master holds, it is not permitted to read them? Rather they are
Rabbi Yose and the Tanna who taught the law about the Egyptian script.

Is Writing Permitted?

Our rabbis taught: Benedictions and amulets, though they contain letters of the Divine Name and many passages of the Torah, must not be
rescued from a fire but must be burnt where they lie, they together with
their Names. Hence it was said, they who write down Benedictions are
as though they burnt a Torah.

Anecdote

It happened that one was once writing in Sidon. Rabbi Ishmael was
informed thereof, and he went to question him about it. As he was
ascending the ladder, he (the writer) became aware of him, so he took a
sheaf of benedictions and plunged them into a bowl of water. In these
words did R. Ishmael speak to him: The punishment for the latter deed
is greater than for the former.

Writing and Translation

The Resh Galutha (head of the exile in Babylonia, the exilarch) asked
Rabbah, son of Rav Huna: If they are written with paint (dye), *sikrah*

(a red paint), gum ink, or calcanthum, in Hebrew, may they be rescued from a fire or not? This is asked whether on the view that we may save[1] or that we may not save. It is asked on the view that we may not save: that may be only if they are written in Targum or any other language; but here in that they are written in Hebrew, we may rescue them. Or perhaps even on the view that we may save them, that is, only when they are written in ink, which is lasting; but here, since it (the writing) is not permanent, we may not rescue them? We may not save [them], answered he. But Rav Hamnuna recited, We may save them? If it was taught, it was taught, replied he. Where was it taught? Said Rav Ashi, Even as it was taught: The only difference between the other Books and the *Megillah* is that the Books can be written in any language, whereas a *Megillah* (Book of Esther) must be written in Assyrian, on a scroll, and in ink.

Eighty-Five Letters

Rav Huna ben Halub asked Rav Nahman: A scroll of the Law in which eighty-five letters cannot be gathered, such as the section, "And it came to pass when the Ark set forward . . .,"[2] may it be saved from a fire or not? Said he, Then ask about the section, "And it came to pass . . ." itself! If the section, "And it came to pass . . .," is defective through effacing, I have no problem, for since it contains the Divine Name, even if it does not contain eighty-five letters we must rescue it. My only problem is about a scroll of the Law wherein this number cannot be gathered: what then? We may not save it, he answered.

He refuted him: If Targum is written as *Mikra* (i.e., in original Hebrew), or *Mikra* is written in Targum or in Hebrew characters, they must be saved from a fire, and the Targum in Ezra, Daniel, and the Torah (the Pentateuch) goes without saying. Now, what is the Targum in the Torah? The words *Yegar sahaduta* (Gen. 31:47f); and though it does not contain eighty-five letters it must be saved? That was taught in respect of completing the number.

What Is Reading?

The eighty-five letters, must they be together or even scattered? Rav Huna said: They must be together; Rav Hisda said: Even scattered. An objection is raised: If a scroll of the Law is decayed, if eighty-five letters can be gathered therein, such as the section, "And it came to pass when the Ark set forward . . .," we must save it; if not, we may not save it. This refutes Rav Huna? Rav Hisda expounded it on the basis of Rav Huna's ruling as referring to words.[3]

The Two Nunim: The Book

Our rabbis taught: "And it came to pass when the Ark set forward that Moses said . . .": for this section the Holy One, blessed be He, provided signs above and below, to teach that this is not its place.

Rabbi said: It is not on that account, but because it ranks as a separate book. With whom does the following dictum of Rabbi Samuel ben Nahmani in Rabbi Jonathan's name agree? She (Wisdom) has erected her seven pillars" (Prov. 9:1); this refers to the seven Books of the Law. With whom? With Rabbi. Who is the Tanna that disagrees with Rabbi? It is Rabbi Simeon ben Gamaliel. For it was taught, Rabbi Simeon ben Gamaliel said: This section is destined to be removed from here and written in its right place. And why is it written here? In order to provide a break between the first account of erring and the second account of erring. What is the second account of erring? "And the people were as murmurers. . . ." The first account of erring? "And they moved away from the mount of the Lord,"[4] which Rabbi Hama ben Rabbi Hanina expounded as meaning that they turned away from following the Lord. And where is its rightful place? In the chapter on the banners.[5]

Are the Blank Spaces a Book?

The scholars asked: The blank spaces (or margins) of a *Sefer Torah*, may we rescue them from fire or not?

Come and hear: If a *Sefer Torah* is decayed, if eighty-five letters can be gathered therein, such as the section "And it came to pass when the Ark set forward," we must save it; if not, we may not save it. But why so? Conclude that it may be saved on account of its blank space?[6] That which is decayed is different.

Come and hear: if a *Sefer Torah* is effaced, if eighty-five letters can be gathered therein, such as the section, "And it came to pass when the Ark set forward," we must save it; if not, we may not save it. But why so: conclude that we must save it on account of its blank space?

As for the place of the writing, I have no doubt, for when it was sanctified it was on account of the writing, and when its writing goes its sanctity goes too. My problem is only in respect of the blank spaces above and below, between the sections, between the columns, and at the beginning and the end of the scroll. Yet conclude that it must be saved on that account?[7] It may mean there that one had cut off the blank spaces and thrown them away.

Come and hear: The blank spaces above and below, between the sections, between the columns, at the beginning and at the end of the scroll, defile one's hands. It may be that when they are together with the *Sefer Torah* they are different and should be saved from the fire.

This text is not proof, since we can say that it is the fact that they are in the fire that confers this status on them. The margins are perhaps not in themselves holy!

Come and hear: The blank spaces and the books of the *Minim* (sectarians, heretics) may not be saved from a fire, but they must be burnt in their place, they and the Divine Names occurring in them. Now surely it means the blank portions of a scroll of the Law? No: the blank spaces in the books of *Minim*. Seeing that we may not save the books of *Minim* themselves, need their blank spaces be stated? This is its meaning: And the books of *Minim* are like blank spaces.

Books Written by Heretics

It was stated in the text: The blank spaces and the books of the *Minim*, we may not save them from a fire. Rabbi Yose said: On weekdays one must cut out the Divine Names that they contain, hide them, and burn the rest. Rabbi Tarfon said: May I bury my son if I would not burn them together with their Divine Names if they came to my hand. For even if one pursued me to slay me, or a snake pursued me to bite me, I would enter a heathen temple for refuge, but not the houses of these people, for the latter know of God yet deny Him, whereas the former are ignorant and deny Him, and of them the Writ says, "Behind doors and doorposts you have set up your sign (*mezuzah*)."[8] Rabbi Ishmael said: One can reason *a minori*. If in order to make peace between man and wife the Torah decreed, Let my Name, written in sanctity, be blotted out in water, these, who stir up jealousy, enmity, and wrath between Israel and their Father in Heaven, how much more so; and of them David said, "YHVH, do I not hate those who hate you? And loathe those who defy you? I hate them with perfect hatred: I count them as my enemies."[9] And just as we may not rescue them from a fire, so may we not rescue them from a collapse of debris or from water or from anything that may destroy them.

Notes

1. What was said above: "They may be saved even if they are written in other languages."
2. Num. 10:35–36.
3. That is to say that the "gathering" of the *Baraita* refers to the case where

there are complete words that need to be assembled in order that eighty-five letters may be obtained. In this case, Rav Huna and Rav Hisda agree: "they may be saved," because for Rav Huna the letters are "united." So there is no text explicitly against Rav Huna; their discussion deals with separate letters that do not make up complete words.

4. Num. 11:1 and 10:33.

5. From Num. 10:14.

6. Since, in spite of the margins, they are not saved, we have a proof and an answer to the question: "The margins are not saved."

7. In this succession of questions and answers, the *Gemara* decides, as it goes, the meaning of the term "margins": it is a question of the white extratextual spaces.

8. Isa. 57:8.

9. Ps. 139:21.

Remarks on the Translation* _____

LEGIBLE AND ILLEGIBLE

Analysis of the Mishnah

A. All holy writings may be saved from the fire, whether we read them or not. . .

B. (And) even if they are written in any other language, they must be buried . . .

C. And why do we not read these books? Because of the neglect of the *Beit Hamidrash* (study hall)!

The fear of transgression—at the origin of the restriction contemplated—is connected to the fire that, it seems, must continue to burn; there is a will to maintain a fire that limits and separates the positive from the negative, obedience and transgression.

The idea of rescuing must also be analyzed; there again, we find the limit and, perhaps, even more radically, the limit between the life and death of the Book. It is a limit or border of the existence of the Book, beyond—or rather, within—which the Book swings over into the non-book.[1]

A. . . . *WHETHER WE READ THEM OR NOT.* . .

What a strange expression! There are books that are not read! If they are not read, why then were they written? Perhaps there is some sort of illegibility that results from their aging. The parchment cracks, the ink is effaced? "Reading" can also have the meaning of a liturgical reading, a public one. The sentence of the *Mishnah* would then mean "whether we read them in public or not. . ."; if that is the case, one would then have to ask what the hypothesis or prejudice is that would make one think that a book which can be read in private should not be saved from the fire. All these questions can be summed up in the following question: is nonreading a cause that is intrinsic or extrinsic to the Book? Does the fault lie with the Book itself or in the relation to the Book?

Rashi, in the name of his master, Rabbenu ha-Levi, gives the following commentary: "The nonreading concerns the individual"; private

_____

*These remarks are provided by way of an illustration, in order to show the complexities of Talmudic reasoning. Should the reader wish to pass over this chapter, his understanding of the demonstration that follows will not be diminished.

nonreading as opposed to public nonreading. Let us point out that the explanation of public nonreading is also accepted: for there are books that it is not customary to read in public, for example, the *Ketuvim*— the *Writings*[2] (with a few specific exceptions).

It is not the form nor the state of the book that is the cause of the prohibition against reading the book.

But, as the *Mishnah* teaches, the reason for the prohibition of reading —there is a commandment to read, and there is also a commandment that forbids reading—lies in "the fear" of the *Bitul beit hamidrash*. This expression, which can be translated literally by "the abolition of the study hall," has absolutely nothing to do with the fire. It is not a matter of an impossibility of reading, resulting from the fire in the library, but of a *"halakhic" illegibility*, the interdiction of having a relationship with the Book in order not to arrive at the point where the "study hall is abolished," by abandoning of the place of study, by giving up listening to the oral teaching. Rashi asserts: "Books are exciting and attract (the heart). Oral teaching was given to the study hall for people who work during the week and, as a result, do not have the chance to study. The content of this teaching is 'halakhic': permission and interdiction, acquittal and guilt, the pure and the impure, etc. It is preferable for these people to listen rather than to read the *Writings—Ketuvim*."

We can outline two readings of this commentary by Rashi. Rashi means that the teaching of *Halakhah* is preferable to that of *Aggadah*; a correct and logical interpretation: for people who do not study, it is good for them to be taught—in the little tuition they receive—what they must and must not do, a teaching they can immediately put to practical use. The second reading—which does not exclude the first— says: "The ear is more important then the eye." It is better to listen to the *master* than to read the *book*.

According to this commentary, nonreading is not simply the negation of the relationship to the Book, but the instituting of the master-disciple relationship.

This analysis that Rashi makes is a synthesis of the reflection that the *Gemara* offers a few pages later. An important discussion pits two masters—Rav and Samuel—against each other:

> And why do we not read certain of the sacred writings? Because of neglect of the *Beit Hamidrash*. Rav said: The interdiction of reading applies only to the opening hours of the *Beit Hamidrash* but, outside the opening hours, we can read. Samuel said: Even outside the opening hours we cannot read. The *Gemara* suggests another version of this discussion. "Rav said: The interdiction of reading applies only to the space of the *Beit Hamidrash*; outside the latter, we are allowed to read. Samuel said: Within the space of and outside the *Beit*

Hamidrash, at the hour of study (in the *Beit Hamidrash*), we may not read; outside of these hours of study, we can read.

The *Gemara*, through the voice of Rav Ashi, accepts the first version.

We shall not go into the details of these discussions here, but let us note in passing that the first version is built around a problem of the time of study, whereas the second brings into play a contrast between the time and space of study. We should also mention the interpretation of Rabbi Nehemiah. "Rabbi Nehemiah said: Why did they say that we should not read holy books on Shabbat? So that people will make the following argument: since we cannot read holy writings, all the more reason for not consulting other books (profane)."

To sum up, there are two reasons for nonreading:

1. *Bitul beit hamidrash* (or abandoning of the study hall) (Rav and Samuel)

2. The restriction of Rabbi Nehemiah

B. . . . (AND) EVEN IF THEY ARE WRITTEN IN ANY OTHER LANGUAGE, THEY MUST BE BURIED . . .

The remarks that follow deal with the structure of the *Mishnah*.

The *Gemara* examines the possibility of linking sentence B to sentence A. The expression "even if" seems to indicate a logical continuum between A and B, which gives the following reading.

First Reading

"All sacred writings may be saved from a fire, whether we read them or not; even if they are written in any other language. . . ." The problem of such a reading is the break made after "language," syntactically isolating the expression "they must be buried," which loses its reference; "they must . . ."—who is "they"? By deleting the "even if," interpreters make A and B independent. In this way they avoid the syntactical break in the middle of B and the internal logic of B is restored.

Second Reading

A. All holy writings, whether we read them or not, should be saved from the fire.

B. The holy writings translated into other languages must be buried.

Whether it be in the first or second reading, there is a problem. In the first reading, we said, "they must be buried" is syntactically isolated, having no sense in the general economy of the *Mishnah*.

In the second reading, the internal logic of B is restored, but to the detriment of the general sense of the *Mishnah*. There again an isolation appears and perhaps to an even more important extent than in the first reading. The sentence B is understood by itself, but what relation does it have to A and to C?

The *Mishnah* has a ternary structure A, B, C.[3] B—(BI or BII)—creates a separation between A and C, which, logically, should have followed one another. The expression "books that are not read" logically calls for the question "why?" if we have to use all the words of the *Mishnah*, i.e., if we keep the wording in the form of a question, we obtain the following:

A. All sacred writings may be saved from a fire, whether we read them or not.

C. And why do we not read them? Because of the neglect of the *Beit Hamidrash* (study hall).

However, if A can and should logically be followed by C, the explicit wording of the interrogation "and why" is not necessary; we can write:

A. All sacred writings may be saved from a fire whether we read them or not . . .

And so we can say that B:

1. introduces the necessity for an explicit wording of the question "and why?";

2. by its presence, defers the questioning in the time and space of the text of the *Mishnah*.

We could state, provisionally, that the search for the definition of the Book passes via the production and the delaying of the questioning of nonreading.

Up to this point, we have used B in a formal way, but what is its meaning? What is behind this production of the interrogative? This displacement?

B. Even if they are written in other languages (BI), they must be buried (BII).

The problem of translation is analyzed mainly in the *Megillah* tractate (8b f.). The commentary of the *Gemara* on our *Mishnah* explicitly refers to these texts. The *Mishnah* in *Megillah* teaches:

MISHNAH. There is no difference between books of the Scripture and *tefillin* and *mezuzahs* save that the books may be written in any language whereas *tefillin* and *mezuzahs* may be written only in Assyrian. Rabbi Simeon ben Gamaliel says that books of the Scripture also were permitted by the sages to be written only in Greek.[4]

The *Gemara* of this *Mishnah* also asks if these translations should be written in Hebrew characters or in their original characters.

It also explains the privilege of the Greek language upon which Rabbi Gamaliel confers a particular dignity, etc. Whatever the case may be, there are translated books.

Another question is grafted onto that of translation: once these books are translated, are they authorized to be read or not? (The *Gemara* in *Shabbat* uses the expression "to be given to be read".) According to Tanna Kama, since their translation is authorized, their reading is also. For Rabbi Simeon ben Gamaliel, the interdiction of translating (with the exception of Greek) leads to the impossibility of reading.

So here is a new possibility for understanding the expression "books that are not read."

The quotation that we have just provided allows us to now approach the passage of the *Gemara* that comments the *Mishnah* (beginning with the words) "All sacred writings."

> It was stated: If they are written in Targum (Aramaic) or in any other language—Rav Huna said: They must not be saved from a fire; while Rav Hisda ruled: They may be saved from a fire.

Here is a discussion between *amoraim* (masters of the *Gemara*) on the saving or not of translated books, in the event of a fire on the Shabbat. BI therefore does have a relation with the general theme of the *Mishnah*.

According to Rav Huna, reading acquires an important power in the possibility for a book to exist, in its constitution, in its definition. Rav Hisda does not seem to reject the importance of legibility-illegibility, but he reminds us that the translated book refers to something else, and that, in return, the reference confers on the book its status as a book. The *Gemara* continues:

> The *Mishnah* taught: "All sacred writings may be saved from the fire, whether we read them or not," and even if they are written in any other language. Surely "whether we read" them refers to the Prophets (*Neviim*), while "or not" refers to the Writings (*Ketuvim*), "and even if they are written in any other language," though they may not be read, yet the Tanna teaches that they "may be saved," which refutes Rav Huna?

The "surely" introduces in the *Gemara* a question of form: it is obvious that this means that, and yet . . . here is another text that expounds the opposite. The question is simple and obvious: how can Rav Huna maintain that the illegible-translated books should not be saved when the teaching of the *Mishnah* insists on precisely the opposite opinion?

The *Gemara* continues:

> According to the opinion "books written in foreign language are authorized to be read" (literally: given to reading) all agree that they must be saved.

So Rav Huna and Rav Hisda do not expound, as we might have thought at the beginning, a personal thought, but they comment our *Mishnah* in the light of the *Mishnah* of the *Megillah* tractate. The opinion cited is that of Tanna Kama, who authorizes both the translation and the reading of these translated books. So, according to this opinion, the books should be saved, either according to Rav Huna, or according to Rav Hisda.

> The question remains, however, if we consider the opinion "Translated books are not authorized to be read." Rav Huna says: We may not save them, since they may not be read. Rav Hisda says: We must save them, because of the disgrace to Holy Writings.

Reading or nonreading becomes a criterion essential to the possibility for a book to exist or not. The illegibility—here it is juridical, but Rav Huna certainly thinks the same thing in the case of material illegibility—condemns the book. An illegible book ends its existence in the flames, without anyone's being able to intervene to save it.[5]
"And even if they are translated and so illegible, we may save them from the fire."[6] Rav Huna is not present to reply; however, the *Gemara* imagines the answer he might have given:

> Rav Huna can answer you: Is that logical? Consider the second clause, "They must be buried" (and I make the following reasoning): seeing that they must be saved (from the fire), need burying be mentioned?

The author of the question posed to Rav Huna uses a version of the *Mishnah* that establishes a break after "languages," a break that has the consequence of isolating "they must be buried." Rashi comments as follows. I read the end of the sentence: according to your version "even if they are written in any other language" refers to "they may be saved"; when I read the end of the sentence, the latter appears as something apart (*beanepei nafshah*). The teaching of the end of this sentence—that these books need to be buried during the week—is obvious. In fact, if we save them from the fire, it is logical to bury them if they have been damaged.
Rashi means that not only is the sentence isolated, but, moreover, it is superfluous, since the teaching it offers is already a logical consequence of that which precedes.
The fact that they merit saving confers on these books the status of a book and so, like any book, they should be buried in the event of dam-

age. Rashi seems only to be paraphrasing the text of the *Gemara*. However, he adds a small but interesting word: *behol*, "during the week." It is a judicious remark: the burying of the book takes place during the six days of the week and not on the Shabbat; it is a *Halakhah* that does not concern *"Shabbatical" time.*

The reading Rav Huna objects to, because he considers it illogical, is the one where B is reduced to BII; even though it is challenged, it is, from the point of view of the structure of the *Mishnah*, of cardinal interest. If we only consider the different times during which, virtually or actually, the actions of the *Mishnah* take place, we notice, on the one hand, that there is a contrast between sacred and profane time and, on the other hand, that profane time (too) creates a break within sacred time.

> **A.** (A + B): "Shabbatical" time (books-fire)
> **B.** (BII): profane time (books-burying)
> **C.** (C): "Shabbatical" time (relation to the book / relation to the master–study hall).

In his explanation, Rashi has us understand that the phrase "they must be buried" has a meaning which is incomprehensible in the general context of the *Mishnah*, meaning that "translated books, even if they are written in another language, i.e., even if they are written in an illicit manner and are forbidden to be read, merit burying in the case—which has absolutely nothing to do with the Shabbat—where they are materially unreadable."

Refusing this reading, where BII makes a break, Rav Huna suggests another:

> Rav Huna explains it in accordance with his view, while Rav Hisda explains it according to his. Rav Huna explains it in accordance with his view. "Whether we read them," i.e., the Prophets (*Neviim*); "or not," i.e., the Writings (*Ketuvim*). That is only if they are written in the Holy Tongue (Hebrew), but even if they are written in any other language, we may not save them, yet even so they must be buried.

Rav Hisda gives the following version:

> "Whether we read them," i.e., the Prophets, "or not," i.e., the Writings; "even if they are written in any other language," we must still save them. And this is what he states: And even their worm-eaten material must be buried.

The grounds for the divergence between Rav Huna and Rav Hisda lie in the interpretation of the extension introduced by the "even if."

A. Rav Huna: "Even if they are written in any other language, we may not save them, yet even so they must be buried."

B. Rav Hisda: "Even if they are written in foreign languages, we must still save them from the fire."

The main part of the discussion in the *Gemara* stops here; we too, shall close our "halakhic" exposition here and continue with the actual "aggadic" aspect of the text.

Notes

1. What is likely to be forgotten in this reading of the *Mishnah* is the specificity of the time in which the Book is thought out. We will formulate a question: why is the Book thought out particularly in Shabbatical time? Is there a relationship between the Shabbat and the Book? On these questions, cf. particularly *Yakrah deshabtah*, by Rav Nahman Sterin (Jerusalem, 1974; in Hebrew; reedition).

2. The Bible is divided into three parts (cf. Book One, "Talmudic Landmarks"):

—The Torah
—The Prophets
—The Writings (or *Hagiographa*)

3. B could be BI or BII. BI: even though they are written in other languages; BII: they must be buried.

4. Cf. E. Lévinas, "Pour une place dans la Bible," in *La Bible au présent*, Colloque des intellectuels juifs de langue française (CIJLF), (Paris: Gallimard, 1982), "Idées," p. 309 (analysis of *Megillah* 7a) and particularly: "La Traduction de l'écriture" in *Israël: le judaïsme et l'Europe*, CIJLF (Paris: Gallimard, 1984), "Idées," pp. 331f. (analysis of *Megillah* 8b and 9a–9b). "Does not the law (*Halakhah*) authorize the translation of the very verses that fix it and does it authorize, consequently, the presentation of Scripture, the Hebrew text of tradition, in a foreign language, without compromising its spiritual dignity and import?

Does the translation of Scripture preserve the religious virtues of the original? Is it not profanation?

. . . Would not a foreign language introduce echoes of foreign worlds into the traditional text, handed down with so much care?"

On the privilege of the Greek language, cf. pp. 351f.

5. We should not forget that the interdiction to extract it from the fire is only a barrier to prevent one from exposing oneself to the use of fire, forbidden on the Shabbat.

6. The sentence takes on the meaning of a *Hidush*, as Rashi points out.

COMMENTARY

I

The Two *Nunim*

HERE is the central part of the passage from the *Shabbat* tractate:

> Our rabbis taught: "And it came to pass when the Ark set forward that Moses said . . ." (Num: 10:35–36): for this section the Holy One, blessed be He, provided signs above and below, to teach that this is not its place. Rabbi said: It is not on that account, but because it ranks as a separate book. With whom does the following dictum of Rabbi Samuel ben Nahmani in Rabbi Jonathan's name agree: "She (Wisdom) has erected her seven pillars" (Prov. 9:1): this refers to the seven books of the Law? With whom? With Rabbi. Who is the Tanna that disagrees with Rabbi? It is Rabban Simeon ben Gamaliel. For it was taught, Rabban Simeon ben Gamaliel said: this section is destined to be removed from here and written in its right place. And why is it written here? In order to provide a break between the first account of erring and the second account of erring. What is the second account of erring? "And the people were as murmurers. . . ." The first account of erring? "And they moved away from the mount of the Lord,"[1] which Rabbi Hama ben Rabbi Hanina expounded as meaning that they turned away from following the Lord. And where is its rightful place? In the chapter on the banners.[2]

Recapitulation of the History of the Writing of the Book

The text of the Hebrew Bible, and that of the various books it includes, was handed down over a very long period, in the single form of a *consonantal text without addition of vowels or punctuation marks of any kind*. This period, the first in the handing down of the biblical text, stretches from the era when the works of the centuries preceding our era were written until the period of the Massorets. The masters of the *Massorah*, the first Hebrew exegetes and grammarians, practiced their science in the schools of the land of Israel and Babylon. Their work, which stretches over several centuries, was finished, at its peak, during the tenth century C.E., and directly precedes the works of the masters of grammar, the commentators and annotators of the Bible.

The scriptural handing-down of the sacred texts, in their original form, was carried out—and is still carried out in our day for the liturgical texts—in the form of *volumina* (sing.: *volumen*), which are scrolls made of tanned leather or of parchmented leather. On these scrolls, made up of strips of skin sewn one to another and ruled horizontally and vertically with an awl, the sacred texts are copied with the use of a reed calamus in the East and a goose quill in the West. These copies are scrupulously executed according to the traditional rules and *without any particular sign being added to the consonantal text* that might have suggested to the reader a particular way of vocalizing and so of interpreting the text or of dividing the text into logical or semantic units, to make it perceptible to the reader. Any sign added to the body of a scroll would have expressed a particular exegetical choice that could be accepted as a possible exegesis of the text, but could not be considered as representative of rabbinical exegesis par excellence. As a result, traditional scribal rules have always *prohibited the adding of any graphical signs other than those reserved for the copying of the consonantal text*, and that alone. The oral knowledge of traditional exegesis passed on from the masters to their pupils has, alone, for a long time made up for the absence of a more elaborate graphical system.

It is because of the dispersing of the Jewish people after the exile in Babylonia and after the settling of the Jewish communities throughout the Diaspora that the masters of the tradition had to resort to *scriptural expedients* to preserve an indisputable unity for biblical tradition. This work of conservation had become indispensable after the slow decline of Hebrew as a national tongue, little by little reduced to the state of a sacred and learned language, losing ground in everyday usage to the surrounding vernacular languages: Aramaic, Greek, Latin, then Arabic, adopted by the Jewish communities. With the decline of Hebrew, not only throughout the Diaspora but also in Judea itself, began the decline of national and traditional learning. Hebrew, reduced to the state of a sacred language, could no longer be faithfully preserved, because its transmission also was subjected to the dialectical influences due to the use of vernacular languages and particular customs developed in the dispersed communities. However, to preserve the unity of the reading of the sacred texts and, especially, to allow their exegetical transmission according to traditional rules, it had become indispensable to set very precisely the reading of the Bible so as to preserve its purity according to normative rules.

These customs were set by the masters of the Massoretic schools of Tiberias (tenth century).[3]

This historical outline points out clearly the prohibition of all graphical addition to a purely consonantal text.

Consequently, the two superimposed dots (:), *sof-pasuk*, that mark the division into verses may not appear in any of the scrolls. This division, which was traditionally accepted, had been completed by the *Soferim*—the scribes or "numberers"—teaching in the era preceding that of the *Mishnah*.[4]

Some "Halakhic" Remarks

The traditional writing of the Bible follows rules that are too numerous and complex for us to describe them all here in detail. We shall, however, explain four of them that are particularly important and necessary for our research.[5]

Blanks of Opening and Closing

The text of the Bible has no vowels in its consonantal liturgical writing. Moreover, punctuation does not exist: nothing indicates the rhythm or the transition from one sentence to another; periods and commas are completely absent. Nothing interrupts the flow of words, except, from time to time, *blank spaces*, *empty gaps in the writing*, which appear, to the inexperienced eye, to be holes within the writing. The text between two blank spaces is called a *Parashah*, which means "transition." There are two sorts of *Parashiyot*, according to the position of the blank that precedes the text. When the blank is in the middle of a line, closed in, to the right and to the left, by writing, the passage that follows is said to form a *Parashah setumah*, a "closed" *Parashah*. On the other hand, when the blank is open on the margin side, the passage that follows constitutes a *Parashah petuhah*, an "open" *Parashah*. The blank is at least the length of nine letters[6] for the "closed" *Parashah* and of indefinite length for the "open" one. As will be noticed, the passage bears the name and the attribute of the blank that precedes the opening blank. It should be noticed, in passing, that the margins between the columns are of the width of one finger, the top margins two fingers, and the bottom margins three fingers. The division between the books is marked by a space of four lines.

Instead of punctuation, all these blanks provide a sort of ventilation.[7] The meaning of these blanks, of the margins, will become clear in the course of the analysis of the text of the *Shabbat* tractate that examines the "status of the margins."

Full and Defective Writing

The spelling must be scrupulously respected. But it is not so easy to write correctly, in an "orthodox" manner, when the text of the Bible is concerned. Some words can take four, five, or even a dozen different spellings. This is because of the semivowels in Hebrew. These are consonants that can also play the role of vowels: that is the case, for example, of the *vav* and the *yod*.

In the word *sukot*, for example, the *u* and the *o* can be represented by means of the *vav*, but they can also be absent as vowels.

When the word is written with a semivowel, it is said to be *male*, "full"; if the opposite is the case, it is said to be *haser*, "defective." In the example of the word *sukot*, there are four possible spellings: with two *vav*, with a *vav* before the *kaf*, with a *vav* after the *kaf*, without *vav* . . .

The Layout Known as the "Song" Layout

As we have seen in the first rule, the layout is not left to chance. In the Pentateuch, two passages differ from the others by the originality of their layout. They are Exod. 15:1–19 and Deut. 32:1–43.

The first passage, the "Song of the Red Sea," is written in the following manner:

The second, the song of *Haazinu*, is set out in two columns:

These two layouts are known as "song-form."

Oral and Literal Readings

Some words are read differently from their written form.[8] The most important example is the "unspeakable" Tetragram. The literal reading is called *ktav*; the oral reading *keri*.

Maimonides explains[9] that only the nonrespect of these four rules invalidates the book, makes it *passul* ("unsuitable" for reading). That is to say, if a *male* is transformed into *hasser* or vice versa; if a *Parashah setumah* is changed into a *Parashah petuhah*, or vice versa; if one changes a classical layout into "song-form" or vice versa; if the oral reading is substituted for the written reading: in these four cases the book is *passul*. What is more, "it loses its holiness as the book of the Torah and becomes a simple *Humash* (fragment without holiness) with which one usually teaches small children."

Notes

1. Num. 11:1 and 10:33.

2. From Num. 10:14.

3. G. E. Weil, P. Rivière, M. Serfaty, *Concordance de la cantilation du Pentateuque et des cinq Mégillot* (Paris: Éditions du CNRS, 1978), Introduction, pp. i–viii.

4. *Cf. Kiddushin* 30a. As for the division into chapters, it was carried out in the thirteenth century by Stephen Langton when he was staying at Paris, at the time when the text of the Vulgate was being revised at the Sorbonne. This division, although unanimously accepted—even in the Hebrew Bibles—diverges largely from the ancient Jewish divisions in *sedarim* or pericopes.

5. For details of these rules, cf. *Sofrim*, the "tractate of the Scribes"; for the references we are following the critical edition of Michael Higer (New York, 1937; reedited at Jerusalem, 1971); cf. also Maimonides, *Hilkhot Sefer Torah* (H.S.T.), chaps. 7–10.

6. Corresponding to the possibility of writing three times the word *asher* (*aleph-shin resh*), "that": a relative pronoun.

7. We may mention here the interesting research of H. Meschonnic who has tried to translate the biblical rhythm into French by a typographical procedure introducing "blanks" that mark the main accents of the rhythm; however, it should be noticed that these blanks are different from the "blanks" that mark the *Parashiyot*; Cf. *Les Cinq Rouleaux* (Paris: Gallimard, 1970), pp. 9–18, and his article, "Le Langage dans la Bible," in *La Bible au présent* (Paris: Gallimard, 1982), "Idées," p. 138.

8. Cf. Deut. 28:30; Isa. 13:16; Zech. 14:2.

9. *Hilkhot Sefer Torah* 7, 11.

במדבר

לְצִבְאֹתָ֑ם וְעַל־צְבָ֗א אֱלִֽישָׁמָ֖ע בֶּן־עַמִּיהֽוּד׃ וְעַל־צְבָ֕א מַטֵּ֖ה   כג

בְּנֵ֣י מְנַשֶּׁ֑ה גַּמְלִיאֵ֖ל בֶּן־פְּדָהצֽוּר׃ וְעַל־צְבָ֕א מַטֵּ֖ה בְּנֵ֥י בִנְיָמִ֑ן   כד

אֲבִידָ֖ן בֶּן־גִּדְעוֹנִֽי׃ וְנָסַ֗ע דֶּ֚גֶל מַחֲנֵ֣ה בְנֵי־דָ֔ן מְאַסֵּ֖ף לְכָל־   כה

הַֽמַּחֲנֹ֖ת לְצִבְאֹתָ֑ם וְעַל־צְבָ֕א וְעַל־צְבָ֕אֹ אֲחִיעֶ֖זֶר בֶּן־עַמִּישַׁדָּֽי׃ וְעַל־   כו

צְבָ֕א מַטֵּ֖ה בְּנֵ֣י אָשֵׁ֑ר פַּגְעִיאֵ֖ל בֶּן־עָכְרָֽן׃ וְעַל־צְבָ֕א מַטֵּ֖ה   כז

בְּנֵ֥י נַפְתָּלִ֖י אֲחִירַ֖ע בֶּן־עֵינָֽן׃ אֵ֛לֶּה מַסְעֵ֥י בְנֵֽי־יִשְׂרָאֵ֖ל לְצִבְאֹתָ֑ם   כח

וַיִּסָּֽעוּ׃   וַיֹּ֣אמֶר מֹשֶׁ֗ה לְחֹבָ֞ב בֶּן־רְעוּאֵ֣ל הַמִּדְיָנִי֮   כט

חֹתֵ֣ן מֹשֶׁה֒ נֹסְעִ֣ים ׀ אֲנַ֗חְנוּ אֶל־הַמָּקוֹם֙ אֲשֶׁ֣ר אָמַ֣ר יְהֹוָ֔ה אֹת֖וֹ

אֶתֵּ֣ן לָכֶ֑ם לְכָ֤ה אִתָּ֨נוּ֙ וְהֵטַ֣בְנוּ לָ֔ךְ כִּֽי־יְהֹוָ֥ה דִּבֶּר־ט֖וֹב עַל־יִשְׂרָאֵֽל׃

וַיֹּ֥אמֶר אֵלָ֖יו לֹ֣א אֵלֵ֑ךְ כִּ֧י אִם־אֶל־אַרְצִ֛י וְאֶל־מוֹלַדְתִּ֖י אֵלֵֽךְ׃   ל

וַיֹּ֕אמֶר אַל־נָ֖א תַּעֲזֹ֣ב אֹתָ֑נוּ כִּ֣י ׀ עַל־כֵּ֣ן יָדַ֗עְתָּ חֲנֹתֵ֨נוּ֙ בַּמִּדְבָּ֔ר   לא

וְהָיִ֥יתָ לָּ֖נוּ לְעֵינָֽיִם׃ וְהָיָ֖ה כִּי־תֵלֵ֣ךְ עִמָּ֑נוּ וְהָיָ֣ה ׀ הַטּ֣וֹב הַה֗וּא   לב

אֲשֶׁ֨ר יֵיטִ֧יב יְהֹוָ֛ה עִמָּ֖נוּ וְהֵטַ֥בְנוּ לָֽךְ׃ וַיִּסְעוּ֙ מֵהַ֣ר יְהֹוָ֔ה דֶּ֖רֶךְ   לג

שְׁלֹ֣שֶׁת יָמִ֑ים וַאֲר֨וֹן בְּרִית־יְהֹוָ֜ה נֹסֵ֣עַ לִפְנֵיהֶ֗ם דֶּ֚רֶךְ שְׁלֹ֣שֶׁת

יָמִ֔ים לָת֥וּר לָהֶ֖ם מְנוּחָֽה׃ וַעֲנַ֧ן יְהֹוָ֛ה עֲלֵיהֶ֖ם יוֹמָ֑ם בְּנָסְעָ֖ם מִן־

The passage of the two *Nunim*, Exod. 10:35 (white on black)

II

The Story of the *Nunin*

Three times was God exiled: in the Name, in the bursting
open of the Name, and in the effacing of this bursting
open.
EDMOND JABÈS

THE PRECEDING historical and "halakhic" outlines have raised the
problems posed by additional graphic signs.

However, there is a case where tradition has accepted the inclusion,
in the body of a text, of two signs before and after verses 35 and 36 of
chapter 10 of the book of Numbers. The whole Talmudic passage we
are going to study seeks and examines the meaning of these signs. We
have entitled verses 35 and 36 "the journey of the Ark," an expression
that sums up the content of this passage. We are going to try to reconstitute the "story" of these signs; it will not be a historical research,
even if we weigh up "historically" the various interpretations that have
been put forward on the matter. Our effort aims to enter into a dialogue with the text of the Talmud and with the Masters who speak in it.
To dialogue is, for us, to respond; that also means—and perhaps above
all—to feel responsible for the life of the text we are studying. In order
to respond, it is necessary, first of all, to listen. There is, however, the
risk of "mis-understanding." Then, in turn, we must enter into the saying, we must speak.

We must speak, not in order to repeat, to settle back into the already-
said, but, on the contrary, to reveal "new faces."

What are these signs that mark the "top" and the "bottom" of the
passage of the "journey of the Ark"?

We can classify the hypotheses of the different commentators in three
categories:

1. The signs are the letter *nun*, fourteenth letter of the Hebrew alphabet.
The form of this *nun* varies according to the commentators.[1]

2. These signs are not letters, but simply dots (*nekudot*).[2]

3. There are neither letters nor dots, but blank spaces: an opening and a
closing blank were added around—"at the top" and "at the bottom" of—the
"journey of the Ark."[3]

These three different interpretations are not necessarily mutually exclusive. One particularly shrewd analysis of the text of the *Sifrei* authorizes the following synthetic interpretation:[4] there are not three distinct opinions but three successive stages of a single process. Let us look closely again at the text of the *Sifrei*.[5]

● (ספר) ויהי בנסוע הארון נקוד עליו מלמעלה ומלממה.מפני שלא היה זה
מקומו רבי אומר מפני שהוא ספר בעצמו מיכן אמרו ספר שנמחק ונשתייר בו שמונים
וחמש אותיות כפרשת ויהי בנסוע הארון מטמאה את הידים ר' שמעון אומר נקוד עליו
מלמעלה ומלמטה מפני שלא היה זה מקומו ומה היה ראוי ליכתב תחתיו ויהי העם
כמתאוננים.משל למה הדבר דומה לבני אדם שאמרו למלך הנראה שתגיע עמו אצל

Vayehi binesoa haaron: nakud alav milemaalah ume lematah; "the passage of the journey of the Ark: dotted (above), above and below"

What is this about? In another passage,[6] the *Sifri* gives the list of ten words and groups of words written in the Torah that manifest the distinctive feature of having one or several dotted letters.[7]

Dotted words in Gen. 19:35, Gen. 33:4, Num. 3:39, and Deut. 29:28 (here, in white on black)

To refer to this dotting, the *Sifrei* uses the expression *Nakud al* or *Nakud alav*. So the expression of the *piskah* 26 does mean that the "journey of the Ark" was dotted. "We can assume that the whole passage—verses 35 and 36 of the tenth chapter of Numbers—was marked by dots above and below, from beginning to end, in the same way as certain words of the Torah are crowned with these dots."[8] This punctuation above and below the lines is the first stage of the process. In the second stage, the dots are replaced by a word—the word "dots" or "dotted." In other words, the dot-objects are withdrawn from the space to be no more than (which does not necessarily mean being lesser) the word that signifies them.

This new existence of the dot within the word "dot" implies the existence of a new space that can receive it/them: the existence, or rather perhaps we should say "appearing." According to Rabbi Solomon Luria ("Rashal"), two "blank spaces" appear between verses 10:34 and 10:35, on the one hand, and verses 10:36 and 11:1, on the other. As it is certainly more logical to create these two spaces first (to receive writing) before creating the word "dots," we may suppose that the second stage of the process is logically the movement of spacing, the third stage being the transition (or metamorphosis) from the figure-dot to the word-dot, a transition that is perhaps contemporaneous with the writing—that is to say, with the movement of writing, letter after letter—with the word in the new space.

At this point in the process, we have already combined two interpretations, that of the dots (*Sifrei*) and that of the blank spaces ("Rashal"). It remains to be considered how we arrive at two inverted *Nunim*. We have to imagine the existence of a fourth stage that would be the backwards effacing of the word "dot" or "dotted." In Hebrew writing, where writing proceeds from right to left, the movement of effacing will go from left to right; and so from the word ⌐ן וק נ the ⌐ן, the ו, the ק, the ן, the ק will be successively effaced; the נ, the letter *nun*, the initial, will remain, isolated in the middle of the blank space. A fifth and final stage completes the process: in order that these *Nunim* might not be confused with the letters of the text, they are inverted: we go from the נ to the כ. The following diagram illustrates this process.

1.　　　　　χ χ χ χ̇ χ̣ χ̇ χ̣ χ̇ χ̣ χ̇ χ χ χ
2. χ χ χ　　　　χ̇ χ̣ χ̇ χ̣ χ̇ χ̣ χ̇　　　χ χ χ
3. χ χ χ ⌐ן וק נ χ χ χ χ χ χ χ ⌐ן וק נ χ χ χ
4. χ χ χ　 נ　 χ χ χ χ χ χ χ　 נ　 χ χ χ
5. χ χ χ　 כ　 χ χ χ χ χ χ χ　 כ　 χ χ χ

The form and the space of the *Nunim* represent the final state of the process, as this text shows.

יָמִים לָתוּר לָהֶם מְנוּחָה: וַעֲנַן יְהוָה עֲלֵיהֶם יוֹמָם בְּנָסְעָם מִן־ לֹ

ויהי בנסע הָאָרֹן וַיֹּאמֶר מֹשֶׁה קוּמָה׀ ﬞ   הַמַּחֲנֶה: שש
יְהוָה וְיָפֻצוּ אֹיְבֶיךָ וְיָנֻסוּ מְשַׂנְאֶיךָ מִפָּנֶיךָ: וּבְנֻחֹה יֹאמַר שׁוּבָה לֹ
יְהוָה רִבְבוֹת אַלְפֵי יִשְׂרָאֵל: ﬞ

וַיְהִי הָעָם כְּמִתְאֹנְנִים רַע בְּאָזְנֵי יְהוָה וַיִּשְׁמַע יְהוָה וַיִּחַר אַפּוֹ א יא

The synthetic interpretation that we have developed does not usually appear in current biblical criticism. This was not a historical process; the transition from the dots to the inverted letters, from the figure-dot to the word-dot, then to the letter *nun*, is a part of the text that we are undertaking. In other words, the *nun* signs are not only a reminder of the existence of the transition from the "dot" to the "letter," but they actually embody the transition itself. We shall see later the consequences of this remark.

It is necessary, first of all, to understand the meaning of the "dots" in their "figure-dot" state. We saw that certain words and expressions, ten in all, were crowned with dots. Dotting differs with each case, and the rules of interpretation vary according to these differences. Four situations are possible:[9]

1. The "dot" < the "written."
2. The "dot" > the "written."
3. The "dot" = the "written."
4. The "written" = 0.

On this subject the Talmud teaches:[10]

> The Masters said: When the "written" is superior to the "dot," you interpret the "written" and you do not take the "dot" into account; when the "dot" predominates over the "written," you interpret the "dot" and ignore the "written."
> Rabbi said: Even if a word has only one dot, you must interpret the "dot" and not take the "written" into account.[11]

According to this Talmudic text, the role of the "dot" is to efface. Whether the "dot" be superior to the "written" or the other way round, its presence brings about an effacing. The "dot" introduces a difference into writing. In this "dotted-nondotted" difference, the majority is the criterion. The "dot" determines a majority and a minority. The majority remains the "written" while the minority is effaced.[12]

The effacing of (minority) letters is only a sign, an indication, given by the text to invite us to a rather radical effacing of the meaning of the word in question. This effacing may be a simple diminishing as well as a reversal of meaning.

Some Examples

1. "And the younger went and slept with him; and he was unaware of her coming to bed or her leaving (*uvekumah*)."[13]
This is the episode concerning the daughters of Lot who sleep with their father after having made him drunk. The letter *vav* of the word *uvekumah* (her leaving) is dotted.
The *Midrash* comments:[14] "And they made their father drink wine. . . . And he knew not when she lay down (with him), but he knew (was conscious of it) when she arose (*uvekumah*): this word (*uvekumah*) is dotted, intimating that he did not indeed know of her lying down, but he did know of her arising."
In this example, the dot totally reverses the meaning given.[15]

2. "And Esau ran to meet him . . . and kissed him."[16] *Vayeshakehu* (he kissed): the whole word is dotted. The *Midrash* comments:
a. he bit him;
b. since we know that Esau hated Jacob, we might be tempted to consider this kiss as ironic. The dots teach us that Esau kissed Jacob sincerely with all his heart.
The analysis given here is fairly subtle: (in b.) the dot does not efface the meaning of the word but the opinion we have of the meaning of this word in this context; the dot effaces the opinion and restores the initial, correct meaning.

3. "Altogether the total count of Levites, whom Moses and Aaron numbered."[17] The name Aaron is completely dotted. The *Midrash* explains that Aaron was not included in the counting of those numbered (he counted but was not himself counted). Because of the dotting, Aaron is excluded, effaced.

4. "Things hidden belong unto the Lord our God; but things revealed are ours and our children's for all time."[18] The letters of "ours and our children's" are dotted. The commentary given by the *Midrash*[19] is rather obscure. However, we can draw two important items of information from it:
a. the eleven dotted letters are not those which should be. These eleven dotted letters are substituted for the eleven letters of the two names LYHVH ELoHeYNU that could not be dotted;

b. we can suppose that the dots efface the letters which carry them. Two other items, in fact, come to light: since the role of the dots is to efface, the (divine) Names could not be dotted because they could not be effaced.

In fact, in giving these examples, we have jumped ahead, because we have not explained the rules of interpretation of the cases: "written" = "dot" and "written" = 0; and yet the examples given allow us to better understand what is going to follow.

In cases 3 and 4, the difference between dotted letters and nondotted letters does not exist at all, or not really.

The difference lies, in fact, in the greater number, absent in the equation "written" = "dot," and in the nonexistence of the "written."

Rabbi Simeon ben Eleazar studies the case of the completely dotted word in Gen. 33:4. The case of the whole word's being dotted may be considered as an extension of the case $P > W$, and the dotted letters have to be taken into account, that is to say, the whole word. We could then say that the word's being dotted or not dotted does not change anything.

But there is a rule that says: "If the word is completely dotted, it abandons its usual meaning, or the opinion we have of its usual meaning."[20]

The effacing of the "dot," or the effacing role played by the "dot" above the letter(s), should allow us to better grasp what is happening in these two verses 35 and 36 of Num. 10. But an important remark is necessary. In these two verses, there are dots above and below each letter. So there is a sort of effacing of effacing (double negation) or, in other words, an assertion of writing (the same way as, in French, the double negation can mean a reinforced assertion).

Let us go back over the process: the function of the dots above each letter of these two verses is to efface them. Once effaced, these two verses no longer exist, but, as a result, their effacing and the meaning of this effacing are themselves effaced, forgotten. Therefore the effacing should be done without effacing, and we should perhaps write indicating the effacing, leaving a trace of the existence of this intention of an impossible effacing.

It is certainly true that the lower dots efface the effacing prompted by the upper dots. The presence of the upper and lower dots was sufficient to achieve this trace of effacing. However, we notice that these dots disappear from space. The "world of dots" can no longer survive.[21]

However, this impossibility of existing in the form of objects, as figures in space, does not mean their suppression but their transformation. The dots do not disappear but are transformed by uniting in letters that immediately form a word. This word maintains the existence of the dots

—in another form, it is true—since they are "dot" words (*nekudot*). So the word, as an association of letters, exists before the letter alone.

It is only after the effacing (perhaps in reverse) that the letter exists independently of its participation in the word.[22] The transition from the dot-object to the dot-word is a marking out, a naming. This stage of the process is important, and we must explain the origin and the meaning of this transition.

It seems that this transformation of the dots can be included with the shifting that example 4 showed us. Let us explain: when a word or a group of words cannot be dotted, which is the case for the name—it is perhaps the only case!—the dots are shifted to an equivalent number of letters of other words (in this case there is a relation between the "undottable" word and its substitute).

We may then suppose that the text of the "journey of the Ark" belongs to this category of "undottable" words, which would explain the shifting. However, for a reason that remains to be explained, the shifting is not carried out here by the transferring of the dots onto the letters of other words, but by the transformation of dots as objects into dots as words. We shall attempt an explanation of this nomination in a later stage of our development.

Once dots exist in the word "dot," this word is then effaced in its turn. The dot remains active in its effacing role right into its very literal existence. The word "dot" is dotted since it says the dots; so it is effaced. However, a necessary trace remains of the whole process: the initial of the word "dot," the *nun*, which will be inverted so as not to enter into the text.[23]

Notes

1. It is mainly the opinion of Rashi (cf. *Rosh-Hashanah* 17b); cf. also Rabbi Solomon Luria, *responsum* no. 63, who attests having consulted an authentic manuscript of Rashi's commentary in which the inverted *nun* explicitly appears; cf. also the commentary of "Rashba" on *Shabbat* 103a.

2. It is the opinion of the *Sifrei*; cf. *Sifrei Bamidbar*, "*Behaalotekha*," *piskah*, no. 26.

3. Cf. Rabbi Solomon Luria, *responsum* no. 63; quoted by Isaac Ratsbi in *The Extraordinary Letters of the Torah* (Jerusalem, 1978; in Hebrew); for the different opinions, cf. also "Maharam" of Lublin, *responsum* no. 75, "Maharan" of Lozano in *Or Torah (Behaalotekha), Noda Biyeudah*, responsum (first part) no. 74, *Yoreh de'ah*.

4. Cf. Nehema Leibowitz, *Studies in Bamidbar* (Jerusalem, 1980); cf. also S. Lieberman, *Hellenism in Jewish Palestine*, "Critical Marks in the Hebrew Bible—The Inverted Nuns" (New York: The Jewish Theological Seminary, 1962), p. 38.

5. Here we give the text according to Horowitz's edition: *Siphrei de Rab, fasciculus primus; Siphrei ad numeros, adjecto Siphrei zutta, cum variis lectionibus et adnotationibus* (Leipzig, 1917) the numbering of the chapters in this edition differs from that of other editions; the text quoted here is the *piskah* 84 according to Horowitz and 26 in the edition with the commentary of the *Netziv*.

6. *Sifrei* on *Badmidbar*, *piskah* 11, in the *Netziv* edition; cf. also *Midrash Rabbah* on Num. 3: 39 and 9:10; cf. also *Masekhet Sofrim* (the Scribes' tractate) 6, 2 on the rules for the interpretation of these dots; cf. especially *Midrash Rabbah* on Gen. 48:17; T.B., *Bava Metsia, Tosefot, "Lamah Nakud,"* T.B., *Pesahim* 9, 2.

7. (1) Gen. 15:5; (2) Gen. 18:9; (3) Gen. 19:33; (4) Gen. 33:4; (5) Gen. 37:12; (6) Num. 3:39; (7) Num. 9:10; (8) Num. 21:30; (9) Num. 29:15 or Num. 28:21; (10) Deut. 29:28.

8. Leibowitz, *Studies in Bamidbar*, p. 89.

9. In a word, all the dotted letters are called in the texts *nekudah*, which means "the dot"; all the nondotted letters are called the "written," *ktav*.

10. *Pesahim* 9, 3 (Jerusalem Talmud).

11. On the meaning of Rabbi's words, there are two opposite explanations: (a) according to Rabbi Moses Margaliot of Amsterdam, author of the *Penei Mosheh* commentary, it is a case where the word has only two letters, and so where a "dot" = "written"; it is in this case that Rabbi would say that the dot should be taken into account (and will thus be the object of analysis); (b) according to Rabbi David Frankel of Berlin, author of the *Korban Haeda* commentary (he was Moses Mendelssohn's master), Rabbi is in discussion with the masters; it is a case of "written" = "dot" that implies an analysis of the "written," according to the masters, and of the "dot" according to Rabbi. That is to say, R. D. Frankel points out, that it is neither the "written" nor the "dot," but the entire meaning of the word that is shifted to another context.

12. The term that comes up the most often for the role of dotting is *laakor*, "to uproot": the dot uproots the existence of the letter and meaning. R. M. Margaliot says, concerning the word *Mesalek* (that we have translated as "putting aside," "not taking into account"): "one should act as if the dotted letter was not written."

13. Gen. 19:33.

14. *Midrash Rabbah* and *Sifrei*, previously quoted.

15. By using an expression from popular language, we could translate the dotting (in this case) by "My eye! Really! He didn't know anything? Pull the other one!" The dot calls the meaning into doubt, into question. It dots the i's, so to speak . . .

16. Gen. 33:4.

17. Num. 3:39.

18. Deut. 29:28.

19. *Numbers Rabbah* 3, 13.

20. Cf. *Netziv* on *Sifrei*, previously quoted.

21. At this point in our interpretation, there is certainly a convergence between the Cabalistic texts of Isaac Luria and the Talmudic text we are com-

menting. In fact, there is, in the doctrine of Luria, a process of emanation, the three important phases of which are the "world (of dots) united in a dot" (*olam haakudim*), the "world of dots" (*olam hanekudim*), and the "world of divided dots" (*olam haberudim*). The "world of dots" does not subsist (*olam hane-kudim ein metsiut kayam, ela hayah venitbatel*); cf. *Kol ha-Nevuah*, Rabbi David ha-Kohen, M. Kook, 1978, p. 294.

22. On the subject of the independent existence of the letter, cf. R. Moses Grossberg, *Tsefunot Harogashevi*, 2d ed. (Jerusalem, 1975; in Hebrew); chap. *Otiyot umilim* (Letters and words), and cf. below, section entitled "The Second Error: The Refusal of the Manna."

23. On the impossibility for the name to be dotted that we explain as the corollary of the interdiction of effacing the divine Name, cf. *Sanhedrin* 43b in Rashi's commentary, *Vehaniglot lanu . . .*; cf. also the commentary of the Tosafists, *Melamed . . .*; finally, cf. Rabbenu Behayeh, *Commentaries on the Torah* (Mossad Harav Kook ed., in Hebrew) (Jerusalem, 1977), 3:435.

III

Dots, Coronets, and Letters

BEFORE going any further with the analysis of the *Shabbat* text, we would like to pause once again, for a paragraph, to consider the meaning of these dots, in the context of the place they occupy in the general economy of the Torah's graphical organization. Now that we have studied several rules of layout, here is the smallest element of the page: the letter.

As Rabbi Zadoc ha-Kohen[1] points out, there is an essential difference between the ways of writing Hebrew and Latin characters.[2] It has to do with the position of the letter in its relation to the guiding line.[3] In Lating writing,[4] the letter rests on a lower line, for example:

But in Hebrew writing, the letter is suspended from the upper line, for example:

The upper guiding line is the limit of the writing. This limit also has a symbolic meaning, for it traces the limit between writing and writing's beyond.[5] We may notice, as well, that none of the twenty-two letters of the Hebrew alphabet goes beyond this limit.

None, or almost none, for there is one exception: the letter *Lamed*.

The name of this letter encloses the very meaning of its form: *Lamed* is the semantic root of everything that has some relation to study and teaching; literally, the teaching of this letter, *Lamed*, which expresses learning.[6] Learning is entering into the movement that goes beyond the line of writing, "beyond the verse." The Talmud[7] calls this letter a "tower that flies in the air." According to Rabbi Zadoc ha-Kohen,[8] air is the space surrounding the letter: "And it is the meaning of the expression that 'flies in the air,' i.e., in the space situated between the writing."[9]

עַל פָּנָי יְרוֹחוּ וַיַּרְאֵהוּ יְהוָה אֶת כָּל הָאָרֶץ אֶת
הַגִּלְעָד עַד דָן וְאֵת כָּל נַפְתָּלִי וְאֶת אֶרֶץ אֶפְרַיִם
וּמְנַשֶּׁה וְאֵת כָּל אֶרֶץ יְהוּדָה עַד הַיָּם הָאַחֲרוֹן
וְאֶת הַנֶּגֶב וְאֶת הַכִּכָּר בִּקְעַת יְרוֹחוּ עִיר הַתְּמָרִים
עַד צֹעַר וַיֹּאמֶר יְהוָה אֵלָיו זֹאת הָאָרֶץ אֲשֶׁר
נִשְׁבַּעְתִּי לְאַבְרָהָם לְיִצְחָק וּלְיַעֲקֹב לֵאמֹר לְזַרְעֲךָ
אֶתְּנֶנָּה הֶרְאִיתִיךָ בְעֵינֶיךָ וְשָׁמָּה לֹא תַעֲבֹר וַיָּמָת
שָׁם מֹשֶׁה עֶבֶד יְהוָה בְּאֶרֶץ מוֹאָב עַל פִּי יְהוָה
וַיִּקְבֹּר אֹתוֹ בַגַּי בְּאֶרֶץ מוֹאָב מוּל בֵּית פְּעוֹר וְלֹא
יָדַע אִישׁ אֶת קְבֻרָתוֹ עַד הַיּוֹם הַזֶּה וּמֹשֶׁה בֶּן
מֵאָה וְעֶשְׂרִים שָׁנָה בְּמֹתוֹ לֹא כָהֲתָה עֵינוֹ וְלֹא נָס
לֵחֹה וַיִּבְכּוּ בְנֵי יִשְׂרָאֵל אֶת מֹשֶׁה בְּעַרְבֹת מוֹאָב
שְׁלֹשִׁים יוֹם וַיִּתְּמוּ יְמֵי בְכִי אֵבֶל מֹשֶׁה וִיהוֹשֻׁעַ בֶּן
נוּן מָלֵא רוּחַ חָכְמָה כִּי סָמַךְ מֹשֶׁה אֶת יָדָיו עָלָיו
וַיִּשְׁמְעוּ אֵלָיו בְּנֵי יִשְׂרָאֵל וַיַּעֲשׂוּ כַּאֲשֶׁר צִוָּה יְהוָה
אֶת מֹשֶׁה וְלֹא קָם נָבִיא עוֹד בְּיִשְׂרָאֵל כְּמֹשֶׁה
אֲשֶׁר יְדָעוֹ יְהוָה פָּנִים אֶל פָּנִים לְכָל הָאֹתֹת
וְהַמּוֹפְתִים אֲשֶׁר שְׁלָחוֹ יְהוָה לַעֲשׂוֹת בְּאֶרֶץ
מִצְרַיִם לְפַרְעֹה וּלְכָל עֲבָדָיו וּלְכָל אַרְצוֹ וּלְכָל
הַיָּד הַחֲזָקָה וּלְכֹל הַמּוֹרָא הַגָּדוֹל אֲשֶׁר עָשָׂה מֹשֶׁה
לְעֵינֵי כָּל יִשְׂרָאֵל

Dots, coronets, and letters on a passage of the Torah (the final one, which concludes the book of Deuteronomy)

This expression, as we shall see, introduces the notions of freedom, movement, renewal, time, and history.[10] On looking more closely at the letters of the Bible we can make out two distinct elements: the actual letter and one or several marks above certain letters. These marks—all of which are identical—are the coronets: the *Ketarim* or *Tagim*.[11] The meaning of these coronets comes from that of the *Lamed*; but a difference should be noticed: the upper part of the *Lamed* is still part of the body of the letter. The coronets are outside the letter. The space between the "here" and the "beyond" grows, and the transcendence of meaning is reinforced.[12]

The gap increases even more. The "dot" occupies the space beyond the verse's beyond. A question then arises: is not the transition from the "object-dot" to the "word-dot" a returning to the "within" (*en deçà*)? Does not the commentary of the commentary returning to the book of writing (the Written Law) become stranded in the said, in the already-said of writing? Is the transcendence always and ever a failure?

Nevertheless, we shall attempt to answer that the effacing of the word "dot" itself suggests a meaning which is just the opposite of this failure!

Notes

1. Cf. *Mahashavot Haruts* (Pieterkov, 1912), pp. 91 and 92.

2. Latin here is an example.

3. We saw above that the parchment has lines ruled vertically and horizontally with a stylus. So there are guiding lines, which are called *sirtut*.

4. All the letters of a same body occupy the same space: A, B, C, D, E, etc.

5. The *sirtut*-line not only has the role of guiding the scribe; it also is a part of the essential structure of the book, and, because of that, a written book—even if very well written—without lines is said to be *pasul* (unsuitable for use); cf. *Shulkhan Arukh, Yoreh De'ah*, chap. 271, par. 5.

6. In both its immanent and transcendent meanings.

7. Rashi on *Sanhedrin* 106b, *Zohar "Mishpatim"* 102a, *Zohar "Shelah"* 164b; *Zohar "Yitro"* 91a, and *Zohar Hadash "Shir hashirim"* 66a.

8. *Mahashavot Haruts*, p. 92.

9. For Rabbi Zadoc, the meaning of this space, of this "blank," is fundamental. In it lies the essence of the Oral Law: "So, in the Written Law, between each line, can be found in an allusive manner the whole of the Oral Law." Study therefore means the relation between the Oral and the Written Laws. The verse's beyond lies precisely in the existence of the Oral Law. The "blank" encloses meaning. Paradoxically, saying is revealed where nothing is said. Without anticipating too much on further developments, we can refer to the text of the *Gemara Shabbat* 166a: "The scholars asked: The blank spaces of a Scroll of the Law (the blank perigram spaces), may we rescue them from a fire or not?"

10. On the origin of this "monumental" metaphor, cf. *Sefer Yetsirah*. The letters are called "stones" and the words "houses."

11. Only the letters *shin, ayin, tet, nun, zayin, gimel, tsadi* (mnemonic acronym: *shaatnez gats*) have a coronet; one coronet is made up of three lines—cf. *Menahot* 29b.

12. On the relationship between the coronets and the *Lamed*, cf. Rabbi Zadoc, *Mahashavot Haruts*, p. 92.

IV

The Structure of the Text

My effort to comment starts from the hypothesis that
the Talmud is not simply a compilation. Of that I am
persuaded, in spite of the appearances to the contrary,
and I always ascribe my difficulties in discovering this
coherence and this profound logic of the Talmudic
statements to the paucity of my means. Perhaps nothing
should be published under the title of "Jewish thought"
for as long as this logic has not been found.
    E. LÉVINAS

BESIDES the introduction, which poses the problem of signs (as far as
"to teach"), the text is divided into two parts:

1. The first shows the confrontation between an anonymous author,[1]
Tanna Kama, and Rabbi, that is to say, Rabbi Judah ha-Nasi, the last
of the official writers of the *Mishnah*. Two ideas enter into play: that of
the place (or rather of the nonplace) and that of the book. For Tanna
Kama, signs (or the process of which the signs—*Nunim*—are the trace)
indicate the text's atopia. On the other hand, Rabbi does not see an
atopian text in these two verses. For him, the signs reveal, underscore
the book. The question that may be asked at this stage deals with the
relationship between the place and the book. When Rabbi explains that
these two verses make up a book and are where they belong, does that
imply that the nonplace expressed by Tanna Kama excludes the possibility that these two verses might constitute a book?

The question is important, because the direction that the commentary
will take in its wandering analysis depends directly on the answer.

2. The second part repeats, to a certain extent, the discussion of the
first part. The difference lies in the reorganization of the structure.
Rabbi—who is simply a second opinion in the first part—becomes the
center of the text. Everything is reorganized around Rabbi's thinking,
that is to say, around the book. And so the existence of the second part
is already an answer to the question.

Tanna Kama speaks[2] again and develops his thought. It is as if there
were three opinions: those of Tanna Kama, Rabbi, and Rabban Simeon
ben Gamaliel ("Rashbag"); whereas in fact Tanna Kama and Rashbag

are one and the same person.[3] This doubling of the discussion impresses us with the necessity of thinking the "nonplace," atopia, from two different points of view: the first one being before the thought of Rabbi, the second after it. In other words, Tanna Kama certainly does not contest the fact that these two verses form a "book," but he prefers, at first, to think out their atopia independently of this notion. It is interesting to note, also, that Tanna Kama is no longer anonymous after the first book is discovered (or defined, by Rabbi).

The definition of the book allows the anonymous author of the atopia to acquire a name.[4] We shall approach the text by following its suggestion of three opinions: Tanna Kama will not be the author of the explanation in our analysis, that is to say, Rabban Simeon ben Gamaliel. Consequently, we suspect that Tanna Kama is unaware of the place, the real place of these verses.

This gives us the following plan:

Introduction
1.   Tanna Kama
     Rabbi
2.   Author agreeing with Rabbi
     Rabbi
     Author disagreeing with Rabbi

Notes

1. In a "Tannaitic" text, the first author who speaks is called Tanna Kama (i.e., the first *Tanna*) and the second or the last one is called Tanna Batra (the last author); these designations are particularly used in cases where the thoughts are anonymous, which is the case here for the first opinion.

2. Rather than a resumption, we have the impression that he is continuing his initial speech.

3. That is, in any case, Rashi's opinion.

4. We shall see later the comparison that the *Zohar* makes between the book and the name, two words that have the same numerical value.

V

An Atopian Text

The book of wandering could only be the wandering of
the book.
EDMOND JABÈS

Art does not reproduce the visible, it renders visible.
PAUL KLEE

The book is, perhaps, the loss of all place; the nonplace
of the lost place. A nonplace like a nonorigin, a
nonpresent, a nonknowing, an emptiness, a blank.
EDMOND JABÈS

"To teach us that this is not its place . . ."

An extraordinary statement! A text of the Torah, deliberately, has
not been written in the right place. Not being in its place means here the
impossibility of being in a place, the fundamental impossibility of finding a place to settle. This *Parashah* is atopian. We may as well distinguish, right away, atopian and utopian; the distinction is necessary
since it governs the confrontation between Tanna Kama and Rabban
Simeon ben Gamaliel.

Atopia is the refusal of the place without hope of a place. The place
of atopia is, radically, the nonplace (*non-lieu*). On the other hand, utopia is a temporary nonplace, linked to the place by hope, or by demand,
for example.

Why is this text of two verses not in its place? In these two verses, it
is a question of the "journey of the Ark," departure and settling. The
Ark is what contained the Law.[1]

The "journey of the Law" is the journey of meaning; a text from
Exodus (25:15), explaining the construction of the Holy Ark, allowed
for staves to be used for transporting the Ark: "The staves must remain
in the rings of the Ark and not be withdrawn." The Law carried in the
Ark is ever ready for movement; it is not attached to a point in space or
in time, but is, at any moment, able and ready to be transported.[2] This
interdiction of withdrawing the staves from their rings is so important
that it is in itself one of the 613 *Mitzvot*.[3] In our opinion, it is not only a
matter of an "ever-readiness" for traveling, but, in fact, of continuous,

perpetual, incessant movement. The Ark must travel, because the Law, the Torah, is in becoming. Meaning is never there where it is given. A giving meaning is automatically nonsense. Thematized meaning is dead. The "journey of the Ark" is, actually, the *dynamism of meaning*.

Tanna Kama expresses the following: the meaning of the Torah is the dynamism of its meaning; being is becoming. Being, for the Torah, is to be journeying. And the journey is not limited to a place. Journeying is a nonplace.

Some will most probably object that the "story" of the journey is only a "story," that the journey has settled down in the "said," has been brought together in the synchrony of a written text, is not yet or no longer a journey, is not lived!

Tanna Kama would refute this objection by the boldness of his reflection: the words that carry (that transport) the "journey of the Ark" cease to be words. The distance separating the "world of real-objects" and the "world of named-objects" is abolished. The word becomes the thing it names.[4]

The word "journey" is no longer simply a word! It is the journey itself. The words of "journey" express the journey of words. The story of the "journey of the Ark" is atopian, for the dynamism of meaning, dynamic in its very essence, refuses to enter into the world of words, refuses the power the Written Text has to bring together synchronically the diachrony of time and of movement.[5]

The saying of the "journey" must not stop, grind to a halt in a "said." The movement of the spoken word cannot be enclosed within the synchrony of the written word.

According to this commentary by Tanna Kama, the Torah pulls off a dazzling tour de force: how can an idea that, by essence, escapes the fixedness of a theme, be written and thematized? How can one write, without this writing's entailing the death of the saying? How can one *say* and *unsay* at the same time? How can one write without writing? The *Nunim*, signs above and below—the dots—by their presence, achieve the demand for tearing away. The *Nunim* tell us: be careful! this text is not written, has never been written. It is unwritten, ever and already effaced. It is "writing in progress," and so forever in the process of being in the movement of writing.

But the "dynamism of meaning" cannot be taken for granted. The Ark does not travel alone. The contribution of man is necessary, the "contribution of readers, listeners, and students."[6]

The dynamics of meaning is contemporaneous with the dynamics of the being-man, of his ability to generate the meaning. The truth of Jewish law is defined in relation to this double dynamic. We can thus say that the nomadic truth, in the process of becoming, is outside of any place.

"To teach that this is not its place."

The law of Judaism, the Torah, is not in its place; it is "in this respect that it stands out against paganism (against all paganism): to be pagan is to settle, to plant oneself in the earth, so to speak, to set oneself up through a pact with permanency that authorizes the sojourn and that certifies the certainty of the soil. Nomadism answers to a relationship that possession does not satisfy."[7]

The "journey of the Ark" has us understand that the "the words exodus, exile, as well as the words heard by Abraham, 'Leave your native place, your kinship, your house,' bear a meaning that is not negative. If we have to set off and wander, is it because, excluded from the truth, we are condemned to an exclusion that bars the entry to all dwelling? Is it not rather that this wandering means a new relationship with the 'true'? Is it not also that this nomadic movement (where the ideas of dividing and separation can be found) reveals itself not as the eternal privation of sojourn, but as a genuine way of residing, of a residence that does not bind us to the determination of a place or to the settling near an already-founded, sure, and permanent reality? As if the sedentary state were necessarily the aim of all behavior! As if the truth itself were necessarily sedentary"![8]

The Ark is the place of the nonplace, the place of divine (and human) speech; the journey of the Ark is the journey of speech![9]

Notes

1. In the Ark were the debris of the first Tables, the second Tables, and a *Sefer Torah*; cf. *Bava Batra* 14b.

2. E. Lévinas, *L'Au-delà du verset* (Paris: Éditions de Minuit, 1982), p. 163.

3. Maimonides, *Sefer Hamitzvot*, *"Mitzvot lo ta'aseh,"* no. 86; *Tosafot* in *Yoma 72a*, which suggests the existence of two additional staves that were there simply to mark the notion of traveling, "notional" staves that bore the "transport."

4. André Neher, *L'Exil de la parole. Du silence biblique au silence d'Auschwitz* (Paris: Seuil, 1970), pp. 99–100. The word *davar* means "thing, fact, object, word, event, revelation, commandment, etc." What a contrast between the prodigious unity of the *davar* and the Latin dichotomy of *res* and *verbum*!

5. E. Lévinas, *Otherwise Than Being*, (The Hague: Nijhoff, 1981), p. 36.

6. Lévinas, *L'Au-delà du verset*, p. 164.

7. Maurice Blanchot, *L'Entretien infini* (Paris: Gallimard, 1969), p. 183; it is in this sense that we interpret Rabbi Nahman's "burnt book." The impossibility

for the truth to find a place must go as far as the abandoning of all place, as far as its destruction as an utterance in the language that is the first (original) place of its truth.

8. Ibid., pp. 185–86.

9. The relationship between the nonplace and the (divine) Name should be thought out here, *Sotah* tractate, 42a and b and 43a; the Ark contains the Name: "The Name and its other names are in the Ark." Cf. also 2 Sam. 6:2; cf. also *Yerushalmi Sotah* 8, 3.

VI

The Book: The Verse's Beyond

> Rabbi said: The reason for these signs is not the one that
> has just been given. These signs are to teach us that the
> passage of the "journey of the Ark" ranks as a separate
> book. . . .

LET US go back to the question of the *Gemara*: why are verses 35 and
36 of Numbers 10 flanked by the graphical signs that tradition has
identified as being two inverted *nun* letters?

In the preceding section, we saw that Tanna Kama interpreted these
signs as parentheses, whose function was to remove this passage of the
"journey of the Ark" from the place—from any place, from the fixedness of a place.

Rabbi intervenes: the reason given by Tanna Kama is not the one to
invoke; for this text is in its place in the overall organization of the texts
of the Torah. The real reason is quite different: the *Nunim* are there to
teach us that verses 35 and 36 are a *book* in their own right, as are
those of Genesis, Exodus, Leviticus, and Deuteronomy. The *Nunim* create a break in the book of Numbers,[1] where there is a sort of breaking
up of the book into three parts that could be called *Bamidbar I*, verse 1
to chapter 10, verse 34, inclusive; *Bamidbar II*, verses 35 and 36 of
chapter 10; and *Bamidbar III*, chapter 11 to the end of the book. The
Torah would thus no longer be a pentateuch (five books) but a hep-
tateuch (seven books).

This tradition of the seven books, less well known than that of the
five books, is, however, confirmed by a teaching of Rabbi Samuel bar
Nahmani, in the name of Rabbi Jonathan.

> What does verse 1 of chapter 9 of the book of Proverbs mean: "Wisdom
> has built herself a house, she has erected her seven pillars"? They are the
> seven books of the Torah!

Hokhmah[2] implies a breaking up of the text of the book. The transition from five to seven books certainly has a precise meaning,[3] but what
seems to be important here is the spreading out, the extension. The
existence of the book implies this generating of the book. If the book
exists, it is not alone, for in it, through it, other books become neces-

sary. It is precisely the possibility of other books that, in turn, reveals the book. Up to this point, we have hesitated to ascribe a capital letter to the word "book." We can perhaps begin to do so, as we are starting to sense, more and more, what the Book is. This bursting of the Book into books (and perhaps into other Books) means that its "power of saying" (*pouvoir dire*) exceeds its actual "intention of saying" (*vouloir dire*, lit.: meaning to say). In his book *L'Au-delà du verset* (The verse's beyond)—whose title is none other than a brillant translation of the fact that the *lamed* (in which all study, in its strongest sense, takes root) goes beyond the line of writing—Lévinas expresses the definition of the Book.

The book is not defined by its theme, but by its structure: "the structure of the Book of books inasmuch as it allows exegesis, enjoying the privilege of containing more than it contains. . . ."[4]

"What is it that makes a book institute itself as the Book of books? Why does a book become a Bible?"[5] We could say that a Book is worthy of this name, worthy of the capital letter that can be ascribed to it, if its "power of saying goes beyond its intention of saying," if it "contains more than it contains," if "a surplus of meaning, perhaps inexhaustible, remains enclosed in the syntactical structures of its sentences, in its word groups, in its terms, phonemes, and letters, in all this materiality of the book, potentially forever meaning."[6] In the Book, "the meaning immobilized in the characters already starts tearing open the texture that holds it in." In the propositions of the verses of the Book "a voice that is other resounds among us, a second tone covering or tearing apart the first."[7] In the Book, there is "another meaning that pierces the immediate meaning of the intention-of-saying."[8] The bursting open of the book of *Bamidbar*[9] is the bursting of the "lesser" that contains the "greater," putting us en route for the experience of the thinking of Infinity.

The "greater" within the "lesser" that is revealed in the Book is the most eminent manner that Judaism has of living transcendence.[10]

What is important to consider is not the extraordinary fact of the Infinite's being able to reside in the finite, but the overflowing that is nothing more than the benediction (*berakhah*).

The book is thus the scene of a paradox—or of a meeting; it receives the Infinite (*Tsimtsum*), but it immediately unveils its incapacity for this reception, showing that the Infinite will not allow itself to be encompassed, will not allow itself to be enclosed in a presence over which we would have an ascendancy. There is an overflowing, a breaking up (*shevirah*) of the Book into three books.

Interpretation is none other than the creation of a surplus of meaning that allows breaking up and transcendence. The paradox is the following: the Book is a Book when it is no longer a Book.[11]

Notes

1. So their role is to transform the blanks of the opening and closing of a *Parashah* into the blanks of opening and closing of a book; cf. above, the section entitled "Blanks of Opening and Closing."

2. We shall see in the "Visible and Invisible" opening the meaning of this term as a form of questioning; we shall see later more precisely what this means.

3. Cf. *Midrash Vayikra Rabbah, Parashah* 11, 1.2.3.4. The teaching of R. Nahmani and R. Jonathan is given by Bar Kafara.

4. E. Lévinas, *L'Au-delà du verset* (Paris: Éditions de Minuit, 1982), p. 135.

5. Ibid., p. 137.

6. Ibid., p. 135.

7. Ibid.

8. Ibid.

9. Which can also be read in the manner of a *Midrash—Bam-Dabar:* "in them (the plural of books and not the book), speech"; in them, that is to say, in this book which is a Book, because "it contains more than it contains." We should remember also the "Hasidic reading" of *Bam. Beit* is the first letter of the word *Bereshit,* the first word of the Torah. *Mem* is the first letter of the word *Meeymatai,* the opening vocable of the Talmud as a whole. So *Bam* means the "Written Law" with the "Oral Law."

(We can notice that the whole of this chapter of Joshua speaks essentially of the journey of the Ark; in verse 14 an echo can be heard of Num. 10:35: *Vayehi binesoa ha'am.* This chapter cites the expressions of the Torah that indicate the Revelation and the preparation for the Revelation: cf. Josh. 3:5, *Hitkadeshu ki mahar ya'aseh hashem bekirbekhem niflaot,* and Exod. 19:10; the similarity is striking. The *Midrash* studies the meaning of the expression *Goshu henah,* which appears only once in the book of Joshua. What is the meaning of this "here" [*henah*]? Where is "here"? Rav Huna says: "He held all Israel bowed down between the two staves of the Ark"; the Masters say: "He concentrated them between the two staves of the Ark." To sum up, there are three different ways of standing between two staves or, to speak more "Talmudically," three ways of living in the *Nirin Veeyn nirin* [the "visible and the invisible"] and the dynamics of meaning: (1) *Zekafan,* (2) *Semakhan,* (3) *Tsimtseman.* The *Midrash* continues: "Joshua said to them: by the fact that the two staves of the Ark have contained you all, you know that the Presence of the Lord is among you, as it is said, 'Hereby you shall know that the living God is among you'" [Josh. 3:10]. "Hereby" [*bezot*], that is to say: this situation where a small space was able to contain a multitude of people, and so "a lesser that contains a greater.")

10. Cf. *Midrash Rabbah Bereshit* 5, 6, the principle of "the least that contains

the most," in Hebrew, *Muat shemahzik et hamerubeh* (in the text of the *Midrash*, the expression introduced in the form of a conclusion is *ela mikan heyhehhezik muat et hamerubeh* and is deduced from the six following situations: (1) Gen. 1:9, (2) Num. 20:10, (3) Exod. 9:8, (4) Exod. 27:18, (5) Josh. 3:9, (6) Jer. 3:17 (cf. also for the sixth case: *Avot* 5, 5 and *Yoma* 21a).

We quote only, here, the fifth case, which particularly interests us because it provides a link between our text from *Shabbat* and our text from *Yoma*: "And Joshua said to the children of Israel: come here (*goshu henah*) and listen to the words of YHVH your God, and Joshua said: Hereby (*bezot*) you shall know that God is living among you. . . ."

11. That is what can be shown from an analysis of the text of the *Gemara* on the margins and the texts of Rabbi Nahman's "burnt book." On the other hand, we can immediately see the close link between the Book and interpretation, for the Book exists only if there is interpretation, i.e., overflowing.

VII

An Open Work

WHAT IS important for us is the continual presence of meaning, the guarantee of the existence of the Book. The particular structure of the Talmudic text, the original mode whereby Talmudic thought is expounded, is also what makes the lasting meaning of the Book possible. The Book should be sought in the Talmud, rather than in the Bible.

The Talmud, by its specific problematics, its concern for opening, is the place where the lesser contains the greater; the error many Talmudists make is not to see where the fundamental stakes of this text lie. What needs to be understood is that the philosophy of the Talmud should not be sought in the different themes one encounters but in the problematics that underlie the expounding of these themes. In the Talmud, beyond the various themes described, lies the question of opening, of ever-present meaning.

We shall now examine this particular mode of Talmudic expression: *Mahloket*, "Talmudic discussion."

The reader of the Talmud, when he studies one of these texts for the first time, is surprised by the multiplicity of opinions that are expressed about the same subject: Hillel and Shammai, Rabbi Akiva and Rabbi Ishmael, Rav and Samuel, Rav Huna and Rav Hisda . . . There are incessant debates where reconciliation is not sought; on the contrary. So, if the term "dialectic"—often used in discussion of the Talmud—is to be used, the word "open" should be added, for no synthesis, no third term, intervenes to efface the contradictions. Everything does not subside in the "same," in the equivalence of the identical and the nonidentical. *Mahloket* is not only a way of saying but is also a way of thinking the refusal of synthesis and system; it represents an antidogmatism that, alone, makes a living truth possible.

Speaking of the discussion between the Sages, the Talmud itself says: "The words of some and the words of others are words of the living God" (*Elu veelu divrei Elohim hayyim*); this sentence should be understood in its conditional form: if there are words of some *and* words of others, then they are words of the living God, living words. The Talmud does not conceive a word of God that would be heard in one single fashion. The divine speech is a plural speech.

Mahloket is the expression of a certain conception of truth and a certain way of thinking knowledge. Truth is a thought that cannot be possessed, a thought that thinking cannot be satisfied with. *Mahloket* undermines satisfaction, "knowledge where thought is always shown as true to type."[1] Talmudic *Mahloket* shows that thought is not conceptual; in conceptual thought, the diverse is brought together in the presence of representation. In this way the diverse accepts synchrony, confirms its aptitude for entering into the unity of a genre or a form. Everything allows itself to be thought together at once: it is a thought of presence. *Mahloket* shows that everything cannot be resolved into the same, cannot lend itself to synchrony and synthesis, that perception is not only an understanding, a graspable; it bursts open the immanent structure of synthetic and simplistic thought, shakes up the tranquillity of a single and unique truth that slumbers and is forgotten because it is no longer thought out.

The logical structure of *Mahloket* is that of the Book: writing and effacing, saying and unsaying. As soon as a Master proffers his thought, his interlocutor shakes his position, his positivity (and vice versa). There is an incessant destabilizing: *Mahloket* is an athetic thought that resists synchronization and prepares for a sojourn in Infinity.

We can now better understand the role of thinking-in-community. The Talmud teaches us, first of all, that only community studying bears fruit: "True thinking is not a silent dialogue of the soul with itself, but a discussion between thinkers."[2] Truth always begins with two people.[3]

Here, a remark is necessary concerning the relationship of study, which is primordial in Talmudic tradition. The study relationship, *havruta*, is not a gathering of interlocutors who share the same opinion. There is no unfortunate scattering that would have to be countered. The multiplicity of consciousnesses is not the deficiency of a previous or final unity.[4] The questions and answers of an exchange of ideas between Masters are not intended to come to an agreement on a truth or on Truth, which could very well be embraced by a single consciousness, or worse, be outside the two consciousnesses present.[5] A well-known text from the *Bava Metzia* tractate, 84a, forcibly asserts the refusal of what could be called the "immanent dialectic." Rabbi Johanan, famous for his legendary beauty,[6] had a codisciple named Resh Lakish.[7] After the latter's death, Rabbi Johanan sank into despair; the Masters of the day wondered whom they should send to succeed Resh Lakish in the function of study companion.

Resh Lakish dies, and Rabbi Johanan was plunged into deep grief. Said the rabbis, "Who shall go to ease his mind? Let Rabbi Eleazar ben Pedath go, whose disquisitions are very subtle." So he went and sat before him; and on every dictum uttered by Rabbi Johanan he observed: "There is a Baraita that supports you." "Are you the son of Lakisha?" he complained: "When I stated a law, the son of Lakisha used to raise twenty-four objections, to which I gave twenty-four answers, which consequently led to a fuller comprehension of the law; while you say, 'A Baraita has been taught that supports you'; do I not know myself that my dicta are right?"

In this fundamental text we learn three things:

1. That study and thinking are possible only in the context of a dialogical experience
2. That dialogue is not a simple exchange of ideas, but "questions-answers" (*sheelot u-teshuvot*)
3. That the question and the answer of such thinking do not unfold within the same sphere of thought

We could suggest for Talmudic *Mahloket* the expression "transcendent dialectic." The Other of the Talmudic dialogue is not just a stylistic device, as is the case with Plato where the interlocutor has the function of showing the speaker up to advantage; in many Platonic dialogues, the interlocutor merely says, "Yes!" "No," "That's right," "I think so," "That's how it is," etc. It is the central character of the dialogue who pronounces the questions and answers himself. Everything takes place within a single consciousness; it is an internal discourse where thinking splits—artificially—giving the appearance of questioning and answering itself, but where, in the end, everything comes together.

In the "immanent dialectic"—non-Talmudic dialogue—thinking "remains the same. It goes from one term to the opposite term, but the dialectic where it finds itself is not a dialogue or, at least, it is the dialogue of the soul with itself, proceeding by questions and answers; it is an internal discourse in which the mind, in thinking, remains nonetheless single and unique, in spite of the steps taken and its coming and going where it confronts itself."[8]

Rabbi Johanan "already knows"; so his study does not aim to confront previous knowledge; on the contrary, he seeks to be shaken, disturbed, put in check, overwhelmed. There is not, as in Platonic philosophy, a knowledge-already-there, in the student's mind from all eternity. This text from the *Bava Metzia* teaches us that "teaching is a discourse in which the master can bring to the student what the student does not yet know."[9] Talmudic dialogue, as it is described in *Mahloket*, is not oriented toward synthesis, unity, a Truth that is One.

So, in the relationship of study, an "exorbitant relationship" is created; a relationship that includes the absence of a common measure, the absence of a common denominator, something like the absence of relationship between the terms, an "unrelating relation."[10]

This resistance to a synthesis between the terms implies that the relation between the terms passes through speech, but speech that is expressed through a certain mode. Speech that is to maintain an infinite relationship between two interlocutors should have "the concern of marking, either the interruption and breaking off, or the density and fullness of the field that results from difference and tension."[11] This speech is a *questioning speech*:[12] "All language in which it is a matter of questioning and not of answering is a language that is already interrupted."[13]

The speech of *Mahloket* is a question, but it does not seek an answer (even if an answer is often given): *Sheelah* without *Teshuvah*! It introduces nonrepose, unsettling, and so the security of accomplishment and foundation is brought into question. In *Mahloket*, the speech of the question is "the first fissure visible in the psyche of satisfaction."[14] The refusal of satisfaction, of contentment, or, in other words, of a totality is one of the essential characteristics of *Mahloket*. The question shatters the totality, the concept; it is an opening and a way toward (and of) transcendence; it is the source of *Hidush*, of transcendent knowledge.

Notes

1. E. Lévinas, *De Dieu qui vient à l'idée* (Paris: Vrin, 1982), p. 239.

2. E. Lévinas, *L'Au-delà du verset* (Paris: Éditions de Minuit, 1982), pp. 67f., particularly his rereading of Jer. 50:36: "A sword for loners, they lose their wits!" a remarkable substitution of "liar" for "lone thinker"; cf. also *Taanit* 7a.

3. This eminence of the Talmudic dialogue certainly continues an idea introduced right from the first letter of the Bible: "In the beginning was the second letter, the *beit*, a sign of duality and breaking apart"; cf. André Neher, *Le Puits de l'exil* (Paris: Albin Michel, 1966), p. 35. In this book, Neher sets out very well the meaning of *Mahloket*. He shows how *Mahloket* is a criticism of one of the fundamental principles of Aristotelian philosophy: the principle of noncontradiction, the impossibility of the coexistence of two opposites, "the impossibility of the coexistence of two opposites in the same subject" (p. 171).

4. Lévinas, *De Dieu qui vient à l'idée*, p. 240.

5. Perhaps we should say that truth is not in the theme of the words exchanged, but in the exchange itself, in the event of the relation itself.

6. This same page of the Talmud says: "He who desires to see Rabbi Johanan's beauty, let him take a silver goblet as it emerges from the crucible, fill it with the seeds of red pomegranate, encircle its brim with a chaplet of red roses, and set it between the sun and the shade; its lustrous shade is akin to Rabbi Johanan's beauty."

7. He was first of all his student, then his study companion, *haver* (they were brothers-in-law). Resh Lakish first met the brother, by chance, and then married his sister who was even more beautiful (*Bava Metsia* 84a).

8. Lévinas, *De Dieu qui vient à l'idée*, p. 216.

9. E. Lévinas, *Totality and Infinity* (Pittsburgh: Duquesne University Press, 1988), p. 180.

10. Ibid., p. 295.

11. M. Blanchot, *L'Entretien infini* (Paris: Gallimard, 1969), p. 7.

12. Cf. also below, the analyses on the manna.

13. Blanchot, *L'Entretien infini*, p. 7.

14. Lévinas, *De Dieu qui vient à l'idée*, p. 166.

VIII

The *Talmid Hakham* and the Wise Man: *Hokhmah* and Wisdom

"WISDOM PHILOSOPHY is a philosophy of the answer—it is the answer that counts; it is the *result*, as Hegel says. . . ."[1] This idea of Western philosophy—Greek philosophy in this case—should be contrasted with Talmudic thought, where the question is considered a "a thought that thinks more than the doxical proposition of the answer."[2] *Hokhmah* and Wisdom thus contrast with each other, and so do, consequently, the *Talmid Hakham* and the wise man. "As far as the definition of the wise man is concerned, all philosophers agree. It is very simple and can be given in a single sentence: the wise man is he who is able to answer in an intelligible and satisfactory manner all the questions one might ask him about his actions, and answer in such a way that the sum of his answers forms a coherent discourse. Or else, which amounts to the same thing: the wise man is the man who is fully and perfectly conscious of himself."[3] Synthetically, three definitions of the wise man can be given.

The wise man is, first, "the man-of-absolute-knowledge," the man who is perfectly conscious of himself, omniscient (potentially, at least). (The Book of the wise man can only be encyclopedic.) The second definition of the wise man is "the man-perfectly-satisfactory-for-what-he-is." He wants nothing, desires nothing, wishes to change nothing either in himself or outside of himself; so he does not act. He simply *is*, and is not *becoming*; he maintains himself in identity with himself and is satisfied in and by this identity. There is a third definition in which wisdom is identified with moral perfection. The wise man is thus "the morally-perfect-man." In one way, these three definitions are complementary.[4]

The wise man is the world of the "same."

The *Talmid Hakham* is not a man who wants to become a wise man, because the state of wisdom would halt becoming, the dynamics of meaning.

If wisdom is the *art of answering* all questions that can be asked about human existence, *Hokhmah* is the *art of asking them*. The *Talmid Hakham* always ends up by asking a question that he cannot answer. In this way, he cannot be satisfied; that is what drives him to become. For if conscious satisfaction can be translated by identity with oneself, the consciousness of nonsatisfaction stimulates and reveals a change: the *Talmid Hakham* is essentially the man who changes.[5] The *Talmid Hakham* and *Hokhmah* contrast profoundly with the wise man and wisdom: *Hokhmah* is a mode of being that refuses absolute knowledge and self-satisfaction!

Notes

1. Lévinas, *De Dieu qui vient à l'idée* (Paris: Vrin, 1982), p. 136.
2. Ibid.
3. A. Kojève, *Introduction à la lecture de Hegel* (Paris: Gallimard, 1947), p. 271.
4. Ibid., p. 275.
5. Ibid., p. 281.

IX

The Book and the "Manual"

IN THE PRECEDING pages, we showed, from the idea of the bursting open of the book, that the Book can be defined by its privilege of containing more than it actually contains. Now we have to describe in more detail the relationships of the wise man with the "book" and the relationships of the *Talmid Hakham* with the "Book."

The wise man, the man-of-absolute-knowledge, knows only a single book, his book, where the totality of science is brought together. The wise man's book is the place of the *Begriff*, of the concept.[1]

Begriff, the concept, is derived from *Be-greifen*: "Perception is an ascendancy and the concept, the *Begriff*, a com-prehending."[2] (This capturing of the concept, this conceptual seizure, certainly directs the man who thinks in these categories toward the heart of violence.)

If we have made this detour via "the hand," it is in order to understand more acutely why the book is what is commonly called a "manual." The "manual" is the book that is present, available, that the hand can hold and grasp at each moment, a *main-tenant* (hand holding; *maintenant*: now). Time, as present, as memory of the past and anticipation of the future, is "dead time," time that "no longer passes." The book, as a "manual," is the death of time and the book.

The Book of the *Talmid Hakham*, bursting open the book, reveals a centrifugal movement, opposite to synchronization and the will to gather together. The time of the Book is not a "time that is synchronizable in a re-presentation by memory or history."[3]

On the contrary, the Book of the *Talmid Hakham* is creative, productive of time and history. The "dynamics of meaning" renew the Book: "New meanings arise in its meaning, and their exegesis is an unfolding, or history before all historiography."[4]

The vocation of the *Talmid Hakham* is "to save a text from its misfortune as a book" (Lévinas). It is this rescuing of the Book that, each in his own way, Lévinas, Derrida, Blanchot, Laporte, Jabès, and particularly Rabbi Nahman try to carry out. The "burnt book" is the "saved" book.

The Book of the *Talmid Hakham* is the scene of "nonreason." For "reason is sought in the relationship between terms, between the *one* and the *other* showing themselves in a *theme*. Reason consists in ensuring the coexistence of these terms, the coherence of the one and the other despite their difference, in the unity of a theme; it ensures the agreement of the different terms without breaking up the present in which the theme is held. This coexistence or accord between different terms in the unity of a theme is called a system."[5]

The bursting of the Book (a book that is three books), the explosion of the Book, means "that the book is not the laborious gathering of a totality finally obtained, but its being is a clamorous, silent bursting which otherwise would not occur (would not assert itself) while belonging itself to the shattered being, violently overwhelmed, thrown out of being; it designates itself as its own violence of exclusion, the lightning refusal of the plausible: the outside in its fragmentary becoming. . . ."[6] Blanchot is commenting, here, a sentence by Mallarmé: "The only explosion is of a book."[7] This sentence is the heart of the whole book, a heart that does not form a center but shifts throughout the book, appearing at each page in the same term or in the name of "disaster," "dislocation," "fragmentary," etc.; several important fragments[8] shed light on the project of fragmentary writing as a criticism of the Work as a totality.[9]

Notes

1. A. Kojève, *Introduction à la lecture de Hegel* (Paris: Gallimard, 1947), p. 271.

2. E. Lévinas, *De Dieu qui vient à l'idee* (Paris: Vrin, 1982), p. 236; cf. also pp. 163, 169; *Totality and Infinity* (Pittsburgh: Duquesne University Press, 1988), pp. 158–68: ten very beautiful pages devoted to the phenomenological description of the hand.

3. Lévinas, *De Dieu qui vient à l'idée*, p. 242.

4. E. Lévinas, *Otherwise Than Being* (The Hague: Nijhoff, 1981), p. 169.

5. Ibid., p. 165.

6. Blanchot, *L'Écriture du désastre* (Paris: Gallimard, 1980), p. 190.

7. Initially quoted by Blanchot in *L'Écriture du désastre*, p. 16.

8. Pp. 96–101. The call for the "fragmentary" and the "disaster" (bearing in mind that the disaster is not only the disastrous) in Blanchot aims at the same project. Cf. also the essential idea of "the absence of book" in *L'Entretien infini*; cf. also R. Laporte, mainly *Fugue 3* (Paris: Flammarion, 1976) and "Une Oeuvre mort-né," in *Digraphe* 18–19 (April 1979): 17–76, wherein operate the concepts of "counterwriting," "unwriting," "crossing-out," "whitening," which efface in advance that which is being written. Derrida's "dissemination" and Lévinas's "unsaying" (*dédire*, lit.: retract, recant) are also situated in this critique of reason, critique of the philosophical discourse. *Otherwise Than Being*, mainly in the penultimate part entitled "The Exposition," gives one possible version of the "burnt book": the setting of the paradox of the philosophical

discourse criticizing the philosophical discourse (the impossibility of the philosophical discourse). This is the impossibility that the Book of the *Talmid
Hakham* realizes: "Saying and unsaying." Cf. also J. Derrida, "En ce moment
même dans cet ouvrage, me voici," in *Textes pour Emmanuel Lévinas* (Paris:
Jean-Michel Place, 1980).

9. We can note a remark on the 613th *Mitzvah* of the Torah. The last of these
Mitzvot teaches the obligation for every man and woman to write a Book of the
Torah. This "*Mitzvah* of the Book" is deduced from the verse "Now write this
song . . ." (Deut. 31:19).

X

Time and Interpretation

> Greek time, as a metaphysical dimension, cannot give
> birth to anything; it can only be reflected in perfectly
> identical pictures, whereas Hebrew time renews itself by
> childbirth in unforeseeable futures: *child-time* depends on
> *parent-time* for its birth, but it has its own physiognomy
> and its own particular content.
>   Hebrew time does not start over again like Greek time;
> it engenders.
>   ANDRÉ NEHER, *L'Essence du prophétisme*

THUS the Book is not a "compilation," a "manual." It is not the scene
of a gathering together of signs; it is not a system. The Book is the scene
of the "impossible simultaneity of meaning," of the "nonassemblage,"
of the unsynchronizable.

The relation of the Book and time appears, then, as a fundamental
relation by the fact that the Book is—or should be—the breaking up of
the synchronizable, that is to say, of the recollectable. The temporality
of the Book is transcendence.

The Book will always be the future book, the "book yet to come" (*à-venir*) or, simply, the future (*avenir*). The Book, by its impossibility of
settling down in the "now," helps us to attain discontinuity and time-as-discontinuity. The Book introduces us into a time that "adds something
new to being, something absolutely new."[1]

The Enigma of the Eighty-Five Letters: The Book

"Rabbi said: it is a Book in its own right. . . ."

Rabbi does not give any explanation. Rashi and the commentators do not
suggest any, either. However, all the texts that expound the definition of the
Book refer to this teaching of Rabbi and to the "journey of the Ark" . . .

In tackling these texts on the Book, we might expect to find a reflection on the content, on the meaning of the words of verses 35 and 36.
Not at all . . .

In one way, the *Gemara* works to seek out a definition of the Book without seeking to understand the theme expounded. Paradoxically, Rabbi encounters the Book in its form and not in its meaning.

It is the formal structure of the Book that is analyzed. All the texts that refer to the "journey of the Ark" allude to the number of letters that make up this passage.

> Rav Huna ben Haluv asked Rabbi Nahman: A *Sefer Torah* in which eighty-five letters cannot be gathered, such as the section, "And as the Ark set out," etc., may it be saved from the fire or not?
>
> The eighty-five letters necessary for saving the book, must they be together (in the same passage) or can they be counted even if they are scattered?

And further on:

> Come and hear: If a *Sefer Torah* is decayed, if eighty-five letters can be gathered therein, such as the section "And as the Ark set out," we must save it; if not, we may not save it.

A parallel version given by the *Yadayim* tractate[2] is interesting in other respects, for it compares the Book (eighty-five letters) and the hand.[3]

The commentators who have examined the number 85 are rare. Yet it is extraordinary that a book—that the Book—be defined not by its semantic content but by its literal architecture. The excessive simplicity, the obviousness of this idea may have embarrassed the commentators.

Eighty-five! This number, like any explicit number of a text of the Torah or of the Talmud, says "*Darsheni*": Interpret me! We shall call upon the *Gematria* here, the rule of Talmudic hermeneutics[4] that supposes a link between figures and letters. The two letters that make up the number 85 are *Peh* and *Heh*,[5] which are read as *Peh*: "mouth."

The Book is the Book if it has eighty-five letters, that is to say, if it is a "mouth": a scene of speech. In the very structure that expresses it—in writing—the Book is orality.

The *Torah shebikhtav* is a Book (a written law) in and by the *Torah she-be-al Peh* (the Oral Law). The Book has/is a "mouth." The Book speaks and so makes us speak.

Hence, the Book is the relationship to the Book: the relationship of man and the Book. The Book is not actually the Book, the text, or man—the reader-of-the-Book; it is the relationship of one to the other, of one for the other. This relationship is set up in the *Torah she-be-al Peh*: the Oral Law. The structure of the Book, the fact of its containing more than it can contain, makes the relationship to the book possible—reading and interpretation—a relationship that "comes and frees in the signs of writing a spellbound meaning that smolders under the characters or that is coiled up in all this literature of letters."[6]

To say that "the Book is a mouth" implies an intimate and reciprocal relationship between writing and the mouth. The book is a Book if it is the source of the opening of a mouth, if it creates, generates speech. A mouth speaks only, speech speaks only if they create meaning. The creation of meaning is known as *Hidush*, in Hebrew. The speech that the "mouth of the Book" is to pronounce is necessarily a *Hidush*, "speaking word."[7] "One might draw a distinction between the *word in the speaking* and the *spoken word*. The former is the one in which the significant intention is at the stage of coming into being. Here existence is polarized into a certain 'significance' that cannot be defined in terms of any natural object. It is somewhere at a point beyond being that it aims to catch up with itself again, and that is why it creates speech as an empirical support for its own not-being. Speech is the surplus of our existence over natural being. But the act of expression constitutes a linguistic world and a cultural world, and allows that to fall back into being which was striving to outstrip it. Hence the spoken word, which enjoys available significance as one might enjoy an acquired fortune."[8]

Consequently, interpretation cannot be repetition.[9] The creation of meaning is a creation-production of time. We could be brought around to define a new time that is not the measurable time of the "watch or the calendar," but that of the creativity of interpretation. We could talk about "*Hidush* time" or about "Talmudic time." In this way we would think, not about the change that is produced by time, but about time through change, and change through the speech of *Hidush*; "*Hidush* time" is the founding of History, of the World and Being. It is no longer a subjective or internal time, where time accelerates or slows down with the intensity of life, and of the events that fill existence. It is an ontological time. It is a time that "adds something new to being, something absolutely new."[10]

The *Hidush*-word-in-the-speaking is not only the actualization of language (of the system of signs), but the event or the advent of a new meaning, the movement from one meaning to another meaning: an exegesis that carries one toward possible modes of being opened up by the spoken word.

The importance of *Hidush* lies in the fact that it introduces a discontinuity into the rhythm of consciousness and into the process of being: it shatters the block of being.

The *Lamed*: The Letters and the Coronets or the Tradition of the New

In considering Franz Rosenzweig's "creation," "revelation," and "liberation" triad,[11] one might be led to think that Tradition is an action which creates a synthesis of these three stages.

Tradition[12] should be understood, not only as an action of reception and passing on, but as (re-)creation of meaning. This re-creation is Revelation. Revelation is not in the receiving of a revealed word—a spoken word—but in its renewing. This Creation-Revelation is also a Liberation, for it tears being away from its sinking into the already-there (*déjà-là*).

We can therefore distinguish two types of men who hand on tradition: the first type is the one who frequents schools; he is a purely passive bearer of tradition; he conserves it without adding the slightest feature of his own initiative. He hands tradition on, but the latter is not enriched; he is only an instrument that is called upon. He plays the role of a "memory of meaning." But tradition, considered as the passing on of a *depositum*, remains a dead tradition if it is not the continuous interpretation of this deposit. The real master is more than a memory; his relation to Tradition is not purely passive. He receives established meaning but never feels he has the right to pass it on without contributing his personal *Hidush*. "The Cabala has given us this judgment that has been widely accepted: 'The Torah has a special face for each Jew.' The Torah bears a particular meaning that can be grasped only by him; and consequently, each Jew can only fulfill his own vocation once he has met this face and is able to contribute it to tradition."[13] Revelation is not a specific and positive communication.[14]

A teaching from the *Midrash Rabbah*[15] about Exod. 31:18 may be considered as a basic reference for this manner of understanding Revelation; the *Midrash* says:

> Could Moses have learned the whole Torah? Of the Torah it says: "The measure thereof is longer than the earth, and broader than the sea" (Job 11:9): could then Moses have learned it all in forty days? No; but it was the principles (*kelalim*) thereof that God taught Moses.[16]

What Moses hands on are the keys that allow us to open the text of the Torah.[17] It is then clear that *Cabala* "reception," is *not receiving*, but *building*: "The role of the commentator is not to explain a (con)text, but to build it. The relationship of the commentator to the text is obviously not one of deduction (the commentary is not deduced; it is not drawn from the text), but one of an application to the text: it is projected as a new grid that allows new things to be read in the old text."[18]

At this stage, it is not uninteresting to point out the difference between Jewish and Christian exegesis. This comparison does not aim to start up a controversy: it is simply an illustration to insist—in the contrast—on what Tradition-Revelation as *construction-creation* of meaning represents. "The Middle Ages witnessed the development of the theory of *allegorism* whereby Holy Scripture (then, by extension, poetry and the figurative arts) could be interpreted according to four different meanings: literal, allegorical, moral, and anagogical. This theory . . . originated in Saint Paul. . . . Continued by Saint Jerome, Augustine, Scotus Erigena, Bede, Hugo and Richard of Saint-Victor, Alain of Lille, Bonaventure, Thomas, and many others, it is the key to medieval poetry. A work conceived on this principle is incontestably endowed with a certain degree of 'opening'; the reader knows that each sentence, each character, envelops multifarious meanings that it is incumbent on him to discover. According to his frame of mind, he will choose the key that seems best and will 'use' the work in a meaning that will perhaps be different from that adopted in the course of a preceding reading. Here, 'opening' does not mean 'indetermination' of communication, 'infinite' possibilities of form, freedom of interpretation. The reader simply disposes of a range of possibilities that have been carefully determined and conditioned so that the interpretive reaction never escapes the author's control."[19] If we take a verse (an event of biblical history) and call on the four meanings of writing, "the licit readings are exhausted: the reader can chose one meaning rather than another, within a verse that unfolds on four distinct levels, but without escaping prefixed and univocal rules. The meaning of allegorical figures and emblems that the medieval reader is likely to encounter is already prescribed by his encyclopedias, bestiaries, and lapidaries: their symbolism is objective and institutional."[20]

In the Talmudic conception of interpretation, the Text is undefined, ever open to new interpretations. We find the four meanings of Scripture, but these meanings remain polyvalent; they are not guaranteed by any encyclopedia. The most diverse interpretations—philosophical, symbolical, psychoanalytical, psychological, sociological, political, linguistic, etc.—exhaust only a portion of the possibilities of the Text; the latter remains inexhaustible and open because its structure is that of the "visible-invisible."[21]

The text itself is complete; not one letter could be missing, not one additional letter can slip in, and, in spite of this completeness, the Text is infinitely open.

The numberless points of view of the interpreters and the numberless aspects of the Text echo, meet, and shed light on each other, so that the interpreter, in order to reveal the Text in its entirety, must grasp it in one of its particular aspects, and, conversely, a particular aspect of the Text must await the interpreter capable of perceiving it, thus giving the entirety of the Text a renewed interpretation. All of these interpretations are definitive in that each one is, for the interpreter, the Text itself; but at the same time they are provisional, since the interpreter knows that he will have to deepen his own interpretation indefinitely.

Inasmuch as they are definitive, these interpretations are parallel, with the result that one excludes the others, yet without refuting them.[22]

And so Revelation is the gift of the keys of interpretation. Tradition is, on the one hand, the passing on of these keys, on the other hand, of an established meaning—a spoken word—but at the same time renewed by the Master as the bearer of Tradition-Revelation-Creation. The fact that Revelation is not the effective communication of a positive, substantial, and explainable given helps us to understand the existence of a plurality of interpretations, of a polysemy of meaning: the word is "like the hammer that strikes the rock, sending up innumerable sparks."[23]

Interpretation is not just perception; it is the creation of meaning.

All these remarks allow us to understand the meaning of this text from the *Menahot* tractate, 29b (one of the most famous of the Talmud), describing Moses and Rabbi Akiva.[24]

> Rav Judah said in the name of Rav, When Moses ascended on high he found the Holy One, blessed be He, engaged in affixing coronets (*taggim*) to the letters. Said Moses, "Lord of the Universe, who stays Your hand?" He answered, "There will arise a man, at the end of many generations, Akiva b. Joseph by name, who will expound upon each tittle heaps and heaps of laws (*halakhot*)." "Lord of the Universe," said Moses; "permit me to see him." He replied, "Turn around." Moses went and sat down behind eight rows and listened to the discourses upon the law. Not being able to follow their arguments he was ill at ease, but when they came to a certain subject and the disciples said to the master, "Whence do you know it?" and the latter replied, "*Halakhah le-Mosheh mi-Sinai*" (It is a law given to Moses at Sinai), he was comforted. Thereupon he returned to the Holy One, blessed be He, and said, "Lord of the Universe, You have such a man and yet You give the Torah by me!" He replied, "Be silent, for such is my decree." Then said Moses, "Lord of the Universe, You have shown me his Torah, show me his reward." "Turn around," said He; and Moses turned around and saw them weighing out his flesh at the market stalls. "Lord of the Universe," cried Moses, "such Torah, and such a reward!" He replied, "Be silent, for such is my decree."

Notes

1. E. Lévinas, *Totality and Infinity* (Pittsburgh: Duquesne University Press, 1988), p. 283.

2. Chap. 3, *Mishnah 5*.

3. On this subject, cf. Lévinas in Colloque des intellectuels juifs de langue française, *La Bible au présent* (Paris: Gallimard, 1982), "Idées," pp. 327f.

4. Even more common in the "mystical" readings of the *Zohar* and Hasidism.

5. Respectively, the seventeenth and fifth letters of the alphabet.

6. E. Lévinas, *L'Au-delà du verset* (Paris: Éditions de Minuit, 1982), p. 135.

7. We are using the distinction made by Merleau-Ponty between "word in the speaking" and "spoken word." Cf. *Phenomenology of Perception*, trans. Colin Smith (London: Routledge and Keagan Paul, 1962), p. 197.

8. Ibid.

9. Except, perhaps, in the meaning that Blanchot gives to this exercise in *L'Entretien infini* (Paris: Gallimard, 1969), pp. 570f.

10. Ibid., p. 260.

11. We prefer the term of liberation to that of redemption used by F. Rosenzweig (*L'Étoile de la rédemption* [Paris: Seuil, 1982]).

12. In Hebrew, *Kabbalah* (reception) or *Masoret* (transmission).

13. Cf. G. Scholem, *Le Messianisme juif. Essais sur la spiritualite du judaïsme*, trans. B. Dupuy (Paris: Calmann-Lévy, 1974), p. 417.

14. Ibid., p. 417; cf. also p. 399.

15. Exod. 41:6.

16. There is a "play on words" between *kekaloto*, which means "when he had finished," and *kelalim*, which means "principles." In fact, according to Mandelkern, *Veteris Testamenti hebraïcae atque Chaldaïcae Concordantiae*, p. 561, *kalah* (terminate, exterminate) and *kelal* (totality, summary, principle) are of the same family. So the verse from Exod. 31:8 should not be read, "Then he gave Moses, when he had finished talking to him, on Mount Sinai, the two tables of the Testimony, tables of stone inscribed by the finger of God"; but, "Then . . . , when he had given him the general principles. . . ."

17. H. Atlan, in "Niveaux de signification et athéisme de l'écriture," in *La Bible au présent* (Paris: Gallimard, 1982), "Idées," pp. 82f., speaks of formal teaching, of a grid, sources of interpretations.

18. Ibid., p. 84.

19. U. Eco, *L'Oeuvre ouverte* (Paris: Seuil, 1979) "Points," pp. 19–20; like the "beyond of the verse," the "open work" is a fundamental concept-title of Talmudic hermeneutics.

20. Ibid.

21. Eco speaks of ambiguity. It should be emphasized that the "four meanings" of the Talmud do not correspond to the "four levels" of medieval tradition; on this subject, cf. G. Scholem, *La Kabbale et sa symbolique* (Paris: Payot, 1980), pp. 63–77. Scholem sets out and examines the resemblance between this fourfold aspect of the Torah and the meaning of Christian exegesis. He concludes that the latter influenced Jewish exegesis, but shows the metamorphosis of the approach when one goes from one tradition to the other. He also describes the other important Jewish tradition according to which each word and even each letter has seventy facets (faces): cf. p. 74; cf. also Atlan, "Niveaux de signification," which is, in our opinion, the better reflection on the topic.

22. Cf. Atlan, "Niveaux de signification," ". . . Apart from the *Peshat*, there are no discussions or confrontations between the different commentaries, even if they are contradictory: they are simply juxtaposed . . ." (p. 70).

23. *Taanit* 7a, quoted by Lévinas in *L'Au-delà du verset*, p. 204.

24. Quoted by Scholem in *Le Messianisme juif*, p. 398; by Lévinas, *L'Au-delà du verset*, pp. 162, 164; by Atlan, "Niveaux de signification," p. 55.

XI

Violence and Interpretation

> Who is the Tanna that disagrees with Rabbi?
>
> It is Rabbi Simeon ben Gamaliel. For it was taught in a *Baraita*, Rabbi Simeon ben Gamaliel said: This section is destined to be removed from here and written in its right place.
>
> And why is it written here?
>
> In order to provide a break between the first account of erring and the second account of erring.
>
> What is the second account of erring? "And the people were as murmurers . . ." (Num. 11:1f.).
>
> What is the first account of erring? "And they moved away from the mount of the Lord" (Num. 10:33).
>
> Rabbi Hama, son of Rabbi Hanina, expounded as meaning that they turned away from following the Lord.

RABBI Simeon ben Gamaliel continues the reflection about the Book started by Tanna Kama and Rabbi. His disagreement with Rabbi concerns the place. The Book is not in its place at the present time; the definition of the Book is going to be pinned down more precisely here, by means of an examination of the role of the Book.

The Book: a separation not between good and evil, but between evil and evil. The Book: that which hinders violence from lending violence assistance; the Book is thus an interruption.

Rabbi Simeon ben Gamaliel has us think out the Book as an interruption of the same: "To separate the first from the second account of erring."

The Second Error: The Refusal of the Manna

The *Gemara* first cites the second error: "And when the people complained, it displeased the Lord."[1] In his commentary, Rashi sums up the error in these words: "The desire for meat." "For the three days of their journey, they expressed a desire by complaining about the meat in order to rebel against God."[2] So, according to Rashi, *the* error is situated in verses 4, 5, 6 of chapter 11:

> A group of people in their midst were seized by covetousness, and even the children of Israel began to cry; they said: "Who will give us meat to eat? We

remember the fish that we ate freely in Egypt, and the cucumbers, and the melons, and the leeks, and the onions, and the garlic! And now, our throat is parched: there is nothing, nothing but manna before our eyes!"

Did the violence originate in a badly prepared menu? These verses smelling of stew that may make us smile seem a long way from the preoccupations being studied. What is wrong? Where is the war or murder? Is the nostalgia for old times prohibited? Perhaps . . .

There are two attitudes to the past. One is the conservative attitude, which preserves the past and returns to it. It is nostalgia: this attitude is not faithful to tradition. The other, faithfulness to tradition, is an active attitude that transfigures the past. Paradoxically, faithfulness to the past is oriented toward the future. It is a matter of being faithful not to time past but to the consciousness of time that the ancients had. The Cabala, that is to say, the reception of tradition, is essentially reception of this particular consciousness of time. The Cabala is not a semantic content, but an attitude to meaning, an attitude of creativity. It is a matter of being a "man of *Hidush*."[4]

In fact, it is the first teaching of the Torah. If the text of Genesis starts with the story of Creation, an obvious *Halakhah* can be drawn from this opening: man must look after Creation—creating—and its renewal.[5]

The first stage of erring is in the mistaken assumption of the past. The "desire for meat," the nostalgia for a past that may never even have existed, derives from a misunderstanding of the past, and hence of time in general.

Remembering in itself is not an offense; it is even a *mitzvah*: there is, for example, the obligation to remember the leaving of Egypt, the revelation on Sinai, of the Shabbat, etc. . . .[6]

The problem we encounter here is that of the "eternal return of the Same," where everything that is already has been, but in the sense that all action—and more particularly all "halakhic" action—is always identical to itself. How can the repetition of an action—often an action linked to the past—generate time, futurity? How can time unfold in an eternal repetition of the identical? The manna is, for tradition, what represents this identity: a food consisting of identical white grains. Every day, the same menu is served up. Manna on Monday, manna on Tuesday, etc. It is the eternal return of the identical. And the children of Israel, in the desert, faced with this infernal and insipid cycle react: Enough! We don't want any more manna. "Our throat (*Nefesh*: soul) is parched: nothing but manna before our eyes!"

There it was! In uttering this last sentence, the fault was committed: *the refusal of manna!*

Did they react badly? Was it abnormal?

Certainly! But in order to understand, we must analyze in detail the meaning of the manna. Let us return to its first appearance in the text of the Torah:

In chapter 16 of Exodus, all Israel is in the desert and already the (first) complaints can be heard:

> And the whole community of the sons of Israel began to complain against Moses and Aaron in the wilderness and said to them, "Why did we not die at YHVH's hand in the land of Egypt, when we were able to sit down to pans of meat and could eat bread to our heart's content! As it is, you have brought us to this wilderness to starve this whole company to death! (Exod. 16:2, 3)

So God said to Moses:

> "Now I will rain down bread for you from the heavens. Each day the people are to go out and gather the day's portion; I propose to test them in this way to see whether they will follow my law or not." (Exod. 16:4)

A little further on, in verses 13, 14, 15:

> And in the morning there was a coating of dew all round the camp. When the coating of dew lifted, there on the surface of the desert was a thing delicate, powdery, as fine as hoarfrost on the ground. When they saw this, the sons of Israel said to one another, *Man-hu* ("What is that")? not knowing what it was.

And further on, in verse 31:

> The House of Israel named it "manna." It was like coriander seed; it was white and its taste was like that of wafers made with honey.

Manna, is the question, questioning: "What is it?" The refusal of manna is expressed by a refusal of questioning: the offense lies in this refusal which is so serious, no weighty, that the book must appear to stamp out the inflation of meaning which followed the refusal of the manna, of the "what is it?"

The refusal of the "what is it?" is also the refusal of *Hokhmah* wisdom: *koah-Mah* (the force of the "What?"); refusal of thinking: *Mahashavah* (*Hashav-Mah*); thinking is always—or should always be—the thinking of the question, a questioning. Not questioning for the sake of questioning, not an arbitrary process, but a remarkable occurrence, an event.[7]

The manna, the "what is it?" is not a game; nor is it a vain, pretentious speculation on verbal meanings devoid of content.

The question arises to disturb being in its tranquillity, in the obviousness of the "everything is normal," in considering that "everything is settled." It is the awaking of the consciousness to the necessity of the

transition from the "spoken word" to the "speaking word." The *Mah*
or the "manna"[8] is the primordial interrogative attitude that makes man
a man: *Adam, Mah.*[9]

The questioning is not to do with *one* particular question; it is not *to
do with*. Questioning is not interested in the object, but above all in the
man who questions. I question, I mean: I question myself, I disturb
myself. Questioning is a movement where one is disturbed, but not for
nothing. "To question is to break with something; it is to establish an
inside and an *outside*."[10] Outside, that is to say, outside of order. "We
go beyond that which is the order of the day. We question over and
beyond the ordinary and the 'in-order' that is well ordered in everyday
life."[11]

This interrogative attitude is that of the philosopher, the "man who
never ceases living, seeing, conjecturing, hoping, dreaming of extra-or-
dinary things. . . ."[12]

The *Mah*-man is the philosopher. The latter does not aim at attaining
wisdom or the status of wise man; he refuses the conclusion, any conclusion.[13]

Implicitly, there is the refusal of absolute knowledge and at the same
time the refusal to consider that the supreme value is in self-knowledge.
The man who possesses the *Hokhmah/koah-mah* is a *Talmid Hakham*—a disciple—wise man—this is to say that the final state, that of
absolute knowledge, does not exist; the master always has something of
the disciple in him: a possibility of entering into questioning. In one
way, to the question "Who am I?" one should reply, "I am not; I am
becoming."[14]

The manna and the acceptance of the manna imply a certain conception of time and being as well as a certain conception of truth.

But is there not a contradiction in this description of the manna? At
first, the manna appeared as a collection of white identical grains. Then,
we saw the manna as a "what is it?" as the becoming-by-the-question.
On the one hand, there is the identity of the identical, on the other,
change and becoming. Is there repetition or difference? "Is" the manna,
or is it "becoming"? Is there an error? A text from the *Midrash Rabbah*
and from the Talmud will help us resolve the difficulty.

In *Shemot Rabbah* (25:3) we read:

> It is written, "You open Your hand, and satisfy every living thing with will"
> (*poteah et yadekha umassbia lekhol hay ratzon*, Ps. 145:16). It does not say,
> "Every living thing with *food*" (*mazon*), but with "*will*" (*ratzon*), that is, He
> grants to each one his request. In the millennium, too, God will grant the
> request of each individual. Should you wonder at this, then see what He has
> done for Israel in this world, when He brought down for them the manna, in
> which all kinds of flavors lodged, so that each Israelite could taste therein

anything he particularly liked, for it is written, "These forty years YHVH your God has been with you; you have lacked nothing"[15] (*davar*).

What is the meaning of "you have lacked nothing" (*davar*)?

When a man desired anything special to eat, he had only to say, "I wish I had a fat capon to eat," and the morsel of manna in his mouth immediately acquired the taste of fat capon. They had only to say the word (*davar*) and the Lord performed their will.[16]

Rabbi Abba said: They were even spared the utterance of their wish, for God fulfilled the thought still in their heart and they tasted their heart's desire. A proof that it was so? For Ezekiel says, "The bread I gave you, the finest flour, oil, and honey, with which I used to feed you" (Ezek. 16:19). One verse tells us, "Now, I will rain down bread for you from the heavens (Exod. 16:4), and another verse says, "It was like coriander seed; it was white and its taste was like that of wafers made with honey" (Exod. 16:31).

And another verse: "The people went round gathering it, and ground it in a mill or crushed it with a pestle; it was cooked in a pot and made into pancakes. It tasted like cake made with oil" (Num. 11:8). How do you reconcile these three verses? The young tasted therein the taste of bread, the old the taste of honey, and the babies the taste of oil.

Another text from the Talmud, *Yoma* 75a, gives a parallel and more general version:

> *The cucumbers and the melons.* Rabbi Ammi and Rabbi Assi were disputing its meaning. One said: They found in the manna the taste of every kind of food, but not the taste of these five (cucumbers, melons, leaks, onions, garlic); the other said: Of all kinds of food they felt both taste and substance, but of these the taste only without the substance.

In this *Midrash* and this Talmudic text that echoes it, a theory of the sign and of signification is developed. The manna is a sign; not just any sign, but a perfect sign, the paradigm of all signs. The manna is a signifier that does not refer to any particular signified: an empty sign or else an absolutely full sign! A sign completely open to meaning, signifying only to the extent that it is given a meaning.

Here the *Midrash* poses the problem of *Ta'am*. In Hebrew, *Ta'am* is both "taste" and "meaning."[17] The manna has no more "taste," complain the children of Israel. The signs are empty and have no meaning. "Our throat is parched; there is nothing, nothing but manna." That is the mistake: allowing the sign to lose its meaning(s). And the *Midrash* explains the origin of this loss: "Our throat is parched; there is nothing, nothing but manna." There is the first important point: the relation of "taste"—that is to say, of "meaning"—to will!

There is no taste without will, no meaning without desire to confer

meaning. The expression of the *Midrash* is interesting: we nourish ourselves with will. It is as if food did not satisfy one's hunger but whetted
it![18] The first aspect of the error resides in this: the acceptance of the
manna as a food (*mazon*) and not as will (*ratzon*). There is thus a
will—a desire—for meaning that is above all a will to will. But the will
does not reveal meaning: the emergence of meaning reveals the will.
The manna is the scene of the test.[19] In the same way as the *Mitzvah* or
the Text, it is always identical to itself. There is always the same act to
accomplish; there is always the same Text to read. Is it possible to think
that life is the scene of repetition? Is living the eternal repetition of the
identical? Is it a circular movement of totality within a totality?

The analysis of the manna we have carried out is based on a certain
understanding of the world and of life as "becoming."[20] The will to will
is the basis of becoming, and therefore of life. To will is to reach out
toward something; but the will does not aspire to what it wants as
something it does not yet have. Of course, the new meaning does not
yet exist; and yet it is important to understand that the new meaning is
a means whereby the will is able to will.

The new meaning allows the will to will itself. The will is thus defined
as willing to will: it can, in that case, surpass itself. The "what is it?"
the first meaning of the manna, is the basis of the becoming of meaning.
Thus the error, the refusal of the "what is it?" lies in the fact that the
children of Israel considered the manna as something, in the sense of
something stable and firmly established. In one way, they erected the
truth of the world into something, in itself, constant, unchanging, and
eternal. But since the world is changing and fleeting and because its
essence is in what is the most fleeting among that which disappears and
is unstable, then truth—in the sense of that which is firmly established
—is only a pure fixation of that which, in itself, is becoming, and this
fixation compared with what is becoming does not adapt to it but de-
forms it.

The action, the text, do not have—or should not have—a meaning
that is fixed once and for all. The error of the children of Israel is that
of noncomprehension and nonapplication of the dynamism of signification.

This theory of the sign is a corollary of a conception of time. That is
what the *Midrash* would have us understand when it says that the
"taste-meaning" is different for babies, adolescents, and old people.
Here is a mistake to avoid: it is not the transition from one stage to
another, from one age to another, that is the source of the change in
meaning. On the contrary, the "dynamism of meaning" generates time
and history. In order for the meaning of a single sign to evolve—volun-
tarily—there has to be interpretation. History and interpretation are

therefore two inseparable terms. We can compare, in this context, the manna and the coronets that the tractate *Menahot* 29b speaks of, mentioned previously. Like the manna, the coronets are empty signs—or absolutely full ones. The *Gemara Menahot* 29b has us understand that the future, that is to say history,[21] depends on the interpretation and the contribution of new meanings (Moses does not understand what Rabbi Akiva says). We can therefore say that it is not man who is in time, but time that is in man. The time of history depends on the time of man, which is the opening up of *Hidush*. Time defined as incessant renewing of the instant is subordinated to the incessant renewing of meaning. The gaze turned longingly back toward Egypt, to the tastes and meanings of Egypt, describes exactly the opposite movement to this history anchored in the becoming of meaning.

The First Error: A Reading Mistake

Rashi explains that the first and second error are identical. The *Tosefot*, in the name of *Midrash*, explain it in the following way:

> What does "They departed from the mount of the Lord, three days' journey" (Num. 10:33) mean? That means that the children of Israel fled from Mount Sinai like a child who flees school after having learned too much.

The *Tsafnat Paneah* (by Rabbi Yossef Rozin) explains this *Midrash* as follows:[22]

> Like a child who flees school, that means: they did not want to learn the letters of the Torah as separate entities, but preferred (to read and study) whole words.

Each letter is a world, each word, a universe. To read letter after letter is to understand the constitution of things in their essence; it is to seize the first faltering attempts of a language in the process of being created, opening up to the light of the world. To read words is to shut oneself up in a totality, without having traveled the difficult road of the joining up of letters one to another, without understanding the secret progression of their creation. The first and the second error are identical, as Rashi explains: they lie in what we could call, with Lévinas, the "failure of transcendence." This failure originates in "a theology that thematizes the transcending in the logos, assigns a term to the passing of transcendence."[23]

But can one really speak of an error? Can there be any question of responsibility? Is it not the irremediable destiny of the other of being to lead nowhere, to be immediately hemmed in by being?[24] Is it "their" fault if the other than being—the transcendent—finds itself betrayed by the said dominating the saying that it utters?[25] The system is necessary for the intelligibility of the message.[26]

That being the case, should we criticize this reaction of reason that seeks to understand the intelligible through an already-formed linguistic structure? Is not the reading of words more intelligent? Would not that of the letters simply be poetic dreaming? Did not God Himself write with His hand, engrave, inscribe, fix His word? And did He not pass it on in a volume, in a Book, in a system, in a totality? So where is the error? What does "not having read the letters but the words" mean? Perhaps we could say that the "fleeing from Sinai" or the "refusal of the manna" indicates a certain basic failure to understand Revelation. What the children of Israel did not understand is that "the *otherwise than being* is stated in a saying that must also be unsaid in order to thus extract the *otherwise than being* from the said in which it already comes to signify but only a *being otherwise*" was not understood.[27] The reading of letters means the demand of the simultaneity of the saying and the unsaying (or at least, if the simultaneity is too great a demand, the necessity of contemplating this unsaying). The reading of letters expressed "the possibility of a tearing-away from the essence" that goes as far as seeking the nonplace,[28] because this tearing-away contests the unconditional privilege of the question "where?"[29]

The "reading of letters" means that "the statement of the beyond being, of the name of God, does not allow itself to be walled up in the conditions of its enunciation."[30] The Book reaches toward the impossibility of existing, for "the transcendence of a named God cannot be set out in a theme."[31] Of course, thematization is inevitable for meaning itself to come to light.[32] The Saying is incessantly concealed in the Said. But the Saying must constantly seek to unsay this concealment. In the first part of this research we showed that the text is "visible-invisible." This visibility-invisibility is enigma, ambiguity, the very domain of transcendence. Already, in the Text, the "system" carries in itself the seeds of its effacing; the work contains the forces of its unworking.[33]

The "refusal of the manna" is the refusal of being unsaid; it is the settling down in the lap of being, the closure of the road that leads beyond being.

The Book—the eighty-five letters—is a mouth that sets in motion "a movement going from said to unsaid in which the meaning shows itself, eclipses and shows itself. In this navigation the element that bears the embarcation is also the element that submerges it and threatens to sink it."[34]

Consequently, the Book is always the fore-Book or, as Jabès would say, the fore-fore-Book: the preface.

"The word by way of preface . . . belongs to the very essence of language, which consists in continually undoing its phrase by the foreword or the exegesis, in unsaying the said, in attempting to restate without ceremonies what has already been ill understood in the inevitable ceremonial in which the said delights."[35]

We can then understand why the foreword is always necessarily written after the book, for "it is not a repetition, in an approximative language, of the rigorous exposition that justifies a book. It is able to express the first, and urgent, commentary, the first 'that is to say'—which is also the first unsaying—of the propositions where, present and gathered together, is absorbed and expounded, in the *Said*" that which signifies as *Saying*.[36]

It is doubtless possible to understand now that Revelation passes through the medium of the gift, not of one Torah but of two *Torot*, written and oral, "said-Saying" (*Dire-dit*) and "Unsaying" (*Dédire*, lit.: to recant, retract).

The Book could have only the mouth as a structure—the eighty-five letters.

Manifestation and withdrawal, inscription and effacing, "visible and invisible."

Notes

1. Num. 11:1.

2. Rashi, *Shabbat* 116a.

3. Cf. also Num. 11:13 and 11:18.

4. Rav Yossef Dov Soloweichik, *L'Homme de la Halakha* (Jerusalem: W.Z.O., 1979), p. 105.

5. Ibid., pp. 112–30.

6. The main festivals of the liturgical calendar are set around these rememberings. There is also a "mystical" habit of reciting the "four memories" after the morning prayer (the exodus from Egypt, the Revelation, Amalec, Myriam).

7. Cf. M. Heidegger, *Introduction à la métaphysique* (Paris: Gallimard, 1967), "Tel," p. 17.

8. The difference between these two terms is the letter *nun*! Well, well . . . Here we are again on familiar ground!

9. The texts of the Cabala underline the numerical parity of these two terms: man is a question. "The Jew not only asks questions; he himself has become a question." E. Jabès, *Du désert au livre* (Paris: Belfond, 1980), p. 112.

10. Ibid., p. 105.

11. Heidegger, in the first pages of the *Introduction à la métaphysique*, treats a particular question, "Why is there something instead of nothing?" and then examines the reasons for this question. It is a magnificent meditation on ques-

tioning in general (and on the meaning and role of philosophy); we retain here only the general aspect of this meditation.

12. F. Nietzsche, *Ainsi parla Zarathoustra*.

13. A. Kojève, *Introduction à la lecture de Hegel* (Paris: Gallimard, 1947), mainly pp. 271–91.

14. Thus the *Mah*-man, the one who accepts the manna, "is" not: "that which is becoming is not yet. That which no longer needs to become, that which 'is,' the being, has left all becoming behind him, if ever we can say that he has ever become or could have become. That which 'is,' strictly speaking, resists all impulse of becoming." Heidegger, *Introduction à la métaphysique*, p. 104.

15. Deut. 1:7.

16. The word *Davar* is thus understood as a "thing" and as a "word"; on this subject, cf. A. Néher, *L'Exil de la parole* (Paris: Seuil, 1970), pp. 99–100.

17. Cf., for example, Ps. 119:66 and Prov. 26:16.

18. Cf. the analysis of metaphysical desire in E. Lévinas, *Totality and Infinity* (Pittsburgh: Duquesne University Press, 1988), pp. 33–34.

19. Exod. 16:23.

20. In the classical alternative that has us choose between Parmenides and Heraclitus, we situate our reflection (and, thereby, Talmudic thought) in the wake of Heraclitus: "Being is not; it becomes."

21. The text insists on this orientation of time by the repetition of terms that mark the future: (*Atid, Besof kamah dorot*, etc.).

22. Editions of the "Tsafnat Paneah" Institute (Jerusalem, 1960), 4:110.

23. Lévinas, *Otherwise Than Being* (The Hague: Nijhoff, 1981), p. 5. This whole book can be read as a quest for the definition of the Book.

24. Ibid., p. 5.

25. Ibid., p. 7.

26. Ibid., p. 132.

27. Ibid., p. 7.

28. This is not its place, says Tanna Kama.

29. Lévinas, *Otherwise Than Being*, p. 8.

30. Ibid., p. 156.

31. E. Lévinas, *L'Au-delà du verset* (Paris: Éditions de Minuit, 1982), p. 152. This whole article on the names of God is a commentary of this question of saying and unsaying.

32. Lévinas, *Otherwise Than Being*, p. 151.

33. Cf. M. Blanchot, *L'Entretien infini* (Paris: Gallimard, 1969), pp. 620–36, as well as *L'Écriture du désastre* (Paris: Gallimard, 1980).

34. Lévinas, *Otherwise Than Being*, p. 181; cf. also *De Dieu qui vient à l'idée* (Paris: Vrin, 1982), p. 141: "But I will also say that Saying should immediately be accompanied by an unsaying and the unsaying should also be unsaid in its own way and there, there is no stopping, there is no definitive formulating."

35. Lévinas, *Totality and Infinity*, p. 30.

36. E. Lévinas, *Humanisme de l'autre homme* (Paris: Fata Morgana, 1972), p. 11.

Second Opening

VISIBLE AND INVISIBLE;

OR,

EROTICISM AND TRANSCENDENCE

כל הדרה מאי כל הדרה הדדה אתה מאי אתה אומר נגנז נגנז שנאמר ויאריכו הבדים וגו׳ אמר ליה רבה לעולא מאי משמע דכתיב ויהיו שם עד היום הזה וכל היכא דכתיב עד היום הזה לעולם הוא והכתיב וישב הגר בנימן בירושלם עד היום הזה נמי דלא גלו הרתנוא ר׳ יהודה אומר חמשים ושתים שנה לא עבר איש בהודה שנאמר על ההרים אשא בכי ונהי ועל נאות מדבר קינה כי נצתו מבלי איש עבר ולא שמעו קול מקנה מעוף השמים ועד בהמה נדדו הלכו בהמה בגימטריא חמשין ושתים הוו ותניא ר׳ יוסי אומר שבע שנים נתקיימה גפרית ומלח בארץ ישראל ואמר רבי יוחנן מאי טעמא דרבי יוסי דכתיב ברית לרבים שבע ובתיב יוסי אתיא ברית ברית כתיב הכא והגבר ברית לרבים כתיב התם את בריתי...

[Main body: dense Talmudic text in multiple columns surrounding the central text — Rashi and Tosafot commentaries in side columns, Rabbeinu Chananel and Tosefot Yeshanim below, with marginal glosses]

Translation

Yoma Tractate, 54a

A. Rav Judah contrasted (*Rami*) the following passages: "They length-ened the staves (*badim*); the ends of the staves could be seen from the Holy of Holies in front of the Sanctuary" (1 Kings 8:8). It is also writ-ten: "And they could not be seen without. They are there to this day."

How is this contradiction possible? Visible and invisible!

B. A *Baraita* teaches thus:

I could have thought that the staves were not moved from their place! The verse refutes this hypothesis when it says: "They lengthened the staves."

I could have thought that they tore the curtain and showed forth. The verse refutes this hypothesis when it says: "They could not be seen without."

How then can we explain this contradiction?

They pressed forth and protruded as the two breasts of a woman, as it is said: "My beloved is a sachet of myrrh lying between my breasts" (Song 1:13).

C. R. Kattina said: Whenever Israel came up to the Festival, the cur-tain would be removed for them and the *Keruvim* (Cherubim) were shown to them, whose bodies were intertwined with one another, and they would be thus addressed, Look! You are beloved before God as the love between man and woman.

R. Hisda raised the following objection: "But they shall not go in to see the holy things as they are being covered" (Num. 4:20), in connec-tion with which Rav Judah in the name of Rav said, It means at the time when the vessels are being put into their cases?

R. Nahman answered: That may be compared to a bride. As long as she is in her father's house, she is reserved in regard to her husband, but when she comes to her father-in-law's house, she is no more reserved in regard to him.

Layout of the Commentary ───────────

Those who camp every day further off from their place
of birth, those who pull up their barque every day on
other shores, know better each day the course of things
illegible. . . .
  SAINT-JOHN PERSE

  —*. . . Where are you going, master?*
  —*I don't know, I said. I only want to leave here,*
    incessantly leave here; only thus will I reach my goal.
  —*So, you know your goal?*
  —*Yes, I replied, have I not already told you? My goal*
    is to leave here. . . .
  FRANZ KAFKA

THE PASSAGE analyzed here is taken from the *Yoma* tractate of the Babylonian Talmud. *Yoma* is the Aramaic word that means "the day." "The day," the day par excellence, the Great Day: *Yom Kippur* (Day of Atonement). So, it is a tractate on *Yom Kippur*: we find there a detailed description of all the laws and rituals of this day, a reflection on pardon and repentance (*Teshuvah*). The ceremonies of this day take place mainly within the confines of the Temple. We find, in passing, in the middle of the tractate, several passages concerning the architecture of the Temple, the utensils that can be found there, etc. Our text is a part of the latter. We can distinguish three parts: The first, from "Rav Judah" to "invisible" (A), is a text from the *Gemara* whose author, Rav Judah, is an *amora*. The second part, "A *Baraita* . . . between my breasts" (B), is a *Baraita*, and thus a Tannaic text whose author is a doctor of the *Mishnah*.

The third part (C) is a discussion between *amoraim*. It constitutes the whole of the final section of the text, starting from "Rav Kattina. . . ."

FIRST PART (A)

Rav Judah introduces the following contradiction:

It is written, on the one hand: "The ends of the staves
were visible." And on the other hand it is also written:
"They could not be seen without." How is this
contradiction possible? Visible and invisible!

I

Architecture

THE ABOVE text makes up one and a quarter lines of a page of the traditional edition (the Vilna edition) of the Talmud: i.e., sixteen words. Sixteen words to describe transcendence!

Before we broach this theme, it is necessary, first of all, to explain the immediate meaning of the text. The latter functions by a series of more or less direct references. The biblical or Talmudic quotation in a text of the Talmud is an open door leading from the textual space of one book to the textual space of another. This intertextuality, this practice of quoting, confers on each text—even if there are only sixteen words—an infinite density.

It is as if Rav Judah were playing on a two-manual keyboard, never playing one note without playing the corresponding note on the other manual. The first of these manuals is the book of Kings, chapter 8, verse 8; the second is chapter 25 of the book of Exodus.

First Reference: 1 Kings 8:8

> And they lengthened the staves, so that the ends of the staves were seen out in the *Kodesh* (holy place) before the *Devir* (oracle), and they were not seen without: and there they are unto this day.

The verse recounts the end of the episode of the transferring of the Holy Ark (*Aron ha-kodesh*) from the hill of Zion to that of Jerusalem, at the time of the inauguration of the Temple (*Beit hamikdash*) built by King Solomon. The Holy Ark was brought to the place assigned to it, the Holy of Holies (*Kodesh-Kodashim*); the text then says: "They enlarged the staves. . . ."

Second Reference: Exod. 25:1–22

Architectural Background

The part of the book of Exodus entitled *Terumah* describes in detail the materials, the plans, the measurements of the different items used in the construction of the sanctuary, the *Mishkan*.

To sum up, we learn that the Holy Ark is a rectangular box of acacia wood covered in pure gold outside and inside, two and a half *Amot*[1] (1.25 meters) long by one and a half *Amah* (0.75 meters) wide and high. The Ark contains the Law. Two carrying staves, the *Badim*, are fitted and not fixed in the rings (*Taba'ot*) on the shorter side. The staves too are made of acacia wood and covered with pure gold. A pure gold lid covers the Ark: the *Kaporet*. Two cherubim (*Keruvim*) emerge from this cover. The cherubim and the cover are made of one piece (*Miqshah*). The cherubim, situated at either end, face each other: "Their faces look one to another." A strange gaze. Oblique. A double gaze toward the Law and toward Others.

Topographical Background

The central and main part of the *Mishkan* and of the *Beit ha-Mikdash* is the *Ohel-Mo'ed*: the "meeting tent" or (Tabernacle). It is made up of two unequal areas—a large area, the *Heykhal* or the *Kodesh*; a small area, the *Devir* or the *Kodesh-Kodashim*—the Holy and the Holy of Holies. A heavy veil, the *Parokhet*, creates a separation between these two spaces.[2] The Holy Ark, its staves, and its lid are situated in the *Kodesh-Kodashim*.

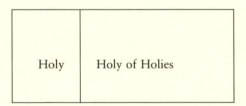

Notes

1. *Amot*: plural of *Amah* = cubit ≃ 50 cm.
2. Exod. 26:31.

II

Visible and Invisible:
The Contradiction

"Rav Judah Rami . . ."

The expression *Rami* introduces a contradiction between two parts of a single verse, an internal contradiction, or between two distinct verses, an external contradiction.

In our text the contradiction is internal. In practical terms, what is this contradiction?

To speak of visible and invisible is to refer to a person, a viewpoint, a subject of vision, a point of origin. The verse of the book of Kings says: "in the holy place before the oracle." The point sought is situated in the *Kodesh* in sight of the *Devir*. In sight of: that means where the line of sight leads toward . . . Toward the *Devir*; in the direction of the veil.

Verse 22 of chapter 25 of Exodus helps us to define this point. This verse follows those which describe the Ark, its lid, and its staves; verse 22 says:

> And there (*Sham*) I shall come to meet you; there, from between the cherubim
> . . .

The *there* (*Sham*) of this verse indicates the meeting point. The analysis of the different commentaries shows the coincidence of the viewpoint and this "meeting point."

Sham is the place of transcendence![1] We shall call "being-in-the-*there*" the fact of being situated at this point.

"Being-in-the-There" as the Scene of Contradiction

The carrying staves (*badim*) are the objects offered up for "seeing" and not for "not-seeing." Verse 8 of the book of Kings can be read as an answer to the question: What can a person situated in the veil perceive of the staves of the Holy Ark? The detailed answer of verse 8 can be expressed as follows: *first part*, the ends of the staves are visible; *second part*, the ends of the staves are not visible—thus prompting the question. The simultaneity of the visibility and invisibility of the same thing arouses questioning: How is it possible? How is the case set out? Contrary to the classical approach of the Talmud, which solves the contradiction by dissociating the conflicting cases into two separate cases (a spatial or temporal difference is evoked), Rav Judah answers the contradiction with another contradiction:

—Visible and invisible?
—How is it possible?
—Visible and invisible!

The will to make the two opposites coexist at the same time, the refusal of the diachronization of the cases, opens up a dialectic of the Visible and Invisible that is not resolved by a third term and whose force and meaning arise in the infinite tension underlying it.[2] The "Being-in-the-there" belongs to the Visible-Invisible contradiction. Being-in-the-movement-of-transcendence consists in seeing and not seeing at the same time. The *Nirin-veeyn-nirin* is the expression of transcendence.

Notes

1. The meaning of the word *sham* is in the verse "here" and "there." When God is speaking to Moses of the projected meeting, *sham* indicates a time posterior and a future place (since the *Mishkan* has not yet been built) and so an "over-there" in time and space. But at the time of the actual meeting, the "here" of the meeting is still the *sham*; the "here," the place of transcendence, can only be a "there." In these two letters, *sham* reveals all the distance, the radical separation that the metaphysical relationship implies. In the *sham* there is the necessary rupture for the relationship of alterity.

2. We shall show, later, that in fact it is not a question of a dialectic, in the Hegelian sense of the word.

III

Different Modes of Perception of Revelation

Listening and Seeing

Talmudic tradition suggests two principal orientations concerning the possibility of perceiving the Word of Revelation: *listening* and *seeing*. These two modalities are introduced into Midrashic literature concerning the verse: "And all the people saw the voices . . ." (Exod. 20:18).[1]

The *Mekhilta—Midrash Halakhah* on Exodus—teaches:

> And the whole people saw the voices. . . .
> Rabbi Akiva was discussing with Rabbi Ishmael:
> Rabbi Ishmael said: This verse means that the people saw what was to be seen and heard what was to be heard (*Roin hanireh veshomein hanishma*).
> Rabbi Akiva said: This verse means that the people saw and heard the visible (*Roin veshomein hanireh*)[2]

What can a verse setting out the "seeing of voices" mean, wonders Rabbi Ishmael? Nothing, a priori; so we have to understand that the verse is elliptical. The word "hear" is missing. Hearing is not mentioned, perhaps to indicate that real listening is always situated in the "unsaid of the said," in the "saying-between" (*entre-dire*) or in the "inter-dict" (*inter-dit*). At first, the interpretation of Rabbi Akiva seems more audacious: let the text be as given, he says. Its meaning is that of the "seeing of voices" and the "listening to images." The voice becomes an image and the image a voice. . . . It is not only a question of poetry. Dealing with this verse, the *Zohar*[3] speaks of voices that are embodied. Historically, this would mean that there was, during the epiphany at Sinai, a vision of the letters of the revealed word, in other words, a miracle. The teaching of Rabbi Akiva and that of Rabbi Ishmael, seen in this light, would be a historical revelation of the events that took place during the Revelation. But the frequenting of Talmudic texts has taught us that the teaching of the Talmudic Masters only secondarily concerns the historical event. The Revelation commented on by the *Midrash* or the Talmud is never the historical revelation (whatever actually took place at the foot of Mount Sinai remains of secondary importance).

The questions raised by Rabbi Akiva and Rabbi Ishmael are: What is the meaning of the idea of Revelation in general? What is the meaning of transcendence? What are its modalities? What is the manner (or manners) of being necessary to participate in them? Listening or seeing? *Mahloket*, again! In this discussion, rather than the radical exclusion of one of the two terms, it is the insistence on one of the two that is is emphasized. Rabbi Ishmael insists on the idea of listening . . .

To say "listening" is to evoke the "mouth-ear" relationship: orality. In Deut. 4:15, Moses says: "Take great care what you do, therefore: since you saw no shape on that day at Horeb when YHVH spoke to you from the midst of the fire."

We can also read: "Face-to-face, God *spoke* to you." In the text quoted from Deuteronomy, the Master of Revelation insists on the fact that Revelation is speech and not an image offered up to the eyes. And if, in Scripture, the words referring to Revelation are borrowed from visual perception, the appearing of God is reduced to a verbal message (*Dvar Elohim*) . . . Even Moses, upon whom the Torah confers the dignity of the greatest of prophets, even Moses, who had the most direct relationship with God—called "face-to-face" (Exod. 33:11)—is refused the vision of the divine Face. Only the "back parts" of God are revealed.[4] Hence: listening . . . Prophetic listening or internal listening . . .

Rabbi Akiva asserts that the approaching of Revelation is carried out through the idea of vision.

Before we go any further with this analysis, it would certainly be profitable to remember that Rav Yehuda—author of the *Nirin veeyn Nirin*—is the "grand-disciple" (in the way we speak of a grandson) of Rabbi Akiva.[5]

That being the case, the question of Revelation in visual terms is addressed as much to Rabbi Akiva as to Rav Judah. The expression "visible and invisible" should doubtless be situated in the wake of the "seeing of voices." Rabbi Akiva and Rav Judah refer to the same tradition. What does it teach? The simplicity, or even the banality, of the answer we offer may seem disconcerting if all its implications are not weighed up.

The "seeing of voices," the "flesh of the letter," is *writing*. The material aspect of writing. The voice that becomes flesh is the *text*. The voice that can be seen is the *letter*.

Emmanuel Lévinas[6] says, concerning this discussion of the *Mekhilta*, that, for Rabbi Ishmael, this seeing of the visible and this listening to the audible means that

> revelation is hearing the audible, hearing a saying, no longer seeking the unknown in a visible form, no longer grasping in the form of an image. It is a voice that orders and commands, that narrates and teaches. Transcendence appears in the dimension of the discourse and in the hindthoughts (*arrière-pensées*) of meaning—which are not mythological worlds behind the scene

(*arrière-mondes*)—and proximity is promised as listening, that is to say, as meditation and questions, obeying and, doubtless, justice. But revelation and truth probably also come down both to seeing that which is shown and, when it comes to seeing, keeping strictly to that which is seen in its rigorous univocity without introducing anything legendary and/or bookish.[7] It is a transcendence without idols and an experience without mythology, true religion and authentic knowing. It is the division of the mind into Jewish wisdom and Greek wisdom.

The expression of Rabbi Ishmael, apparently tautological, insists on the fact that Revelation "should never be a suspending of good sense or the confusion of senses."

As for Rabbi Akiva, for whom "the people saw and heard the visible," seeing is the major part of Revelation. Rabbi Akiva refines his expression, adding this: "There is no word that came out of the mouth of the Almighty and that was not engraved on the tables, as it is said: 'The voice of YHVH divides the flames of fire.'"[8] The voice engraved in stone. "The visible would then be the voice become writing! To hear the voice of the Lord at Sinai would be to pass via letters! So it is a matter of a passing from the visible of the world to the audible of language that tells of the world and discovers its meaning or lends it to the visible; but, also, it is a transition from the audible of language to the visible of the book."[9]

Rav Judah continues in the *Nirin veeyn Nirin* the reflection of Rabbi Akiva. For these two Masters, the purely visible is an insignificant and bare space, still a desert. Through the verse and the book, the desert becomes a world that will "tell the glory of an invisible God." It is through the unfolding of the Book that the desert literally bursts open, explodes, to become, in turn, a book.

Does not the incarnation of the voice that the *Zohar* speaks of offer, in a way, a denial of repressing, forgetting, the scorn of the body that Rabbi Ishmael outlined? Is not the body of the voice, in one way, a rehabilitation of writing in its material form? Is that not a way of elevating it above a secondary and instrumental function?

The "relation to the book," promoted to the rank of a philosophical and ontological category by Revelation, is a "relation-with-the-materiality-of-the-book." That is, perhaps, the teaching of Rabbi Akiva.

Notes

1. It is the verse that follows immediately after the "Ten Words"; it is, in the Bible, the verse that is the closest to the Revelation. The grammatical anomaly should also be pointed out: the subject (people) is in the singular; the verb (to see) is in the plural (*roim*).

2. A. Y. Heschel, *Theology of Ancient Judaism* (New York: Soncino, 1962), cf. 2:22.

3. 3:81a and b, par. 296, *Hasulam* edition.

4. E. Lévinas, *L'Au-delà du verset* (Paris: Éditions de Minuit, 1982), p. 174.

5. *Kiddushin* 72b.

6. "Exégèse et culture," notes on a verse, *Cahiers du Nouveau commerce* no. 55 (Spring 1983): 89–94.

7. Lévinas translates thus the expression of Rabbi Ishmael.

8. Ps. 29:7.

9. Lévinas, "Exégèse et culture."

IV

The *Parokhet*: The Text, the "Trace"

WHAT IS the *Parokhet*, this veil that separates and bears the visible and the invisible? In fact, the *Parokhet* constitutes, in itself, the visible and the invisible. The invisible in question is not a "world beyond," a world that is not and never will be given to be known; "the invisible is writing in abeyance" (Edmond Jabès). The *Parokhet*—the veil, the fabric, the texture—is the text. The visible-invisible is that which is given to be seen in the gaze directed toward the veil. The text is the scene of the "visible-invisible."[1]

The "invisible, writing in abeyance," is somewhat like a woman who is expecting, with the difference, however, that giving birth to the invisible is not an event in life but life itself.

The invisible is the word that lives secretly beneath the word, the text beneath the text, the text in the word, the book(s) within the book; the "seeing of listening" is the reading of words behind the words.

Rabbi Ishmael said: "We have to hear what there is to be heard and see what there is to be seen." In other words, we should not seek to hear or to see beyond what is given: it is basic, simple listening, immediate seeing. Rabbi Ishmael translates his own attitude by the expression: *Dibrah Torah Kileshon benei adam* (the Torah speaks the language of men). For Rabbi Akiva and Rav Judah, the invisible is *beyond the text*: *sham*, both here and there. The semantic duality given in verse 22[2] confers on the word *sham* the possibility of expressing the simultaneity of the here and the elsewhere, of the "here" of the text and its "over there" (*là-bas*), of its visible and its invisible. Consequently, the most accurate translation of the "being in the *sham*" would be: "being-in-the-here/there."[3]

The transcendence described by the *Nirin veeyn Nirin* is a relation to the text where a meaning that is "other" filters through the literal meaning. "Seeing without seeing" defines faith, the acceptance of the existence "of a possible meaning (*pouvoir-dire*) in the intended meaning (*vouloir-dire*)." The "meaning other"—the *Drash*—hidden in the visible text, shows itself without showing itself, appears without appearing, is revealed without being revealed; visible and invisible: it is the Enigma.[4]

We can probably say that Rav Judah agrees with Abbaye who, in the name of Rabbi Joshua ben Levi, attributes to the interpretation of *Midrash* (soliciting of meaning) the power of forcing open the secret of transcendence.[5]

Rav Judah confronts one contradiction with another in an infinite dialectic. The "meaning other" remains irremediably invisible; the other meaning, even if it is unveiled—if it passes through the veil—is ever absent. The *Nirin veeyn Nirin* is unveiled as being unveilable. The contradiction now lies in a relation to the text that "is a relation with an absence radically withdrawn from unveiling and dissimulation." In short, the *Nirin veeyn Nirin* is the Talmudic expression for Lévinas's "trace."

The "Verse's beyond" means that

> the utterance being commented exceeds the intended meaning (*vouloir-dire*) it originates from, that its possible meaning (*pouvoir-dire*) goes beyond its intended meaning, that it contains more than it contains, that a surplus of meaning, possibly inexhaustible, remains enclosed in its groups of words, in its vocables, phenomena, and letters, in all this materiality of saying, ever virtually signifying.[6]

The "trace," that is to say, the visible-invisible contradiction, means that the surplus of meaning contained in the *Nirin* is never exhausted. The *Eyn Nirin* is inexhaustible, infinite. Consequently, in Lévinas's sentence, we should strike out the "perhaps" of the "perhaps inexhaustible." The exhausting of the meaning other would destroy the idea of trace and transcendence. The exhausting of the *Eyn Nirin* would make the extraordinary fall back into order and so the *Other* would be absorbed into the *Same*. The exhausting, the death of the *Eyn Nirin* would mean the thematization of the so-called first meaning—or the last meaning other—and hence its own death. The distance that separates the *Nirin* from the *Eyn Nirin* is infinite; never will the invisible become stranded in the visible.

The *Nirin veeyn Nirin* is the only place where transcendence is the "one opening where the meaning of the transcendent does not annul the transcendence to make it enter into an immanent order, but where, on the contrary, the transcendence is maintained as a transcendence ever 'gone by' of the transcendent."[7]

Notes

1. Even more radically, we could say that the *Nirin veeyn Nirin* is the modality whereby the text is a text.

2. Cf. n. 1, chap. 2.

3. That we could also call "being utopian."

4. In Lévinas's sense of the word, *En découvrant l'existence avec Husserl et Heidegger* (Paris: Vrin, 1974), p. 209.

5. Cf. E. Lévinas, *L'Au-delà du verset* (Paris: Éditions de Minuit, 1982), p. 135.

6. Ibid.

7. Lévinas, *En découvrant l'existence avec Husserl et Heidegger*, p. 198.

V

New Faces

Rabbi Eliezer said: If all the seas were made of ink, all the ponds planted with calamus reeds, if the sky and the earth were parchments, and if all men practiced the art of writing, they would not exhaust the Torah I have learned, whereas the Torah itself is only diminished as much as the tip of a brush dipped into the sea.
  Avot by Rabbi Nathan, chap. 25.

THE INEXHAUSTIBILITY of meaning is made possible, first, by the very specificity of the Hebrew language. This specificity consists in a purely consonantal writing; the invisibility expresses a certain relationship with the visible in the way that absence refers to presence. The vowels are there in their absence: "this writing punctuated by absence" opens up to transcendence. Even the first text does not exist but has to be created; reading is in itself an act of creation. The *Nirin veeyn Nirin* is the continuous creation of reading, of successive readings. No reading should be identical to the preceding one. Each reading, each study, gives birth to "new faces."

This idea allows us, in one way, to understand why the thinking of the "visible-invisible" is essentially structured around the carrying staves (*badim*). The latter should never be removed, in accordance with the verse "The staves shall be in the rings of the Ark: they shall not be taken from it (*lo yasuru mimenu*)."[1] The interdiction of taking out the staves even when they are not in use confers on them a symbolic character. The journey of the Ark is never over; it is an infinite journey of meaning that we call the "dynamism of meaning." The "dynamism of meaning" is the impossibility of exhausting the meaning of an idea, of a law, of a *Mitzvah*. It is, above all, a supreme refusal of thematization.

Note

1. Exod. 25:15 and cf. also Maimonides, *Sefer Hamitzvot*, "*lo ta'aseh*," no. 86.

VI

Confronted with the Text . . .

> To be is to interrogate.
> It is to interrogate in the labyrinth of the question we
> ask others and God and that does not bear any answer.
> EDMOND JABÈS

THE *Nirin veeyn Nirin* as an enigma places man in an interrogative attitude before the text. The search for *Drash*, for the meaning other, is carried out by questioning. Only an "interrogative thought" makes the verse's beyond, the dynamism of meaning, the new faces possible. Confronted with the text, man (*Adam*) does not say, "I think, therefore I am," but *"I question, therefore I am."* Questioning brings man and the world into existence;[1] the thinking of the Cabala goes even further in this assertion: the *Adam*-being is the question itself (the *Mah* of *Adam* and the *Mah* of the question are identical).[2] That being the case, we can say that the "being-in-the-there" is "being-in-the-*Mah*." In one way, the expression is a pleonasm, since being is already defined by *Mah*. Questioning makes the text and man exist in that it makes them confront each other and, in the same tearing away, level themselves out.

The revelation of the text and the revelation of interrogative reality are one and the same revelation. Questioning tears the "other meanings," the "other faces," from beyond the text where they hide. Thus, interrogation promotes the existence of the text, of the world, and of man. Confronted with the text, man is *Adam-Mah*, an interrogative existence that gives rise to the total possibility of possibilities; it is the text as a total possibility of possibilities that rises up, called up by the interrogative; it is to the present totality that the interrogation is addressed, even if it concerns only precise points; human (*Adam*) reality is a questioning of the text to bring it back to life, make it present, elevate it to existence. The *Nirin veeyn Nirin*, or the presence-absence of meaning. The presence of a "face" is an interrogation of the absence of "other faces."

The interrogation of the "being-in-the-there" realizes transcendence. Questioning enables being to attain the status of "being-in-the-there." Not only does the appearance of interrogation distinguish human real-

ity from other existents, but, even more, within this human reality it
creates a split between man and *Adam*-man. The *Adam*-being withdraws himself from all the forms he could take on. Perpetually beyond,
he escapes, in his incessant search for "new faces," all positivity, all
thematization, all given.

The concept of "new faces" (*Panim Hadashot*) is essentially "halakhic." It means that a transformation—internal or external—of an object or of a living being implies a change in the "halakhic" status of this
object or living being. It is particularly concerning the "pure and impure" and the "edible and inedible" that this concept intervenes.[3] In all
these cases, the term "face" is considered figuratively and means the
appearance, the modality, the expression. "New faces" can then be understood as a "new appearance" or "new modality."

There is, however, a case where the face preserves its literal meaning.
Moreover, it is interesting to note that the author of the expression in
this precise case is Rav Judah bar Yeheskel, the author of *Nirin veeyn
Nirin*. We can read in the *Ketuvot* tractate, 7b and 8a: "Our rabbis
taught: The blessing of the bridegrooms (*sheva berakhot*) is said in the
presence of ten persons on each of the seven days. Rav Judah said: And
that is only if new guests (faces) come." That means that the "seven
benedictions" recited during the first week of the marriage after each
meal can be pronounced only in the presence of a *minian* (ten persons),
on the one hand, and, on the other, of "new faces." Each day of the
week, with each new meal, a person who was absent the day before
should be present at the meal, thus constituting "new faces."

The fact that *Panim Hadashot* is a concept developed in the Talmud
from a more general social relationship (ten people being the archetype
of social existence) and the fact that these social gatherings are organized around the meal should be analyzed. In Jewish tradition, the meal
is considered as a rite of renewal. In fact, "eating" is the accomplishing
of the fundamental act of the renewing of life. By absorbing and assimi-
lating external matter, the body carries out an operation of the "conversion of energy where the worn organic elements are replaced by new
ones, thanks to which it ensures its own renewal. In Judaism, eating is a
fundamental ritual act. To this ritual meaning of the act of eating, the
meal eaten in community adds the dimension of a social rite. When people
gather together to eat, a specific community is created between them
where each one, while preserving his own individuality, shares with the
others the same fundamental experience, that of the renewing of life."[4]

Of all meals, only that of the *Sheva Berakhot* necessarily requires the
presence of ten persons (for the other meals, the presence of ten persons
is desirable, but not necessary). The meal (rite of renewal) in the presence of ten people (the Jewish archetype of society) creates, as concerns
these "seven nuptial benedictions," an atmosphere of the renewal of

society. In other words, there is a setting that allows the bride and groom, the smallest social unit, to be conscious of the necessity, or even the obligation, of renewal in the relationship. The "new faces" of the guests should be viewed by the bride and groom as their own faces.

The notion of *Panim Hadashot* can also be understood in another way. The first week of marriage symbolically prefigures the time to come of the relationship. This time to come of the relationship will also be marked by a renewal which is even more radical than that of the meal: the birth of children. In this prefiguration of the time to come (*à-venir*), which is the first week, the presence of one child, of the "new face," is already there, in one way.

The newcomer, the being yet to come (*à-venir*), is not simply an additional person but a person who counts, who is counted, who makes up the number (*minian*). The weight of the person should, according to Rav Judah, be symbolically marked, but also effectively in the time of the project of the inaugural week. The person who presents his *Panim Hadashot* makes the weight of his presence felt, by the very fact of his newness, by the necessity of his newness. Without him the group loses its meaning as a group. The presence has a meaning because it is revealed. A presence that is already present becomes a nonspecific presence, and thus absence. The "new faces" mean that the appearance of an Other, radically other, must be envisaged in the context of the relation to Others. This radicality is symbolically made possible here by the existence of an inside and an outside. The "new faces" are significant if they come from outside the ready-made social field (the ten persons). It is by this coming from outside that the person has the status of "new faces." But in this passing from the outside to the inside, the new person is integrated into the group and thereby loses his present presence. This loss of the meaning of the presence is due to time, since it is only the "following day" that there is a non-sense. Rashi points this out: "who were not there the preceding day."

The Tosafists' commentary adds an important element: "On the *Shabbat* day, the *Panim Hadashot* are not necessary, for the *Shabbat* is, in itself, *Panim Hadashot*."

The author of the book *Ta'amei Haminhagim* (The meanings of the customs), Rabbi Abraham Isaac of Lvov, adds that the *Drasha*, the commentary (certainly in the sense of *Hidush*, the renewal of meaning), is also an equivalent of the *Panim Hadashot*.

Notes

1. J. Delhomme, *La Pensée interrogative* (Paris: PUF, 1954), pp. 8–9; cf. also G. Bernheim: "La Voix et l'Écriture," in *La Bible au présent* (Paris: Gallimard,

1982), pp. 219f.: "There are two main schools of thought in rabbinical tradition: that of *theological thought* and that of *interrogative thought*. Theological thought attempts to answer men's questions. When interrogative thought functions, usually—I do not mean only—it turns out afterwards that there is no form of answer to the questions that men ask, but simply a form of reinterrogation, of putting back into shape of the questions that the Scripture of Revelation poses. We are confronted with anxiety, with the questioning of men, and the questioning of Revelation. The relations between these two questionings call upon new concepts. That is the case of Hasidic thought and, even more so, of the Cabala of the nineteenth and the beginning of the twentieth centuries in Lithuania."

2. Introduction to the *Tikkunei Zohar*.

3. Cf., for example, *Zevahim* 96a and *Avodah Zarah* 75b, especially in the commentaries of the Tosafists.

4. S. Moses, *Système et révélation. La philosophie de Franz Rosenzweig* (Paris: Seuil, 1982), p. 199.

VII

The "There" and the Name

> Never say that you have arrived; for, everywhere, you will
> be a traveler in transit.
> EDMOND JABÈS

IT IS NOT without interest to ask oneself why the scene of transcendence, the scene of questioning, the *sham*, also means (in some respects) the Name. The two letters *shin* and *mem*, which make up the word *sham*, express both a place when it is punctuated by an *a* and the Name (or name) when it is punctuated by an *e*.

The *Nirin veeyn Nirin* is thought out from a particular space: that of the *Kodesh/Kodesh-Kodashim*; why?

The remarks that follow may help us to answer these two questions. The masters of the Cabala[1] teach the relation of the "Name" and the "place." Through a play on figures and letters, these masters tell us that the *Hekhal* or *Kodesh* is a Name (is the Name); in the same way the *Devir* or *Kodesh-Kodashim* is a Name (is the Name). Yet a distinction has to be made between these two Names, for *Ha-Shem* (the Name) has two Names:

1. The Name known as *Shem-Havayah*, usually translated by the Tetragram

2. The Name known as *Shem-Adnut*, which can also be translated by the Tetragram since it has four letters

And yet only the first one receives this name. In fact, it is better not to translate them and to keep them in the form of the expressions *Shem-Havayah* and *Shem-Adnut*. The former, which is also called *Shem Hameforash*, the "Name explained," is written as *Yod-Heh-Vav-Heh*. The second one is written *Aleph-Dalet-Nun-Yod*.

The masters teach that the *Shem-Havayah* is the space of the *Kodesh-Kodashim*, whereas the *Shem-Adnut* is that of the *Kodesh*. The *Shem-havayah* has a privilege "that consists in this strange condition for a name, which is never to be pronounced. The *Shem-Adnut* that, in turn, should never be pronounced in vain is the Name. The Name has a Name!"[2]

Emmanuel Lévinas rightly remarks that "the name here has the value of a proper noun and so the revelation by the proper noun is not only a corollary of the oneness of being; it leads us further perhaps, beyond being. First, through the proper noun, it is the assertion of a relation which is irreducible to knowing that thematizes or defines, or synthesizes; it is to understand revelation as a modality which, paradoxically, preserves the transcendence of that which reveals itself."[3]

The *Nirin veeyn Nirin*, expressed in a place that is a *name*, and in particular a *proper noun*, says precisely this particular form of transcendence that is revealed without being shown. The *Nirin veeyn Nirin* is this withdrawal that is contemporaneous with presence.

The duality of the Name—written and said—introduces a gap, a distance, separation (holiness), and alterity: an abyss between writing and reading. The *Parokhet*-text is the support of this abyss.

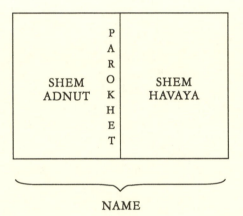

NAME

The inexistence of the veil represents the suppression of the gap between the "said" and the "written," between the *Torah she-be-al peh* and the *Torah shebikhtav*. The "here," as the hither side of the beyond (owing to the veil), means that the *Nirin veeyn Nirin* is situated in the tension between the "said" and the "written."[4] The "there" has its place in orality, in the commentary.[5] This orality should be understood in its reference to a writing. The *Shem Adnut* is sense-less (*in-sensé*) without the *Shem Havayah*. All the problems of the relation of the Written Law to the Oral Law should be thought out in this light. Transcendence by the *Nirin veeyn Nirin* can and should be thought through only in the context of this problematic. "The Text-*Parokhet*, writing punctuated by absence, outlines a sort of modality of transcendence. The square letters are a precarious dwelling whence the revealed Name is already withdrawing. But this uncertain epiphany, on the verge of evanescence, is just the one that man alone can grasp. And that is why

he is the essential moment of this transcendence and of its manifestation."[6] Let us note further that the *Shem Havayah* is also called *Shem
Mah* (according to the numerical value of its letters when developed).[7]
The Name that is written without being pronounced is the question of
questions, the question par excellence and the foundation of all questions. The *Nirin veeyn Nirin* is transcendence because the *Mah* reflects
the *Mah*.

Notes

1. Cf. *Shaarei ora*, by Rabbi Joseph Gikatillia (Warsaw ed.), p. 24.
2. E. Lévinas, *L'Au-delà du verset* (Paris: Éditions de Minuit, 1982), p. 150.
3. Ibid., p. 148.
4. It is in fact this tension itself.
5. Since topographically (and typologically . . .) in the *Shem Adnut*.
6. Lévinas, *L'Au-delà du verset*, p. 149.
7. Cf. *Kol Hanevua*, Rabbi David ha-Kohen, M. Kook, 1978, p. 224.

SECOND PART (B)

"*A* Baraita *gives a parallel teaching . . .*"

The parallel teaching of a Baraita is never a mere repetition of the preceding passage. Under the appearance of being very close to the parallel text, it is in fact a commentary of the latter. The *Baraita*, commenting verse 8 of chapter 8 of the first book of Kings, is going to work from two hypotheses that are, in turn, refuted. The Talmudic expression of the refuting-hypothesis is *Yakhol . . . Talmud lomar.*

Yakhol introduces the hypothesis and means "we could," which is an abbreviation of the expression "we could have said" (believed, thought).

Talmud lomar introduces the refutation by a verse (or a quotation).

I

The Structure of the Text

The Two Hypotheses

Hypothesis I

> I could have thought that the staves were not moved from their place. The verse "They lengthened the staves" refutes this hypothesis.

From the fact that the staves were visible, according to the verse "The ends of the staves were visible," *Yakhol*, I could have thought that they were visible without being moved, and so without being slid in the rings. The verse that teaches the visibility of the staves does not say in what position they were visible. Perhaps they were visible in their usual position? And yet another part of the verse teaches (refutation-teaching) *Talmud lomar*: "They lengthened the staves," and so it was necessary to slide the staves in the rings in order for them to be seen.

Hypothesis II

> I could have thought that the staves tore the curtain and protruded. The verse "They could not be seen without" refutes this hypothesis.

From the preceding conclusion where we learn that the staves were slid in the rings, *Yakhol*, I could have thought that the staves tore the veil and protruded so they could be seen from outside, as is said in the verse "The ends of the staves were visible." *Talmud lomar*, they were not visible from outside; refutation, the veil was not torn, and the staves could not be seen from outside according to the verse "They could not be seen from without."

The Contradiction and the Solution Suggested

The conclusions and the refutation-hypotheses are contradictory. First, we concluded that the staves were visible and that it was necessary to slide them. Second, we concluded that they were not visible from the outside. We end up with the contradiction expressed by Rav Judah, to the same questioning: *Ha Ketsad?* "How is the case presented? How is it possible?"

Same subject, same problematics—that of the visible and invisible; the *Baraita* differs from Rav Judah's thought in two important aspects. First in the procedure: it takes a detour via the refutation-hypotheses. Then by the question that the *Baraita* outlines in an attempt to solve the contradiction: "the image of the breasts." It is the analysis of these two points that makes the *Baraita* a commentary of the thought of Rav Judah.

The Detour via the Refutation-Hypotheses

Rav Judah	Baraita
—The ends of the staves are visible	A: —Hypothesis: the staves do not slide. —Refutation: they lengthened the staves.
—The ends of the staves are not visible	B: —Hypothesis: the veil was torn. —Refutation: they could not be seen from without

The difference between the first statement (Rav Judah) and the second (the *Baraita*) lies in the contrasts involved. In the first statement there is a single contrast, that of "seeing" and "nonseeing": visible/invisible. In the second statement, two contrasts:

1. slide/do not slide
2. torn/not torn (expressed by the nonvisible).

Which contrast is the second statement talking about? The fundamental contrast: visible/invisible, which, however, is not very clear. The detour via the refutation-hypotheses consists in turning away from, bypassing, "seeing" (positive or negative). Does this mean to say that it is impossible to approach visibility/invisibility without first turning away? The *Baraita* seems to attest it.

Here are the different stages of this detour:

—do not slide
—slide
—tearing of the veil
—nonvisible

It should be noted that hypothesis number 2 is based on the refutation of number 1: "sliding" implies "seeing," but this "seeing" is not stated. Only "nonseeing" is utterable. Seeing, it implies, is unutterable, since it is already invisible. (We should say, rather, "under-written"— *sous-écrit*, and not "under-stood"—*sous-entendu*, lit.: implied.)

This saying and nonsaying (or the unsaid of the said) teaches that the visible is already withdrawn at the moment it is revealed. The seeing that is concerned in the *Nirin veeyn Nirin* is at the limits of evanescence; the refutation-hypothesis is a form of reflection that goes forward and withdraws: revelation and withdrawal. Through the detour of the refutation-hypotheses, the *Baraita* describes its thinking in the structure that expresses it. The visible is not said, because it is situated outside the *Yakhol-Talmud lomar* structure. The verse "The staves are visible" comes before the first *Yakhol*. It is doubly outside:

1. outside the manifestation-withdrawal structure
2. its withdrawal exposed by the manifestation-withdrawal

The *Baraita*, we said, is commentary. The commentary is thus silence; the visible is silenced because it is outside the demonstration.

II

An Erotic Image

THE DETOUR via the refutation-hypotheses allows the *Baraita* to incorporate in the very structure of its saying the meaning of transcendence as presence-absence. But the interesting and specific contribution of the *Baraita* lies outside of the dialectic of advance and withdrawal. The nodal thought of the *Baraita* is the suggestion of the relationship between transcendence and the erotic:

> They pressed forth and protruded in the veil and were visible as the two breasts of a woman.

After having slid in the direction of the veil, the staves appear in the *Parokhet* as two breasts of a woman. For a person situated in the *Sham*, the vision of the *Nirin veeyn Nirin* takes shape. The picture of the breasts does not resolve the contradiction of the visible and invisible; this image of the breasts that appear under the tunic is not the third term which suppresses the dialectical antinomy. Quite the contrary, the "image of the breasts" defines the tension that unites the terms "visible" and "invisible," the tension existing in the relation of the "here" and the "beyond." In short, the "image of the breasts" defines transcendence. In his commentary, Rashi underlines the fact that the breasts are visible "under a tunic." The breasts are not *bared* but are visible behind the veil of the item of clothing. So the comparison is complete. It is not the form of the breasts that counts, but the form of the breasts hidden from the gaze by a veil. Modesty? Not at all, on the contrary . . . The breasts beneath the veil present a nudity even more naked than that of naked breasts. Paradoxically, this nudity more naked than nudity itself is clothed—nudity under the veil. This nudity is called the erotic: "Is not the most erotic part of the body the part where the clothing gapes? It is intermittency that is erotic, that of the skin which sparkles between two items, between two edges. It is this very sparkling that seduces or else the staging of an appearing-disappearing."[1] The *Nirin veeyn Nirin* is the erotic. Transcendence is this movement in the direction of a "not-yet-being" that will never be; because, as we have said, the invisible never becomes stranded in the visible, without immediately disappearing, retreating. The suppression of the "not-yet" would not promote being; on the contrary, more than a decline, it would be a negation.

Transcendent Being, on the border of being and nonbeing, closer to non-being than to being, "withdraws into [its] future, beyond every possible promised to anticipation."[2]

The *Nirin veeyn Nirin* text and the *Nirin veeyn Shekhinah* is revealed as erotic, as a "not-yet-being" where the "not-yet" is never severed from being. To say that the essence of the *Nirin veeyn Nirin* is the erotic means that the tension which unites the "here" with the "beyond" is *desire*. But this erotic desire should be understood as metaphysical desire; metaphysical desire reaches toward the "not-yet-being" that will never be; it is thus an infinite desire that is never satisfied.[3]

How could one resist . . . the desire to quote, in its entirety, a passage from *Totality and Infinity* entitled "Desire of the Invisible" on the basis of which the relation between the categories of the erotic and transcendence can be thought out:[4]

> Metaphysical desire desires beyond everything that can simply complete it. It is like goodness—the Desired does not fulfill it, but deepens it.
>
> It is a generosity nourished by the Desired, and thus a relationship that is not the disappearance of distance, not a bringing together, or—to circumscribe more closely the essence of generosity and of goodness—a relationship whose positivity comes from remoteness, from separation, for it nourishes itself, one might say, with its hunger. This remoteness is radical only if desire is not the possibility of anticipating the desirable, if it does not think it beforehand, if it goes toward it aimlessly, that is, as toward an absolute, unanticipatable alterity, as one goes forth unto death. Desire is absolute if the desiring being is mortal and the Desired *invisible*.[5]
>
> Invisibility does not denote an absence of relation; it implies relations with what is not given, of which there is no idea. Vision is an adequation of the idea with the thing, a comprehension that encompasses. Nonadequation does not denote a simple negation or an obscurity of the idea, but—beyond the light and the night, beyond the knowledge measuring beings—the inordinateness of Desire. Desire is desire for the absolutely other.
>
> Besides the hunger one satisfies, the thirst one quenches, and the senses one allays, metaphysics desires the other beyond satisfactions, where no gesture by the body to diminish the aspiration is possible, where it is not possible to sketch out any known caress or invent any new caress. A desire without satisfaction that, precisely, understands [*entend*] the remoteness, the alterity, and the exteriority of the other. For Desire this alterity, nonadequate to the idea, has a meaning. It is understood as the alterity of the Other and of the Most-High. The very dimension of height is opened up by metaphysical Desire. That this height is no longer the heavens but the *Invisible*[6] is the very elevation of height and its nobility. To die for the invisible—this is metaphysics. This does not mean that desire can dispense with acts. But these acts are neither consumption, nor caress, nor liturgy.[7]

The "being-in-the-*there*" establishes a relation to the Other mediated by the Text and a relation to the Text mediated by the Other. This double relation is supported by a desire that can be described as erotic insofar as the alterity is not altered, is not impinged upon by any satisfaction, any possession; the Other is "foreign" and therefore free. The metaphysical relation as an erotic relation is liberty.[8]

The relation to the Text is erotic because "being-in-the-*there*" accepts the Text as a manifestation of presence-absence. The "being-in-the-there" confronted with the *Parokhet*-text is *Adam-Mah*: a being in question and a being of the question. An interrogative being, he untiringly calls meaning into question. So we can say that his relation to the text is a "caress," in the sense where "the caress consists in seizing upon nothing, in soliciting what ceaselessly escapes its form toward a future never future enough, in soliciting what slips away as though it *were not yet*. It *searches*, it forages. It is not an intentionality of disclosure but of search: a movement unto the invisible."[9] This calling into question of meaning is aimed at the nonappropriation of meaning—i.e., *of a meaning*—the refusal of thematization. In the relation to the text defined as erotic, the signifying (*significance*) is inexhaustible by virtue of the fact that "the essentially hidden throws itself toward the light, without becoming signification." The infinity of signifying is at the limits of nonsignifying. The text, essentially violable, is inviolable: it is virgin.[10]

The relation to the text is erotic because by its nonthematization, a consequence of the dynamics of meaning, the meaning that is discovered does not lose its mystery. The *Parokhet*-text has an erotic nudity—visible and invisible—that expresses the unutterable. The unutterable is revealed in such a way that its manifestation is its nonmanifestation. Its saying is silence. Erotic, the saying is equivocal.[11] The equivocality of meaning goes beyond the possibility of several meanings. Here "the equivocal does not play between two meanings of speech, but between speech and the renouncement of speech."[12]

The image of the breasts has introduced the category of the erotic into the *Nirin veeyn Nirin*. However, in one way, all these developments on the erotic character of the Text are already contained in the presence-absence dialectic. The commentary of the *Baraita* consists in defining the *Nirin veeyn Nirin*. But the image of the breasts is not simply a metaphor of presence-absence making a place for Eros within transcendence; it tells us—possibly in the first place—that the metaphysical event of Transcendence is accomplished in a relation with the Feminine, that the extreme closeness of feminine alterity is transcendence itself.[13]

Notes

1. Roland Barthes, *Le Plaisir du texte* (Paris: Seuil, 1973), pp. 18–19.
2. E. Lévinas, *Totality and Infinity* (Pittsburgh: Duquesne University Press, 1988), p. 258.
3. Ibid., p. 33.
4. This passage introduces and anticipates a later development entitled "Phenomenology of Eros," pp. 256–66.
5. My italics.
6. My italics.
7. Lévinas, *Totality and Infinity*, p. 34.
8. Ibid., p. 265: "Nothing is further from *Eros* than possession."
9. Ibid., pp. 257–58; my italics.
10. "The feminine is essentially violable and inviolable; the 'Eternal Feminine' is the virgin or an incessant recommencement of virginity, the untouchable in the very contact of voluptuousness, future in the present." Lévinas, *Totality and Infinity*, p. 258.

The light of the *Nirin veeyn Nirin* in the formulation of *Totality and Infinity* sets out the body-of-the-text and the body-of-the-woman in a relationship of equivalence. The relation-to-the-text as the relation to the feminine body is explicit in a Talmudic text from the *Eruvin* tractate, 54b: "With reference to the Scriptural text, 'fair as a hind, graceful as a fawn' (Prov. 5:19), why were the words of the Torah compared to a 'hind'? To tell you that as the hind has a narrow womb and is loved by its mate at all times as at the first hour of their meeting, so it is with the words of the Torah. They are loved by those who study them at all times as at the hour when they first made their acquaintance."

Two important ideas should be underlined: (1) The analogy of study and sexual intercourse; (2) The existence of an erotic and sexual enjoyment—like that of the first time—given by the study of the Torah.

It is actually a question of the "incessant renewal of virginity" here; as a proof, we could quote this commentary by Rabbi Joseph Hayyim of Baghdad: "It is because of the narrowness of its genitals that it is dearer in the eyes of its partner who ever enjoys the taste of virginity, so the Torah, the Holy One, blessed be He, has closed it and occluded it with numerous 'rings,' so that a man can attain its words with truth only by the new faces he innovates (*al yedei hidush hapanim shemehadeshim bah*) . . . ," in: *Sefer Ben Yehoyada* on *Eruvin* 54b (Jerusalem, 1964); *Kol hahalomot holkhim ahar ha-peh*. The analysis of the dream-text as penetration of the object-dream: let us recall that, for the Talmud, interpretation in general and the interpretation of dreams carry out the same movement, unfold the same space.

Another famous text has its place here; it is this Talmudic page from the *Kiddushin* tractate, 30b.

"Rabbi Ishmael taught: My son, if this repulsive wretch (the *yetser hara*: the Evil Desire) assail thee, lead him to the study hall: if he is of stone, he will dissolve; if iron, he will shiver into fragments, for it is said, 'Is not my word like a fire? says the Lord; and like a hammer that breaks the rock in pieces?' (Jer. 23:29)." Rabbi Joseph Hayyim of Baghdad, *Sefer Ben Yehoyada* on *Kiddushin* 30b, asks the following question: "Why lead him and not leave him outside and flee 'without him' to the study hall?" What can be done with the repulsive wretch in the study hall?" The answer is set out by means of a quotation from the *Zohar* (1:138a):

"Rabbi Isaac, son of Rabbi Yose, was going from Kaputkin to Lod. Rabbi Judah met him on the way. Rabbi Issac said to him: 'Tell me, is it true that the companions, the masters of the *Mishnah*, have discussed and concluded that the evil desire will disappear from the world with the exception of the moment of sexual intercourse?' He replied: 'My word! The evil desire is as necessary for the world as rain, because without the evil desire the pleasure of study would not exist. . . .'" R. Joseph of Baghdad comments: "If you meet the wretch who wants you to desire, be jealous, covet earthly pleasures, do not reject and repel him entirely, but lead him to the study hall and use him for a good thing, for there you will make the students of the Torah jealous and your desire will be to expound a reflection and innovate commentaries, and the enjoyment of study will result; for when a thing is closed and difficult to the point that the masters could not explain and clarify it, and you succeed in explaining it by the effort that you put in, it is about this that David said in the Psalms: 'I rejoice in your word, like someone on finding a vast treasure' (Ps. 119:162)."

11. Lévinas, *Totality and Infinity*, p. 255. The originality of the erotic is the equivocal par excellence.

12. Ibid., p. 260.

13. Cf. Chalier, *Figures du féminin* (Paris: Éditions La Nuit surveillée, 1982).

III

Eroticism and Transcendence

A Verse from the Song of Songs

Visible like the two breasts of a woman as it is said: "My
beloved is a sachet of myrrh lying between my breasts."
  Song 1:13

The *Baraita* calls on a verse from the Song of Songs. It is not surprising:
"Of course, the Song of Songs has a mystical interpretation, but for
informed—or uninformed—eyes, because the mysticism of the Song is
not a mystification, it is an erotic text."[1] It is a love song, where the text
is a woman's body and the woman's body unfolds in the text. The Song
is a text-body, and the relationship that the reader has with it is as
much a relationship with the text as a relationship to the body, to the
female body. But the "body" of the song is difficult to catch. It is an
incessant game of hide-and-seek; if there is contact, it is in the caress.
The woman runs after her beloved without ever catching him. The "I
opened . . . he had disappeared" of chapter 6 is a perfect expression of
the relation that is in question in this text: a relation where that which
is revealed immediately retreats. The Song of Songs is an erotic text that
can appropriately "illustrate" the thinking of the *Baraita*. But it would
be interesting to understand, now, why the author of the *Baraita* chose
this verse: "My beloved is a sachet of myrrh, etc." To comprehend the
contribution of this verse, we must understand that "the image of the
breasts" is above all a production of the verse, and not the reverse. In
other words, it is not the "image of the breasts" that evokes the verse;
the verse produces the image, and we shall see how the image *is* in the
verse. The meaning of the image will be analyzed in its production from
the verse, and not only from reality. One might say that the reality of
the text is more real than the visual perception itself. The verse the
Gemara refers to does not have the role of an illustration (as, in fact, is
the case of all quotations), but of a commentary.

  In an initial reading, we shall examine the perfume: "My beloved is a
sachet of myrrh." According to another verse of the Song of Songs, we
can assert that the perfume represents the intangible, the impalpable.
We read, in verse 5 of chapter 5:

Then I rose up to open to my beloved; myrrh ran off my hands, light myrrh off my fingers, on to the handle of the lock.

Rashi comments, the light myrrh, literally the myrrh that passes or the subtle myrrh (*mor over*): the "perfume passes and disperses on all sides." Evanescent is the beloved; an idea which confirms that of the following verse: "I opened . . . he had disappeared." According to this explanation, the quotation appears rather as a repetition of the ideas of the *Baraita*. In fact, the commentary of the verse is not to be found in the notion of perfume. "Maharsha"[2] will, in only *two words*, emphasize the essential aspect of the verse in its relation to the *Baraita; Beyn Shadai*, he says, refers to *Shenei Badei*, or the same letters that spell "between my breasts" (*Beyn Shadai*) also spell "two staves" (*Shenei Badei*). *Beyn Shadai* is spelled *Beit-Yod-Nun Shin-Dalet-Yod*. In the same way, *Shenei Badei* is spelled *Shin-Nun-Yod Beit-Dalet-Yod*.

Is this merely an allusion, a play on words in order to establish a connection between the "staves" and the "breasts"? This commentary does not exclude this idea. But, in following this approach, the allusion tells us nothing new; it only confirms the relation previously described. In fact, "Maharsha" invites us to understand that the important point in this verse lies in the word *Shadai* and leads us, in the same way, to examine the particular polysemic character of this word.

Shadai, read as "my breasts" in the verse of the Song, is immediately understood as *Shadai*, the ninth of the divine Names, according to the *Zohar*.[3] It is interesting to note that this verse from the Song is the only verse where "*Shadai*-breasts" is identical to "*Shadai*-Name."[4] The identification of "*Shadai*-breasts" with "*Shadai*-Name" means that there is a mutual illuminating of the categories of the erotic and transcendence.[5] The quotation from the Song becomes a commentary and loses its simple illustrative character, by the shifting from "*Shadai*-breasts" to "*Shadai*-Name." This shifting is not irreversible, since the commentary lies in the double reading that can be made of *Shadai*, in the relation of eroticism and transcendence. Hence, it is in the analysis of the Name *Shadai* that the verse of the Song completes the information of the *Baraita*. We should add, before going ahead with the study of the Name *Shadai*—as one should do before any investigation of the divine Names —that for the Talmud "the Hebrew terms of the Bible that we translate as God or *Deus* or *Theos* are understood as proper nouns; . . . it is a consequence of monotheism where there is no divine species or generic word to identify it. . . . To approach [God] through a proper noun is to assert a relation which is irreducible to a knowledge that thematizes, defines, or synthesizes it, and that, thereby, signifies the correlative of this knowledge as being, as finite, and as immanent. It is to understand revelation as a modality that, paradoxically, preserves the transcendence of that which is manifested and, consequently, as that which is beyond the capacity of intuition and even of a concept."[6]

Moreover, as Lévinas points out again, quoting Maimonides: "The word designating the divinity is precisely the word *Shem*, a generic word in relation to which all the different names of God are individuals."[7] The other terms that name God—besides the proper nouns which name him, for example: "*ha-Kadosh-Barukh-Hu*," "*Shekhinah*," "Master of the World," "King of the World," etc.—are terms that express relations and not the essence.[8] The proper nouns themselves, such as the Name *Shadai*, name a mode of being or a beyond being rather than a quiddity.[9]

We should now examine the specific meaning of the Name *Shadai*. Several explanations have been advanced on this subject; we shall retain the one that the Talmudic tractate *Hagigah*[10] cites in the name of Resh Lakish:

> Resh Lakish said: What does "I am *El-Shadai*" mean? I am he who said to the world: Enough!

Resh Lakish analyzes *Shadai* by breaking it up into two parts: *She-dai*, literally: "that-enough." The *shin* takes one of its usual meanings, which is that of the relative pronoun; *dai* then adopts the form of the adverb "enough." *Shadai* loses its status as proper noun to take on the form of a relative clause.

> Resh Lakish comments the Name *Shadai*, I am he who said to the world: Enough!

This teaching backs up a thought of Rav Judah in the name of Rav:[11]

> Rav Judah said in the name of Rav: when the Holy One, blessed be He, created the world, the latter stretched out to infinity—like the threads of a loom that endlessly intertwined; then they stopped as it is said: "The pillars of the heavens tremble, they are struck with wonder when he threatens them" (Job 26:11).

The name *Shadai* thus expresses limitation. *Limitation*: the majority of Hasidic masters comment the Name *Shadai* in relation with the *Tsimtsum*. Rabbi Isaac of Berdichev writes:

> *El-Shadai moreh al ha-tsimtsum, al haremez deamrinan bigemara, El Shadai, mi sheamar la-olam: dai!*

Which means, the "Name *El-Shadai* should be understood in relation with (literally: designates) the *Tsimtsum*, according to the allusion (*remez*) of the *Gemara, El Shadai*, he who said to the world: enough!"[12]

Rabbi of Sokhotshov, the author of the *Shem Mishmuel*, wrote, even more radically:

Shadai hu shem ha-tsimtsum.

Which means, "*Shadai* is the Name of *Tsimtsum.*"[13]

We shall be coming back to this idea of *Tsimtsum*, but first we shall make a second remark. In the verse of Exodus[14] where the Name *Shadai* appears, the latter is compared with a term expressing sight (*Reiyah*), which in turn contrasts it with the Tetragram-Name in relation with a term meaning knowledge (*Yediyah*). The verse says:

To Abraham and to Isaac and to Jacob, I appeared as *El-Shadai*, I did not make myself known to them by my Tetragram Name.

The Name *Shadai*: a Name of seeing, a Name that is given to be seen. It is a visible Name: the Name *Shadai* is the Name whose modality of revelation is *Nirin veeyn Nirin*.

Above, we evoked the relation between *Shem Adnut/Shem Havayah* and that of *Kodesh/Kodesh-Kodashim*. The Name *Shadai* would thus be the intermediary Name achieving the transition, the limit between the Name *Havayah* and the Name-*Adnut*. The Name *Shadai* "would be" the *Parokhet*. (In "Hasidic Hebrew," we would say: *ha-Parokhet hi mibelinat Shem Shadai*). According to our preceding analyses, the *Parokhet* is the Text, Writing. The Name *Shadai* would then be the divine Name which expresses the Text, that is to say, not that which expresses the essence of Writing—*Shadai* is not Writing—but the modality Writing uses to reveal itself. If *Shadai* is, on the one hand, "the Name of the *Tsimtsum*" and if, on the other hand, *Shadai* "is" the *Parokhet*-Text, we can say that the Text is *Tsimtsum*.

What does the proposition "the Text is *Tsimtsum*" mean? To answer this question, we have to know first what we mean by *Tsimtsum*.

Tsimtsum: numerous definitions, numerous commentaries follow one after another, confront each other, or complement each other depending on the different schools, the different tendencies of the Cabala. Very simply, we can say that *Tsimtsum* is an idea of Cabalistic speculation developed by Rabbi Isaac Luria in his fundamental work, the *Ets Hayim*.

According to this author, *Tsimtsum* is the idea of the "original contraction" of the Divine that allowed the antinomy of the omnipresence of God and the being of the creature outside of God to be solved. If God is the Totality, how can anything other than him exist? The notion of *Tsimtsum* answers this question, stating that "God contracted himself prior to the creation, to make a place, beside himself, for something other than himself"[15] (We must insist, and repeat: *Tsimtsum* should never be understood in the context of a cosmology. The notion of *Tsim-tsum* is ontological).

According to the author of the *Kuntras Maamarim*,[16] the *Tsimtsum* means the fact of the "infinitive light" (*Or habeli Gevul*), not becoming finite, but *unveiling* itself as "finite and limited light." *Tsimtsum*, in one way, appears as the transition from the Infinite to the finite, and hence the possibility for the Infinite to be perceived. This perception—finite—is almost a paradox in itself; how can Infinity be conceived in a finite way? Absolute Infinity is revealed to man in the unpronounceable Tetragram. Although unpronounceable, the Tetragram is unfaithful to Infinity, because "infinity is more concealed than any secret, and is not to be named by any name, not even the Tetragram, not even by a part of the smallest letter."[17]

The "infinite Light" contracts (*hi metsamtsemet et atsmah*); some authors speak of a "withdrawal," others of "dimming." The contraction of the Infinite leaves a trace, called *Reshimu*. All finite entities bear the trace of the Infinite. This trace is not a new creation; it exists within the Infinite. The Infinite, being infinite, also contains the possibility of finiteness; this possibility is the trace. *Tsimtsum* is the revelation, in the finite, of the trace of the Infinite.[18] The proposition "The text is *Tsimtsum*" is in fact a fundamental idea of the Cabala. The *Ein-Sof*, the divine Infinite, contracts into letters of the Torah in order to be revealed; the text of the Torah is the finite-Infinite. Each letter, each finite element, reveals the trace of the Infinite it contains. That is what the Cabalists mean in the expression "The Torah is the Name of God."[19]

The text-*Parokhet* is the limit-place where infinity borders on finiteness. So the *Parokhet* is the scene of transition, the door to infinity; the *Parokhet-Shadai* is limitation and revelation of infinity. Rabbi Isaac Luria points out that the Name *Shadai* has the particular characteristic of containing another Name. The *ne'elam*, the hidden of the letters *Shadai*, spells the Name *Tsevaot*, by numerical identification; *Shadai: Shin-Dalet-Yod*. Each letter can be spelled out in turn: (*Shin/Yod-Nun*) (*Dalet/Lamed-Tav*) (*Yod/Vav-Dalet*). The numerical value of *ne'elam*—(*Yod-Nun*), (*Lamed-Tav*), (*Vav-Dalet*)—is 500, identical to the numerical value of the Name *Tsevaot*.

The name *Tsevaot* indicates infinite multiplicity (the "classical" translation, "Lord of hosts," does not mean anything at all). So to say *Shadai* is to understand, at the same time, *Tsevaot*. To say limitation (*She-Dai*) amounts to expressing nonlimitation, Infinity. The text-*Parokhet* is the "finite-infinity," the "visible-invisible."

We are now armed to grasp in depth the real meaning of the verse from the Song of Songs. Through the semantic duality of the word *Shadai*, the erotic vision of the breasts behind the veil is commented by an analysis of the finite-infinite relationship. The verse introduces the word *Shadai*, whereby it is no longer possible to think the erotic without transcendence, and vice versa.

Notes

1. E. Lévinas, *Quatre Lectures talmudiques* (Paris: Éditions de Minuit, 1968) p. 162.

2. Rabbi Samuel Eliezer Ha-Levy Edels of Lublin (1560–1631); classical commentaries, printed at the end of the Talmudic tractates.

3. *Zohar*, 3:116a, *Maamar Asarah Shemot*. According to Maimonides— *Livre de la connaissance, Hilkhot Yesodei Hatorah*, chap. 6, par. 2—the number of the divine Names is seven. In this enumeration, the Name *Shadai* occupies the sixth place, the seventh place being occupied by the Name *Tsevaot*. Cf. also E. Lévinas, *L'Au-delà du verset* (Paris: Éditions de Minuit, 1982), p. 146n.4.

4. Cf. Mandelkern, *Veteris Testamenti hebraïcae atque Chaldaïcae Concordantiae*, p. 1150.

5. On the legitimacy of this identification, cf. *Sefat Emet* (Jerusalem, 1971), 2:15. The *Sefat Emet* sees in the "breasts" the "Name," even when the breasts appear in a form other than that of *Shadai*: for example, in *Shadayikh*, i.e., "your breasts," it reads: "your two Names *Shadai*."

6. Lévinas, *L'Au-delà du verset*, p. 148.

7. Ibid., p. 147.

8. Ibid., p. 148.

9. Cf. among others, *Pitei She'arim*, by Rabbi Isaac Aizik Haver (Tel Aviv, 1964), 2b.

10. *Hagigah* 12a.

11. Rav Judah is the author of the *Nirin veeyn Nirin*.

12. *Kedushat Levi* 33a (Jerusalem, reedited 1965).

13. *Shem Mishmuel, Shemot* (Jerusalem, 1974), 1:106, 108.

14. Exod. 6:3.

15. Lévinas, *L'Au-delà du verset*, p. 200.

16. Rabbi Joseph Isaac Schneersohn, *Otsar Hassidim* (1930), p. 131.

17. *Nefesh haHayyim*, 3:2.

18. Cf. *Kol hanevuah*, by Rav David ha-Kohen (Mossad Harav Kook ed.) (Jerusalem, 1970), p. 268, chapter entitled: "*Ha-tsimtsum, ha-Reshimu, vehakav*"; cf. also the *Hundred and Thirty-Eight Doors of Wisdom*, by R.M.H. Luzzatto (Warsaw, 1888), door 24 and the following.

19. Cf. G. Scholem, *La Kabbale et sa symbolique* (Paris: Payot, 1980), p. 55.

IV

Eroticism and Prophecy

The Verse That Was Not Quoted

Throughout this research, we have tried to orient our analysis so as to show up the possibility of a type of commentary whose unifying idea would be the divine Names. The originality of this approach consists in its application to the Talmud, inasmuch as it has been reserved until now—for a large number of commentators—for the texts of the Cabala. It is not a matter of tacking on, at all costs, preexisting reflections on the different divine Names, by means of vague allusions encountered here and there in the lines of the *Gemara*, but of demonstrating that the fundamental structure of the text can be shown to be a Name, Names, or relationships between these different Names.

In this perspective, there suddenly appears a reflection that, in the chronology of the text, is situated before the section "A Verse from the Song of Songs," yet without finding a place in the passage entitled "An Erotic Image." In "An Erotic Image," the image of the breasts was studied without any reference to Hebrew terms; we did not concern ourselves with knowing how the breasts were named. In "A Verse from the Song of Songs," we opted for the opposite attitude, since the whole study dealt with the reference of *Shadai*, my breasts, to the divine Name *Shadai*. The third approach we have here is also going to be based on the Hebrew passage that the breasts refer us to.[1] One remark is essential: in the quotation from the Song of Songs, the word meaning "breasts" is different from that used by the *Baraita*. In the latter, it is the word *Dad* and not *Shad* that denotes the breast. And so, in one way, the verse from the Song of Songs is inadequate, since it differentiates itself from the terminology of the *Baraita*. This remark should orient the research in two ways: first, we should ask ourselves if the use of the word *Dad* by the *Baraita* does not refer to a precise meaning other than that of the *Shadai*-Name/*Shadai*-breasts relation; second, and as a consequence of the first point, we have to find out what is at stake in the existing difference between *Dad* and *Shad*, that is to say, on the one hand between the letters *Dalet* and *Shin* and, on the other hand, between the reference of *Dad* (that we do not know, for the moment) and that of *Shad*, i.e., the Name *Shadai*. The confrontation will turn out to be particularly interesting if the reference of *Dad* proves to be also a divine Name. That is the case: a new relation to the Name is going to emerge, and this name is *Elohim*.

From a methodological point of view, the present analysis diverges radically from the preceding for the following reason: in the *Baraita*, the quotation from the Song of Songs is a part of the text of the *Gemara*; the verse is given. As a result, the breast-Name relation is immediate: to say *my breasts* immediately makes us think of the divine Name. This simultaneity is absent here, because no verse is present to make us perceive some sort of homophony or allusion. And yet this verse exists; but, we shall see, no relation exists a priori between this verse and the breasts and, all the more, no relation between the breasts and the divine Names. It is from an analysis—of a very particular kind—of one or several words of this verse that the breasts and the Name will be highlighted. Our commentary lies in the comparison of this verse, and the analysis made by Rabbi Isaac Luria,[2] with the teaching of the *Baraita*. For complete understanding of this commentary, it is necessary to quote in its entirety the context of the verse in question. It is a passage from the book of Numbers in which the children of Israel in the desert rebel against Moses and demand a more varied food than the manna; they cry out for meat! Moses has difficulty putting up with these demands:

> Where am I to find meat to give to all this people, when they come worrying to me so tearfully and say, "Give us meat to eat"? I am not able to carry this nation by myself alone; the weight is too much for me. If this is how you want to deal with me, I would rather you killed me! If only I had found favor in your eyes, and not lived to see such misery as this!
>
> YHVH said to Moses, "Gather seventy of the elders of Israel, men you know to be the people's elders and scribes. Bring them to the Tent of Meeting, and let them stand beside you there. I will come down to speak with you; and I will take some of the spirit that is on you and put it on them. So they will share with you the burden of this nation, and you will no longer have to carry it by yourself.
>
> Moses went out and told the people what YHVH had said. Then he gathered seventy elders of the people and brought them around the Tent. YHVH came down in the cloud. He spoke with him, but took some of the spirit that was on him and put it on the seventy elders. When the spirit came on them they prophesied, but not again.
>
> Two men had stayed back in the camp; one was called Eldad and the other Medad. The spirit came down on them; though they had not gone to the Tent, their names were enrolled among the rest. These began to prophesy in the camp. The young man ran to tell this to Moses; "Look," he said, "Eldad and Medad are prophesying in the camp." Then said Joshua the son of Nun, who had served Moses from his youth, "My Lord Moses, stop them!" Moses

answered him, "Are you jealous on my account? If only the whole people of YHVH were prophets, and YHVH gave his spirit to them all!" Then Moses went back to the camp, the elders of Israel with him. (Num. 11:13–30).

The key verse of this passage is "One was called *Eldad* and the other *Medad*." Before quoting the analysis of Rabbi Isaac Luria, we pose, along with the *Gemara*,³ three essential questions:

1. How did Moses choose the seventy elders?
2. What is distinctive about Eldad and Medad that made them merit a prophetic gift superior to that of the other elders?
3. What is the content of their prophecy?

1. The problem of the seventy elders has drawn the attention of numerous commentators. The twelve tribes should supply the assembly of seventy equally. Now, if each tribe has six representatives, the assembly will have seventy-two persons, two too many. Ten tribes must therefore have six representatives and two of them have to make do with five. How is the choice to be made? Why favor one tribe over another? Moses works out a system of drawing lots (*goral*): he takes seventy-two small tablets, on seventy of which he writes *zaken* (elder), and leaves two of them blank (*halak*). Of the seventy-two persons who draw a tablet, two must inevitably "come across" a blank tablet and thereby be excluded from the assembly. The *Midrash*, quoted by the *Sanhedrin Gemara* (17a), helps us understand verse 26 of this chapter 11, which says of Eldad and Medad, "*Vehemah baketuvim,*" which means, "They are in the writing." This obscure sentence takes on meaning through the *Midrash* quoted. They are among those who drew a tablet on which was *written Zaken*. In other words, Eldad and Medad are actually part of the assembly of seventy. (It is from this episode that the Talmud draws the rule that the great Sanhedrin must consist of seventy-one persons: seventy plus Moses.)⁴ Eldad and Medad refuse this choice; they refuse to be a part of the great Sanhedrin. In a way, they act as if they had drawn blank tablets, wishing to contest the verse "*vehemah baketuvim.*" They withdraw from writing.

2. By different indications in the text, we understand that, paradoxically, Eldad and Medad receive a prophetic spirit superior to that of the elders of the assembly. It is said of them, "They prophesy," in the present, a present that the *Gemara* interprets as a nontemporary gift of prophecy; whereas of the elders it is said, "They prophesied," in the past: a prophetic gift of a moment. Whence comes the prophetic superiority of these two men? The same text of the *Gemara* continues: "At the moment when the Holy One, blessed be He, said to Moses, 'Gather seventy men for me,' Eldad and Medad said, 'We do not deserve such

an honor.' The Holy One, blessed be He, said: 'Since you are diminished, I shall add greatness to your greatness.' And what greatness did
he add? All the other prophets prophesied and stopped, but they received the gift of prophesy forever."[5]

3. Of the content of their prophecy, three hypotheses are put forward:
   a. According to the sages, "Eldad and Medad said: 'Moses is dead,
Joshua, take Israel into the land!'"
   b. Aba Hanin says, in the name of Rabbi Eliezer: "They prophesied
about the quails; they said: 'The quails are rising, the quails are rising.'"
   c. According to Rav Nahman, they prophesied about Gog and Ma-
gog. (According to the *Targum Jonathan* and the *Targum Yerushalmi*,
Eldad was the author of the first prophecy, Medad the second, and both
together authors of the third).[6]
These different quotations allow us now to formulate the problem
more clearly. Let us return to the key verse:

One was called Eldad and the other Medad.

The analysis of "*Ari*"-*zal* (an acrostic referring to Rabbi Isaac Luria)
is based on a simple and fascinating play on words. His thought can be
summed up in one sentence: "*Da', ki Eldad u Meydad hem Sod shenei
dadim hamozegim ha-halav*";[7] which means: "Know that Eldad and
Medad are the Secret of the two breasts which give milk." It is thus a
matter of showing how, from these two names, we end up seeing, reading: "two breasts."
Prepared by these two preliminary remarks, the attentive ear will
sound Eldad and Medad more carefully. So here is, at a first reading,
the meaning of the statement: "Eldad and Medad are the secret of the
two breasts." Rabbi Isaac Luria continues the analysis, relating the two
breasts to the divine Name *Elohim*. When *Dad* is removed from Eldad
and Medad, the letters *Aleph* and *Lamed* remain: *El*; and *Mem* and
Yod: Mi (the "e" of Medad includes a *Yod*, which is transcribed in English
as *i* in the Name *Elohim*). Now these four letters are centered on an axis
formed by the letter *Heh*—absent—to spell the Name *Elohim*:

Aleph-Lamed-Heh-Yod-Mem

E   Lo   H   I   M

Two Remarks

The first remark has to do with the relation between Eldad and Medad,
who are historical characters, and the meaning of their names. The sec-

ond deals with the meaning of the Name *Elohim*, which the word *Dad*, used by the *Baraita*, sought, without any doubt, to reveal.

Man, standing before the *Parokhet* (i.e., before the Text), perceiving the image of the breasts and hearing them as *Dadim*, is referred back— but not simultaneously—to a historical situation whose main characters are called Eldad and Medad. Rabbi Isaac Luria's commentary, which reveals the unsuspected richness of these two names, should first be studied in its relation to history: the reading, in Eldad and Medad, of "two breasts" and of *"Elohim"* should not make us forget the original historical meaning that these names convey. By conjugating the information of the biblical texts—both Midrashic and Talmudic—we can understand that the notion called into play in the episode of Eldad and Medad is that of prophecy. We may say that Eldad and Medad attain prophetic status precisely by refusing prophecy. The texts of the *Sanhedrin Gemara* are very enlightening on this subject: "Since you are diminished, I shall add greatness to your greatness."[8]

Eldad and Medad withdraw from the field of speech and thereby attain speech (a more detailed analysis of this passage would show that there is withdrawal not only from the field of speech but also from the field of writing). Not accepting membership in the assembly of the seventy elders amounts to challenging the verse *"veheimah baketuvim,"* "they are in writing." Their behavior effaces the inscription *"zaken."*

That being the case, Eldad and Medad would be present in order to teach the manner of being that man should have before the Text-*Parokhet*: the necessity of withdrawing from the possibility of speech in order to give it over to the Text and Others. Withdrawing from before the text, without refusing the relation to the text, signifies the will to be questioned by the latter. The *Dad*, which is without doubt a nourishing breast, is still understood as "the meaning other which arises from under the initial meaning." If we seek out all the biblical occurrences of *Dad*, we notice that the meaning of this term is always the breast, considered from an aesthetic, sensual, and erotic angle,[9] whereas *Shad* means both the nourishing and the erotic breast. Once we have described the vision of the breasts as an erotic one, we have also expressed the modality whereby the text is revealed. The reference to *Shadai* and to the *Tsimtsum* is thus essentially aimed at the text and not—or, in any case, in a much more secondary manner—at man faced with the text. We can now state that the second reference to *Elohim*, working backwards, is aimed at man faced with the text. In other words: the Name *Shadai* expresses the essence of the text, whereas the Name *Elohim* expresses the relationship man has with the text.

It may be noticed that in *Shadai*, the image of the breasts refers to the two staves, the supports of the Ark, of the Torah, of the text; on the other hand, in *Elohim*, the image of the breasts is contained in the names of persons, which confirms the *Shadai/Elohim* distinction.

The withdrawal of Eldad and Medad, this will to be questioned, should be understood and interpreted in the light of this very famous passage from the prologue to the *Zohar*:

> In the beginning, Rabbi Eleazar opened his discourse with the text: "Lift up your eyes on high and see; who has created these?" (Isa. 40:26). "Lift up your eyes on high": to which place? To that place to which all eyes are turned, to wit, *Petah 'Enaim* ("eye-opener"). By doing so, you will know that it is the mysterious Ancient One, whose essence can be sought, but not found, that created these, to wit, *Mi* (Who?), the same who is called "from (Heb. *mi*) the extremity of heaven on high," because everything is in His power, and because He is ever to be sought, though mysterious and unrevealable, since further we cannot inquire. That extremity of Heaven is called *Mi*, but there is another extremity that is called *Mah* (What?). The difference between the two is this. The first is the real subject of inquiry, but after a man by means of inquiry and reflection has reached the utmost limit of knowledge, he stops at *Mah* (What?), as if to say, what knowest thou? What have thy searchings achieved? Everything is as baffling as at the beginning. In allusion to this, it is written, "What (*Mah*) shall I testify against you, etc."[10] (Lam. 2:13)

This text from the *Zohar* not only gives us the meaning[11] of the Name *Elohim* but will also allow us to define the difference of approach of the terms *Shadai* and *Elohim*. In the process, it is not uninteresting to make a detour via some general reflections concerning the different levels of interpretation united in the term *PaRDeS*, the anagram of *Pshat, Remez, Drash*, and *Sod* (the word *Pardes* itself means "orchard").

Pshat is the literal meaning; it concerns the immediate meaning. *Remez* is the allusive meaning; it deals with the allusions in the text given by different reading grids, different codes such as the *Gematria* (numerical value of the letters) and the *Notarikon* (anagram). *Drash* is generally translated as "symbolic meaning." In fact, the commentators do not distinguish between *Remez* and *Drash*; however, we may say that *Remez* is allusion and *Drash*, the interpretation that is made of this allusion. Finally, *Sod*, which means "secret," is applied to mystical commentaries that are encountered in the texts of the Cabala and Hasidism. *Sod* differs from *Drash* only by its content (we could point out that the *Zohar* is also called *Midrash*); the methodological approach is identical. We could even reduce *Pardes* to the *Pshat/Drash* duality and translate *Drash* as symbolic interpretation, as distinct from the literal interpretation of *Pshat*. According to this presentation, the text becomes a "symbol." This radical dichotomy of *Pshat* and *Drash* has the advantage of broadening the hermeneutic field; but does not the excessive broadening become simplistic? Does the symbol cover only the double or multiple meaning? It seems to be necessary and possible to restore at least the three levels *Pshat, Drash*, and *Sod* (while seeing *Remez* as the origin of *Drash*). This restoration can be effected through a refinement of the notion of symbol. In a passage from the *Livre à venir* entitled the "Secret of the Golem," Maurice Blanchot underlines the distinction to be made between allegory and symbol:

> These two ways of reading are celebrated and they originated centuries ago: to cite only one example, one led to the rich commentaries of the Talmud, the other to the experiences of prophetic Cabalism linked to the contemplation and manipulation of letters.[12]

Blanchot continues:

> Allegory has a meaning, many meanings, a greater or lesser ambiguity of meaning. The symbol does not express anything, does not mean anything. . . . Each symbol is an experience, a radical change that has to be lived, a leap that has to be made. There is no such thing as a symbol, only a symbolic experience.[13]

This difference between allegory and symbol can adequately serve to express that which separates *Remez-Drash* from *Sod*. It is not, as is often said, *Drash* that is symbolic but *Sod*. To sum up, *PaRDeS* (where *Remez* is included in *Drash*) contains three levels: *Pshat*, literal meaning, which refers only to itself; *Remez-Drash*, which opens up to other sources; and finally *Sod*, which does not express anything, does not refer to any meaning, any language. The *Zohar* itself, and all the texts of the Cabala and of Hasidism, insofar as they are discourses on . . . , are at a *Pshat* level of *Sod*, at the *Drash* of *Sod*, but not yet *Sod* (let us remember that the *Zohar* is also known as *Midrash Ha-Zohar*).[14]

We can thus extend the distinction between the *Shadai reading* and the *Elohim reading* outlined above. *Shadai-Tsevaot* indicates the way a text can be understood *intellectually*. Through *Shadai*, there is the possibility of grasping the thread, the semantic architecture of the text; it is a knowledge that leads to a certain discourse. Transcendence, the content of this discourse, is not sufficient to leave the domain of language. *Shadai*-breasts refers to *Shadai*-Name, but this Name is itself an explanation of limitation, of *Tsimtsum*. Real transcendence is an *experience* of transcendence. *Sod*, and must refer only to something ultimate about which all discourse becomes impossible. *Elohim*, which is attained by *Dad* and by the Names of Eldad and Medad, is still a discourse, but expresses precisely the impossibility of all discourse. It is a limit-word on the border of silence.[15]

In the text of the *Zohar*, the *Mah* is the being here below and the *Mi*, the transcendent being; the *Mah* is defined as the being whose question is *Mi*. This quest for the *Mi*, this aiming for the *Mi*, is expressed by an interrogative movement in the direction of the *Mi*. What Eldad and Medad reveal is not the *Mi*, nor *Elohim*, but the *El-Mi*, the "toward-whom?" "In the direction of whom?"—but the *Heh* is absent. It is the voluntary absence of a letter, the silence of the letter, that accomplishes the writing of the divine Name, for only in silence is transcendence possible. The letter *Heh* creates a link between *El* and the *Mi*; silence is that which allows one to attain the transcendent being. However, does silence itself allow one to attain the *Mi*? The *Zohar* says:

> When a man by means of inquiry and reflection has reached the utmost limit of knowledge, he stops at *Mah* (the what?), as if to say, what have you understood? What have thy searchings achieved? Everything is as baffling as at the beginning.

Man in quest of the *Mi* comes across the *Mah*; and so finds himself (*Mah Adam*). This meeting up with himself is also an encounter with the question mark.

The "What have you understood?" is not a negative result of the cognitive procedure: the "what?" adorned with its question mark is the positive result that should be achieved. We can say that "the essence of reason consists not in securing for man (*Mah*) a foundation and powers, but in calling him into question (*Mah?*)."[16] The idea to be drawn from this text of the *Zohar* is: the *Mi* cannot be impinged upon.

In the text of *Yoma* 54a, this inviolability of the *Mi*, or, to put it differently, of the *Eyn Nirin*, calls into question the very idea of dialectic evoked above concerning the "visible-invisible":

> Can we say that the invisible (the *Mi*) is determined in its opposition to the visible, that is to say, in its dialectical unity with it, not as the concept of a separate essence, but in the fluidity of the passage where it is incessantly constituted as that which ceases to elude it?[17]

In the alternative described above, like the author we opt for the second proposition. But it is here that we differ, since he applies it to Christianity. We read (p. 564):

> The antagonism of the visible and the invisible, far from implying their inclusion in the dialectical unity of a single process, is expressed, on the contrary, as an opposition of the real and the unreal, the radical ontological heterogeneity of their essences, and finds, in it, its foundation.

The radical heterogeneity of the visible and the invisible—the second proposition of the alternative that we accepted to integrate into our analysis—cannot be thought of, in the context of Judaism, as the difference between real and unreal. In Judaism, there is not one world that is real and another that is not. If two worlds exist and coexist, the *olam hazeh* and the *olam haba*, the reality of one has no cause to be jealous of the reality of the other . . . There is not a true and a false world, nor is there a distinction between a world of appearances and one of essences.

Should we not rather assert that the essence of the invisible has nothing in common with that of the visible, that "they differ, on the contrary, in the irreducible heterogeneity of their structures"?[18] Consequently, the invisible and the visible cannot be transformed, one into the other; no transition, no time joins them, but they remain, one separate from the other, each in its own assertion and status.

These remarks shed, not a different, but, after all, a reinforced light on the teaching of the "visible-invisible" of Rav Judah and the *Baraita*. This idea of the absolute separation of the visible and the invisible is the central theme of the whole first section of *Totality and Infinity*; Lévinas calls this separation "atheism"[19] and, to highlight the paradox, calls this unrelating relation by the name of "religion";[20] he insists on this atheism that "conditions a true relation with a true God." Lévinas, as a reader of the passage quoted from the *Zohar*, would say that the *Mah* exists in the solitude and the independence of the being-oneself, that the *Mah* is a separate being which maintains itself alone in existence "without participating in the Being from which it is separated."[21] The *Mah* is atheistic: in its relation to the *Mi*, it "is not annihilated on contact, neither is it transported outside of itself, but remains separated and keeps its as-for-me [*quant à soi*]. Only an atheistic *Mah* can relate himself to the *Mi* and already *absolve himself* from this relation."[22]

The relation of transcendence that reveals the structure of the *Nirin veeyn Nirin* distinguishes itself from union, by participation,[23] with the transcendent; that is the meaning of the sentence of the *Zohar*: "But everything remains as baffling as at the beginning."

Continuing in this reading of Lévinas, we read, heightening the paradox, on the enigma of the relation without relation: "To be sure, the atheism of the *Mah* marks the break with participation and consequently the possibility of seeking a justification for oneself, that is, a dependence upon an exteriority without this dependence absorbing the dependent being, held in invisible meshes. This dependence, consequently, *at the same time* maintains independence."[24]

The ultimate structure that is "religion results in the ultimate situation which is the 'face to face.' "[25]

It is a situation that unfolds at the heart of the teaching of Rav Kattina in the third part, which follows.

Notes

1. But a different reference from that of *Shadai*.

2. A teaching of R. I. Luria recounted by Rabbi Hayim Vital in *Likkutei Torah* (Research Center of Kabbalah ed., in Hebrew) (Jerusalem, 1970), p. 208. In the first analysis, we started off with the verse from the Song of Songs to end up with the image, or rather the word, *Shaddai*. Now we are going to trace from the word *Dad* to a verse that has this word concealed in it.

3. *Sanhedrin* 17a.

4. *Sanhedrin* 2a.

5. *Sanhedrin* 17a. On the diminishing and effacing before . . . Cf. *Hulin* 60b.

6. A fourth opinion says that their prophecy is written and is a part of the prophetic literature: that would be the meaning of "And they are among the (prophetic) writings." And what is this book? Verses 35 and 36 of chapter 10 of the book of Numbers; cf. *Midrash Haserot vayeterot* in *Batei midrashot*, 2:74. This fourth opinion is fundamental.

7. *Likkutei Torah*, p. 208.

8. *Sanhedrin* 17a.

9. Cf. Ezek. 23:3, 23:8, 23:21, and Prov. 5:19.

10. *Zohar*, trans. C. Mopsik (Paris: Éditions Verdier, 1981), 1:31–32.

11. One of the meanings, at least . . .

12. M. Blanchot, *Le Livre à venir* (Paris: Gallimard, 1959), (folio, essais), p. 123.

13. Ibid., pp. 121–22.

14. On the four levels of meaning, cf. H. Atlan, "Niveaux de signification et athéisme de l'écriture," in *La Bible au présent* (Paris: Gallimard, 1982), "Idées," pp. 55–88. It is doubtless the best article in French written on the subject.

15. Silence, nondiscourse *on* . . . Silence does not exclude the discourse *to* . . . , such as prayer.

16. E. Lévinas, *Totality and Infinity*, (Pittsburgh: Duquesne University Press, 1988), p. 88.

17. M. Henry, *L'Essence de la manifestation* (Paris: PUF, 1963), 2:559.

18. Ibid.

19. Lévinas, *Totality and Infinity*, p. 58.

20. Ibid., p. 80. We can read on the same page: "Religion, where relationship subsists between the same and the other despite the impossibility of the Whole —the idea of Infinity—is the ultimate structure."

21. Ibid., p. 58.

22. Ibid., p. 77.

23. Ibid., p. 48.

24. Ibid., p. 88.

25. Ibid., p. 81.

THIRD PART (C)

Rav Kattina said: Whenever the children of Israel came
up to Jerusalem, during the three festivals of pilgrimage,
the *Parokhet* would be removed for them and the
Keruvim were shown to them, whose bodies were
intertwined with one another, and they would be
addressed: Look! You are beloved before God as the love
between masculine and feminine.

I

Invisible Faces

THE TEACHING of Rav Kattina can be read in two different ways: either by isolating it from its context, from the statements of Rav Judah and the *Baraita*; or by situating it as the continuation of the thinking of the *Nirin veeyn Nirin*. The second hypothesis can, in turn, generally be considered from two contrasting angles: Rav Kattina can complete, reinforce, deepen one or several aspects of the preceding text, or, on the contrary, he can adopt a controversial attitude. The content of Rav Kattina's words could be removed from the context of the page where they are found. We would then have a historical commentary about what happened at the Temple during the three pilgrimage feasts. The situation of this reflection in this page would then originate in an association of ideas from the word *Parokhet*. But we may as well state immediately that the association of ideas—if it actually exists in the logic of the development of Talmudic thought—is not anarchic. An implacable logical coherence cements all parts of the text; the first hypothesis is therefore excluded. As for the second, since no word indicates a controversy, it would seem that Rav Kattina deepens the thought of the visible-invisible rather than contradicting it.

So the teaching of Rav Kattina is not a historical account, a sort of "journalistic" chronicle of what was happening at the Temple at such and such a time. The three pilgrimage feasts—Pesah, *Shavu'ot*, and *Sukhot*—highlights of Jewish time, immediately reintroduce reflection into the context of the "visible-invisible." According to the texts of the Torah and of the Talmudic tractate *Hagigah* that opens it, the essential part of the celebration of the three feasts lies in the act of going to the Temple. This attendance bears the name of *Reiyah*, "seeing." Going to the Temple or, in the words of the biblical verse, "having onself seen": it is therefore a matter of "being seen" and not of "seeing." According to the expression of a passage of the Talmud,[1] there is a relation in terms of looking, or seeing, and of the face, where God is called "*Panim Haroin veeynan Nirin*": "the Faces that see but that are invisible."

Man is before God, "*Panim Hanirim veeynan Roin*," like "visible faces that cannot see."

We should also note that the *Reiyah* indicates the name of the gift that each person who goes up to the Temple should carry with him, to fulfill the verse "And they shall not appear before the Lord empty-handed.[2] "To be seen" is to approach Others with one's hands full; the relation to the Other is fulfilled in the gift. If, as we have seen, man is "visible faces that cannot see," what is the meaning of the gesture of opening the *Parokhet*? Is it an act that makes the invisible visible? No! The invisibility of the invisible exists independently of the Veil. The *Parokhet* does not hide anything. The *Shekhinah* (divine Presence) is "invisible Faces."

That is the meaning of the action of Rav Kattina: showing that the invisible is, not because it is hidden from our eyes, but because it is beyond all vision; it is a matter of a "spiritual perspective" revealed by the *Keruvim*.

The *Keruvim*: that is to say, the face-to-face, the *Panim-El-Panim*. We shall read later the modalities of the face-to-face, as they appear in biblical verses and Talmudic texts. However, let us jump ahead to our conclusions: still with Lévinas, we can assert that the "face-to-face is the ultimate situation of 'religion'" (the latter being understood in the meaning that Lévinas ascribes to it).

The *Keruvim* are set out as a primary and ultimate situation, a horizontal relation—of human faces—that does not overshadow the vertical relation of the visible and the invisible, but determines it. Whether the *Keruvim* have, according to the different commentators, children's, fathers', masters', or women's faces, they mean first, and above all, that the "dimension of the divine opens forth from the human face, that a relation with the Transcendent—which is, however, free from all captivation by the Transcendent—is a social relation."[3]

The opening gesture of the *Parokhet* means that "religion" does not run the risk of confusing the invisibility of God with the mere inaccessibility of a mysterious super-being,[4] that an invisible God means not only an unimaginable God but a God who is accessible in justice.[5]

Rav Kattina, here, is the mouthpiece of the whole Talmudic tradition that may be described by these words: "The alterity of God is not a world behind the scenes. . . . But it is manifested in the humble call of our neighbor who incites us to break out of ourselves."[6] But let us not be mistaken—the face-to-face is not an opening that leads to God: the quotation marks we put around the words atheism and atheist should not be removed (even though Lévinas does not use them). "The Other is not the incarnation of God, but precisely by his face, in which he is disincarnate, is the manifestation of the height in which God is revealed."[7] In short, "the atheism of the metaphysician means, positively, that our relationship with the Metaphysical is an ethical behavior and not theology, not a thematization, be it a knowledge by analogy, of the attributes of God."[8]

Notes

1. "Rabbi and Rabbi Hiyya set off. When they arrived in this place, they said:
—Is there a master here, so that we can visit him?
The inhabitants of the town replied:
—Certainly, there is a master and he is blind.
Rabbi Hiyya said to Rabbi:
—Stay here, do not damage the honor of your rank. I shall go alone to visit the blind master.
Rabbi refused, and they went there together.
As they were taking leave of the blind Master, the latter said to them:
—You have welcomed the "visible faces that cannot see"; you should also merit welcoming "faces that see, but which are invisible."
Rabbi said to Rabbi Hiyya:
—If I had listened to you and not come, I would have missed out on this blessing."
2. Deut. 16:16.
3. E. Lévinas, *Totality and Infinity* (Pittsburgh: Duquesne University Press, 1988), p. 78; on this idea, see also *Makkot* 24a.
4. F. Guibal, . . . *Et combien de dieux nouveaux: Lévinas* (Paris: Aubier-Montaigne, 1980), p. 112.
5. Lévinas, *Totality and Infinity*, p. 79.
6. Guibal, . . . *Et combien de dieux nouveaux*, p. 112.
7. Lévinas, *Totality and Infinity*, pp. 78–79.
8. Ibid., p. 78.

II

The Double Gaze

The *Keruvim*

The *Keruvim*, which English translates as "cherubim," are the paradigm of the face-to-face. Let us try to notice, in the verses that deal with them, the main points of what is the relationship par excellence. We read in Exodus (25:11):

> Further, you are to make [for the Ark] a lid (*Kaporet*), of pure gold, two and a half cubits long, and one and a half cubits wide.
>
> For the two ends of this lid you are to make two golden *Keruvim*; you are to make them of beaten gold. Make the first *Keruv* for one end and the second for the other and fasten them to the two ends of the lid so that they make one piece with it. The *Keruvim* are to have their wings spread upwards so that they overshadow the lid. They must face one another, their faces toward the lid. You must place the lid on top of the Ark. Inside the Ark you must place the Testimony that I shall give you. There I shall come to meet you; there from above the lid, from between the two *Keruvim* that are on the Ark of the Testimony, I shall give you all my commands for the children of Israel.

The first problem that the realization of the *Keruvim* poses lies in the contradiction which seems to arise in relation to the precept "You shall not make gods before me, gods of silver, gods of gold . . . nor graven image, nor any likeness of anything that is in heaven above or that is in the earth below."[1]

Sexual Difference

Rabbenu Behayeh remarks, concerning the verse "You are to make two *Keruvim* . . ." the following grammatical anomaly: it is said "*Veassita shenayim Keruvim*" (You are to make two cherubim"); the *Shenayim* (two) should have been used in the full form, "*shenei-Keruvim*." *Shenei*, Rabbenu Behaye explains, expresses identity and parallelism (*hashvaah*), whereas *shenayim* implies difference and alterity, and this difference immediately takes the form of a sexual difference: "*Shenayim: ki hem haluhin beinyanam, zeh zakhar vezeh nekevah.*" Which means:

"Two: expressed by *shenayim* and not *Shenei*, because they differ essentially, one being masculine and the other feminine."[2]

The interhuman relationship is not a relationship between neutral humans but between a masculine and a feminine. That is the idea of Rav Kattina; he also adds that of transcendence. The relation of otherness, transcendence, takes place on the basis of a difference between sexes. But is that really what Rav Kattina says? Is he not exaggerating when he goes so far as to say that not only is the basic relationship sexual, but the very relationship between man and God proceeds from the same difference?

The Double Gaze

The text says: "And their faces, one man toward his brother . . ." The *Keruvim* express a face-to-face relationship. In this verse, the sexual character is replaced by the notion of responsibility introduced by the word "brother" (*ah*).[3]

The same verse continues: "the faces of the *Keruvim* toward the lid." "Toward the lid": that is to say, toward the Ark of the Covenant, a gaze in the direction of the Law. The face-to-face, the ultimate situation, is a "double gaze." It is a matter not only of a continuation of the *you* toward a *You*, but of the simultaneity of an "I-you" and an "I-You" relationship.

The gaze turned toward the Law does not refer only to the "formality to be accomplished" but also—and primarily—to the Legislator. The relationship of the "double gaze" means that in the interhuman relationship, the exclusion of the divine is unthinkable and that the relationship with the Distant also depends on the fellow man.

The Voice

When Rav Kattina says that love between man and God can be understood on the basis of the love between masculine and feminine, he sets up, to a certain extent, a parallel between the modalities of what may be called a horizontal relationship (between men) and those of a vertical relationship (between man and God). The terms "horizontal" and "vertical" are fairly classical; although Lévinas seems to contest the idea of horizontality to describe the interhuman relationship since it excludes the height that he wishes to introduce into this relationship.

The point about the *Kaporet*, where the two gazes meet, has a particularly important significance. It is there that the "word speaks," according to the verse: "And I shall speak with you from above the *Kaporet*, from between the two *Keruvim*." Speech originates in the heart of the face-to-face, in the place where one gaze meets another. The speech that is in question in this verse is divine; but the preceding remarks about the parallelism of the two relationships allow us to assert that it is also a question of human speech; the horizontal and vertical (both of which are vertical) relations open the dialogue.

However, it is important to insist on the fact that it is not the dialogue that makes the relationship, but the relationship—whose original event is the face-to-face—that founds the dialogue.[4] The relation between the two *Keruvim*—whether these be, according to the different commentators, two men, two brothers, two children, a man and a child, the master and disciple, or a man and a woman (or, more exactly, a masculine and a feminine)—turns out to be a verbal relationship. We may say that the face-to-face is not only an "inter-view" (*entre-vu*, lit.: glimpsed) but also an "inter-saying" (*entre-dire*) (and intercourse—*entretien*—according to the "impossibility of meeting others empty-handed,"[5] signified by the *Korban Reiyah*). In the relationship with the Other, there is an incessant coming and going between "seeing" and "saying." But, as we have said, the "relation to others, whatever the modality it expresses, and primarily in the dialogue or in the gaze or even fleetingly, in the violence of an embrace, allows an unsurmountable distance to arise in the proximity it promotes."[6] This closeness in distance is taught by Rav Kattina in the space created between reality and the interpretation of this reality. The *Keruvim*, made of one block, one at either end, are, in space, radically distinct, separate one from another.[7] If they meet, it is through their gaze, their speech (or the tips of their wings). The physical impossibility of a clasping—one with the other—cannot be questioned. The *Keruvim* cannot clasp one another; and yet . . . Rav Kattina says that they "clasp one another" (*meorim zeh bazeh*), which Rashi does not contradict; on the contrary, since he provides the proof, quoting verses, that *Meorim* is a term which means *devekut*, enfolding, relation, perfect and total adequacy and adhesion, body to body, on the verge of unification (according to Rashi, the term *Meorim* is used to describe the relation between the albumen and the yoke of an egg). The space between reality (absolute separation) and fusion (*devekut*), described by Rav Kattina in his interpretation, is not a contradiction that requires resolving, because the solution is in this very contradiction. The relationship of alterity is this contradiction of "relation without relating." Consequently, the gaze and speech, which form a bridge over an infinite abyss separating the two *Keruvim*, should be approached in a special way. A classical "contradiction," highlighted by all the commentators and particularly by Rashi, will allow us to examine this particularity of speech (and gaze) in the relationship.

According to the verse of Exodus (25:22) that we quoted, speech emerges from the "between-the-two-*Keruvim*." However, another verse—the first one of Leviticus—denies this origin of speech; it is said (Lev. 1:1): "And God spoke to him from the Tent of Meeting." This is contradictory! The "between-the-two-*Keruvim*" is situated in the Holy of Holies, whereas the Tent of Meeting is the Holy. The Holy and the Holy of Holies are separated, we remember, by the *Parokhet* . . . Is the speech heard in the *Kodesh* or in the *Kodesh-Kodashim*"? *Veyavo hash-elishi veyakhria beyneyhem*! As the Talmud says: "A third (verse) is there to solve the contradiction" . . .

We read in the book of Numbers (7:89):

> When Moses went into the Tent of Meeting to speak with Him, he heard the voice that spoke to him from above the lid which was on the Ark of the Testimony, from between the two *Keruvim*. It was then that he spoke with Him.

This contradiction does not originate in the incoherence of a text that has not been fully thought out; rather, it should be understood as the will to conceal, or even to destroy, the existence of a listening place. Of course, the third verse tells us that we have to distinguish between the place whence the voice emanates and the place of the perception of the speech (the voice emanates, as the verse of Exodus says, from "between-the-two-*Keruvim*," but it is perceived in the *Sham*, in the "there," which is situated in the *Kodesh* in front of the *Parokhet*), thus solving the contradiction. Yet that does not hinder this intentional contradiction from containing an important teaching about the space of dialogue or, more precisely, the space of speech. Through a contradiction that draws the attention of the reader, the Torah underlines—heavily—the interval that separates the place of discussion from the place of hearing.

In the text of Numbers, the verb "to speak" is expressed in a form that draws the attention: "*Vayishma et hakol Midaber elav.*" He heard the voice, not speaking to him, as we translated earlier, but speaking to itself. *Midaber* is a reflexive form—the equivalent of a pronominal.

So the exact translation of this verse is: "He heard the voice speaking to itself, to him (addressed)." The voice speaks to itself, an infinite speech, whether or not here be an interlocutor. We need to distinguish between the voice (*kol*) and its content (*dibur* or *amirah*).

According to the *Orah Hayim* commentary, we should understand here that there is no difference between the content of this voice and the voice itself: the voice is already the whole of the message; the voice has precedence over the meaning. This suppression of the meaning, or its secondary status, means that the "dialogue does not consist in a communication of oneself or of something, but in the opening of a hearing. . . . To speak, hear, stand in separation, that is what man is called to.

Here, the voice is more important than the discourse."[8] This precedence of the voice over the meaning allows "the relation to others to be neither self-assertion, nor the seizing or respectful attention to another person, but the experience of alterity as foreignness."[9]

To hear the voice that speaks to itself and that, at the same time, addresses itself to the Other is to feel summoned. It is in this summoning that the relation is a "relation between terms that resist totalization."[10]

We can therefore say that "the claim to know and to reach the other is realized in the relation with the Other that is cast in the relation of language, where the essential is the interpellation, the vocative. The other is maintained and confirmed in his heterogeneity as soon as one calls upon him, be it only to say to him that one cannot speak to him. . . ."[11]

The voice implies the vocative, summoning. What can be heard in the between-the-two-*Keruvim* is the summoning voice; a voice from above, whether it be addressed by God or by a human. This voice that surprises us, summons us, and questions us invites us to answer. The reply can be a reply only if it is situated in the same dimension as the question—that is to say, if it is, itself, a summoning, a *kol*.

The reply is a prayer. Prayer should not be understood as a request, even though this idea is not excluded. The structure of the *tefilah*, or *Shemoneh-Esreh*, is very significant: two categories of saying can be distinguished. The first, itself divided, split in two, in the time and space of prayer, is *kol*, summoning.

In the *Shemoneh-Esreh* prayer, the *kol* embraces the second part, which is the actual request or the saying of a said that is a request. The structure of prayer is thus *Kol-dibur-Kol*.[12]

Another Invisible

We may say that Rav Kattina deepens the meaning of the "visible-invisible" relationship by a reference to the *Keruvim*. If the modalities of this relation are those described above, it is nonetheless undeniable that the important point of the teaching is the analogy of the interhuman relationship with the divine-human relationship, an analogy that concerns the sexual character of the relationship.

The structure of the "visible-invisible" could, in a rapid analysis, be interpreted in an erroneous manner. Rav Kattina seeks to emphasize that the beyond is not "another world," somewhere behind the world. The beyond is, precisely, beyond all unveiling. The action of opening the *Parokhet* does not destroy the idea of *Nirin veeyn Nirin*, as one might suppose, but teaches us that the true invisible is beyond "the world."

There is an insistence on the fact that the visible-invisible expresses a relation distinct from unveiling and dissimulation. The non-unveiling does not mean that this relation is reduced to the recondite, since the recondite that manifests itself takes on meaning. It is a meaning by which the invisible does not become stranded in the visible, the *Mi* is not converted into a *Mah*, and the Other is not absorbed into a Same: the meaning is in the trace.

The *Nirin veeyn Nirin* can be understood as a "trace" in the light that Rav Kattina sheds on the thought of Rav Judah. The *Nirin veeyn Nirin*, *Kodesh-Kodesh Kodashim*, *Pshat-Drash* dualities are comparable, in a preliminary approach (that of Rav Judah), to the signifier-signified duality of the sign where the relation between the two faces of the sign "is of a correlative nature and, consequently, still rectitude and hence an unveiling that neutralizes transcendence."[13]

But the *Nirin veeyn Nirin* text, according to Rav Judah, is not a simple *Pshat-Drash* duality where the raising of the veil reveals a meaning other. For then, the *Pshat-Drash* duality would be that of the sign which reveals and introduces the Absent, signified in immanence. The beyond is not the beyond of the *Parokhet*; the duality of the text is *Pshat-Sod* in the sense that the *Sod* signifies an experience which leads beyond being, out of range of the bipolar game of immanence and transcendence where, as Lévinas says, immanence inevitably prevails over transcendence. By his action, Rav Kattina shows up the *Eyn-Nirin* as a false invisible.

The true *Eyn-Nirin* is situated beyond the *Nirin veeyn Nirin* itself. It is in this sense that the *Nirin veeyn Nirin* is a trace. But Rav Kattina, while explaining Rav Judah, goes even further.

The statement of Rav Kattina could have been read more "briefly" as a simple pretext to the objection of Rav Hisda, an objection that continues the problematics of the visible and invisible by introducing very explicitly the notion of unveiling. But are there ever pretexts in the Talmud?

Notes

1. Exod. 20:23 and 20:3.

2. *Rabbenu Behayeh Al hatorah* (Mossad Harav Kook ed.), (Jerusalem, 1977), 2:275.

3. *Ah*: brother; *ahrayut* (same root): responsibility. Cf. on this subject E. A. Valensi, *Le Temps dans la vie morale* (Paris: Vrin, 1968), p. 203.

4. E Lévinas, *Totality and Infinity* (Pittsburgh: Duquesne University Press, 1988), p. 206.

5. Ibid., p. 75; "To recognize the Other is to recognize a hunger. To recognize the Other is to give."

6. F. Collin, *Maurice Blanchot et la question de l'écriture* (Paris: Gallimard, 1971), p. 105.

7. The verse underlines several times: *mikatseh mizeh . . . umikatseh mizeh*.

8. Collin, *Maurice Blanchot et la question de l'écriture*, p. 100.

9. Ibid.

10. Lévinas, *Totality and Infinity*, p. 97.

11. Ibid., p. 69.

12. *Zohar, Vaera* 25b, where the distinction *Kol* and *Dibbur* is analyzed differently.

13. E. Lévinas, *Humanisme de l'autre homme* (Paris: Fata Morgana, 1972), p. 59.

III

Seeing and Death

The Objection of Rav Hisda

Rav Hisda raised the following objection (*metiv*):

"But they shall not go in and cast their eyes, even for a moment, on any of the holy things; if they did, they would die."[1]

From a technical point of view, this objection does not pose any problem; it is a very classical Talmudic procedure: a verse that describes a contrasting situation or assertion is put forward to contradict a given situation or assertion. In our text, the objection can be expressed as follows: "How can Rav Kattina say that the *Parokhet* would be drawn and the *Keruvim* unveiled? Is it not said, in the Torah, that whoever sees holy objects—the Ark and the *Keruvim*—would die?"

Let us situate the verse in its context. Chapter 4 of the book of Numbers (1 to 20) explains the dismantling of the Sanctuary and the way the priests and Levites proceed, the children of Kohath in particular.

It all takes place in two stages. In the first stage, the *Kohanim* (priests) dismantle and cover up the objects. In the second stage, the *Leviim* (Levites) come and transport them (verses 5, 6, and 15).

When the camp is broken, Aaron and his sons are to come and take down the veil of the screen (*Parokhet hamassakh*). With it they must cover up the Ark of the Testimony (*Aron haedut*). On top of this they must put a covering of fine leather (*tahash*) and spread over the whole a cloth all of violet. Then they are to fix the staves of the Ark.[2]

When Aaron and his sons have finished covering all the sacred objects and all their accessories at the breaking of camp, the sons of Kohath are to come to take up the burden, but without touching any of the sacred things; otherwise they would die. This is the charge entrusted to the sons of Kohath in the Tent of Meeting.

Verses 17 to 20, since they follow the verses that we have just quoted, are easier to understand:

YHVH spoke to Moses and Aaron. He said:

Do not cut off the tribe of the clans of Kohath from the number of the Levites. But deal with them in this way, so that they may live on and not incur death when they approach the most holy things (*Kodesh Kodashim*):

Aaron and his sons must go in and assign to each of them his task and his burden. In this way they can go in and cast yet not their eyes, even for a moment, on any of the holy things; if they did, they would die.

The two stages we have just highlighted were intended to prevent the children of Kohath from dying, not only by directly touching—bare-handed—the *Kodesh Kodashim* (verse 15), but also by seeing it. Touching and seeing are forbidden. The objection of Rav Kattina is quite clear: how is it possible to unveil, when the sight of the Ark entails death—*Karet*?

Notes

1. This death concerns everyone but more particularly the Levites, and, among them, even more particularly the children of Kohath, entrusted with transporting the Ark; cf. the whole chapter 3 and, in particular, verses 14–39 of the book of Numbers and chapter 4, verses 1–20.

2. The *Midrash* points out that the Ark is distinguished from the other objects, during transportation, by two things: (1) It is the only object to be covered by the *Parokhet*, then by a *tahash* skin cover, then a violet cloth. All the other utensils are first covered with a violet cloth, then with a scarlet cloth, and finally with a cover of *tahash* skin; (2) All the other utensils are carried in chariots. The Ark must be carried by men, on their shoulders.

IV

The Body beyond the Body

The Parable of the Fiancée

> Rav Nahman said: "The parable of a fiancée: As long as she is in her father's house, she is reserved in regard to her future husband, but when she comes to her father-in-law's house, she is no longer reserved in regard to him."

Rashi comments: "In her father's house, that means during the engagement; in the same way Israel in the desert was not yet accustomed to the divine presence" (Rashi on *Yoma* 54a).

The time of the desert is the time of the engagement of man and God; the return to the land of Israel, that of the wedding.

Engagement and wedding are terms that bring us back to the problematics posited by Rav Kattina: the analogy of the human-divine relationship with the masculine-feminine relationship.

Here is Rav Nahman's answer:

There are two different situations that imply no comparison, and therefore no contradiction. The time of the engagement cannot be contrasted with that of marriage. If, in the desert, it is impossible to "see," it is because Israel has an attitude comparable to that of the fiancée: reserved and distant—modest, in short. Once in its own land, Israel is like a woman who retires into the intimacy of her home, and there, modesty is replaced by immodesty: immodesty which is not that of the erotic nudity of the visible-invisible, but rather that of a neutral and insignificant nudity. Rav Nahman's answer, although very clear, poses a problem. If the aim is to show, as the Talmud does in its usual manner, that there are two cases, two independent situations—which would solve the contradiction—why explain this by means of a parable that restores the man-woman relationship? Why not simply limit oneself to the classical form of the *hatam* (there) and the *hakha* (here), using a language without images? Why not just say "in the desert . . ." and "in the land . . ."? Why, in short, bring that which was a part of the context of profanation over to these notions of modesty and immodesty, thereby comparing them?

In fact, Rav Nahman is not concerned simply with solving the contradiction, which could have been done without the parable; he turns the reflection around the other way. What was said about the human-divine relationship, in the shadow of the masculine-feminine relationship, is now going to shed light on the man-woman relationship.

The *Nirin veeyn Nirin* is a timeless invariant of the relation, since, whether it be in the desert or in the land, the *Parokhet* sets up the "visible-invisible" structure. The strict analysis of the parallelism, the comparison, and the object of the latter lead to a very significant paradox: the modesty of the fiancée, which institutes separation and distance, proceeds from the *Nirin veeyn Nirin*, that is to say, from the erotic. There is also an erotic modesty. The woman who separates herself, becomes distant, retires, hides, or veils herself is far from absent. Her position is that of an absence designed to reveal a sort of presence-absence. When modest, the woman withdraws from the gaze; when erotic, she reveals herself. When, in her husband's home, modesty is replaced by immodesty, the erotic disappears, and a neutral and insignificant nudity replaces it.

The action of demystification that reveals a beyond, not of the invisible, but of that which took on the appearance of the invisible, is, in return, applied to the man-woman relationship, and the immodest woman should be seen in the light of this action. We can therefore say that an exceptional relationship is realized in a circumstance which, for formal logic, proceeds from a contradiction: the uncovered does not lose its mystery in the uncovering; the concealed is not unveiled; the shadows are not dissipated. The uncovering-profanation is in modesty, even in the form of immodesty; "the clandestine, when uncovered, does not acquire the status of the disclosed."[1]

The indecency of the woman under her husband's roof, in the light of Rav Kattina's action, is inverted into decency, or better, into decency-indecency, into eroticism, in fact.

The whole teaching of the parable lies in the fact that modesty and immodesty, the concealed and the unveiled, must always be understood in the simultaneity of each term. "Immodesty refers to the modesty that it has profaned without overcoming it."[2]

This simultaneity is the essence of what Lévinas calls femininity. Rav Nahman is concerned with teaching that woman offers a body that goes beyond the body, like the "face that goes beyond the faces."[3] The naked body of skin—which should be perceived as a body dressed with skin—shows the way toward the being of light; it refers to something else, "beyond the possible," to the original unpronounced *Aleph* (according to the *Midrash* of Rabbi Meir, the *Ayin* of *Or* [skin] is replaced by an *Aleph* and thereby becomes light).

"The Beloved, at once graspable but intact in her nudity, beyond object and face and thus beyond the existent, abides in virginity."[4]

Notes

1. E. Lévinas, *Totality and Infinity* (Pittsburgh: Duquesne University Press, 1988), p. 260.
2. Ibid., p. 257.
3. Ibid., p. 260.
4. Ibid., p. 258.

BOOK THREE

The Burnt Book

"Tonight, as every night by the light of my candle, I fill a few unsated leaves with exhumed words.

God, on the other side of my table, composes His book whose smoke envelops me; for the flame of my candle serves as his pen.

What will *my* book be, in a short while, but a few ashes on one of the pages of His?

No space is protected for writing," wrote, three centuries ago, an unrecognized rabbi whose name I shall not disclose.

He also wrote: "In each vocable, a wall of fire separates me from God and God is, with me, this vocable."

Fire can be extinguished only in the word it writes. Eternity of the book, conflagration after conflagration . . .

There will only ever be one book thrown to the flames where all books will be sacrificed. So time is written in the ashes of time and the book of God, in the wild flames of our books.

Fire is the virginity of desire.

EDMOND JABÈS

To think is to go beyond.
The best thing in religion is that it creates heretics. . . .
ERNST BLOCH

Rabbi Nahman of Bratslav—or the Hasidic imagination, the celebration of
the word, the apotheosis of the winged legend, inspired and intoxicating.
Rabbi Nahman—or the flight toward the fantastic, danger, and laughter.

His life, rich in exploits, whose dominant theme is paradox and fever, on
the heights or in the abyss, in complete hallucination, and never in security.

Great-grandson of Ba'al Shem Tov (the founder of Hasidism), he quarrels
with all the greats who draw their inspiration from him. An intellectual guide,
he passes on his vision of the world through tales, masterpieces of the genre,
rather than by theories. Too accessible as a Cabalist and not sufficiently so as
a rabbi; ascetic and an enemy of doubt, he frequents so-called emancipated
intellectual circles whose vocation and pastime is to doubt, enjoy, and dis-
pute. An intolerant believer, he plays chess with freethinkers: their faith in
nothingness stimulates him.

When ill, he detests doctors. . . . He forbids his followers to read philosophical works, including Maimonides, but he himself has read them all.

Haughty with some, humble with others (and always with those with
whom he should not be), he is never the same, he is ever the same . . . .

Customs and possessions repel him, they hinder freedom. . . .

He moved from one place to another; he loved movement, changes of scen-
ery. He feared boredom more than illness, repetition more than sin. . . .[1]

THIS BRIEFLY sketched portrait of Rabbi Nahman of Bratslav, borrowed from Elie Wiesel, is typical of the classical image we have of this
character who manages to escape the narrow frame of Hasidism to become one of the figures of world literature.

He is made out to be a storyteller; he is said to be the precurser of
Kafka, the founder of modern Hebrew literature. All these images are
not false, but they tend to end up leaving his work as a whole lost in the
vagueness of all his poorly known works. The whole philosophical part
of his work has been neglected; worse, it has been claimed to be in-
existent. The traditional literature of Bratslav would only be of an apologetic and moralizing nature and, basically, simplistic.[2]

The purpose of this *Burnt Book* is to show up, from the general work
of Rabbi Nahman, the concept of a "burnt book," which denotes not

only the book of Rabbi Nahman that bears this name, but all the related objects or facts that may be related to it according to the explanation that we shall give.

Rabbi Nahman is an author whose philosophy and biography are
closely intertwined (somewhat in the same way as Kierkegaard's), and
call for a detour via some episodes of his life or, we should say, his
adventures.

For the main part, it is enough to know that Rabbi Nahman was
born at Medzibezh, in Podolia, in 1772; on his mother's side, he is the
great-grandson of Israel ben Eliezer Ba'al Shem Tov, founder of Hasidism, and, on his father's side, the grandson of Nahman of Horodenka
(Gorodenka), an important pre-Hasidic figure, close to Baal Shem. He
marries young (at thirteen) and settles, after a second marriage, at Med-
vedevka, in the province of Kiev. There he starts his "career" as a rabbi,
as a spiritual leader of a small group of disciples.

In 1798, he makes a trip (important for the development of his
thought) to the land of Israel, accompanied by his friend and disciple
Rabbi Simeon. The Napoleonic Wars are at their height. He visits
Haifa, Jaffa, Galilee, Safed, among others. He meets Jacob Samson of
Shepetovka and Abraham ben Alexander Katz of Kalisk, both engaged
in a controversy with Rabbi Shneur Zalman of Lyady. Napoleon in-
vades the Holy Land, and Rabbi Nahman decides to quickly leave the
country after having stayed for only a few months (a short period for
the times). Returning to Madvedevka, after an eventful journey, Rabbi
Nahman becomes involved in a local conflict, which prompts him to
develop a theory of the necessity of conflict (*Mahloket*) that he will hold
to all his life and that occupies an important place in his thought. During the summer of 1800, he settles at Zlatopol (near the town of
Shpola) in the province of Kiev. Immediately after his arrival, a conflict
breaks out with Aryeh Leib, nicknamed the "Grandfather of Shpola,"
an important Hasidic leader who was very influential in Podolia and the
Ukraine. Among other accusations, Aryeh Leib denounces the Shabbatean and Frankist character of Rabbi Nahman's teachings. The quarrel
of Zlatopol becoming unbearable, R. Nahman leaves the town and settles at Bratslav in 1802. He will stay there until 1810. There again, his
personality causes controversies among the *Hasidim*. In fact, all the
Hasidic masters of the region come into conflict with him, except his
faithful friend, Rabbi Levi Isaac of Berdichev.

Rabbi Nahman traveled a great deal. All his trips are described in his
biography *Hayyei Moharan* (1875) and *Yemei Moharan* (The life and
days of our master Rabbi Nahman), two books written by his disciple

and secretary Rabbi Nathan Sternhartz of Nemirov, to whom we owe the majority of the texts of Bratslav; in fact, Rabbi Nahman taught, recounted, and spoke in Yiddish and R. Nathan transcribed into Hebrew.[3]

Besides his journey to Israel, the journey to Lemberg (Lvov) in 1808 is also considered as a capital moment. The official reason for the journey: R. Nahman is sick; he is leaving to consult doctors, who will tell him that he has tuberculosis. The more secret reason is linked to his contacts with Frankism . . .

In 1810, he leaves Bratslav and settles in Uman, with the clear intention of dying and being buried there. He dies on 18 Tishri (October) 1811.

If we were to re-create Rabbi Nahman's library in our imagination, we would see a piece of furniture with three shelves. On the first (let us say, the bottom one), there is the first category of books entitled "Book I," all of an exoteric character (*nigleh*, in Hebrew), "readable" in sum; the *Likkutim*, usually called *Likkutei Moharan*, volumes 1 and 2 (now in a single volume), belong to this category. *Likkutim* means "collections." The first volume includes 286 paragraphs, or rather passages (*Torot* in Hasidic language), long or short, some covering several pages, others only in the form of aphorisms. It dates from 1809 (it seems that there was only one edition prior to 1806). The second volume is shorter and has only 125 pages.

In the same "Book I" category, there are the tales and the *Sefer Hamidot*, a book of aphorisms and advice of all sorts, organized into themes according to the order of the letters of the Hebrew alphabet.

On the second shelf up, we would find the category of books entitled "Book II." These books are of an esoteric character (*nistar* or *razin*, "secret"). These books are not manuals, in the etymological sense of the term, because they are not graspable by the hand, and not without cause . . . they constitute the whole of the "Burnt Book" (*Sefer ha-Nisraf*). The shelf is therefore empty.

Further up, on the third shelf, the category of "Books III." Totally esoteric books (*nistar denistar* or *razin derazin*). The reader need not worry about this one either; once again the shelf is empty. "Book III" is entitled the "Hidden Book" (*Sefer ha-Ganuz*).

We are going to examine in detail the text dealing with "the library" that is found in the *Hayyei Moharan*, the biographical book written by

R. Nathan; it includes biographical aspects but also numerous statements by Rabbi Nahman, cited here directly in Yiddish, statements about everyday life, not necessarily intended for publication. The book was published at Lemberg in 1874.

The passage presented here is entitled the "Journey to Lemberg." Rabbi Nahman was then thirty-four years old; he has just learned that he has tuberculosis and is shortly going to die.

The style of the text is repetitive and fairly heavy, but the tragedy and drama are well highlighted.

The "Journey to Lemberg"

At Lemberg, between Purim and Pesah in the year 1808, Rabbi Nahman entered a room and wept; he called Rabbi Simeon (the disciple who had accompanied him). The tears ran down his cheeks. Sighing, he said: "I have no one by me from whom I can seek counsel." He then said that he had in his house a book which was the cause of the death of his wife and son, and of his own situation. He knew not what to do. What is important to understand is that he thought he was going to die at Lemberg and that he thought he could live only if the book in question was burnt. And because of this Rabbi Nahman knew not what to do. What! Burn the extraordinary book to which he had devoted himself entirely . . .

Rabbi Simeon answered: "It is obvious that if your life depends on the disappearance of the book, it is better to burn the book so that you may live." Rabbi Nahman replied: "It is certain that I would be able to go on living for a time if the book were burnt; in spite of that, it causes me great suffering to burn it, for you do not see the importance of the holiness of this book; and I have lost my first wife and my children, and I have been beset by numerous sufferings because of it." And he wept and wept . . .

Then the doctor arrived, and Rabbi Simeon explained the situation to him. The doctor spoke a little with Rabbi Nahman who was still weeping a lot. He then said to Rabbi Simeon: "If it is so, here is the key to my little cupboard. Go quickly, do not weaken, hire a coach for Bratslav. Do not let the rain and the snow slow you down, hasten to Bratslav. When you arrive there, you shall take two books: the first one is in the small cupboard and the second in the box of my daughter Adel; take them and burn them. Hurry, and, above all, do not change anything of what I have ordered."[4]

Rabbi Simeon left straight away for Bratslav. But, as he arrived at Dashiv, which is near Bratslav, he fell and could not rise again. He ordered that he be put in the coach to continue to Bratslav, so he could at least command others to burn the books in his presence. However, once he had arrived at Bratslav, he felt in perfect health. He took the two books and burnt them both. Rabbi Nahman later said that this book would never ever exist again, that it was a shame for this loss that would never come again, and he said that it was necessary to burn this book; but the "collections" would be printed and "distributed throughout the world."

When I wrote the holy book before him, the very one that was burnt on his orders, he said to me as I was writing it: "Do you know what you are writing?"

I humbly answered: "No, of course, I do not know at all." He said to me: "You do not know what you do not know!" (Then follows the Yiddish translation of this sentence: *Di weisst gor nit di weisst nit.*)

He had yet another book of a level greatly superior to the "Burnt Book"; it was a "Hidden Book" of which he said that his body had departed from him as he was writing it. No eye had seen this book. It belonged to the realm of the "secret of secrets," completely esoteric. He said of this book that the Messiah would make a commentary on it. The "Hidden Book" was already completed in 1806, that is to say, five years before his death.

And now, continues R. Nathan, contemplate the greatness he attained after that, for, during his lifetime, he was never at the same level; at each moment, he was in a new situation.

Understand this well: the greatness of the "Hidden Book"; no thought could ever have a hold on it, and the Messiah will make a commentary on it . . .

Before we go any further, here are some points to be kept in mind.

1. The nonmateriality of books, the refusal of the presence of the body, the impossible coexistence of the body and the "Hidden Book."
2. The permanent evolution of the personality of the author ("It is forbidden to be old").
3. The book is not visible.
4. The book is not graspable.
5. The Messiah makes a commentary . . .

He said: concerning the "Burnt Book," only a righteous person (*Tsaddik*), unique in his generation and wise (*Hakham*) in the seven wisdoms, could understand anything of it.

The "Burnt Book" could be understood by at least one person, whereas the "Hidden Book" would not be understood by even one person; only the Messiah would make a commentary on it.

"Book II," also called the "Burnt Book," was made up of four parts. The "Burnt Book" was first passed on to two persons of our group. R. Nahman ordered them to go around the towns of the region and to recite, in each town, a part of the book. He also ordered them to take some leaves of the manuscript of his future *Likkutei Moharan* (vol. 1) and to leave some leaves in each town. This is in 1806. None of his books has yet been published.

The book that the two envoys had with them was the copy which I had recopied. We nickname "Book II" the "Burnt Book," for all the printed books formed "Book I," since they belonged to the esoteric category (*nigleh*).

The book he ordered to be burnt when he was at Lemberg constituted "Book II," an esoteric (nistar) book; I recopied this book in 1806; he gave this copy (mine) to two people to have it go around several towns and be recited bit by bit in each town; he made these people swear not to reveal anything of it.

Then there was a third book: "Book III." That is the "Hidden Book"; no man has touched it, no eye has seen it. Secret of secrets (*nistar denistar*). This book was also finished at the beginning of 1806.

Then Rabbi Nathan explains that there is a link between the "Burnt Book" and the death of R. Nahman's son. Here are some more points to sum up:

1. R. Nahman settles at Bratslav.
2. Before 1803, he started writing the fragments that make up the *Collections* ("Book I").
3. 1803: R. Nathan becomes R. Nahman's private secretary.
4. June 1805: the circle of R. Nahman hears for the first time of "Book II," the future "Burnt Book."
5. 1806 (winter): R. Nathan reads and copies the "Burnt Book."
6. 1806 (summer): R. Nahman sends the two emissaries.
7. 1806 (summer): death of R. Nahman's son, Shlomo-Ephraim.
8. 1808: R. Nathan copies the whole of "Book II."
9. 1808: Journey to Lemberg; "Book II" becomes the "Burnt Book."

Feuille, "leaf," he spelled: *feu-oeil.* But I have never found
out if *feu-oeil* meant for him "dead eye" or, on the
contrary, "eye of fire." The latter fits rather better with
my idea of the white page in whose eye the word is
consumed.

EDMOND JABÈS

The order to burn the book, which transforms "Book II" into the "Burnt Book," is given at a moment of crisis; Rabbi Nahman has known since 1807 that he is going to die; now, in 1808, during the winter at Lemberg, he actually realizes it. We also know that as he left Lemberg, he carried with him the manuscript of the *Likkutim* that he had apparently had R. Nathan prepare for publication before his departure. The idea of burning the books is completely contemporaneous with the idea of having them published . . . Once again we find the revealed-hidden dialectic; the visible-invisible . . .

It is just before his departure for Lemberg that he asks R. Nathan to finish copying by dictation the second copy of the "Burnt Book." They were to be completed . . . in order to be burnt. At a first glance, we might see, in the order to burn, an isolated and circumstantial idea, a consequence of the crisis. However, the study of the whole of Bratslav's texts shows that this action is, at this particular moment, a part of a developed thought, even if it was systematized later. We may thus consider some significant texts, of which these two are characteristic examples.

The first text is a short anecdote recounted in a book written by R. Nathan, a sort of continuation of the *Hayyei Moharan*, which compiles speeches and dreams of R. Nahman not mentioned in the other books; this book is entitled *Sihot Haran* (Words of R. Nahman).

> The disciples entered the room and found R. Nahman, holding a sheet of paper. On the sheet, his writing. He turned to them and said: "Numerous are the teachings of this page and numerous are the worlds that are nourished by its smoke. . . ." He held the sheet of paper against the flame of the candle. . . .

The second text, more important, more systematic, is found in the *Likkutei Moharan*, second volume, passage 32 (henceforth: *LM* 2:32).

It is made up of five unnumbered paragraphs. It is a relatively long, difficult, and enigmatic text, typical of the procedure and style of the *Likkutei Moharan*, using association of ideas, reinterpreted quotations from the Talmud, from the *Midrash*, and from the *Zohar*, and with numerous repetitions. A progression is marked by "because," "but," "however," "also," which follow on, one from the other, without any apparent logic. We give here the first paragraph, without commentary. We shall pick it up again, in a linear fashion, after a general introduction to the main themes of R. Nahman's thought.

> There are hidden righteous men; they know faces in the Torah but have to keep their teaching hidden. . . . Even so with him (i.e., Rabbi Nahman). Sometimes he knows a teaching which has faces, that is to say faces in a teaching, but he must keep it secret and not tell it. Sometimes he does not even write it. At other times he writes it down and then burns it. In fact,

if this teaching were written, it would be a book and the latter would have
its place in the world. In these books, there are Names that should be understood in the sense of the Talmudic expression "My Name written in holiness . . ." (*Shabbat* tractate, 116a). However, the world destroys that and it is
necessary to make it disappear and burn it. But it is good for the world that
these teachings and books be hidden and burnt.

So here: numerous books, which were books, have been effaced and destroyed. It is certain that the righteous, the greats of old, the authors of the
Mishnah and the *Gemara* and the men of this caliber, wrote numerous books
that have been lost. However, it is good for the world, because if it had not
been so, it would have been impossible for us to approach the blessed Name.
For if there are many heretical books (*Sifrei minim*), if they were scattered
over the world, it would be impossible to approach the blessed Name. Thus
Jeroboam ben Nebat who made two golden calves and said: "Here are your
gods, Israel . . ." (1 Kings 12:28) and led the people of Israel astray. Is it
possible that he could have led a whole nation astray with such a trifle?
Worship calves! come, come! However, it is certain that there was a great
display of intelligence and subtlety in this heresy. And if we found now the
smallest leaf of these books, it would remove us from the blessed Name and it
would be impossible to approach him. And because of this, it is good that
holy books disappear and be burnt. . . .

Each page of the *Likkutei Moharan* reveals something new—either in
the interpretation of the Bible, of the Talmud, of the *Zohar*, and the
classical texts of the Cabala, or in the traditional concepts already developed by Hasidism. In order that our study may remain faithful to the
text of Bratslav, here are some fundamental propositions around a single passage of the *Likkutei*, which has the advantage of setting out ideas
that come up fairly often in other passages, with the result that they
form an essential theme.

It is passage 64 from the *Likkutim* 1 (*LM* 1:64), composed of six
parts. We shall be analyzing four of them. We have made the subdivisions a, b, c . . .

64, I, a

For the Name, blessed be He, because of his uterine capacity (*rahmanuto*),
created the world, because he wished to reveal this uterine capacity. Now, if
the world had not been created, to whom could he have revealed his uterine
virtue? And because of this, He created the whole of creation, from the beginning of the emanation, right up to the central point of the material world, in
order to show his uterine capacity.

64, I, b

And when the Name, blessed be He, wanted to create the world, there was no room to create it, because everything was infinite. Because of this, He contracted (*tsimtsum*) the "light" toward the sides and by means of this withdrawal (*tsimtsum*) an "empty space" (*hallal hapanui*) was formed. And inside this "empty space" the days [time] and measures [space] came into existence that constituted the major part of the creation of the world—as is mentioned at the beginning of the book *Ets-Hayim* at the start.

This "empty space" was logically necessary to allow the creation of the world. For without this "empty space," there would have been no room for the creation of the world as we have just said.

In these first two paragraphs, Rabbi Nahman takes up one of the key concepts of the Cabalistic thought of Rabbi Isaac Luria.[5] It is not, however, a question of repetition, since R. Nahman, as we shall see, adds important changes that accomplish the transition from the world of the Cabala to that of Hasidism—the latter having much more affective and existential overtones, compared to concepts that had an almost exclusively theological, theosophical, and metaphysical tone.

The Lurianic universe is based on three main ideas, those of the *Tsimtsum* (Withdrawal), *Shevirah* (Breaking), and *Tikkun* (Reparation).

The theory of the *Tsimtsum* is one of the most surprising and daring concepts ever put forward in the history of Cabalism.[6] *Tsimtsum* originally means "concentration" or "contraction." In Cabalistic language, it is better translated as "withdrawal" or "retreat." Luria begins by asking questions with a realistic or, if one prefers, a rather brutal turn of phrase:

—How can there be a world if God is everywhere?
—If God is "Everything-in-Everything," how can there be things that are not God?
—How can God create the world ex nihilo, if there is no nothingness?

Luria answers by formulating the theory of the *Tsimtsum*, or the "Withdrawal." According to this theory, the first act of the Creator was not to reveal himself to something exterior. Far from being a movement toward the outside, or a coming out from his hidden identity, the first stage was a retreat, a drawing back; God retired "from and within himself" and, by this act, abandoned to the emptiness a place within himself, created a space for the world-to-come.

At a certain point in the heart of the light of the In-finite (*Ein-sof*), the divine essence of "light" was eclipsed; a space was left empty, in the middle. Compared to the In-finite, this space was only an infinitestimal dot, but compared to Creation, it was the whole of cosmic space. God can reveal himself only because, first of all, he withdrew.

עח   מוהר"ן   סד פרעה אל בא סג המילה כונת סוד   ליקוטי

לאחרים בחכמתם, הוא רק בבחי' הליכה, שאינו מעופף ונכנס בעומק לתוך המוח והלב, רק שנדבק קצת להמות, אבל אינו נכנס בעומק לתוך הלב והמות. אבל כשיש להם ח"ו כנפים מדיבורים רעים כנ"ל, אזי שכלם מעופף כנ"ל, וגם מזיק למרחוק, כמו המעופף שמעופף בשעה אחת למרחוק, וגם שמעופף חכמתם המשובשת ונכנס ונדבק בהמוח והלב בעומק גדול מאד: **והנמלה** המונח בתוך פי הנחש, הוא בחינות חכם הדור, שהוא חכם הישר והצדיק, ובעל מדות טובות. ומחמת שהוא חכם גדול דקדושה ונכנס באלו החכמות, אזי כשאלו החכמים נכנסים בחקירתם, לחקור באלו החכמות, אז יש לו צער גדול מאד, ויש לו מלחמה גדולה עמהם, היינו עם בחי' הנחש הנ"ל. כי מתגברים עליו מאד בלבולים ואמונות כוזביות, והוא בחי' מבטח בוגד, שמתגבר עליו במחן בוגד, שאינו במחן שלם ואמת כראוי, שזהו בחי' אמונות כוזביות, וזהו בחינות (משלי כ"ה) שן רועה ורגל מועדת מבטח בוגד, היינו שזה המבטח בוגד היא בחינות שן רועה את החכם, שהוא הנגלה שבתוך פיה כנ"ל. כי מחמת שהוא חכם ונכנס בעבדות ה', מתגברים עליו אלו הבלבלים והאמונות כוזביות ביותר, וצריך לו תמיד מלחמה גדולה עמהם: ובין כשהנחש הולך, ובין כשהוא מעופף, יש לו צער גדול ומלחמה גדולה. רק שבוודאי בעת העפיפה, צערו גדול יותר מאד. ואין לו שום נייחא בין כשהוא הולך, בין כשהוא מעופף. רק שיש ממוצע בין ההליכה ובין העפיפה, הוא בעת שפוסק העפיפה ומוריד עצמו מן העפיפה ממעלה למטה, כדרך המעופף בעת שרוצה לשלש ולהוריד עצמו למטה, ואזי יש להנמלה הנ"ל נייחא, כי אזי אינו הולך ואינו מעופף. היינו, כי יש כמה עתים שהחכמים נייחים ואינם חוקרין, כגון בעת שינה ואכילה, ואז יש נייחא להחכם שהוא בחי' הנמלה שבתוך פיה. כי החכם הוא בחי' נמלה, כמ"ש (משלי ו') לך אל נמלה וגו' חכם, כי זה החכם מלמד דעת ודרכי ה' אל העם:

וזה סוד מה שאמר הסבא (זוהר משפטים דף צ"ה) מאן הוא נחש דפרח באוירא ואזיל בפרודא, בין כך ובין כך אית נייחא לחד נמלה דשכיב בין שינוי. היינו בחינות הנחש הנ"ל. דפרח באוירא, שפריחתו, על ידי האוירים. היינו, על ידי דיבורים רעים, שנעשה לו מהם כנפים. ואזיל בפרודא, היינו שאין לו רק בחינות הליכה, כשכנפים דקדושה הם כתיקונן, ואין להנחש כנפים מדיבורים רעים, אזי אין לו רק בחי' הליכה. וזה ואזיל בפרודא, בחינות (יחזקאל א') וכנפיהם פרודות מלמעלה, היינו בחינות כנפי דקדושה. אזי, ואזי, שאין לו רק בחינות הליכה. כי בחינות הליכה יש לו תמיד, כי הבחירה חפשית להמחקרים לחקור בכל עת שירצו, רק שאין יכולים לעופף בבחי' הנ"ל, כשאין להם כנפים מדיבורים רעים, ואין להם רק

(א) עיין בסוף הס' מובא התר הזאת בנ"א מכתי" רבינו ז"ל בעצמו.

בחי' הליכה כנ"ל : בין כך ובין כך, היינו בחי' הממוצע בין ההליכה והעפיפה כנ"ל, וזה נקרא בין כך ובין כך, שהוא בין ההליכה והעפיפה, ואזי יש לה נייחא להנמלה דשכיב בין שינה כנ"ל: שארי בחבורא וסיים בפרודא, היינו שאלו המחקרים, שהם חכמים להרע, שהם בחינות הנחש כנ"ל, חכמתם וחקירתם הוא, שארי בחבורא, שתחלת חקירתם מתחלת מהמחוברים, מחיבור חומר וצורה. וסיים בפרודא, שמסתיימת חכמתם בשכליים הנפרדים. כי כן דרך כל חקירתם, להתחיל מחיבור החומר והצורה, ועולים ממדריגה למדריגה, מתחילה מחומר וצורה של הגשמיים, ואח"כ מחומר וצורה של הדקים יותר, ואח"כ מחומר וצורה של עילה ועלול, עד שמגיעים ומסיימים בשכליים הנפרדים. ורוצים להשיג בחקירתם האנושיית, המומעת והמשובשת, כידוע להמחקרים בעצמן, הם רוצים להשיג ע"י חקירות הללו, מחיבור חומר וצורה, את שכליים נפרדים, וזה שארי בחבורא וסיים בפרודא:

סד ויאמר ה' אל משה בא אל פרעה כי אני הכבדתי את לבו ואת לב עבדיו למען שתי אותותי אלה בקרבו. ולמען תספר באזני בנך ובן בנך את אשר התעללתי במצרים ואת אותותי אשר שמתי בם וידעתם כי אני ה' וכו'. הנני מביא מחר ארבה בגבולך (שמות י') (א):

א כי השי"ת מחמת רחמנותו ברא את העולם, כי רצה לגלות רחמנותו, ואם לא היה בריאת העולם על מי היה מראה רחמנותו. וע"כ ברא את כל הבריאה מתחילת האצילות, עד סוף נקודת המרכז של עולם הגשמי, כדי להראות רחמנותו. וכאשר רצה השי"ת לברוא את העולם, לא היה מקום לבוראו מחמת שהיה הכל א"ס. ע"כ צמצם את האור לצדדין, ועל ידי הצמצום הזה נעשה חלל הפנוי. ובתוך החלל הפנוי הזה, נתהוו כל הימים והמדות, שהם בריאת העולם (כמ"ש בעל"ח בתחלתו). וזה החלל הפנוי, היה מוכרח לבריאת העולם. כי בלתי החלל הפנוי, לא היה שום מקום לבריאת העולם כנ"ל. וזה הצמצום של החלל הפנוי, א"א להבין ולהשיג, כ"א לעתיד לבא. כי צריך לומר בו שני הפכים, יש ואין. כי החלל הפנוי הוא ע"י הצמצום, שכביכול צמצם אלקותו משם, ואין שם אלקות כביכול, כי אם לא כן אינו פנוי, והכל אין סוף, ואין מקום לבריאת העולם כלל. אבל באמת לאמת, בוודאי אעפ"כ יש שם ג"כ אלקות, כי בוודאי אין שום דבר בלעדי חיותו. וע"כ א"א להשיג כלל בחי' חלל הפנוי, עד לעתיד לבא:

ב ודע, שיש שני מיני אפיקורסית. יש אפיקורסית, שבא מחכמות חיצוניות, ועליו נאמר (אבות פ"ב) ודע מה שתשיב לאפיקורוס. כי האפיקורסית הזאת יש עליה תשובה, כי זאת האפיקורסית בא מחכמות חיצוניות שהם

Likkutei Moharan, 1:64, I a–e

בלא אותיות כנ"ל. וע"כ המבוכות הבאים משם, הם בבחי' שתיקה. וכמו שמצינו במשה (מנחות כ"מ) כששאל על מיתת ר"ע, זו תורה וזה שכרה. השיבו לו, שתוק כך עלה במחשבה. היינו שאתה צריך לשתוק, ולבלי לשאול תשובה ותירוץ על קשיא זו. כי כך עלה במחשבה, שהוא בחינות למעלה מן הדיבור. ע"כ אתה צריך לשתוק על שאלה זו, כי הוא בבחינות עלה במחשבה, שאין שם דיבור ליישב אותה. וכמו כן אלו הקושיות והמבוכות שבאים מחלל הפנוי, שאין שם דיבור ולא שכל כנ"ל, ע"כ הם בבחי' שתיקה, וצריך רק להאמין ולשתוק שם. וע"כ אסור ליכנס ולעיין בדברי האפיקורסית והמבוכות אלו, כ"א צדיק שהוא בחי' פה (שמות ד'), בחי' שתיקה, בבחינות שנקרא כבד פה מן הדיבור. וע"כ הצדיק שהוא בחינות משה, בחינות שתיקה, יכול לעיין בדברי המבוכות אלו, שהם בחינות שתיקה כנ"ל. וצריך דווקא לעיין, כדי להעלות הנשמות שנפלו לשם כנ"ל :

ד ודע, כי מחלוקת היא בחינות בריאת העולם. כי עיקר בריאת העולם, ע"י חלל הפנוי כנ"ל, כי בלא זה היה הכל אין סוף, ולא היה מקום לבריאת העולם כנ"ל. וע"כ צמצם עצמם האור לצדדין, ונעשה חלל הפנוי, ובתוכו ברא את כל הבריאה, היינו הימים והמדות, ע"י הדיבור כנ"ל, בדבר ה' שמים נעשו וכו'. וכן הוא בחי' המחלוקת, כי אלו היו כל הת"ח אחד, לא היה מקום לבריאת העולם. רק על ידי המחלוקת שביניהם, והם נחלקים זה מזה, וכ"א מושך עצמו לצד אחר, על ידי זה נעשה ביניהם בחינות חלל הפנוי, שהוא בחינות צמצום האור לצדדין, שבו הוא בריאת העולם על ידי הדיבור כנ"ל. כי כל הדברים שכ"א מהם מדבר, הכל הם רק בשביל בריאת העולם שנעשה על ידם בתוך החלל הפנוי שביניהם. כי הת"ח בוראים את הכל על ידי דבריהם, כמ"ש (ישעיה נ"א) ולאמר לציון עמי אתה, אל תקרי עמי אלא עמי, מה אנא עבדי שמיא וארעא במילולי אף אתם כך (כמ"ש בזוהר בהקדמה דף ה') : אך צריך ליזהר שלא לדבר יותר מדאי, רק כפי צורך בריאת העולם ולא יותר. כי על ידי רבוי האור, שלא היו הכלים יכולים לסבול ריבוי האור, נשתברו, ומשבירת הכלים היה התהוות הקליפות. כן הם אם אחד מרבה לדבר, מזה גורם התהוות הקליפות. כי הוא בחי' ריבוי האור, שע"ז היו שבירת הכלים, שע"ז התהוות הקליפות:

וזה פירוש המשנה (אבות פ"א) **כל ימי גדלתי בין החכמים, ולא מצאתי לגוף טוב משתיקה. ולא**

המדרש הוא העיקר, אלא המעשה, וכל המרבה דברים מביא חטא. כל ימי גדלתי בין החכמים. בין החכמים, הוא בחי' חלל הפנוי, שנתהוה ונעשה בין החכמים, על ידי הפירוד והמחלוקת שיש ביניהם כנ"ל. וזה בין החכמים דייקא, היינו שיש פירוד ומחלוקת ביניהם. כי אם היו כולם אחד, אין שייך לומר בין החכמים. וע"י המחלוקת נעשה בחינות חלל הפנוי, ובתוך החלל הפנוי הזה נעשה בריאת העולם, היינו **כל ימי גדלתי**, שהיינו מגדל ימי ומדותי, שהוא בחי' בריאת העולם. **בין החכמים**, בין החכמים דייקא, בתוך החלל הפנוי כנ"ל, כי שם נעשה כל הבריאה כנ"ל. וזה **גדלתי**, שהגדלתי ימי ומדותי, מקטנות לגדלות. וזה שקראם **ימי**, כי הם ימים שלו, כי הוא בורא את העולם וכו' כנ"ל. וזה **ולא מצאתי לגוף טוב משתיקה**, כי שם בחלל הפנוי אין בו טוב משתיקה כנ"ל. כי אסור ליכנוס לשם, כ"א מי שהוא בבחינות שתיקה, בחי' משה כנ"ל. וזה שאמר כל ימי גדלתי בין החכמים ולא מצאתי וכו', כי על ידי שאני במדריגה זו, בבחי' שתיקה, כמו שאמר שאין טוב משתיקה. כי אסור ליכנוס שם בחלל הפנוי. כ"א מי שהוא בבחינות שתיקה כנ"ל. וזה **המדרש הוא העיקר אלא המעשה, וכל המרבה דברים מביא חטא.** כי כל מדרשם ודבריהם שאלו החכמים מדברים, אין העיקר המדרש בלבד, אלא המעשה, שיעשו ויבראו על ידי דבריהם את העולם כנ"ל, אל תקרי עמי אלא עמי כנ"ל. אך כל המרבה דברים מביא חטא, כי מריבוי האור נתהוו הקליפות כנ"ל:

ה **ודע**, שעל ידי הניגון של הצדיק, שהוא בחי' משה, הוא מעלה את הנשמות מן האפיקורסית הזאת של החלל הפנוי שנפלו לשם. כי דע, שכל חכמה וחכמה שבעולם, יש לה זמר וניגון מיוחד. שזה הזמר מיוחד לחכמה זו, ומזה הזמר נמשכת החכמה הזאת. וזה בחינות (תהלים מ"ז) זמרו משכיל, שכל שכל וחכמה יש לו זמר וניגון. ואפילו חכמת האפיקורסית, יש לה זמר וניגון המיוחד לחכמה האפיקורסית. וזה שאמרו רז"ל (חגיגה ט"ו ע"ב) אחר מה הוי ביה, זמרא יווני לא פסק מפומיה, וכשהיה קם מבית המדרש, כמה ספרי מינין נופלין ממנו. כי זה תלוי בזה, כי על ידי זמר הנ"ל שלא פסק מפיו, על ידי זה היו הספרי מינין נופלין ממנו, כי זה הזמר היה מיוחד לזה האפיקורסית והמינות שהיה לו. נמצא כל חכמה וחכמה לפי בחינתה ומדריגתה, כן יש לה זמר וניגון השייך ומיוחד אליה. וכן ממדריגה

ליקוטי   בא אל פרשה סד   מוהר"ן

שהם באים ממותרות, מבחינות שבירת כלים. כי מחמת ריבוי האור נשתברו הכלים, ומשם נתהוו הקליפות כידוע. וחכמות חיצוניות באים משם, היינו משבירת כלים, ממותרות פסולת הקדושה. כמו אצל האדם, יש כמה מיני מותרות ופסולת, כגון צפרנים ושער וזיעה, ושאר פסולת ומותרות, כן כל חכמה חיצונה בא ממותרות ופסולת ידועה של הקדושה, וכן כישוף בא ממותרות ופסולת ידוע. וע"כ מי שנופל לאפיקורסית הזאת, אף שבוודאי צריך לברוח ולהמלט משם. אך אעפ"כ מי שנופל לשם, אפשר לו למצוא הצלה לצאת משם. כי יוכל למצוא שם את השי"ת, אם יבקשהו וידרשהו שם. כי מאחר שהם באים משבירת כלים, יש שם כמה ניצוצות הקדושה, וכמה אותיות שנשברו ונפלו לשם כידוע. וע"כ יוכל למצוא שם אלקות ושכל, ליישב הקושיות של האפיקורסית הזאת הבא מחכמות חיצוניות, שהם באים ממותרות משבירת כלים, כי יש שם חיות אלקות, היינו שכל ואותיות שנשברו ונפלו לשם. ועל כן האפיקורסית הזאת יש עליה תשובה, ועליו נאמר ודע מה שתשיב לאפיקורוס: אבל יש עוד מין אפיקורסית, והם החכמות שאינם חכמות. אלא מחמת שהם עמוקים ואינם משיגים אותם, ומחמת זה נראים כחכמות. כמו למשל כשאחד אומר סברא שקר בגמפ"ת, ומחמת שאין למדן ליישב הקשיא שבא ע"י סברא זו, עי"ז נדמה שאמר סברא וחכמה גדולה, אף שבאמת אינו סברא כלל. כן יש כמה מבוכות וקשיות אצל המחקרים, שבאמת אינם שום חכמה, והקשיות בטלים מעיקרא. אך מחמת שאין בהשכל אנושי לישבם, עי"ז נדמים לחכמות וקשיות. ובאמת א"א לישב אלו הקשיות, כי אלו הקשיות של אפיקורסית הזאת, באים מחלל הפנוי, אשר שם בתוך החלל הפנוי אין שם אלקות כביכול. וע"כ אלו הקשיות הבאים משם, מבחי' חלל הפנוי, א"א בשום אופן למצוא להם תשובה, היינו למצוא שם את השי"ת. כי אלו היה מוצא שם ג"כ את השי"י, א"כ לא היה שם פנוי, והיה הכל אין סוף כנ"ל. וע"כ, על האפיקורסית הזאת, נאמר (משלי ב') כל באי' לא ישובון. כי אין שום תשובה על האפיקורסית הזאת, מאחר שבא מחלל הפנוי, שמשם צמצם אלקותו כביכול. רק ישראל ע"י אמונה עוברים על כל החכמות, ואפי' על האפיקורסית הזאת הבא מחלל הפנוי. כי הם מאמינים בהש"י בלי שום חקירה וחכמה, רק באמונה שלימה. כי הש"י ממלא כל עלמין וסובב כל עלמין (ב). נמצא שהוא כביכול בתוך כל העולמות, וסביב כל העולמות. וצריך להיות הפרש כביכול, בין המילוי והסיבוב. שאם לאו, א"כ הכל אחד. אך ע"י בחי' החלל הפנוי, שמשם צמצם אלקותו כביכול, ובתוכו ברא את כל הבריאה. נמצא שהחלל הפנוי מקיף את כל העולם, והש"י שהוא סובב כל עלמין, מסבב גם על החלל הפנוי. וע"כ שייך

(ב) רע"מ פנחס רכ"ה.   (ג) רש"י בראשית ל"ס ע"פ איש עברי.

לוסר ממלא כל עלמין, היינו כל הבריאה, שנברא בתוך החלל הפנוי. וגם סובב כל עלמין, היינו שמסבב גם על החלל הפנוי. ובאמצע מפסיק מחלל הפנוי, שבכביכול צמצם משם אלקותו. והנה ע"י אמונה, שמאמינים שהש"י ממלא כל עלמין. ומאחר שהוא סובב כל עלמין, א"כ שגם החלל הפנוי בעצמו נתהוה מחכמתו ית'. ובוודאי באמת לאמיתו יש שם אלקותו ית', רק שא"א להשיג זאת, ולמצוא שם אלקותו כנ"ל. ע"כ הם עוברים על כל החכמות הקשיות והאפיקורסית הבא משם מחלל הפנוי, כי יודעים שבוודאי א"א למצוא להם תשובה. כי אם היה מוצא להם תשובה, היינו שהיה מוצא בהם את השי"ת, א"כ לא היה חלל הפנוי, ולא היה אפשר להתהוות הבריאה. אבל באמת לאמיתו, בוודאי יש עליה תשובה, ובוודאי יש שם אלקותו ית'. אבל ע"י חקירות נשקעים שם, כי א"א למצוא שם השי"ת, מאחר שהוא בחי' חלל הפנוי. רק צריכין להאמין שהש"י סובב גם עליו, ובוודאי באמת גם שם יש אלקותו ית'. וע"כ ישראל נקראים עבריים, ע"ש שהם עוברים באמונתם על כל החכמות. ואפילו על החכמות שאינם חכמות, היינו האפיקורסית השנית הבא מחלל הפנוי כנ"ל. וע"כ השי"ת נקרא אלקי העבריים (שמות ג'), מלשון (יהושע כ"ד) עבר הנהר (ג), לשון צדדין. היינו שאלקותו מסבב גם על החלל הפנוי, הבא ע"י הצמצום, שצמצם האור לצדדין. וע"כ ישראל נקראים עבריים, שע"י אמונתם שמאמינים שהש"י אלקי העברים כנ"ל, הם עוברים על כל החכמות, ועל שאינם חכמות, היינו האפיקורסית השנית כנ"ל. וע"כ בוודאי מזה האפיקורסית השנית, בוודאי צריך ליזהר יותר ויותר, לברוח ולהמלט משם, לבלי לעיין ולהביט בדבריהם כלל, כי ח"ו בוודאי ישקע שם, כי עליו נאמר כל באיה לא ישובון וכו' כנ"ל:

נ אך דע, אם יש צדיק גדול שהוא בחי' משה, הוא צריך דוקא לעיין בדברי האפיקורסית אלו. ואף שאי אפשר לישבם כנ"ל, על כל זה ע"י עיונו שמעיין שם, הוא מעלה משם כמה נשמות שנפלו ונשקעו בתוך האפיקורסית הזאת. כי אלו המבוכות והקשיות של האפיקורסית הזאת הבא מחלל הפנוי, הם בבחי' שתיקה, מאחר שאין עליהם שכל ואותיות לישבם כנ"ל. כי הבריאה היתה ע"י הדיבור, כמ"ש (תהלים ל"ג) בדבר ה' שמים נעשו וברוח פיו כל צבאם. ובהדיבור יש חכמה, ועל ידם נתהוו כל הדברים של הבריאה, וכמ"ש (שם ק"ד) כולם בחכמה עשית. והדיבור הוא הגבול של כל הדברים, כי הגביל חכמתו באותיות, שאותיות אלו הם גבול לזה, ואותיות אלו הם גבול לזה. אבל בהחלל הפנוי שהוא מקיף כל העולמות כנ"ל, והוא פנוי מכל כביכול כנ"ל, אין שם שום דיבור, ואפילו שכל בלא

Likkutei Moharan, 1:64, I, II, III, IV (cont.)

In the Lurianic writings, the "empty space" is termed *Tehiru*. According to Luria, there remained in this primordial emptiness, or *Tehiru*, a small residue, a trace of the fullness and the divine light, called *Reshimu*.[7]

Rabbi Nahman continues this idea of *Tsimtsum*, insisting on the logical necessity of this withdrawal for the world to be possible; there is no creation without *Tsimtsum*. Rabbi Nahman differs from Luria by radicalizing the theory of the *Tsimtsum*. First by the terminology: the *Tehiru* becomes the *Hallal hapanui*, the "empty (or free) space." The term *Reshimu* no longer appears at all. If the space is really empty of God, there cannot be any trace.

The empty space is "empty of God": radically a-theist, not as a mark of the inexistence of God, but his absence in the midst of the space of the world. The theory of the *Tsimtsum* is opposed to all pantheism. Scholem is right to assert that "nothing is more natural, consequently, than pantheistic tendencies, which started becoming more important in Cabalism, especially after the Renaissance in Europe, and which entered into conflict with the Lurianic doctrine of the *Tsimtsum*, and that attempts were made to reinterpret it to strip it of its meaning."[8]

Rabbi Nahman is one of those who, among the Cabalists and masters of Hasidism, insisted the most on the radicality of the *Tsimtsum*: God is absent from the world. But he does exist beyond the world; so there will always be an infinite distance between man and God, whose surmounting (or nonsurmounting) constitutes one of the essential aspects of the life of man.

Rabbi Nahman introduces an important term, that of *Rahmanut*. What does this term mean? In modern Hebrew, it means "compassion," "mercy," "pity": weaker meanings compared to the original meaning. The term *Rahmanut* comes from the term *Rehem*, the "womb," "uterus." "It describes the uterine nature of the womb, that is to say, the capacity of the uterus to be what it is: to conceive the fetus, the *ubar*. It is the capacity of the *Rehem* to open up, to make an empty space in the heart of fullness of the person and to make room for the embryo, for a being Other. *Rahmanut* is essentially the ability to conceive someone other than oneself."[9] It is by conceiving the emptiness in oneself to receive the alterity of the world; it is by withdrawing from and within himself that God created the world. From this absence of God, the world arose.

The creation of empty space made alterity possible by separation. It is a radical separation between the one who begets and the one begotten (between mother and child). The *Tsimtsum*, by the empty space it introduces, represents the paradigm of the "introduction of the difference in the nondifferentiated." It is an alterity in separation, a distancing, a differentiation that makes fusion no longer possible. One can only throw out a bridge in an attempt to cross the abyss, without ever succeeding.

This idea of *Tsimtsum* and *Rahmanut* can be found, in contemporary philosophy, at the heart of the thought of Emmanuel Lévinas:

> Infinity is produced by withstanding the invasion of a totality, in a contraction that leaves a place for the separated being. Thus relationships that open up a way outside of being take form. An infinity that does not close in upon itself in a circle but withdraws from the ontological extension so as to leave a place for a separated being exists divinely. Over and beyond the totality it inaugurates a society. . . . Society with God is not an addition to God nor a disappearance of the interval that separates God from the creature. By contrast with totalization we have called it religion. Multiplicity and the limitation of the creative Infinite are compatible with the perfection of the Infinite; they articulate the meaning of this perfection.[10]

The absolute separation from God, his absolute transcendence, is the logical condition for the existence of man and the world. For Rabbi Nahman, atheism logically precedes religion, and the latter—an unrelating relation—is never the abolition of the former.[11] Lévinas explicitly says that creation ex nihilo, which he describes as a renunciation, a contraction "leaving room for the separated being," presupposes atheism.[12]

According to Rabbi Nahman, a world without God is inconceivable. Of course, there is "atheism," but there is also "religion." Yes, there is absolute transcendence, but the divine has to be reintroduced, given the possibility of immanence. This reintroduction of the divine into the "space empty of God" is the origin of the fundamental paradox. Two opposite things have to be asserted at the same time: (1) God is absent from the world (as a consequence of the *Tsimtsum*); (2) God is in the world, because the world cannot exist without him. This antinomy is logical, ontological, and existential. Rabbi Nahman is conscious of the difficulty of his development; because of this, he insists on the fact that this paradox, which must be posited logically, does not belong to the realm of intellectual comprehension.

There is an important relationship between this paradox and time. It is only in a future "yet to come" (*à-venir*; *le'atid lavo*) that the possibility of understanding will arise. The future "yet to come," like the Messiah, is not for Rabbi Nahman a stage, a fulfillment of time, but, on the contrary, it is its impossible fulfillment that constitutes it as time. It is the incomprehensibility of the paradox that generates time. Rabbi Nahman says:

64, I, c

This withdrawal that constitutes empty space is impossible to understand and attain, if not in the future to come. Two opposites have to be put forward at the same time: "there is" and "there is not."

For empty space is produced by the withdrawal. He has, so to speak, withdrawn his divinity from this space and, so to speak, no divine aspect is there. For if things are not presented thus, space is not empty and everything remains infinite, and there is no longer any place whatever for the creation of the world.

Here, Rabbi Nahman insists on the logical impossibility of the presence of God in the empty space. "Empty space" means, precisely, "space empty of God." As in all cabalistic literature, the assertions that are rather daring are punctuated by "so to speak," "if we may say so," expressions that dilute the intellectual *Hutspah*[13] but nevertheless allow the expression of thoughts that are "irrelevant to the present day."

In a second stage, and only in a second stage, Rabbi Nahman continues:

64 I, d

But, in fact, according to its truth, it is obvious that there is divinity in spite of that; for it is certain that nothing exists without its vitality.

64 I, e

And, as a result, it is impossible to grasp intellectually the notion of empty space, thus, until the future to come.

The "there is" and "there is not," *yesh veayin*, at the same time, is the foundation of the whole of R. Nahman's thought. It is not a philosophy of the option that chooses either *one or the other* (disjunction); nor is it a thought of *neither one nor the other* (negative conjunction) such as one encounters in the dialectics of antinomies, and which remains on the hither side of the alternative instead of going beyond. Nor is it a question of the Hegelian synthesis, which offers us a *both one and the other* (positive conjunction). There is, with Rabbi Nahman, a *both one and the other* where each element is maintained without disappearing in a synthesis. But with Rabbi Nahman—somewhat in the same way as for Kierkegaard—it is the scandal of the antithesis without synthesis that the commentators have called a "paradox" and that Rabbi Nahman calls *Kushiah*, that is to say, the "question." Rabbi Nahman aims to be "the holder of the question" (*Baal Kushiah*): a holding without domination; the seeking of the question. We can contrast it, typolog-ically, with the *Baal Teshuvah*, which is the "master of the answer," the one who is sure that he possesses the answer.

In this connection, the sociological existence past and contemporary of the *Ba'alei Teshuvah*—which, in everyday language, means the "re-pentant," "those who return to the Torah"—is the logical consequence of a discernible mystico-philosophical current,[14] in which the key con-cept is the immanence of the divine, close to a pantheistic tendency, where the role of the "follower" is to "nullify" himself (*bitul hayesh*) in God and to nullify his personality in face of that of the leader of the movement (through an ideological captivation of the speech and thought by the institution). For the *Ba'al Teshuvah*, the obvious inclina-tion for a certain pantheism ("The sparks of God in man," for example) leads to an acosmic thought, where the world is drowned in God, which is linked to a mysticism of ecstasy or contemplation where it is the God-object who reveals himself and not the man-subject. In short, the *Ba'al Teshuvah* destroys all the distance, separation, and differentiation intro-duced by the *Halal Hapanui*, the empty space of the *Tsimtsum*.

The *Ba'alei Kushiah* ("the askers of questions")—a term that has not yet gathered a following, and rightly so—do not yet have a discernible sociological existence in the palette of the different existing religious movements. Typologically speaking, the category of the *Ba'alei Kushiah* follows on from the Hasidic movement, where the absolute transcen-dence of the divine has precedence over its immanence (or, at least, is in dialectical balance with its immanence). It is the school of Bratslav, of Kotzk: not of ecstasy, not of the abolition of the self; on the contrary, it is the assertion of subjectivity, the right to subjectivity, and an equiva-lent hierarchical place of Master and disciple. We can quote this famous sentence by the Rabbi of Kotzk:

> If I am I, because you are you, then I am not I, and you are not you. But if I am I, because I am I and you are you, because you are you, then I am I and you are you.

In the "both one and the other" of Rabbi Nahman, the "and" that joins one and the other does not mean addition, nor even the synthesis of that which the alternative dissociates, but rather the dialectical reci-procity, the oscillation that ever refers each certainty to its contradic-tion. Not only do the contradictory terms follow one another in becom-ing and coexist at the same time on different levels, but they coincide at the same time as they contradict each other, at the same point. There is a *tension* that is defined by the contradiction of a coincidence and a contradiction.

The play of the complex contradiction goes back and forth between conflict and union, union and conflict, and resolves irrationally, and ad infinitum, the intolerance that makes the contradictory terms refute each other.

With Rabbi Nahman the paradox is logical, ontological, but, above all, existential: it is essentially a question of living.

Moreover, in the eyes of Rabbi Nahman, the *Kushiah* does not originate in a weakness in thinking, in an error of reasoning. It is not a matter of a "subjective paradox"; the *Kushiah* has an ontological status. The antinomies are not antinomies of reason, but of reality. In the words of the Cabala, we would say that the *Kushiah* has to do with Creation (*Beriyah*) and not the creatures (*Nivraim*); it is what we could call an "objective paradox." The antinomies are not only present in reality, they make up its very texture, its fundamental architecture, since they are the primary condition for the emergence of being.

We can formulate the preceding by saying, in a synthetic manner, that "it is not the world which is the scene of the question, but the question which is the scene of the world."[15] The paradox is not a characteristic of being, since it is the primary logical principle of the creation of the world. "To be" and "not to be" at the same time, that is the *Question*[16] . . .

After the description of the logical significance of empty space as the scene of the possibility of a world within the paradox, Rabbi Nahman develops its existential implications. The fundamental problem which preoccupies him is that of belief and atheism, two notions linked with the way of viewing the "question." Rabbi Nahman says:

64 II, a

Know that there are two sorts of heresy (*Apikorsut*). There is a heresy that comes from the "external wise men," and, concerning them, it is said in the *Mishnah Avot*: "*Know what to reply to the heretic (Apikoros).*" For an answer exists for this category of heresy. It comes from the "external wisdom" that comes from "scraps" (*kelippot*) from the domain of the "breaking of the vessels."

Two sorts of heresy, two sorts of questioning. The first category of questions is less interesting for Rabbi Nahman, because it finds an answer. The movement of these questions goes from absolute transcendence (the absence of God) to absolute immanence (the close presence of God): "There is a possibility of finding God."[17] Paradox: it is because there is a philosophical language (*Hokhmah habaah mehokhmot hitsoniyot*) that a linguistic formulation is possible: "There is intelligence and letters"[18] (*Sekhel veotiyot*).

In this paragraph (II, a), Rabbi Nahman alludes to the second stage of the process of Creation in the Cabala of Luria. It is the *Shevirat hakelim*, "the breaking of the vessels," of which here is a brief description.

After the *Tsimtsum*, the divine light gushed forth into the empty space in the form of a straight ray. This light is called *Adam Kadmon*, "primordial Man."

Adam Kadmon is none other than the first figure of the divine light that comes from the essence of the *Ein-sof* (infinite) into the space of the first *Tsimtsum*, not from all sides, but as a ray in a single direction. At first, the lights that emanated were balanced (*or yashar veor hozer*); then the lights that gushed from the eyes of the "primordial Man" emanated according to a principle of separation, atomized or punctiform (*olam hanekudim*). These lights were contained in solid vessels. When these lights emanated later, the impact was too strong for the receptacles, which could no longer contain them, and, as a result, they burst. Most of the light freed from the vessels returned to its higher source, but a number of sparks remained attached to the fragments of the shattered vessels. These fragments "fell" into the empty space, as did the divine sparks that adhered to them. They produced, at a given moment, the domain of *Kelippah*, which Cabalistic terminology calls "the other side."

The "breaking of the vessels" introduces a shifting in creation. Before the breaking, each element of the world occupied an adequate and reserved place; with the breaking, everything is dislocated. Even the *Sefirot*, whose containers should have received a greater influx of light in order to transmit it—according to the laws of emanation—to the levels of lower beings, no longer have their place. Henceforth everything is imperfect and deficient, in a way "broken" or "fallen." Everything is "elsewhere," removed from its proper place, in exile . . .

We can understand, then, the meaning of the third stage of the Lurianic process—the *Tikkun*; it is a matter of restoring, or repairing the breach, in a way, of finding and putting everything back in its place. It is the role of man; that is his story.[19]

In the process of the "breaking," Rabbi Nahman particularly insists on the "scrap" aspect, on what we could call the "excremental" function:

64 II, b

Because of the excessive intensity of the light, the vessels were broken and, thereafter, became "masks" (or peels), *kelippot*.

The "exterior wisdoms" came from this place, that is to say, from the breaking of the vessels, the scraps, the residue of holiness.

For example, with man, there are several sorts of scraps and residues, such as nails, hair, sweat, and other sorts (excrements). In the same way, all "external wisdom" comes from excesses and from the scraps of holiness. Such is the case, for example, with sorcery.

64 II, c

As a result, he who falls into this first category of heresy—that one should flee and avoid—can find a chance to leave it, for he could find God, if he asks and begs for it. For since these wisdoms come from the breaking of the vessels, there can also be found sparks of holiness and letters that are broken and are fallen.

So he could find divinity and thought (*sekhel*) in order to answer the questions of this heresy coming from "external wisdoms" that come from the scraps of the breaking of the vessels. For there is divine vitality, that is to say, thought and letters (*sekhel veotiyot*) that were broken and have fallen.

As a result, there are answers for this first category of questions, and about this it is said: "Know what to reply to a heretic."

The breaking is the interrupting of an economy of internal equilibrium where everything that is taken is utilized. The scrap is the exteriorization of the rupture, its sign. From the point of view of language, this means that the phonetic equilibrium introduces the notion of silence, of neutrality. Each sound emitted is taken up again: the silence that results is the manifestation of the internal equilibrium. Once the emitted sound is not canceled out by its opposite or identical (the double cancels its identical), the sound bursts outside in the form of noise and language. Discourse is, then, the rupturing of the internal equilibrium that exists between being and nonbeing. To say "there is being" without asserting at the same time "there is not being"; if there is "saying" without "unsaying" (*dédire*, lit.: to retract, recant), if there is "signifying" without "designifying," then the "saying" exposes itself, outside, in the form of a residual utterance, in the form of a "spoken word," of a fallen word, of a fallen-out word, that Rabbi Nahman calls "there is God" or "philosophical discourse," or "exterior wisdom." Rabbi Nahman states further on:

64, IV

But one must be careful not to talk more than necessary. Just as much as is necessary for the creation of the world, no more.

By the surplus of light, the vessels were broken, and from the breaking of the vessels came the "masks," the *kelippot*. In the same way, if someone talks too much, he brings about the existence of masks, according to the process: too much light, breaking up, masks.

The "answering word" (*parole de réponse*) is a word that settles into a language which sediments, which becomes institutionalized. In the institution, "God is there" since we "seek him and ask for him." But the answer that is given to this question closes the summoning, stops up the word of opening.

The institution's answer is a dogmatic one; the answer takes the form of *Tikkun*: a gathering of the sparks, a gathering of the Name of God, the reconstruction of the Name: *logos* and *cosmos*. The discourse of the answer can be called a "metaphysical discourse." By saying, "There is God," by finding the divine everywhere, seeing sparks of divine light in everything, one signifies that everything has its meaning in the Whole, so that in fact "Everything is One."

Compared with the shaking of the world, with the shattering and breaking of the *Shevirah*, where the light of the One multiplies into a great number of lights, the metaphysical discourse of the answer is the totalizing discourse on which all political discourse is founded, all ideological discourse that tries to justify that "everyone-should-think-together-in-the-same-way."

Against the "full discourse" of the answer, Rabbi Nahman posits the "broken word" of the *Mahloket* (of the debate, the controversy in dialogue).

---

64 II, d

But there is another sort of heresy. . . . [Here it is not necessary to try to answer.] For, verily, it is impossible to answer these questions. The questions of this type of heresy come from the "empty space" in which there is no divine at all (so to speak).

As a result, it is strictly impossible to find an answer to the questions that come from the empty space, answers here meaning "God." For if God were to be found (there too), the space would not be empty and everything would be infinite and creation would be impossible.

There is thus a second category of questions: "Questions without answers" that come from the "empty space." Assertions such as "God is," "God can be found" are impossible since the space is empty of God. The only discourse possible is silence, *shtikah*.

64 III, b

The questions that come from the empty space are of a silent nature. Reason and language cannot answer them.

and:

64 III, f

The empty space that surrounds all the worlds is empty of everything: no speech is found there, not even "unformulated thought" (*sekhel belo otiyot*). And, as a result, the labyrinthine interrogations (*mevukhot*) that come from there are of a silent nature.

For Rabbi Nahman, silence is the impossible *Tikkun*. The gathering of the sparks, which would reconstruct the Totality, is not possible. It is an imperfect *Tikkun* that does not succeed in being spelled out to the last letter: *Tikku*, that is, silence by status quo in the context of a dialogue. The text is difficult, because Rabbi Nahman tries to confuse the reader, but the sentences that come back like a leitmotiv are clear. "And, in fact, it is impossible to answer these questions, because the questions of this type of heresy come from the empty space: there is no God."

Rabbi Nahman does not like answers. In that respect he is faithful to the whole Talmudic and Cabalistic tradition that defines man-Adam as a "what?" (*Mah?*). Man is a "What is it?" As Jabès remarks very well: "The Jew not only asks questions: he has himself become a question."[20] He is a question without an answer: "To be is to interrogate in the labyrinth of the question that is asked of others and God and does not include an answer."[21] Rabbi Nahman says: "It is necessary to ask questions of God, against God, without answers."[22] Blanchot's statement echoes here: "The answer is fatal to the question."[23]

The philosophy of the question or of questioning—which is how we could describe the thought of Rabbi Nahman and Talmudic thought in general—transforms the world. Through the question, the world that "is" loses all assertion of being; all its certainty of being becomes pure possibility. It is the opening up of time to time (*zeman*, time, also means: here is the question, *zeh-man*), the opening up of being to being.

The real question does not expect an answer. And if there is an answer, the latter does not satisfy the question and, even if it puts an end to it, it does not put an end to the waiting that is the question of the question. Any answer should bear in it the essence of the question, which is not extinguished by the one who answers.[24]

As an echo, by way of an example, here is the very first text of the Talmud, which begins with the question (about time),

From what time?

and its answer is not an answer at all, since it is necessary to question this answer in order to find the answer. This requestioning is only formulated some centuries later, producing a multiplicity of answers, thus allowing the question to find no answer.[25]

———————

The new interpretation that Rabbi Nahman gives of the concepts of *Tsimtsum*, *Hallal hapanui*, and *Shevirat kelim* will allow us to explain the meaning of Talmudic *Mahloket*, the fact that all speech, all Talmudic thought, is always double, reduplicated in a fundamental dialectical situation.

> **64 IV, a**
> *Mahloket* emanates from the creation of the world. The main part of the creation of the world lies in the empty space that suppresses the idea of a "One-Whole-Infinite." So God drew the light toward the sides, creating an empty space in which he created the whole of Creation, time and space, through the use of the word, as it is said, "By the word of God were the heavens made."
>
> The same thing concerns *Mahloket*: if the Masters formed a unity, there would be no room for the creation of the world.
>
> It is only by the *Mahloket* that exists between them—they are thus separated from each other, each one pulling to his side—that the model of the empty space proceeding from the retracting of the light toward the sides, in which the world was created by speech, is produced between them.

The term "Master" to refer to a Talmudic sage does not imply any notion of mastery or violence, quite the contrary: the Master of the Talmud seeks to undo any mastery he may have over his speech, and even more so over that of others. Rabbi Nahman uses the same model of the empty space to explain the forms of the "between-the-masters" relation. By the empty space—withdrawal of the divine—man finds himself totally separated from the divine; it is a separation that is not the solitude of one or the other, but an enigmatic relationship in an unrelating relation. Here intervenes the speech that must try to bridge the insurmountable abyss while still maintaining the separation: "The distance is not abolished; it is not even diminished. On the contrary, it is preserved and pure by the rigor of the speech that sustains the absoluteness of the difference."[26] The empty space "refers to a gap and separation as the origin of all positive value."[27]

Rabbi Nahman makes a leap characteristic of Hasidic thought. He goes from the metaphysical (man-God relationship) to the social (man-man relationship), or, more exactly, he introduces into the social relationship of men the dimension of the relations between man and God.

The relationship "between the Masters," between men, is comparable to the relationship between man and God: "The Masters cannot agree, because in that case they would form a unity." In *Mahloket*, the relationship is such that *one and the other* remain protected from everything that would make them identify *one with another* or would confuse them *with the other* or would transform them both into a middle term.

There is an absolute relationship in the sense that the distance which separates the Masters will not be diminished. On the contrary, it is produced and maintained absolutely in this relationship; the empty space that separates them is irreducible. The transition from the metaphysical to the human, made by Rabbi Nahman in introducing the empty space between the Masters, makes of others the transcendent. As Lévinas says, the other is the "Most High" or the "Completely Other." In *Mahloket*, which is also the model for all relationships, the other "is that which escapes me completely." "The relationship with the other, who is the others, is a transcendent relationship, which means that there is an infinite and, in one way, unsurmountable distance between me and the other who belongs to the other shore, has no homeland in common with me, and cannot, in any way, take up rank in a same concept, a same unity, constitute a Whole, or make up numbers with the individual that I am."[28]

The function of *Mahloket* is to maintain the between-two (*entre-deux*) that, alone, allows creation. The exchange of dialogue does not aim at the confirmation of a unitary truth where the coherent discourse is then confused with its silent reverse; *Mahloket* produces an interruption into which is introduced a waiting, a suspension, which measures the irreducible distance between the two masters. *Mahloket* research is not unifying; on the contrary, it seeks separation, a breach, the interval, which are the other's possibility of being.

Mahloket introduces, into the field of relations, a distortion hindering all direct communication and all relation of unity. The role of speech here is not to reduce but to bear the interval: "nonunifying speech, which accepts no longer being a passage or a bridge, and so abandoning pontifying speech, while still remaining able to cross the two shores that the abyss separates, without filling it in and without reuniting (without reference to unity)."[29]

Thereby, the speech of *Mahloket* really becomes plural . . .

----

64 IV, b

For of all the words that each person pronounces, all are only a progression in view of the creation of the world that takes place through them, within the empty space which is between them.

For the Masters (*Talmidei-Hakhami*) create everything by their words, as it is said (Isa. 51): "And say to Zion, you are my people (*Ami*)." We should not read *Ami* (my people) but *Imi* (with me); "I made the heaven and the earth with words, the same is true for you" (*Zohar* introduction, 5).

64 VI, d

The *Mishnah* explains in the following manner (*Avot*, chap. 1): "All my days, I have grown up between the Masters, and I have not found better for the body than silence. It is not the commentary (*Midrash*) that is the main thing, but action (*Ma'asseh*). And whoever speaks more than is necessary brings sin.

"All my days, I have grown up between the Masters. . . ." Between the Masters, that is to say, inside the empty space which is created between the Masters, by the fact of the separation and the controversy there is between them, between the Masters precisely, that is to say that there is a difference and polemical discussion between them. Because if they agreed there would be no need to say: "*Between the masters.*"

And, as we said, through *Mahloket* an empty space is created, inside which the creation of the world takes place, that is to say, the days (time) and measures (space).

It is not "I have grown up" that should be understood, but "I have made to grow" the days and measures (time and space), that is to say, the main part of the Creation of the world. We should not read *gadalti*, but *higdalti*.

It is said *yamai* (my days), that is to say, "his" days, the time of the one who is speaking; he does not build the world but "his" world, "his time and his space."

By the plural speech of *Mahloket*, room is left for each person to create his own world. It is important to emphasize how Rabbi Nahman reinterprets the whole of the *Mishnah*, basing himself strongly on the existence of the subject, on the priority to be given to subjectivity: "Not the world, but *his* world." The speech of the interval as creative of my world has the function of giving birth to the subject as a differentiated individual. The speech of *Mahloket* consists in introducing differentiation within the undifferentiated. To express it in Talmudic language, it is a matter of leaving the "great mixture" (*Erev rav*) by use of questioning speech, which introduces the difference and produces time (*Man:* "What is it?"; *zeh-man:* here is time).[30]

At this level of Rabbi Nahman's thinking, there emerges a criticism of the institution. In the context, it is a question of the rabbinical institution, which, however, goes well beyond the simple rabbinical field and can be extended to all institutions.

From this criticism follows the entire hermeneutic project of Rabbi

Nahman. To illustrate this criticism and hermeneutic project, here are two small and very enlightening texts. They are taken from the *Sihot Haran* § 226 and 267), written by Rabbi Nathan.

> Rabbi Nahman said that there are rabbinical masters who are famous for their knowledge of the Torah. They possess a wide knowledge of the texts and the interpretations given by their predecessors. But, precisely, as a result they are incapable of innovating (*lehadesh*) in the Torah, because they are too knowledgeable.
>
> When one of these masters goes to innovate something, his immense knowledge immediately disturbs him, closes him up, and he begins to formulate numerous preliminaries and sum up the synthesis of his knowledge on the subject, and, as a result, *his* own words get mixed up and he cannot pronounce any interesting new word.
>
> When someone wishes to innovate new words (new meanings), he should limit his knowledge (literally: accomplish the *Tsimtsum* in his mind), that is to say, evacuate, not hurry into the known preliminary considerations that confuse his mind and that are not necessary for innovating. He should act like someone who does not know and only then can he progressively, and in order, innovate new meanings.
>
> He who wishes to innovate meanings in the Torah is allowed to innovate and interpret everything he wants, everything he will have the opportunity of innovating with his mind, on the condition that he does not innovate new laws.
>
> He may even innovate in the field of the Cabala of R. I. Luria, according to his possibilities, as long as he does not innovate new laws.

In these two texts, Rabbi Nahman puts forward, on the one hand, a methodology allowing one to attain the new speech and, on the other, a virulent criticism of the masters (to be understood here as those who believe they possess a mastery over their own speech and that of others). The method is well known; we are not far from Socrates' *docta ignorantia*: it is the "not knowing," which is a consequence of a *Tsimtsum* of the mind. Man has to withdraw from "himself" in order to attain himself. The first "self" is not the real one; it is constructed, prefabricated by institutions. The subject is always, first of all, the product of an institutional prefabrication: "prefabricated subjectivity." And when the individual begins to speak, he does not speak: he is spoken.

> The speaking individual is spoken; he is spoken by the discourse of institutions, the dogmatic discourse. Even before he is born, every individual is spoken, by the very fact that institutions exist and function.[31]

Here a fundamental question is posed: is there a chance of escaping this situation? Can one extricate oneself from prefabricated subjectivity, from all these discourses that are ready-spoken (*prêt-à-parler*) by everyone and no one? Would not the question without an answer belong to that order too?[32] The ready-to-wear (*prêt-à-parler*) discourse is the discourse of institutions and that of opinion. It is comprehensible since the vocation of the institution is to create opinion and, thus, nonspeech and nonthought.[33]

As Pierre Legendre points out well, a social capturing of subjectivity is instituted. What does that mean? That means that being and the text are profoundly and fundamentally related. That means that "subjectivity is first that: we are born to embody a certain ideality, a juridical ideality, of the human subject, as living examples, ourselves images in the reproduction of this particular species of images that are texts, these texts with which we play our identity in the social descent of truth."[34]

If to be is to be in accordance with the text (institutions), in accordance with the opinion that belongs to "the space where everything that is said has already been said, will continue to be said, will never cease to be said,"[35] then "to be or not to be" no longer poses a question since, in any case, we are not, but simply "are been" (*être été*).

If man is thrown into the impersonal being of the social or religious institution (for Rabbi Nahman, the word of the Masters sure of their mastery) and if it is impossible to bring one's *own* world into being, the question of being no longer has any importance (that is to say, for the holders of this ideology). Considered in this way, man is born before his birth (a nonsensical birth).

Everything we have just been saying belongs to what could be called a philosophy of the Totality and of the Neutral.

It is this totalitarian and neutralist philosophy (neutralization of the subject) that Rabbi Nahman contests. The detotalitarization begins by the setting up of the possibility of multiple beings, radically separate one from another (as in *Mahloket*). From this taking into consideration of the subject as a separate and autonomous being, R. Nahman wishes to call a halt to the capturing of subjectivity by society: a halt to the texts that model the existence of the subject by annihilating it.

The cosmic and ontological *Tsimtsum*, which creates a separation and a fissure within the totality, is followed by a *Tsimtsum* of texts, and thus, of opinion (*doxa*). The "I know not" and questioning speech represent a guarantee against all dogmatic speech. In the face of the totalitarian thought of texts that are already established in a system, the first task of questioning speech (of the *Mah*), which is the essence of man, will be *designifying*.[36]

The first attitude one can have toward tradition is that of contestation; the latter poses an obstacle to the transmission of the characteristic stereotypes of ideological discourses. In a noncontested discourse (those who use this type of discourse wish it to be incontestable), ideas are part of a systematic operation that consists of transforming these ideas into concepts, into totalitarian objects of language, and makes them, in the long run, "terrorist." By "designifying," ideas oppose all semantic actualization and resist becoming object-concepts of a discourse. The speech of the text cannot be listened to through the semanticized and sedimented grid of a discourse: the preliminaries that R. Nahman spoke of. All semantic actualization of a word occasions an occlusion of meaning. The reader who "wants to innovate in meaning" by his speech attacks the semantic actuality of a speech or, in other words, redis-covers for himself the power of words through their "designifying."

A word can only be called "speaking," by contrast with a "spoken word," if it works toward "designifying" the semantic fixations of lan-guage. In one way, the main contribution of the Cabala and Hasidism is a certain deconstructive practice of the language, a poetic practice of "designifying."

Rabbi Nahman says (*Likkutei Moharan*, 1:281):

> Even a simple man, if he takes the time to read, if he looks at the letters of the Torah, can see new things, new meanings; that is to say, by an intensive study of the letters, the latter will begin to "make light," mingle, combine together (cf. *Yoma* 73b) and he will see new arrangements of letters, new words, and he will be able to see in the book things that the author had not at all thought of. And all this is possible even for a simple man, without effort. . . . But this experiment must not be tried out intentionally, for it could be that he sees nothing, even though this also concerns the simple man.

The "simple man" Rabbi Nahman speaks of is the person who, hav-ing carried out the *Tsimtsum* of the mind, finds himself in the situation of the "I know nothing." In accordance with the experience of reading he has just described, many of his reflections are based on these permu-tations of letters, this disarranging and rearranging of letters: *Nota-rikon, Rashei Tevot.*[37] . . . It seems that the designifying-resignifying ex-perience of reading partakes more of an unconscious than a conscious nature, somewhat similar to "free association," since Rabbi Nahman adds that one should not have the conscious intention of undertaking this reading. The "I know not" of designifying removes language and the text from a sort of cadaverization where the words would no longer have the power to signify an affective or emotional actuality.

The *Tsimtsum* of meaning, its withdrawal, "gives speech back to lan-guage; that is to say, it gives it the power of its freedom to create lan-guage, to seek within itself its infinite resources, to set about the hearing within itself of the signifying of things."[38] Speech recovers its laughter and its play.

The act of *Tsimtsum* of the "I know not" is an act of resistance to the "language of institutions." This resistance—a veritable combat—opens words up to their polysemic possibilities. Everything takes place in the fracture, in this act of designifying. The unique, univocal, monosemic language of the institution being the foundation of its totalitarianism, of its intolerance and violence, it is important that by the act of designifying the subject and *his* speech attain or reattain liberty.

Moreover, it is very significant that the festival of *Pesah* (Passover), a time of the transmission to children (and so, the opening up of time to itself), is based on the transmission of the subversive capacity of language. Passing on liberty consists in the possibility of a subversive reading of founding texts. Liberty comes through the possibility of leaving the "engraving" of the Law on the Tables of stone: *Al Tikra Harut ela Herut*[39]—"Do not read 'engraved' but 'liberty.' "

When Rabbi Nahman insists, several times over, on this point—"on the condition that he does not innovate new laws"—it is not the newness of the law that bothers him, but the law itself which, being added on to other laws, reinforces the institutional discourse. The additional law is refused because it reinforces the institution and the guardians of its ideology, instead of weakening and destroying it. Since man builds himself up continually by interpretation, his becoming is possible only in the untiring succession of making and unmaking meaning, or reading and unreading the text. The role of interpretation is clear. It is not a matter of repeating, of paraphrasing the original text, but, literally, of unsticking it, of going "beyond the verse," going from the text to one's personal text; by this creative reading, the reader is really born: after a biological birth, then a juridical, institutional, and social birth, the subject is born as a differentiated individual. There is a transition from a "text without a subject" to a "text with a subject."[40] Rabbi Nahman's action of contestation through his text of the *Sihot Haran* (number 267), which could be entitled "A Small Manifesto for the Right to Subjectivity," is a political act. Through this gesture, the Law and its commentaries are no longer inspired words that belong only to certain mouths, but democratic mouths that belong to every human being.

———————

But does not the new text "with a subject" run the risk of being transformed, in turn, into a "text without a subject"? Does not the thinking of Rabbi Nahman, for example, risk becoming a "Nahmanism" or a "Bratslavism," around which a group of disciples will attempt to appropriate and set themselves up as guardians of the Master's word?

We know that Rabbi Nahman tried to check this phenomenon by hindering the creation of a movement around his person. Contrary to other Hasidic masters of his time, among whom the title of Rabbi was passed on from father to son or to the son-in-law or a disciple, he forbade that anyone succeed him after his death. The historians and opponents of the Bratslav movement called the *hasidim* of Bratslav the *"hasidim* of the dead" or the "dead" *hasidim* (in Yiddish, *Toïte Hassidim*).

Apart from this problem of succession, it seems that the action of "burning the books" is related to this question: is the book, as an object, possible? To elucidate this question, we are going to try to follow Rabbi Nahman, step by step, in the twists and turns of chapter 32 of the *Likkutei Moharan*, volume 2, introduced above:

> There are hidden righteous men; they know faces in the Torah but have to keep their teaching hidden. . . . Even so with him (i.e., Rabbi Nahman). Sometimes he knows a teaching which has faces, that is to say, faces in a teaching, but he must keep it secret and not tell it. Sometimes he does not even write it down. At other times he writes it down and then burns it. In fact, if this teaching were written, it would be a book and the latter would have its place in the world. In these books, there are Names that should be understood in the sense of the Talmudic expression "My Name written in holiness . . ." (*Shabbat* tractate, 116a). However, the world destroys that and it is necessary to make it disappear and burn it. But it is good for the world that these teachings and books be hidden and burnt.

The "hidden righteous man" is Rabbi Nahman himself. It is the Master in becoming, the *Talmid-Hakham*, who cannot appear, because the risk of being a *Tsaddik gamur*, a "completed," "finished"[41] righteous man, is too great.

The righteous person in the process of becoming, he who "refuses to be old," knows the faces of the Torah, the multiple meanings that circulate in the text. He has access to the life of the meanings that make the text an object to be passed on. In spite of this knowledge, he finds himself obliged to conceal his teaching, for "the world spoils that"; "the world" spoils these books that contain the multiple meanings of the order of the multiple Names of God. Here, the whole of the thought of Rabbi Nahman is based on a certain definition of the "world." In the text quoted, the "world" means "people," a term that has passed over into Yiddish.[42] But if "people" are linguistically embodied in "world," it is because their way of being is essentially "worldly." And if we are to

מוהר"ן תנינא   ליקוטי   כח כט ל לא לב

מוהר"ן תנינא

(א). ועל כן כשיש אלו הדמעות הנ"ל, הם עומדים
כנגד ומבטלן. וזה אותיות בכיה ר"ת בני ישראל כחול
הים (תושע ב) מה חול הים מגין מן גלי הים שלא ישטופו
העולם (ב), כן בני ישראל מגין עליהם הבכיה והדמעות,
כנגד גזירות האומות כנ"ל. וזה והיה מספר בני ישראל
כחול הים, מספר היינו מְסַפֵּר הנ"ל, משם בני ישראל
כחול הים, היינו בכיה ודמעות של החידושין שבספר,
שמגין עליהם כנ"ל:

לא על ידי הגנינה, אדם ניכר אם קבל עליו עול תורה.
וסימן, בכתף ישאו (במדבר ז), ודרז"ל
(ערכין יא) אין ישאו אלא לשון שירה, שנאמר שאו
זמרה ותנו תוף. ומקרא זה נאמר במשא בני קהת, שהיו
נושאים בכתף את הארון, היינו בחי' עול תורה:

לב יש צדיקים גנוזים, והם יודעים פנים בתורה, אך הם
צריכים להעלים תורתם, וכמו שמשפרים מעשה
מהבעש"ט עם הדרשן. וגם אצלו, יש לפעמים שיודע תורה
שיש לה פנים, דהיינו פנים בתורה, והוא צריך להעלימה,
ואינו אומרה. ולפעמים אינו כותבה כלל, ולפעמים כותבה,
ואח"כ שורפה. ובאמת אם היתה נכתבת, היה מזה ספר,
והיה בא בתוך העולם. וגם יש בהם שמות, בחי' שמי
שנכתב בקדושה. אך העולם מקלקלין זאת, וצריכין
להעלימה ולשורפה. אבל היא טובה להעולם, מה שנגלם
ונשרף תורות וספרים הללו. כי גם יש כמה ספרים, שכבר
נעשה ספרים, ונמחו ונאבדו מן העולם. כי בוודאי הצדיקים
הגדולים הקדמונים תנאים ואמוראים וכיוצא בהם, עשו
ספרים הרבה, אך נאבדו. אך הוא טובה להעולם, כי אם
לא הי' זאת, לא הי' אפשר לנו כלל להתקרב להשם
יתברך. כי יש הרבה ספרי מינים, שאם היו ח"ו מתפשטין
בעולם, לא היה אפשר כלל להתקרב להש"ת. כי ירבעם
בן נבט שעשה שני עגלי זהב, ואמר הנה אלקיך ישראל
וכו' (מלכים א יב), והטעה כל ישראל אחריהם. העלה
על הדעת, שהטעה עם רב בשטות כזה, לעבוד עגלים.
אך בוודאי, הי' בזה חכמות גדולות מאד מאד של
אפיקורסות. ואם הי' ח"ו ח"ו ר"ל נמצא עתה דף אחד
מספרים הללו ח"ו היו מרחקים מאד מהש"י, ולא הי'
אפשר להתקרב אליו ית' כלל. ובשביל זה, הוא טובה
מה שנתעלמין ונשרפין הספרים הקדושים הנ"ל:

כי הספר הוא בחי' שם ה', בכחי' (משלי יח) מגדל עוז
שם ה' בו ירוץ צדיק ונשגב, ואיתא בזוהר (בראשית
ד' לז ע"ב) שם ה' דא ספר, כי ספר במספר שם כמובא.
כי הספר הוא בחי' שמי שנכתב בקדושה, ונתפשט בעולם
ועושה שם. ודע, שכ"א וא' צריך לשמור את בחי' משיח
שיש לו. כי כל אחד כפי קדושתו וטהרתו, כן יש לו בחי'
משיח. וצריך לשמור מאד, שלא יתקלקל בחי' משיח שלו.
ועיקר הדבר שבו תלוי בחינות משיח, הוא שמירה
מניאוף. כי משיח הוא בחינת חותם, בכחינות (איכה ד)
רוח אפינו משיח ה'. וניאוף תלוי בחותם, כ"ש (שמות כ)
לא

כח כט ל לא לב   **ליקוטי**

וכו': נמצא שעל ידי שמסתכלין להעריך כ"א כראוי,
עי"ז זוכין להתרת נדרים, ועי"ז ניצולין מד' מדות הנ"ל,
כנ"ל. והבן:

כח דע, שיש חילוקים בין התורות, כי יש תורה שלא
ניתנה אפי' לדרוש. ויש תורה שניתנה לדרוש,
ולא ניתנה לכתוב. ויש שניתנה לכתוב. וכמו שמצינו
שארז"ל (גיטין ס' ע"ב), דברים שבע"פ אי אתה רשאי
לאומרם בכתב וכו'. ומי שיודע להבחין ולהכיר בין
התורות, איזהו ניתנה לכתוב, ואיזהו לא ניתנה לכתוב.
הוא יכול להכיר את איש ישראלי בין האומות, ואפי' אם
א' מישראל עומד בין כמה אומות, יכול להכירו. וסוד זה
מרומז בפסוק (הושע ח) אכתוב לו רובי תורתי כמו זר
נחשבו (א), היינו כשכותבין רובי תורתי, היינו רב יותר
מהראוי, דהיינו שכותבין מה שלא ניתן ליכתוב כנ"ל.
אזי, כמו זר נחשבו. היינו, שאין יכול להכיר את הישראל,
וכמו זר נחשב אצלו, שנדמה לו לזר ולנכרי. וכן להיפך,
שיכול למעות על הנכרי שהוא ישראל כנ"ל. כי עיקר
ההבדל שבין ישראל לאומות, הוא בבחי' מה שלא ניתן
לכתוב בחי' תורה שבע"פ. כמו דאיתא (ב) שבשביל זה
ניתנה תורה שבע"פ, מחמת שצפה שיהיו ישראל בגלות,
ויעתיקו האומות לעצמן תורה שבכתב, ע"כ נתן לנו
תורה שבע"פ. שזה אינם יכולים להעתיק, מחמת שהוא
בעל פה. נמצא שעיקר ההבדל והיתרון של ישראל על
האומות, הוא בבחי' תורה שבע"פ, שלא ניתן לכתוב.
ויש בכ"א וא' מישראל, חלק מבחי' תורה שבע"פ, שלא
ניתן לכתוב. וע"כ מי שמכיר בין התורות שניתנו לכתוב
ושלא ניתנו לכתוב, הוא יכול להכיר בין ישראל בין אומות,
כי זה עיקר ההבדל כנ"ל:

כט כשאירע שאלה בבית האדם, ע"י תערובת איסור
בהיתר, ואין בהיתר כדי לבטל את האיסור,
בזה מראין לו שפגם באיזהו יחוד של מעלה, כי כל
היחודים והזווגים הם בחי' ביטול איסור. וזה בחי' ואסר
לנו את הארוסות והתיר לנו את הנשואות, נמצא שמאיסור
נעשה היתר. כי בתחלה היא ארוסה, ואז היא אסורה,
ואח"כ נעשית היתר בנשואין. ע"כ גם בזווג התחתון
של זה העולם, נאמר (תהלים סח) אלקים מושיב יחידים
ביתה, היינו זווגים, כשדרז"ל (סוטה ב) זה הפסוק לענין
זווגים אזי, מוציא אסירים בכושרות, היינו שנעשה
האיסור כשר והיתר, בחי' ביטול האיסור כנ"ל. וע"כ
כשאין נתבטל האיסור, והשאלה אסורה, היא סימן שפגם
ביחוד של מעלה, כי היחוד הוא בחי' ביטול האיסור
כנ"ל:

ל כשבא ספר חדש לעולם, וזה מבואר אצלנו שיש
חידושים שנעשין ע"י דמעות (כמובא בסי'
רסב). אזי אלו הדמעות של החידושין, שמהם נעשה
הספר החדש, הם עומדים כנגד גזירות האומות, ומבטלן:
והדבר מבואר, כי כל כחם היא מן הדמעות של עשו

(א) ילקוט שם. (ב) ע' ס"ר תשא פ' מז הובא בתוספות גיטין ס ע"ב ד"ה אתמהה וע' בירושלמי פאה פ"ב. (א) ע' זוהר שמות יב. (ב) ע' זוהר
פקודי רכה. ובמדרש תהלים ב.

מוהר״ן תנינא כד   לב לג   ליקוטי

כדי לסלק הרוח קנאה. כי הרוח קנאה, הוא רוחו של
משיח, שהוא שורה על אנפי אורייתא, דהיינו הספרים
כנ״ל. נמצא, כשנשרפין ונאבדין הספרים, ממילא נסתלק
הרוח קנאה, שהוא רוחו של משיח, ששורה על הספרים
כנ״ל. וזהו סוד שמי שנכתב בקדושה ימחה, כי הספר
הוא בחי' שם ד', בחי' שמי שנכתב בקדושה כנ״ל. ואסרה
תורה שימחה ויאבד, כדי להטיל שלום בין איש לאשתו,
דהיינו זוג הקדוש הנ״ל. שבשביל השלום שביניהן, נמחין
ונאבדין הספרים, שהם בחי' שמי שנכתב בקדושה כנ״ל.
ואזי נושאין ק״ו למעלה, (כשארז״ל שבת קמו) ומה
שמי שנכתב בקדושה, אמרה תורה ימחה, שהוא להטיל שלום וכו'. ספרי המינין,
שהם ממלין שנאה ותחרות בין ישראל וכו', עאכ״ו
שימחו ויאבדו ויעקרו מן העולם, שימח ויעקר זכרם מן
העולם. נמצא שע״י אבידת הספרים הקדושים, בא טובה
שנאבדין ונעקרין ספרי המינין, ואזי יכולים להתקרב אליו
ית'. אמן:

לג (שמות י״ח) ויחד יתרו על כל הטובה וכו', וארז״ל
(סנהדרין צד) שנעשה בשרו
חידודין חידודין. כי כל השמחות הם רק בשעתן, כגון
למשל, שמחה של חתונה או ברית, השמחה הוא רק
בשעתן. ואם יסתכל על הסוף, אין שום שמחה בעולם,
כי סוף אדם וכו' (ברכות יז). אבל אם יסתכל על הסוף
של הסוף, אז יש לו לשמוח מאד. כי סוף כל סוף, דהיינו
התכלית, הוא טוב מאד. והנה, זהו רק מצד הנשמה,
שממצדה המות טוב מאד, כמו שארז״ל (ב״ר פ' מ) והנה
טוב מאד זה וכו'. כי הוא טוב מאד, שעל ידו בא אין לתכלית
הטוב. אך מי שהוא צדיק, ואפילו נופו נקי וקדוש מאד,
אזי יכול לשמוח גם עם נופו, אפי' אם מסתכל על הסוף.
מאחר שגם נופו טהור וקדוש. כ״ש (תהלים נט) באלקים
במחתי מה רשעין לי, כ(א)הבשר דהיינו הגוף אינו יכול
לעשות לי שום היזק. וכ״ש (תהלים טו) אף בשרי ישכון
לבטח, שהצדיק בטוח שגם נופו יהי' טוב מאד. וע״כ
יכול לשמוח גם עם נופו, אפילו כשמסתכל על הסוף. אבל
מי שאין נופו נקי וקדוש כ״כ, בפרט גר, שאע״פ שנשמתו
גבוה מאד, אעפ״כ נופו נוצר מטפה טמאה, ואיך אפשר
לשנות זאת. נמצא, שזה האיש שאין נופו קדוש כל כך
בפרט גר, אי אפשר לו לשמוח עם נופו, כשמסתכל על
התכלית. וזהו, ויחד יתרו על כל הטובה, פי' אפי' שמח
על כל הטובה, פי' אפי' כשהסתכל להלאה מן הטובה.
וזהו, על כל הטובה, למעלה, ולהלאה על הטובה. אעפ״י
שהסתכל על זה, היינו להלאה מן הטובה, היינו על
הסוף, אעפ״כ, הי' שמח מאד. כי מצד הנשמה, אף
כשמסתכל על הסוף, הוא טוב מאד כנ״ל. אך, שנעשה
בשרו חידודין חידודין. בשרו דייקא, דהיינו הגוף. כי
מאחר שהי' גר, לא הי' שמחתו בגופו, כשהסתכל על
הסוף כנ״ל. וזהו, נעשה בשרו חידודין חידודין, בשרו
דייקא כנ״ל:

ויחד

לא תנאף, ואיתא במדרש (רבה פ' נשא פ' יוד) לא תהנה
אף, וצריך לשמור עצמו מאד אפי' מריח ניאוף, כי הוא
פונם בחי' משיח שלו, שהוא בחי' חותם כנ״ל. ובחי'
משיח הוא שורה על אנפי אורייתא, דהיינו הספרים
הקדושים שמנלין הפנים של תורה. ושם מרחף רוחו של
משיח, בבחי' (בראשית א) ורוח אלקים מרחפת על פני
המים. רוח אלקים, דא רוחו של משיח (זוהר ויחי ד'
ר״ם ע״א), שמרחף על פני המים, ומים הוא התורה
כמובא (א):

ודע, שבחי' רוח אפינו משיח ה', נעשה רוח קנאה,
שהולך ומקנא, בכל מקום שמוצא שם ניאוף, הוא
נעשה רוח קנאה, ומקנא על זה, לנודל קדושתו ומהרתו:
ופעמים מקנא והיא נמצאה, או עבר עליו רוח קנאה
וכו' והיא לא נמצאה (במדבר ה). כי לנודל עוצם קדושתו
ומהרתו, אעפ״י שלא נמצאה, הוא מקנא על הסתרה
לבד, כי נחשב פגם כנגד מהרתו של הרוח קנאה,
ונעשה ע״ז לפעמים גם. וע״כ נקרא הגם ספר כריתות
(דברים כד), כי נעשה ע״י הספר, ששם שורה רוחו של
משיח, שהוא רוח קנאה כנ״ל. או שמשקין אותה מים
מאררים, ואזי נבדקת אם נמצאה וכו'. ואם לאו, אזי
אדרבא ונקתה ונזרעה זרע וכו':

ודע, שיש יהודא תתאה שבזה העולם, שהוא בכשרות
גדול בקדושה ובמהרה כ״כ, עד שבו תלוי יהודא
עילאה. שהוא, דהיינו האיש והאשה כשרים כ״כ, שהיא
כשרה מאד ואין בה שום שמץ פסול, וגם הוא כשר מאד,
ווזוונם בכשרות ובקדושה כ״כ, שבו תלוי יהודא עילאה.
כי איש ואשה זכו שכינה שרוי' ביניהם (כשרז״ל סוטה
יז), כי יש בו יו״ד ובה ה', שזהו יהודא עילאה. וזה הזיוונג
והיחודא תתאה הוא יקר מאד מאד, מאחר שבזה העולם
נעשה יחודא תתאה בקדושה כזו, שבו תלוי יהודא עילאה.
והנה הרוח קנאה, שהוא בחי' רוחו של משיח כנ״ל, שהוא
מקנא על ניאוף, מה הוא עושה כאן, מאחר שהם קדושים
ומהורים מאד. אך דע, שכאן בא הרוח קנאה, בשביל
אהבה. כי איתא בזוהר (ויחי ד' רמה ע״א) כל רחימותא
דלא קשיר עמה קנאה, לאו רחימותא רחימא, הה״ד כי
עזה כמות אהבה קשה כשאול קנאה. כי הקנאה מורה
על אהבה, כי מחמת גודל האהבה הוא מקנא בה אל
תסתרי, כדי שלא יתקלקל האהבה ח״ו. וזה פועל כאן
רוח קנאה הנ״ל, בשביל אהבה כנ״ל. אך מחמת
שאעפ״כ זה היהודא תתאה הוא בזה העולם, יוכל
להתקלקל השלום שביניהם ח״ו, ע״י הרוח קנאה. כי
הקנאה אע״פ שהיא בשביל אהבה, יכולה להטיל מחלוקת
ח״ו, ע״י שמקנא לה וכו':

וע״כ דע, שבשביל זה צריכין הצדיקים הגדולים להעלים
תורתם, לשורפם ולהאבידן כנ״ל. כדי שיהי' נסתלק
הרוח קנאה, שלא יקלקל ח״ו שלום הזוג הקדוש הנ״ל.
כי יהודא תתאה שלהם יקר מאד, וכשנתקלקל שלום
שביניהם, ע״י הרוח קנאה כנ״ל, הוא הפסד גדול מאד.
וע״כ מוכרחין שיהיו נאבדין התורות והספרים הנ״ל.

(א) תענית ד. ב״ק י״ז.

Likkutei Moharan, 2:32 (cont.)

understand Rabbi Nahman, we have to determine what he means by "world."

Rabbi Nahman follows here an idea that is found in the Talmud,[43] where the "world" (*le'olam*, literally: "for the world," usually translated by "forever") is defined as *that which refuses to disappear*. This "world" that refuses to disappear is criticized by the Talmud. The latter prefers a world that withdraws, that retires, in a *Tsimtsum*. *Le'elem* is substituted for *le'olam*, "to disappear." The "world" that the Talmud, and later Rabbi Nahman, criticizes is the one that sits before us, with violence and immodesty, revealing itself clearly to our sight! It is that which belongs to the possibility of being grasped by sight, thought, or the hand! It is that which is given in a present, in a "now," that I can make mine by a gesture of appropriation!

The "world," being that which I can know, that which I can take and possess, is of an "ever-present" nature. If the characteristic of time is to make newness arise,[44] the "world" is not in time. It is not, because it is always already (*toujours déjà*) here; it is still already (*encore déjà*) there. It maintains itself in its present, in its *main-tenant* ("hand-holding," *maintenant*: "now"). In the "world," time does not make meaning emerge, but spreads it out and unfolds a meaning that is always anticipated. To have a "world" in the sense of *le'olam* is to escape the uncertainty characteristic of the future. The "*olam*-world" is the Greek world, the world in its Greek way of being, and in its Greek way of being said. It is the *logos*. What does this term mean? Heidegger untiringly repeated that the *logos* is related to being (*einai*). "The latter term, which corresponds to the Latin term *esse* and to the German *sein*, means: 'when approached, to unfold its being in a presence' (*an wesen*). Explained in the sense of the Greek word, "to be" means: to appear in the nonocculted, to be approached and to shine, and, in shining, to endure and remain."[45]

The "world" is unveiled as a *logos*. *Logos* means the utterance and the word, in the precise sense of "to cause to appear, to make a thing appear with the face that belongs to it, to show it in the way it looks at us, and that is why, by saying it, we see clearly into it."[46] "To name means: by calling, to make appear. That which is gathered together and laid down in the name is found, through the very fact of this laying down, to-be-laid-out-before and to appear. To name (*onoma*), if one thinks of this act from the *legein*, it is not to express the meaning of a word, but to leave laid-out-before in the light where a thing stands by the very fact that it has a name."[47]

It could be objected that this Greek "world" is also related to concealing, a love for that which is hidden: "The being of things loves to hide,"[48] but the "hiding" is in a dialectical relation with the unveiling; it exists for the disclosing."[49] "The dis-closing needs the concealing in order to unfold its being as it is, which is: as disclosing."[50] And it is the dis-closing that makes up the world: "The coming of clarity that liberates is called a world. Lighting . . . is disclosing; it resides in the concealing. The latter belongs to it as the very thing that finds its being in the disclosing and so can never be in a simple effacing in occulting, never a disappearance."[51]

It is this laid-out "world" that Rabbi Nahman contests. The world, in the Talmudic sense of the word, is the opposite of the Greek world, *logos* and *phusis*. *Le'elem* signifies disappearance, being en route toward effacing. The *le'elem* where the world disappears no longer allows itself to be mastered, comprehended in a now (*main-tenant*). When Rabbi Nahman criticizes the masters who know, when he says, "I do not know . . . the main thing in knowing is to not know anything," he does not mean that some people can know, or that they will be able to know. For him, knowing is called into question, radically. In one way, the questioning of the question without an answer repeats, untiringly, this doubting. What Rabbi Nahman seeks is of a "nonworldly" nature. Not *le'olam* (for the world) but *le'elam* (for the disappearance of the world). The world is there without being there: it is a "nonworld."

In the Talmudic text cited (*Kiddushin* 70a) the problem posed is that of the possibility or not of pronouncing the divine name and the handing on of this possibility. Everything takes place in the speech-writing duality, in the text and its reading. It is spelled *le'elem* (for the disappearance-effacing), but we read *le'olam* (for the world).

It is through reading that there is a transition from the secret to the world. But, as for the Name of God, what is read is not what is written, as if all reading consisted already in rewriting another legible text, one more legible than the first, which always remains in its silence. There arises this oddity, this enigma, upon which we must incessantly reflect: when the reader reads the text of the Bible, each time he comes across a Tetragram name of God (Y-H-V-H), he goes from a relationship with the writing of the text to a relationship with the writing of his memory, instituting blanks, gaps in the text. To say the Name is to efface it as a written Name.[52] The problem becomes clearer for Rabbi Nahman, since he says later: "The Book is the Name" (*LM 2:32*).

For Rabbi Nahman, reading is not the gathering of the world within a word, but its bursting apart. Talmudic reading, as opposed to the Greek *logos*, does not seek to harvest, to put under shelter and preserve.[53] As R. Yosef Rozin[54] says: we need to distinguish the "reading of words" and the "reading of letters"; we have to give letters the possibility of being letters in spite of the existence of words. Think of Saussure's anagrams, in which a proper noun, a hero or a god, can be found beneath the text. The name can be found in every text in the form of a theme. The word-theme is diffracted throughout the text, dissolved into its simple elements, decomposed, dispersed. "It is not a matter of another way of being the Same, of a reintegration or of a paraphrase, of clandestine metamorphosis of the original name of God. But, rather, it is a question of a shattering, of a dispersion, or a dismembering where this name is annihilated . . . far from reinforcing the signifier in its being, or repeating it positively, this metamorphosis in these scattered members is the equivalent of its death as such, of its annihilation."[55] In other words, we may say: there is a *Shevirat kelim* and not a *Tikkun*. The act of reading is never in a return (*teshuvah*), never a retotalization after alteration, in a resurrection of identity; on the contrary, it always consists of an extermination of the conclusion, in a dispersion with no return. It is a question without an answer. Let us remember that the divine Name means question. We say *Shem Mah*, the "Name-what?"

Talmudic reading[56] is not a linguistic operation that tries to reduce the saying to an intention of saying, bringing it back to the shadow of a meaning, breaking up the utopia of language, bringing it back to the topic of discourses. Talmudic reading is an operation of dissemination that restores life, movement, and time to the very heart of words. Here, words are no longer finalized by the meaning; reading breaks up the authority of meaning and all the elements of the text echo and converse with each other: words, syllables, consonants, vowels. We find in this manner of reading the "Small Manifesto for the Right to Subjectivity"[57]; we find again the political act of Rabbi Nahman: his revolution! The life given back to language in the effacing reading of the Name is a revolution "compared to an order where nothing, no one, words or men, their bodies, their eyes are permitted to communicate directly, but all must transit as values through the models that beget and reproduce them in a total 'foreignness' one to another. . . . The revolution is everywhere an exchange is instituted that breaks the finality of the models— this exchange, were it infinitesimal, of phonemes, syllables, in a poetic text, or that of thousands of men who speak in a city in insurrection."[58]

When Rabbi Nahman explains his way of reading in the *Likkutim* (1:282), he insists on the disarranging much more than on the synthesis. It is correct to speak of an ana-theme instead of a word-theme, to speak of an ana-seme rather than of semes, an "anathematic" and "anasemic"[59] reading. The text is not the showing up of a word-theme, nor is it its development, multiplication, prolonging, or echo; it is its dissemination, its dismembering, its deconstruction—it is analysis and not synthesis. The intensity of the poetic character of a text "is never in the repetition of an identity; it is in the destruction of an identity." Rabbi Nahman's reading, as well as the world that is read, can be called poetic. But we should add what we mean by poetic: "The poetic stakes are not production, or even the combinative variations on a theme, or an 'identifiable subgroup.' In that case, it would enter quite well, in fact, into a universal mode of discourse. The stakes are in the anagrammatical work, the point of no return to any kind of end or theme. . . . The main thing is not to consider the poetic as its mode of appearing but as its mode of disappearing."[60]

Le'elem and not *le'olam*. *Shevirah* and not *Tikkun*.

The whole of Rabbi Nahman's problem lies in the possibility of uttering a new, unheard-of, completely original word, a word without reference to the past, without reference to the "world." In modern terms, we could say that Rabbi Nahman is seeking to utter a "signifier" without a "signified." He is seeking a "new signifier," a "signifier" that is not received but invented. In short, he is seeking a *Hidush*. The real *Hidush* does not consist in substituting a new signifier for an old one. It is not a matter of "doing up" or "giving a face lift" to old monuments, bringing them into line with current tastes to make presentable values of them (that is a problem of marketing and ideological propaganda). The "dynamism of signifying"[61] of *Hidush* does not have its roots in memory; "the invention of a signifier is something different from memory."[62] *Hidush* is that which breaks with transmission and tradition, while still, paradoxically, constituting them. *Hidush* is that which founds atradition and atransmission while still being the foundation of tradition and transmission (of breaking up). The word of *Hidush* is not received, then retransmitted. An ability to invent is passed on but not a meaning. *Hidush* speech is created, invented, but, because of this, it is *senseless* (*insensé*, lit.: insane, demented). *Hidush*, as a new signifier, cannot have any sort of meaning, and that is its richness; this is where a meaning for the prophetic speech should be sought. The author of *Hidush* speech generates himself as a separate subject, thus creating an empty space (*Hallal hapanui*) between his world that he is in the process of constituting and the world of others, between *his* world and the "world."

Rabbi Nahman is the "hidden righteous man" who cannot show himself as "righteous" without running the risk of destroying himself.

Rabbi Nahman himself, in his person, does not want to become a
"world": he withdraws. And yet, he has a great deal to say. "But the
world destroys that" and he must, paradoxically, hide the teaching in
order to allow it to live and be passed on, to give it the chance to be an
object of transmission.

But how can a speech that does not belong to the "world" be passed
on? What can be done with a speech that can be heard only as a sense-
less sound? Would it not be better to be silent? to keep it to oneself? Is
this not the logical solution, since if this new *im-monde* speech (*monde*:
"world") were pronounced and audible, i.e., comprehended, it would
thereby be reduced to a "worldly" meaning, a repeatable and institutional word, and thus devoid of meaning?

Hence, one should not speak too much (*LM* 64, IV, c) . . .

The difference evoked between the world (*olam*) and the world (*elem*)
will allow us to perceive one of the meaning of fire.

In Hebrew, *the object* is introduced by the particle *et*, which is spelled
Aleph-Tav: the first and last letters of the Hebrew alphabet. *Et* thus
indicates, literally, the totality of the world (in English we would say,
"from A to Z"). The *et* can introduce the object, because the latter is
finite, constituted of and by the literal path in the world of letters, from
the first one to the last.

To say that an object is there is to say that it has become a speakable
and comprehensible "world"—graspable: perfect from *Aleph ad Tav*.
The first *et* of the text introduces the heavens and the earth, the world-
cosmos (*et hashamyim veet haaretz*) divine creation: perfect (before the
Shevirah). But it is possible to imagine another world that is not yet
finished, not yet speakable, not yet graspable, where there is still, before
the end and before perfection, an infinitesimal but insuperable distance,
hindering us from ever seizing the world, so that we can only caress it.[63]

Rabbi Nahman contrasts the graspable "perfect-object," which is a
"world," with the imperfect-object,[64] the latter being inaccessible as a
perfect-object. The relation to the object is no longer from *Aleph* to
Tav, a complete run, but a caress, an *almost perfect run*: "fire."

"Fire," in Hebrew, is *esh* (*Aleph-Shin*), "from the first to . . . the
second-to-last letter." "Fire" is that which introduces in a caressing relation an "almost object." There is still a "something" (*je-ne-sais-quoi*;
lit. "I know not what"), and "almost nothing" (*presque rien*), as Jankélévitch would say, which is an opening up to infinity. Fire, as a relation to the world, as an impossible relation to the world, creates a space
inside which time is possible as the unfolding toward the "yet to come"

(*à-venir*), toward the future (*avenir*) of time. "The relationship with the world is an absence from the world; not pure and simple absence, not an absence of pure nothingness, but an absence in the context of a future, an absence that is time."[65]

What can be done with this new word—a signifier without a signified— that is to be "withdrawn from the world" (*leaalimah*)?

Rabbi Nahman suggests three solutions.

1. Not to say it, but write it.
2. Neither speak nor write it.
3. Write it and burn it.

The word is not speakable in any of these three hypotheses. Any formulation would reintroduce this word into the "world." At first the idea of writing seems to be the only solution. But history tells us that he opted for the third solution: to write and burn.

So here is the solution: "the books should be burnt." Have them pass from the state of objects to that of "almost objects." Efface the *Tav*; make the lack, the empty space, the hole appear. Make fire appear in order to stop books from being consumed in the totality of the world.

The "nonbook" (neither spoken nor written in the second solution) is not interesting because it does not allow the empty space to appear. Emptiness has a meaning only when it is surrounded by fullness; it is thus the solution of the "almost-book" that is retained and becomes the paradigm of the whole of Rabbi Nahman's thinking: a thinking of the caress and of infinity; a thinking of time opening up to time, a thinking of the question without an answer, a thinking of the empty space of the gap.

Rabbi Nahman says:

> So here it is: numerous books, which were books, have been effaced and destroyed. It is certain that the righteous, the greats of the past, the authors of the *Mishnah* and the *Gemara* and the men of this caliber have written numerous books that have been lost. And yet it is a good thing for the world, because if it had not been so, it would have been impossible to approach the blessed Name. Because there are many heretical books (*Sifrei minim*); if they spread throughout the world, it would be impossible to approach the blessed Name.

Rabbi Nahman puts forward an original hypothesis. According to him, the thinking of the "burnt book" is an ancient tradition that can be found in all periods of the history of the book, whether it be in the

Torah, in the episode of the woman suspected of adultery (or in the breaking of the Tables), or whether it be with the Masters of the Talmud (the *Tanaim* and the *Amoraim*) or even the great modern masters.

The "burnt book" thus belongs to an ancient tradition that is rooted as much in the Bible as in the Talmud. Does that mean that all these texts should be burnt? Yet we have them; we can seize them, hold them in our hands, and even make *manuals* of them!

And yet we assert: all books end up being burnt! And the holy books that are not yet burnt should be! But how can we assert the inexistence of books that we can obviously see around us?

This is the paradox: we have books that speak of their own absence —"The book is the manifestation of the absence of the book."[66] By means of all the technical procedures used, such as *Mahloket, Gezerah shavah, Gematria, Notarikon*, etc., by the Written Law—orality dichotomy, books escape all possible ascendancy over them. The speech of these books is always taken up, but never comprehended. It tears not only language away from orality, but also the discourse from continuity, refusing itself to the realm of reasons and the finality of the demonstration, making the ungraspable shimmer without ever being captured, in a sort of linguistic nonbeing. The Talmud[67] says that it is forbidden to write down the Oral Law. But this prohibition was abolished, for fear of forgetting and nontransmission. But what if writing were, on the contrary, simply past memory and not life?

According to Rabbi Nahman, this authorized writing down was not a writing and these books were not books. The Masters invented a writing without writing, a book absent from itself that he called the "burnt book." Fire (*esh*) transforms the "book" into an "almost-book" (*presque-livre*). The essence of the "almost" originates in the empty space between the "almost whole" and the "whole." The "almost" is an empty space, a blank The burnt text lives on these blanks. As Mallarmé said:

> The intellectual framework of the poem is hidden and—takes place— stands in the space that isolates the stanzas and within the white of the paper; a significant silence that is no less beautiful to compose than verse.[68]

The Hebrew text is determined by the blanks that open and close (while still opening) it. The Hebrew term that designates a textual entity is *Parashah*, that is to say, "cut," "separated" by two blanks, an opening one and a closing one. A text is caught between-two-empty-spaces. But the text lives through other empty spaces, those between the letters, words, and sentences. According to the *Halakhah* (the law that validates and invalidates), if one of these blanks is not respected, the book loses its status as a book and will be considered as "illegible."[69] We now understand why, for an entire page,[70] the Masters of the Talmud examine the status of the margins of the books. Should the margins be considered as a book or not? This is a juridical question and not at all a poetic or rhetorical one! This is the text that Rabbi Nahman quotes. He is fascinated by these margins, by these frontiers where nothing more is said, and yet where everything seems to be at stake. And, for him, everything becomes clear. The book he is seeking to write is the one that is written in the margins, the one which, through its writing, becomes margins. The book is burnt; it becomes margins, empty space—*Hallal hapanui*—which creates the absolute separation between man and God, allowing the (unrelating) relation that we spoke of. Rabbi Nahman writes his text in such a way that "holy books" are confused with "books written by heretics," so that one wonders which books he is talking about: holy books or books written by heretics? It is not only, as one might think, heretical books that hinder the approach of the divine—on the contrary, since they create, by questioning, the empty space of the interval that makes the relation possible.[71] It is so-called holy books that bar the way to re-ligion (relation). They offer what they cannot offer, absoluteness and Infinity. They accomplish the opposite of the necessary movement; they go from the "almost book" to the "book" and thereby destroy it (negatively). Holy books that exist as books are of the same nature as the idol, the "golden calf":

> Thus Jeroboam ben Nebat who made two golden calves and said: "Here are your gods, Israel . . ." (1 Kings 12:28) and led the people of Israel astray. Is it possible that he could have led a whole nation astray with such a trifle? Worship calves! come, come! However, it is certain that there was a great display of intelligence and subtlety in this heresy. And if we found now the smallest leaf of these books, it would remove us from the blessed Name and it would be impossible to approach him. And because of this, it is good that holy books disappear and be burnt. . . . (*LM* 2:32)

The fact that Rabbi Nahman alludes to Jeroboam ben Nebat and his golden calves, and not to the "golden calf of Sinai," can be explained by an important controversy that he engaged in with Jacob Frank and Frankism,[72] and, thereby, with Christianity.

The problems raised by Rabbi Nahman are those of incarnation and messianism. (False messianism was a crucial problem at this time: the epics of Sabbatai Tsevi and Jacob Frank were not taken lightly. They shook the whole of Jewish history, and out of them came the whole of Jewish modernity.[73] We may consider, for example, that Hasidism is the result of a Shabbatean influence and a Lurianic influence; while adding, on the other hand, that the Shabbatean concepts have been reevaluated positively.)

When we say "Judeo-Christian," we do not mean an amalgam of Judaism and Christianity but, rather, that which makes the difference between Judaism and Christianity. Here, we are considering this Judeo-Christian controversy on a precise point: on the problem of reading and interpreting texts that particularly interest us in the context of the "burnt book."

The "burnt book," that is to say, now, the action of burning the book, is a theatrical representation of Moses' act of breaking the Tables of the Law when he learned of the existence of the golden calf.

The breaking of the tables is not the destruction of the Law; it is, on the contrary, the gift of the Law in the form of its breaking. That is the improved meaning of the Talmudic expression "the abolition of the Law is its very founding." This is the expression that was at the heart of the Pauline, and particularly the Frankist, doctrines (*bitulah shel Torah Zehu kiyumah*),[74] but interpreted in a totally nihilistic and destructive way. The breaking of the Law is eminently positive; it signifies the refusal of the idol. Moses does not pass on, at first, the Law but its shattering:[75] its impossibility of being an idol, the place of perfection, a "total book." "If this breaking of the Law is to be taken seriously . . . then the real Book does not exist; its broken-up copies that run everywhere at the dawn of time show up writing in a call to speech which fissures it and invents stories for it."[76]

The speech that fissures writing, that breaks the Tables and burns the book, is the speech of interpretation, and this is what is at stake in the whole Judeo-Christian controversy. The event of Jesus Christ lies in the fact that a man arose and said: "I am come to fulfill Scripture." The New Testament is "an order of writings entirely organized around quotations; at each gaping in the text, when the thread that bears it is pierced, immediately a quotation comes along like a stitch that sews it up and acts as a basis.[77] The refrain that often punctuates the Gospels is "so that the Scriptures may be fulfilled. . . . The 'new' is said to be the accomplishing of the 'old.' All so-called old writing is reworked so that the new will be its accomplishment, *the* truth."[78]

"In the 'new' text, the staging we find there has us understand that there is saying awaiting in the Scriptures, an enigmatic saying that has been neglected and that was vaguely expected to take place, or of which it was not even known that it could ever be the object of a fulfillment, and here comes a man who fulfills it and reveals afterward that this word was for him, and he for it, and that he is, with his name and his body, the equivalent of that which he fulfills. . . . A body fills in the hole in the Law. . . . The New Testament claims to be the fulfillment of the Old, filling in the holes in its writing that it embodies and blocks up."[79]

The main upheaval brought by Christ—as far as the problematics of hermeneutics are concerned—"is not so much that he embodies the word, but that he identifies himself with that which is missing in the word, is left in suspense, and which Christ comes to fill in, plug, or rather identify with his person, to bring an end to that which is missing in any word, to that which disappoints in that which speaks when speech is uttered."[80]

Biblical speech is a prophetic speech, speech that has not yet finished its course. And when someone comes to defeat the infinite opening of the word to the opening of time "by unveiling the end" in a desire for "apocalypse" (disclosing," in the etymological sense), the closing of the text imposes a closing of the mouth with a double bolt so that it is forgotten that there ever was an opening. That is the case, for example, for Jacob in chapter 47, verse 28, of the book of Genesis.[81]

The Hebrew text and its Hebrew reader realize what could be called an "anti-Christic coup." By introducing "blanks," even where there are none, he makes time enter into the word to give it the chance of remaining in the planning stage, open to its impossible completion. The whole messianic problem is at stake in this precise point.

(It is not superfluous to note that, in the text of the Talmud on which Rabbi Nahman bases his reflection—the text of the *Shabbat* tractate, 116a—it is a question of the status of the margins, the blanks in the texts, and . . . of the Gospels. Rabbi Meir ventures a play on words: he reads *Evangelion* ("Gospel") as *Avon-Gilayon*, "an error in the margins," the destruction of the "marginal word" by the existence of the Christic word. This text, itself, was for a long time deleted by Christian censorship and has only just been restored in the contemporary editions of the Talmud[82]. . .)

Speech of Rabbi Nahman (second part of the *LM* 2:32):

For the book proceeds from the Name of God, to be understood in the sense of the verse of Proverbs (18:10): "A strong tower is the Name of God, in it the righteous runs and rises up." Concerning this we can read in the *Zohar* (Genesis, 37 b): "The Name of God is the Book, because the Book and the Name have the same numerical value" (340).[83] For the book can be understood according to the Talmudic expression (cf. *Shabbat* 116a): "My Name is written in holiness . . ." It is scattered throughout the world and it forms a name.

And know this, that each man should preserve the messianic dimension he has. For each man according to his holiness and his purity has a messianic dimension. . . .

For Rabbi Nahman, the messianic era is not the *Tikkun*, a repairing that effaces the fissure (*Shevirah*). The messianic era is not the time when the Messiah is here. On the contrary: it is the time during which the Messiah is awaited. To exaggerate a little: the Messiah is made for not coming . . . and yet, he is awaited. The Messiah allows time to be continually deferred, to generate time. The messianic era is of the order of the withdrawal (*Tsimtsum*) where the empty space does not exist in order to be healed up.

The messianic dimension of Rabbi Nahman is desire and project. Messianic man (the one who is waiting) constantly projects himself into the "yet to come" (*à-venir*) of the future; he produces a difference, a suspense. It is a break within writing, as if, at the end of each sentence (of each word), there were three ellipsis points that opened up to . . . In this suspension of meaning, time is forever projected toward the yet-to-come by an act of anticipation. But this anticipation does not foresee anything; there is no fulfillment at the end of the road. It is the anticipation of an anti-anticipation. It is in this sense that Rabbi Nahman says: "All my teachings are only introductions. . . ."

To be in messianic time and preserve one's messianic dimension is to suspend oneself, literally to become a question (*Adam-Mah*) and to be incapable of saying the "last word."[84]

Notes

1. Elie Wiesel, *Célébration hassidique* (Paris: Seuil, 1972).

2. Among the more recent works on Hasidism, the following are worth mentioning: J. Weiss, *Studies in Braslav Hassidism* (Mossad Bialik, 1974); Mendel Piekarz, *Braslav Hassidism* (Mossad Bialik, 1972); Yoav Elstein, *In the Footsteps of the Lost Princess: A Structural Analysis of the First Tale by R. N. of Braslav* (Bar-Ilan University, 1984) (with a good bibliography); A. Green, *The Tormented Master: A Life of Rabbi Nahman of Braslav* (Montgomery: University of Alabama, 1979).

3. At present, the *Tales* have been edited in a bilingual edition with Hebrew above and Yiddish below. Some texts of the *Likkutim* are by R. Nahman in Hebrew. It is easy to tell the difference between his style and that of R. Nathan. In any case, it is indicated when the text is by R. Nahman.

4. They are two copies of the same book, one written by R. Nahman himself, the other recopied by R. Nathan. He orders that both be burnt.

5. Rabbi I. Luria Ashkenazi, nicknamed "Ari" zal (Jerusalem, 1534–Safed, 1572), founder of the so-called modern Cabala that bears his name: Lurianic

Cabala; cf. G. Scholem, *Les Grands Courants de la mystique juive* (Paris: Payot, 1950), p. 261, and *Le Messianisme juif* (Paris: Calmann-Lévy, 1974), p. 91.

6. According to Scholem, this notion is borrowed from Joseph Alkastiel of Jativa in a treatise written around 1480; cf. Scholem, *Les Grands Courants de la mystique juive*, p. 412.

7. *Lireshom*: to make a trace, mark, inscribe; according to Luria, there is a succession of *Tsimtsum* in the very heart of the *Reshimu*.

8. Scholem, *Les Grands Courants de la mystique juive*, p. 279.

9. S. Trigano, *Le Récit de la disparue* (Paris: Gallimard, 1977), p. 25.

10. E. Lévinas, *Totality and Infinity* (Pittsburgh: Duquesne University Press, 1988), p. 104. For the definition of religion in Lévinas's thought, p. 80: "For the relation between the being here below and the transcendant being that results in no community of concept or totality—a relation without relation—we reserve the term religion."

11. Lévinas has certainly never considered that his thought might be close to that of a Hasidic thinker. We are not at all exaggerating the comparison. The texts speak for themselves. . .

12. Lévinas, *Totality and Infinity*, p. 88.

13. Insolence, audacity . . .

14. The leaders of this trend would be, for example, R. Dov Baer of Mezrich and R. Schneur Zalman of Lyad.

15. Weiss, *Studies in Braslav Hassidism*, p. 121.

16. The empty space is the logical possibility of the world and the scene of the paradox, because the world is necessarily based on two contradictory theses: the immanence of God in the world and his transcendence beyond the world. There is, at the same time, being and nonbeing of God in the world; these two demands contradict each other and this contradiction is, precisely, the essence of the empty space.

17. Cf. below, § 64, 2, e.

18. Ibid.

19. For all these ideas, cf. Scholem, *Le Messianisme juif*, pp. 101-38.

20. E. Jabès, *Du désert au livre* (Paris: Belfond, 1980), p. 112.

21. Ibid., p. 109.

22. *LM* 2:52.

23. M. Blanchot, *L'Entretien infini* (Paris: Gallimard, 1969), p. 15.

24. Ibid., p. 16.

25. Talmud *Berakhot* 2a: "From what time in the evening is the *Shema* recited? From the time when the priests enter their homes to eat their *Terumah* (Heave-offering)." In fact, this time is unknown. The *Gemara* has to ask, in turn: "The priest's time, what is it exactly?"

26. Blanchot, *L'Entretien infini*, p. 187.

27. Ibid.

28. Ibid., p. 74. The whole of Lévinas's thought on others is summed up in this sentence, which can, without any doubt whatsoever, also sum up the thought of R. Nahman on *Mahloket*.

29. Ibid., p. 110; see also p. 116.

30. The sins in the history of Israel very often consist in denying the empty

space by a refusal of the difference and a will to turn back as a result of the ontological impossibility of continuing to produce time: that is what we have called "the refusal of the manna"; cf. First Opening.

31. P. Legendre, *L'Inestimable Objet de la transmission* (Paris: Fayard, 1985), p. 75.

32. Legendre says: "The space of the question without an answer is occupied, filled in, mastered, without fault by the embodied power."

33. On the opinion, cf. Blanchot, *L'Entretien infini*, pp. 26–27.

34. Legendre, *L'Inestimable Objet de la transmission*, p. 91.

35. Blanchot, *L'Entretien infini*, p. 15.

36. The concept of designifying was introduced in psychoanalysis by Nicolas Abraham in an article in the *Revue critique*, February 1968, under the title "L'Écorce et le noyau." This concept was taken up and extensively developed by P. Fedida, *L'Absence* (Paris: Gallimard, 1978), pp. 322–26. We give the main points of his analysis.

37. Cf. Book One: "Words within words."

38. Fedida, *L'Absence*, p. 324.

39. *Mishnah Avot.*

40. Legendre, *L'Inestimable Objet de la transmission*, p. 129.

41. A play on words: *gamur* means finished, accomplished; the same ambiguity exists in this word as in the English "finished," which means both to have arrived at the peak of one's possibilities and terminated, dead.

42. In French, *monde* ("world") also denotes a group of people: *"Il y a du monde . . ."* ("there are some people").

43. *Kiddushin* tractate, 70a.

44. *Zeman* (time) *zeh-man*: introduction of the difference in the undifferentiated, the production of radical otherness, like the son with relation to the father.

45. M. Heidegger, *Le Principe de la raison* (Paris: Gallimard, 1962), p. 229. Cf. also *Essais et conférences* (Paris: Gallimard, 1958), pp. 249–78 and 311–41, "the world is *logos* and *phusis*"; cf. *Le Principe de la raison*, p. 162, "disclosure belongs to what is proper to being," and p. 233.

46. Heidegger, *Le Principe de la raison*, p. 232.

47. Heidegger, *Essais et conférences*, p. 270.

48. Ibid., p. 327.

49. Ibid., p. 328.

50. Ibid., p. 328.

51. Ibid., p. 334.

52. Cf. E. Lévinas, *L'Au-delà du verset* (Paris: Éditions de Minuit, 1982), pp. 143f. Cf. also the two Openings of this book.

53. Cf. Heidegger, *Essais et conférences*, p. 252.

54. On *Beaalotkha*, 10, 35–36.

55. J. Baudrillard, *L'Échange symbolique et la mort* (Paris: Gallimard, 1976), p. 290.

56. And also Hasidic and Cabalistic reading.

57. The passage on the *Sihot Haran* (no. 267).

58. Baudrillard, *L'Échange symbolique et la mort*, pp. 298–99. It should be

pointed out that we are using Baudrillard's ideas without entering into the controversy he has with Starobinski on the interpretation of Saussure.

59. The term is from Nicolas Abraham, "L'Ecorce et le noyau."

60. Baudrillard, *L'Échange symbolique et la mort*, p. 308.

61. Cf. the First and Second Openings.

62. Cf. A. Juranville, *Lacan et la philosophie* (Paris: PUF, 1984), p. 369, and Legendre, *L'Inestimable Objet de la transmission*, pp. 44–45.

63. Is the world accessible or else do we consider the world as being inaccessible? Obviously, it is a question of attitude and not of reality, a manner of being in the world that allows for alterity; on a philosophy of the caress, cf. E. Lévinas, *Le Temps et l'Autre* (Paris: Fata Morgana, 1979), pp. 80f., and *Totality and Infinity*, "The Phenomenology of Eros."

On the imperfect object, cf. Legendre, *L'Inestimable Objet de la transmission*, pp. 40–41.

64. This is to say that it is the relationship which is imperfect, unabsolute. The object is what it is, inaccessible. We ought to have the Lacanian distinction between "thing" and "object" intervene here.

65. According to Lévinas, *Le Temps et l'Autre*, pp. 83–84; cf. also p. 64.

66. Cf. Blanchot, *L'Entretien infini*, last part, "L'Absence de livre."

67. *Gitten* 60a and b.

68. Quoted by J. Derrida, *La Dissémination* (Paris: Seuil, 1972), p. 260.

69. Cf. First Opening.

70. *Shabbat* tractate, 116a. See the translation at the beginning of the First Opening.

71. Cf. H. Atlan, in *La Bible au présent* (Paris: Gallimard, 1982), "Idées," p. 85.

72. Cf. Weiss, *Studies in Braslav Hassidism*, pp. 24–27. Jeroboam is the veiled expression that denotes Frank and Frankism (on Frankism, cf. Scholem, *Le Messianisme juif*). According to Weiss, R. Nahman tried to carry out the *Tikkun* of the soul of Frank as Baal Shem Tov tried to carry out the *tikkun* of the soul of Sabbatai Tsevi.

73. On this subject, cf. S. Trigano, *La Demeure oubliée* (Paris: Lieu Commun), 1984.

74. Cf. Scholem, *Le Messianisme juif*.

75. D. Sibony, *La Juive. Une transmission d'inconscient* (Paris: Grasset, 1983), p. 240.

76. Ibid., p. 267. Sibony calls this intrinsic facturing the "Moses effect."

77. Ibid., p. 269. Sibony calls this way of proceeding the "Christic coup."

78. Ibid., p. 270.

79. Ibid.

80. Ibid., pp. 295–96.

81. Cf. Maharal of Prague, *Gur Arie*, on this verse.

82. Steinsaltz ed. (1976), *Shabbat* tractate, p. 511. We can also find there a play on words by Rabbi Johanan.

83. Name: *Shem* = *shin* (300) + *mem* (40); Book: sefer = samekh (60) + *peh* (80) + *resh* (200).

84. This speech where the last word will not be uttered is called messianic or prophetic. It is also a conduct; we call it "caress."

In the relationship with the world and the other man (woman), the caress is of a messianic nature, because it refuses to make itself master of the world and the body of the other, of its freedom. It is from this point of view that R. Nahman reinterprets the whole biblical and Talmudic passage on the woman suspected of adultery. It is a completely positive interpretation where he reintroduces the necessity of suspicion as the condition of desire and of relationships. In the part that follows, Rabbi Nahman quotes a passage of the *Midrash Rabbah (Parashah nasso)* that decomposes the word *lo tin'af* (you shall not commit adultery) into *lo tehaneh af* (you shall not profit by, you shall not enjoy), with the nose (*af*). He then quotes Gen. 1:3, "And God's spirit hovered over the water," in parallel with the text from the *Zohar Vayehi* 240a which explains that God's spirit is the breath of the Messiah; the water is the Torah (cf. *Taanit* 4a and *Bava Kana* 17a).

In the third and fourth parts, the references are the following: Num. 5:11–31. As a commentary: even though it is forbidden to efface the Name, there is a case "where the Name can only be traced with a view to its effacing." There is a long passage treating this question in the *Sotah* tractate (53a). The woman suspected, without proof, of adultery by her husband should be brought by the latter to the priest of the temple and be submitted to a test: "the priest will take the holy water in an earthenware vessel and the priest will take some dust from the ground of the dwelling, he will place it in the water. . . . Then the priest will write these imprecations in a book and will efface them in the water of bitterness. . . ." In this effacing the Tetragram written in view of this effacing will also be effaced.

Then R. Nahman quotes the text of the *Gemara Sotah* 17a: in the relationship between man and woman there is a certain relationship with fire; "Rabbi Akiva expounded: When husband and wife are worthy (pure or translucent), the Presence (*Shekhinah*) abides with them; when they are not worthy the fire consumes them." Rashi comments as follows: "What does 'they are pure' mean?: 'they are faithful one to another'? that 'the Presence is between them'; that is to say that He has distributed the letters of his Name; He has placed the letter *Yod* in the word *Ish* (man) and the letter *Heh* in the word *Ishah* (woman). If they are not pure, a fire consumes them: i.e., the Holy One, blessed be He, withdraws his name from between them and on either side all that is left is fire." Rabbi Akiva is playing with letters. The word "man" is spelled *Aleph-Yod-Shin*, and the word "woman" is spelled *Aleph-Shin-Heh*. If we remove the *Yod* and the *Heh*, which spell the Name *Yah* ("God"), from these two words, we are left with *Aleph-Shin* or "fire" on both sides.

In the fifth part, Rabbi Nahman quotes the *Shabbat* tractate, 116a. He says: "And it is the deep meaning of the Talmudic expression 'Let my Name written in sanctity be blotted out in water.' For the book proceeds from the Name, from the Name written in sanctity; yet the Torah says that it is to be blotted out and destroyed in order to make peace between man and wife, which is the holy couple. It is to make peace between them that the books which proceed from 'my Name written in sanctity' are effaced and destroyed.

"We can thus give the following explanation: if already, concerning 'my Name written in sanctity'—i.e., holy books—the Torah says it should be blotted out in order to restore peace . . . books written by heretics who incite hatred and enmity between the children of Israel and their Father . . . should be, even more so, blotted out and uprooted from the world.

"To conclude, it turns out that by the destruction of holy books good is produced, because heretical books are destroyed and uprooted, and so we can come closer to Him. . . ."

Glossary

Of Hebrew Words Used in This Work

Aggadah — Talmudic or "Midrashic" history, of a nonjuridical character

Aharonim — Juridical masters of the modern period, from the seventeenth century onwards

Amora — Master of the *Gemara* living in Babylonia or in Israel, between the first and fifth centuries

Babli — "Babylonian," an adjective that defines the origin of the Talmud. *Talmud Babli*: the Babylonian Talmud as distinct from the Jerusalem Talmud

Baraita — A text parallel to that of the *Mishnah*

Beit hamidrash — Study hall, a place of creativity

Bina — One of the Three modes of intelligence; the ability to distinguish between two things; the differential character of thought, or to be situated between the masters

Cohen — The priest practicing at the Temple of Jerusalem

Dibbur — The word, speech

Esh — Fire

Gemara — The commentary of the *Mishnah* elaborated between the second and fifth centuries by the *Amoraim*

Gematria — A reading procedure whereby the numerical values of the texts are taken into account

Gezerah shavah — Intertextuality

Hakham — A wise man, master

Halakhah — The process of thought in the juridical field

Hidush — Intellectual innovation

Hokhmah — Wisdom, the ability to question

Ketuvim — the *Writings*, third part of the Jewish Bible

Kodesh — Sacred, or, rather, holy

Mah — "What?" Numerical value of Man-*Adam*; the setting of the question

Mahashava — Thought

Mahloket — Controversial discussion between Masters of the Talmud

Manna — "bread from heaven" in the desert, food sent by God; the scene of the trial of questioning

Midbar — The desert; setting of the appearing of Speech

Midrash — Exegetical commentary of the Bible

Mishkan — The portable temple in the desert

Mishnah — The Oral Law written down in the second century by Rabbi Judah ha-Nasi, thought dating from the second century B.C.E. up to the second century C.E.

Mitzvah (pl.: Mitzvot) — commandments to be accomplished; actions to do or not to do

Neviim — The Prophets, second part of the Hebrew Bible

Ohel-moed — The Tent of Meeting, central space of the *Mishkan*

Parashah — A biblical passage

Passuk — A biblical verse

Rabbi — Title given to Masters of the *Mishnah* and other masters of the *Germara* of Babylon

Rashi — commentary of the Bible and the Talmud by Rabbi Solomon ben Yitshaki, born at Troyes in 1040

Rishonim — Juridical masters from the tenth to the sixteenth century

Shabbat — Seventh day of the week, day of rest (Sabbath)

Shem — The name; in general refers to the Name of God, *Hashem*

Shevirat-Kelim — "The breaking of the vessels," in the cabalistic theory of Luria

Sidra — A biblical passage read on Shabbat at the synagogue

Talmid — Student, disciple

Talmid-hakham — literally: "disciple–wise man"; scholar, master

Talmud — The whole of the *Mishnah* and the *Gemara*

Tanakh — The Hebrew Bible (initials of *Torah, Neviim, Ketuvim*)

Tanna — Author of the *Mishanh*; plural: *Tannaim*

Tikkun — Repairing, the last phase in the cabalistic theory of Luria

Torah — The first part of the Bible, the Five Books of Moses; in general, the Law

Torah she-be-al peh — The Oral Law: Talmud, *Midrash*, and commentaries

Torah shebikhtav — The Written Law: the Bible

Tosafot — Commentary of the Talmud, situated in the Talmudic page, developed by the disciples of Rashi, following him, in France and Germany

Tsimtsum — Contraction, withdrawal of the divine in the theory of Luria

Yerushalmi — "from Jerusalem"; the Palestinian Talmud, as opposed to that of Babylonia

Yeshiva — Talmudic school

Yoma — Talmudic tractate concerning the day of Yom Kippur

Bibliography

Works in French and in English

Abécassis, A. *La Lumière dans la pensée juive*. Paris: Berg International, 1988.
———. "Le Midrash entre mythos et logos." *Les Études philosophiques*, no. 2 (1984).
———. *La Pensée juive*. 3 vols. Paris: Le Livre de poche, 1987.
Abécassis, A., and J. Eisenberg. *A Bible ouverte*. Vol. 1, *A Bible ouverte*. Vol. 2, *Et Dieu créa Ève*. Vol. 3, *Moi, le gardien de mon frère?* Vol. 4, *Jacob, Rachel, Léa et les autres*. Paris: Albin Michel, 1978, 1979, 1980, 1982.
Abraham, N. *La Dialectique de la raison*. Paris: Gallimard, 1983.
———. *L'Écorce et le noyau*. Paris: Aubier-Flammarion, 1978.
———. *Jonas*. Paris: Aubier-Flammarion, 1981.
———. *Rythmes*. Paris: Flammarion, 1985.
———. *Le Verbier de l'homme aux loups*. Paris: Aubier-Flammarion, 1976.
Adorno, T. *Jargon de l'authenticité*. Paris: Payot, 1989.
———. *Minima moralia*. Paris: Payot, 1983.
———. *Modèles critiques*. Paris: Payot, 1984.
———. *Prismes*. Paris: Payot, 1986.
———. *Trois Études sur Hegel*. Paris: Payot, 1979.
Amado Levy-Valensi, E. *La Communication*. Paris: PUF, 1967.
———. *Le Dialogue psychanalytique*. Paris: PUF, 1963.
———. *Le Grand Désarroi aux sources de l'énigme homosexuelle*. Paris: Vrin, 1971.
———. *Isaac, gardien de son frère?* Paris: Privat, 1968.
———. *Lettres de Jérusalem*. Brussels: Cirel, 1983.
———. *Le Moïse de Freud ou la Référence occultée*. Paris: Éditions du Rocher, 1984.
———. *La Nature de la pensée inconsciente*. Paris: Vrin, 1978.
———. *Les Niveaux de l'être, la Connaissance et le Mal*. Paris: PUF, 1963.
———. *La Onzième Épreuve d'Abraham*. Paris: J.-C. Lattès, 1981.
———. *La Racine et la source*. Paris: Éditions Zikarone, 1968.
———. *Le Temps dans la vie morale*. Paris: Vrin, 1968.
———. *Le Temps dans la vie psychologique*. Paris: Flammarion, 1965.
———. *Les Voies et les pièges de la psychanalyse*. Paris: J.-P. Delarge, 1971.
Antelme, R. *L'Espèce humaine*. Paris: Gallimard, 1957.
Arendt, H. *La Condition de l'homme moderne*. Paris: Calmann-Lévy, 1961.
———. *La Crise de la culture*. Paris: Gallimard, 1972.
———. *Eichmann à Jérusalem*. Paris: Gallimard, 1966.
———. *Essai sur la révolution*. Paris: Gallimard, 1967.
———. *L'Impérialisme*. Paris: Fayard, 1982.
———. *Sur l'antisémitisme*. Paris: Calmann-Lévy, 1973.
———. *Le Système totalitaire*. Paris: Seuil, 1972.

————. *La Tradition cachée*. Paris: C. Bourgois, 1987.

————. *La Vie de l'esprit*. 2 vols. Paris: PUF, 1981, 1983.

————. *Vies politiques*. Paris: Gallimard, 1974.

Atlan, H. *A tort et à raison*. Paris: Seuil, 1986.

————. "Créativité biologique et auto-création du sens." In *Création et créativité*. Paris: Éditions Castella, 1986.

————. *Entre le cristal et la fumée*. Paris: Seuil, 1979.

————. "État et religion dans la pensée politique du Rav Kook." In *Israël, le judaïsme et l'Europe*. Paris: Gallimard, 1984.

————. "Une mystique du langage aux origines de la science: continuité et rupture." In *Symbiose des cultures juive et française*. Paris: Éditions de la Fondation européenne des arts et de la culture, 1988.

————. "Niveaux de signification et athéisme de l'écriture." In *La Bible au présent*. Paris: Gallimard, 1982.

————. *Tout, non, peut-être. Éducation et vérité*. Paris: Seuil, 1991.

Aulagnier, P. *La Violence de l'interprétation. Du pictogramme à l'énoncé*. Paris: PUF, 1975.

Austin, J.-L. *Quand dire, c'est faire*. Paris: Seuil, 1970.

Bachelard, G. *La Philosophie du non*. Paris: PUF, 1940.

————. *La Poétique de l'espace*. Paris: PUF, 1957.

Badiou, A. *L'Être et l'évenement*. Paris: Seuil, 1988.

————. *Peut-on penser la politique?* Paris: Seuil, 1985.

————. *Théorie du sujet*. Paris: Seuil, 1982.

Bakhtine, M. *L'Oeuvre de François Rabelais*. Paris: Gallimard, 1970.

Balmary, M. *Le Sacrifice interdit*. Paris: Grasset, 1986.

Banon, D. *La Lecture infinie*. Paris: Seuil, 1987.

Barbaras, R. *La Dimension comme être du phénomène: sur l'ontologie de Merleau-Ponty*. Paris: Millon, 1991.

Barthes, R. *L'Empire des signes*. Paris: Skira, 1970.

————. *Le Grain de la voix*. Paris: Seuil, 1981.

————. "Introduction à l'analyse structurale du récit." *Communications*, no. 8 (1988).

————. *Le Plaisir du texte*. Paris: Seuil, 1973.

————. *Writing Degree Zero*. Translated by Annette Lavers and Colin Smith. New York: Hill and Wang, 1967.

Baudrillard, J. *L'Échange symbolique et la mort*. Paris: Gallimard, 1976.

Baumgarten, J., trans. *Commentaires sur la Tora, de Rabbi de Janov*. Paris: Verdier, 1987.

Belohradsky, V. "La modernité comme passion du neutre." *Le Messager européen*, no. 2 (1988): 21–79.

Benamozegh, E. *Israël et l'humanité*. Paris: Albin Michel, 1961.

Berdiaeff, N. *Cinq Méditations sur l'existence*. Paris: Aubier-Montaigne, 1936.

————. *Le Sens de la création*. Paris: Desclée de Brouwer, 1955.

Bergson, H. *La Pensée et le mouvant*. 91st ed. Paris: PUF, 1975.

Bernheim, G. "Israël et les soixante-dix nations." In *Les Soixante-dix Nations*. Paris: Denoël, 1987.

————. "Médiations partielles." In *Idoles*. Paris: Denoël, 1985.

———. "La Voix et l'écriture." In *La Bible au présent*. Paris: Gallimard, 1982.

Binsvanger, L. *Analyse existentielle et psychanalyse freudienne*. Paris: Gallimard, 1970.

———. *Le Cas S. Urban*. Paris: Éditions Gérard Montfort, 1988.

———. *Mélancolie et Manie*. Paris: PUF, 1987.

Blanchot, M. *La Communauté inavouable*. Paris: Éditions de Minuit, 1983.

———. *De Kafka à Kafka*. Paris: Gallimard, 1981.

———. *L'Écriture du désastre*. Paris: Gallimard, 1980.

———. *L'Entretien infini*. Paris: Gallimard, 1969.

———. *L'Espace littéraire*. Paris: Gallimard, 1955.

———. *Le Livre à venir*. (Folio, essais.) Paris: Gallimard, 1959.

———. *Le Pas au-delà*. Paris: Gallimard, 1973.

———. "Une voix venue d'ailleurs." "Sur les poèmes de Louis-René des Forêts." *Ulysse fin de siècle*. Dijon, 1992.

Bloch, E. *L'Athéisme dans le christianisme*. Paris: Gallimard, 1978.

———. *L'Esprit de l'utopie*. Paris: Gallimard, 1977.

———. *Experimentum mundi*. Paris: Gallimard, 1978.

Bochurberg, C. *Une approche ostéopathique de l'angoisse*. Paris: Maloine, 1988.

———. *Mémoire et Vigilance*. Paris: Le Liséré bleu, 1985.

———. *La Relation inachevée: une approche phénoménologique de la relation*. Paris: L'Harmattan, 1991.

———. *Rubrique mémoire*. Paris: AJ Presse, 1992.

———. *Traitement ostéopathique des rhinites et des sinusites chroniques*. Paris: Maloine, 1986.

———. *La Vieille Femme qui passait*. Paris: Bibliophane, 1991.

Bochurberg, C., and J. Baldran. *A l'écoute infinie de la nuit*. Paris: L'Harmattan, 1990.

———. *Brasillach ou la Célébration du mépris*. Paris: AJ Presse, 1988.

———. *L'Histoire baufouée ou la Dérive relativiste*. Paris: L'Harmattan, 1992.

Bouchurberg, C., and E. Morin. *Jeux de mains, jeux de vie*. Paris: Seuil, 1983.

Borges, J.-L. *Fictions*. Paris: Gallimard, 1957.

Bourdieu, P. *L'Ontologie politique de Martin Heidegger*. Paris: Éditions de Minuit, 1988.

Brehier, E. *Histoire de la philosophie*. 3 vols., Paris: PUF, 1981.

Breton, A. *Arcane 17*. Paris: UGE, 1965.

Brenner, F. *Jérusalem: instants d'éternité*. Paris: Denoël, 1984.

Buber, M. *Le Chemin de l'homme: d'après la doctrine hassidique*. Paris: Éditions du Rocher, 1989.

———. *Je et tu*. Paris: Aubier, 1957.

———. *Les Récits hassidiques*. Paris: Éditions du Rocher, 1978.

———. *Une terre et deux peuples*. Paris: Lieu Commun, 1985.

———. *La Vie en dialogue*. Paris: Aubier, 1964.

Canetti, E. *Auto-da-fé*. Paris: Gallimard, 1968.

Castoriadis, C. *Les Carrefours du labyrinthe*. Paris: Seuil, 1978.

———. *Domaines de l'homme*. Paris: Seuil, 1986.

———. *L'Institution imaginaire de la société*. Paris: Seuil, 1975.

Certeau,M. de. *L'Écriture de l'Histoire*. Paris: Gallimard, 1975.

————. *Histoire et psychanalyse, entre science et fiction*. Paris: Gallimard, 1987.

————. *La Table mystique*. Paris: Gallimard, 1982.

Chalier, C. *L'Alliance avec la nature*. Paris: Le Cerf, 1989.

————. *Figures du féminin: lecture d'Emmanuel Lévinas*. Paris: Éditions La nuit suveillée, 1982.

————. *L'Histoire promise*. Paris: Le Cerf, 1992.

————. *Judaïsme et altérité*. Paris: Verdier, 1982.

————. *La Persévérance du mal*. Paris: Cerf, 1987.

Charcosset, J.-P. *Merleau-Ponty, approches phénoménologiques*. Paris: Hachette, 1981.

Chertock, L. *L'Hypnose*. Paris: Payot, 1965.

Chertock, L., and Isabelle Stengers. *Le Coeur et la raison: l'hypnose en question, de Lavoisier à Lacan*. Paris: Payot, 1989.

Chestov, L. *Athènes et Jérusalem*. Paris: Flammarion, 1967.

Clément, C. *Vies et Légendes de Jacques Lacan*. Paris: Grasset, 1981.

Collin, F. *Maurice Blanchot et la question de l'écriture*. Paris: Gallimard, 1971.

Colloque des intellectuels juifs de langue française. Paris: PUF, 1963, 1965, 1971, 1971, 1972, 1973, 1975, 1975, 1976, 1977, 1978, 1979; Gallimard, 1981; *Nouveaux cahiers* no. 70 (Fall 1982); Gallimard, 1982, 1984; Denoël, 1985, 1986, 1987.

Comte-Sponville, A. *Le Mythe d'Icare*. Paris: PUF, 1984.

————. *Vivre*. Paris: PUF, 1988.

Darmesteter, A. "Le Talmud." In "Aspects du génie d'Israël." *Cahiers du sud*, 1950.

Debray, R. *Critique de la raison politique*. Paris: Gallimard, 1981.

De Dieguez, M. *Une histoire de l'intelligence*. Paris: Fayard, 1986.

————. *De l'idolâtrie*. Paris: PUF, 1969.

————. *L'Idole monothéiste*. Paris: PUF, 1981.

————. *Le Mythe rationnel de l'Occident*. Paris: PUF, 1980.

————. *Science et Nescience*. Paris: Gallimard, 1970.

Deleuze, G. *Différence et Répétition*. Paris: PUF, 1981.

————. *Foucault*. Paris: Éditions de Minuit, 1986.

————. *Logique du sens*. Paris: Éditions de Minuit, 1969.

————. *Nietzsche et la philosophie*. Paris: PUF, 1962.

————. *Le Pli*. Paris: Éditions de Minuit, 1988.

————. *Proust et les signes*. 6th ed. Paris: PUF, 1964.

Delhomme, J. *La Pensée et le réel*. Paris: PUF, 1967.

————. *La Pensée interrogative*. Paris: PUF, 1954.

————. *Vie et Conscience de la vie. Essai sur Bergson*. Paris: PUF, 1954.

Derczanski, A. "Itinéraire de Gerschom Scholem." *Recherches de science religieuse* 64 (1976): 271–84.

————. "Le judaïsme face à la modernité: l'imaginaire ou la norme: *Halakha ou Haggada*." *Recherches de science religieuse* 63 (1975): 185–96.

————. "Langue et religion: le yiddish. Note pour une théologie de la langue." *Recherches de science religieuse* 66 (1978): 617–22.

———. "La Révolution française: matrice du judaïsme moderne?" *Archives de sciences sociales et religieuses* 66 (1988): 113–24.

Derrida, J. *La Carte postale*. Paris: Aubier-Flammarion, 1980.

———. "Circonfession." In *Jacques Derrida*. Paris: Seuil, 1991.

———. *De la grammatologie*. Paris: Éditions de Minuit, 1967.

———. *De l'esprit. Heidegger et la question*. Paris: Galilée, 1987.

———. *La Dissémination*. Paris: Seuil, 1972.

———. *L'Écriture et la différence*. Paris: Seuil, 1967.

———. *Edmund Husserl's "Origin of Geometry": An Introduction*. Translated by John P. Leavey, Jr. Lincoln: University of Nebraska Press, 1978.

———. "En ce moment même dans cet ouvrage, me voici." In *Textes pour Emmanuel Lévinas*. Paris: Jean-Michel Place, 1980.

———. *L'Éthique du don: Jacques Derrida et la pensée du don, Colloque de Royaumont décembre 1990*. Paris: A.-M. Métaillé, 1992.

———. *Feu la cendre*. Paris: Des Femmes, 1987.

———. *Glas*. Paris: Galilée, 1974.

———. *Marges de la philosophie*. Paris: Éditions de Minuit, 1972. Translated by Alan Bass as *Margins of Philosophy*. Chicago: University of Chicago Press, 1982.

———. *Points de suspension. Entretiens*. Paris: Galilée, 1992.

———. *Psyché, invention de l'autre*. Paris: Galilée, 1987.

———. *Ulysse gramophone, deux mots pour Joyce*. Paris: Galilée, 1987.

———. *La Vérité en peinture*. Paris: Flammarion, 1978.

———. *La Voix et le phénomène*. Paris: PUF, 1967.

Descartes, R. *Oeuvres et lettres*. Paris: Gallimard, 1992.

Descombe, V. *Le Même et l'Autre*. Paris: Éditions de Minuit, 1979.

Drai, R. *Oeil pour Oeil, le mythe de la loi du talion*. Paris: Éditions J. Clims, 1986.

———. *La Politique de l'inconscient*. Paris: Payot, 1979.

———. *Le Pouvoir et la Parole*. Paris: Payot, 1981.

———. *La Sortie d'Égypte. L'invention de la liberté*. Paris: Fayard, 1986.

———. *La Traversée du désert. L'invention de la responsabilité*. Paris: Fayard, 1989.

Ducrot, O., and T. Todorov. *Dictionnaire encyclopédique des sciences du langage*. Paris: Seuil, 1972.

Dufrenne, M. *La Poétique. Pour une philosophie non théologique*. Paris: PUF, 1973.

Dupuy, B. "Unité et tension de la Halakha et de la Aggada." In "Mélanges à la mémoire de M. H. Prévost. Paris: PUF, 1982.

Duvignaud, J. *Hérésie et subversion*. Paris: La Découverte, 1986.

Eco, U. *Lector in fabula*. Paris: Grasset, 1985.

———. *Les Limites de l'interprétation*. Paris: Grasset, 1991.

———. *Le Nom de la rose*. Paris: Grasset, 1983.

———. *L'Oeuvre ouverte*. Paris: Seuil, 1979.

———. *Sémiotique et philosophie du langage*. Paris: PUF, 1988.

———. *La Structure absente*. Paris: Mercure de France, 1973.

Eisenberg, J., and A. Abécassis. *Une histoire du peuple juif*. Paris: Fayard, 1974.

Eisenberg, J., and B. Gross. *Un messie nommé Joseph*. Paris: Albin Michel, 1983.

Eisenberg, J., and A. Steinsaltz. *Le Chandelier d'or*. Paris: Verdier, 1988.

Eisenberg, J., and E. Wiesel. *Job ou Dieu dans la tempête*. Paris: Fayard-Verdier, 1986.

Éliade, M. *Images et symboles*. Paris: Gallimard, 1952.

Elstein, Y. *In the Footsteps of the Lost Princess: A Structural Analysis of the First Tale by R. N. of Braslav*. Bar-Ilan University, 1984.

Énegren, A. *La Pensée politique de H. Arendt*. Paris: PUF, 1984.

Fedida, P. *L'Absence*. Paris: Gallimard, 1978.

———. *Crise et contre-transfert*. Paris: PUF, 1992.

Fedida, P., and Jacques Schotte. *Psychiatrie et existence*. Paris: Millon, 1990.

Feron, E. *De l'idée de la transcendance à la question du langage: l'itinéraire philosophique de Lévinas*. Paris: Millon, 1992.

Ferry, L. *Heidegger et les Modernes*. Paris: Grasset, 1988.

———. *Le Nouvel Ordre écologique. L'arbre, L'animal et l'homme*. Paris: Grasset, 1992.

Ferry, L., and A. Renaut. *La Pensée 68*. Paris: Gallimard, 1985.

———. *Philosophie politique*. 3 vols. Paris: PUF, 1984–1985.

———. *68–86: itinéraire de l'individu*. Paris: Gallimard, 1987.

———. *Systèmes et Critique*. Brussels: Ousia, 1985.

Finas, L., et al. *Écarts, quatre essais à propos de J. Derrida*. Paris: Fayard, 1973.

Fink, E. *De la phénoménologie*. Paris: Éditions de Minuit, 1974.

———. *Le Jeu comme symbole du monde*. Paris: Éditions de Minuit, 1966.

———. *La Philosophie de Nietzsche*. Paris: Éditions de Minuit, 1965.

Finkielkraut, A. *L'Avenir d'une négation, réflexion sur la question du génocide*. Paris: Seuil, 1984.

———. *La Défaite de la pensée*. Paris: Gallimard, 1987.

———. "Le jour et la nuit, relecture de H. Arendt." *CIJLF*, no. 23 (1984).

———. *Le Juif imaginaire*. Paris: Seuil, 1979.

———. *La Mémoire vaine*. Paris: Gallimard, 1989.

———. *La Sagesse de l'amour*. Paris: Gallimard, 1985.

Forthomme, B. *Une Philosophie de la transcendance: La métaphysique d'Emmanuel Lévinas*. Paris: La Pensée Universelle, 1979.

Foucault, M. *L'Archéologie du savoir*. Paris: Gallimard, 1969.

———. *Histoire de la folie à l'âge classique*. Paris: Gallimard, 1961.

———. *Histoire de la sexualité*. 3 vols. Paris: Gallimard, 1976.

———. *Les Mots et les Choses*. Paris: Gallimard, 1966.

———. *L'Ordre du discours*. Paris: Gallimard, 1971.

———. *Surveiller et Punir*. Paris: Gallimard, 1975.

Fourastié, J. *Le Rire, suite*. Paris: Denoël-Gonthier, 1983.

Freed, L. *La Danse des fidèles*. Paris: Le Chêne, 1984.

Funkenstein, A. *Maïmonide. Nature, Histoire et messianisme*. Paris: Éditions du Cerf, 1988.

Gadamer, H. G. *L'Art de comprendre*. Paris: Aubier, 1982.

———. *Qui suis-je et qui es-tu*. Arles: Actes Sud, 1987.

———. *Vérité et méthode*. Paris: Seuil, 1976.

Gargani, A. *Le Hasard et l'étonnement*. Paris: Éditions de l'Éclat, 1988.

Genot-Bismuth, J. "De l'Idée juive du sens." In *Hommage à G. Vajda*. Louvain, 1980.

Girard, P. *Les Juifs de France de 1789 à 1860*. Paris: Calmann-Lévy, 1976.

———. *Les Juifs et la Révolution*. Paris: Fayard, 1989.

———. *Pour le meilleur et pour le pire*. Paris: Éditions Bibliophane, 1986.

Glucksmann, A. *Descartes, c'est la France*. Paris: Grasset, 1987.

———. *Les Maîtres Penseurs*. Paris: Grasset, 1977.

Green, A. *The Tormented Master: A Life of Rabbi Nahman of Braslav*. Montgomery: University of Alabama, 1979.

Greisch, J. *L'Age herméneutique de la raison*. Paris: Éditions du Cerf, 1985.

———. *Herméneutique et Grammatologie*. Paris: CNRS, 1977.

———. *La Parole heureuse*. Paris: Beauchesne, 1987.

Grossberg, R. M. *Tsefunot Harogashevi* (in Hebrew). 2d ed. Jerusalem, 1975.

Guibal, F. . . . *Et combien de dieux nouveaux: Lévinas*. Paris: Aubier-Montaigne, 1980.

Habermas, J. *Connaissance et intérêt*. Paris: Gallimard, 1976.

———. *Le Discours philosophique de la modernité*. Paris: Gallimard, 1988.

———. *Profils philosophiques et politiques*. Paris: Gallimard, 1974.

———. *La Technique et la science comme idéologie*. Paris: Gallimard, 1973.

———. *Théorie de l'agir communicationnel*. 2 vols. Paris: Fayard, 1987.

Haddad, G. *Les Biblioclastes*. Paris: Grasset, 1991.

———. *L'Enfant illégitime*. Paris: Hachette, 1980.

———. *Manger le livre*. Paris: Grasset, 1984.

Hansel, G. "Et vous craindrez mon sanctuaire." In *Idoles*. Paris: Denoël, 1985.

———. "Le Talmud, le folklore et le symbole." In *Israël, le judaïsme et l'Europe*. Paris: Gallimard, 1984.

Hayoun, M. R., *Maïmonide*. Paris: PUF, 1987.

Hegel, G.W.F. *La Phénoménologie de l'esprit*. Paris: Aubier, 1941.

———. *Précis de l'Encyclopédie*. Paris: Vrin, 1978.

Heidegger, M. *Acheminement vers la Parole*. Paris: Gallimard, 1976.

———. *Chemins qui ne mènent nulle part*. Paris: Gallimard, 1962.

———. *Essais et Conférences*. Paris: Gallimard, 1958.

———. *L'Être et le Temps*. Paris: Gallimard, 1964.

———. *Introduction à la métaphysique*. Paris: Gallimard, 1967.

———. *Nietzsche*. Paris: Gallimard, 1971.

———. *Le Principe de la raison*. Paris: Gallimard, 1962.

———. *Qu'appelle-t-on penser?* Paris: PUF, 1973.

———. *Qu'est-ce qu'une chose?* Paris: Gallimard, 1971.

Henry, M. *La Barbarie*. Paris: Grasset, 1987.

———. *L'Essence de la manifestation*. 2 vols. Paris: PUF, 1963.

———. *Généalogie de la psychanalyse*. Paris: PUF, 1985.

———. *Philosophie et phénoménologie du corps*. Paris: PUF, 1965.

———. *Voir l'invisible*. Paris: Éditions F. Bourin, 1988.

Heschel, A. Y. *Les Bâtisseurs du temps*. Paris: Éditions de Minuit, 1969.

———. *Dieu en quête de l'homme*. Paris: Seuil, 1968.

———. *Theology of Ancient Judaism*. 2 vols. New York: Soncino Press, 1962.

———. *Le Tourment de la vérité*. Paris: Éditions du Cerf, 1976.

———. *The Torah from Heaven* . . . (in Hebrew). New York: Soncino Press, 1965.

Huber, G. "Une conversion rétroactive." *Confrontation*, no. 9 (1983).

———. "Le divan voyageur." *Le Bucentaure*, no. 9 (1986).

———. *L'Égypte ancienne dans la psychanalyse*. Paris: Maisonneuve et Larose, 1986.

———. *L'Énigme et le délire*. Paris: Osiris, 1988.

———. "Sur Lacan." In *Conclure, dit-il*. Paris: Galilée, 1981.

Huber, G., and M. Bydlowski. "Les nouvelles procréations entre biologie et psychanalyse." *Psychanalyse à l'Université* 12, no. 47 (1987).

Husserl, E. *Idées directrices pour une phénoménologie*. Paris: Gallimard, 1969.

———. *Méditations cartésiennes*. Paris: Vrin, 1953.

———. *L'Origine de la géométrie*. Paris: PUF, 1962.

Irigaray, L. *L'Éthique de la différence sexuelle*. Paris: Éditions de Minuit, 1984.

———. *Parler n'est jamais neutre*. Paris: Éditions de Minuit, 1985.

———. *Sexes et parentés*. Paris: Éditions de Minuit, 1987.

Jabès, E. *Aely*. Paris: Gallimard, 1972.

———. *Cahiers Obsidiane*, no. 5 (1982). Special issue devoted to E. Jabès.

———. *Ça suit son cours*. Paris: Fata Morgana, 1975.

———. *Dans la double dépendance du dit*. Paris: Fata Morgana, 1984.

———. *Du désert au livre*. Paris: Belfond, 1980.

———. *El, or the Last Book*. Translated by Rosemary Waldrop. Middletown, Conn.: Wesleyan University Press, 1984.

———. *Elya*. Paris: Gallimard, 1969.

———. *L'Ineffaçable, l'inaperçu*. Paris: Gallimard, 1980.

———. *Je bâtis ma demeure*. Paris: Gallimard, 1975.

———. *Le Livre des questions*. Paris: Gallimard, 1963.

———. *Le Livre des ressemblances*. Paris: Gallimard, 1976.

———. *Le Livre de Yukel*. Paris: Gallimard, 1964.

———. *Le Livre du dialogue*. Paris: Gallimard, 1984.

———. *Le Livre du partage*. Paris: Gallimard, 1987.

———. *Le Livre lu, en Israël*. Paris: Éditions Point Hors-Ligne, 1987.

———. *Le Parcours*. Paris: Gallimard, 1985.

———. *Le Petit Livre de la subversion hors de soupçon*. Paris: Gallimard, 1982.

———. *Récit*. Paris: Fata Morgana, 1981.

———. *Le Retour au livre*. Paris: Gallimard, 1965.

———. *Le Soupçon le désert*. Paris: Gallimard, 1978.

———. *Yaël*. Paris: Gallimard, 1967.

Jacques, F. *Dialogiques, recherches sur le dialogue*. Paris: PUF, 1979.

Jankélévitch, V. *Bergson*. Paris: PUF, 1959.

———. *Critique* 45, nos. 500–501 (1989). Issue devoted to V. Jankélévitch.

———. *Le Je-ne-sais-quoi et le presque-rien*. Paris: PUF, 1957.

———. *Quelque part dans l'inachevé*. Paris: Gallimard, 1978.

———. *Sources*. Paris: Seuil, 1984.

Jaspers, K. *Nietzsche*. Paris: Gallimard, 1950.

———. *Philosophie: orientation dans le monde, éclairement de l'existence metaphysique.* Translated by J. Hersch. Paris, Berlin: Springer Verlag, 1986.

Jauss, H. R. *Pour une herméneutique littéraire.* Paris: Gallimard, 1988.

Juranville, A. *Lacan et la philosophie.* Paris: PUF, 1984.

Kafka, F. *Oeuvres complètes.* Translated by A. Vialatte. Paris: Gallimard, 1984.

Kaplan, J. *Redaction of the Talmud.* Jerusalem, 1973.

Kaufmann, P. *L'Expérience émotionnelle de l'espace.* Paris: Vrin, 1969.

Koestler, A. *Le Cri d'Archimède.* Paris: Calmann-Lévy, 1965.

Kofman, S. *Lectures de Derrida.* Paris: Galilée, 1984.

———. *Nietzsche et la métaphore.* Paris: Payot, 1972.

———. *Paroles suffoquées.* Paris: Galilée, 1987.

———. *Pourquoi rit-on?* Paris: Galilée, 1986.

———. *Socrate(s).* Paris: Galilée, 1989.

Kojève, A. *Introduction à la lecture de Hegel.* Paris: Gallimard, 1947.

Kristeva, J. *Étrangers à nous-mêmes.* Paris: Fayard, 1988.

———. *Révolution du langage poétique.* Paris: Seuil, 1973.

———. *Sémeiotikè.* Paris: Seuil, 1969.

Kundera, M. *L'Art du roman.* Paris: Gallimard, 1986.

Lacan, J. *Écrits.* Paris: Seuil, 1966.

———. *L'Éthique de la psychanalyse.* Paris: Seuil, 1986.

Laporte, R. *Diagraphe,* nos. 18–19 (1979).

———. *Fugue.* Paris: Gallimard, 1970.

———. *Fugue, supplément.* Paris: Gallimard, 1973.

———. *Fugue 3.* Paris: Flammarion, 1976.

———. "Pourquoi?" In *Une voix de fin silence,* vol. 2. Paris: Gallimard, 1967.

———. *Quinze Variations sur un thème biographique.* Paris: Flammarion, 1975.

———. *La Veille.* Paris: Gallimard, 1963.

Lardreau, G. *Fictions philosophiques et science-fiction.* Arles: Actes Sud, 1988.

Laruelle, F. *Les Philosophies de la différence.* Paris: PUF, 1986.

———. "Projet d'une philosophie du Livre." *Cahiers Obsidiane,* no. 5 (1982).

Lefort, C. *Essais sur le politique, XIX–XXe siècle.* Paris: Seuil, 1986.

———. *Un homme en trop.* Paris: Seuil, 1986.

———. *L'Invention démocratique. Des limites de la domination totalitaire.* Paris: Fayard, 1981.

Legendre, P. *L'Amour du censeur.* Paris: Seuil, 1974.

———. *Jouir du pouvoir.* Paris: Éditions de Minuit, 1976.

———. *Leçons II. L'Empire de la vérité.* Paris: Fayard, 1983.

———. *Leçons IV. L'Inestimable Objet de la transmission.* Paris: Fayard, 1985.

———. *Leçons VII. Le Désir politique de Dieu.* Paris: Fayard, 1989.

———. *La Passion d'être autre. Étude pour la danse.* Paris: Seuil, 1978.

Leibowitz, N. *Studies in Bamidbar.* Jerusalem, 1980.

Leroi-Gourhan, A. *Le Geste et la parole.* 2 vols. Paris: Albin Michel, 1964, 1965.

Lévesque, C. *L'Étrangeté du texte. Essai sur Nietzsche, Freud, Blanchot et Derrida.* Paris: UGE, 1978.

Lévinas, E. *A l'heure des nations*. Paris: Éditions de Minuit, 1988.

——. *L'Au-delà du verset*. Paris: Éditions de Minuit, 1982.

——. *Cahiers Emmanuel Lévinas*. Paris: Verdier, 1984.

——. *De Dieu qui vient à l'idée*. Paris: Vrin, 1982.

——. *De l'évasion*. Paris: Fata Morgana, 1982.

——. *De l'existence à l'existant*. Paris: Vrin, 1947.

——. *Difficile liberté*. Paris: Albin Michel, 1976.

——. *Du sacré au saint*. Paris: Éditions de Minuit, 1977.

——. *En découvrant l'existence avec Husserl et Heidegger*. Paris: Vrin, 1974.

——. *Entre nous. Essais sur le penser-à-l'autre*. Paris: Grasset, 1991.

——. *Éthique et Infini*. Paris: Fayard, 1982.

——. "Exégèse et culture." *Cahiers du nouveau commerce*, no. 55 (Spring 1983).

——. *Hors sujet*. Paris: Fata Morgana, 1987.

——. *Humanisme de l'autre homme*. Paris: Fata Morgana, 1972.

——. *Noms propres*. Paris: Fata Morgana, 1975.

——. *Otherwise Than Being or Beyond Essence*. Translated by Alphonso Lingis. The Hague: Nijhoff, 1981.

——. "Pour une place dans la Bible." In Colloque des intellectuels juifs de langue française, *La Bible au présent*. Paris: Gallimard, 1982.

——. *Quatre Lectures talmudiques*. Paris: Éditions de Minuit, 1968.

——. *Sur Maurice Blanchot*. Paris: Fata Morgana, 1975.

——. *Le Temps et l'Autre*. Paris: Fata Morgana, 1979.

——. *Totality and Infinity: An Essay on Exteriority*. Translated by Alphonso Lingis. Pittsburgh: Duquesne University Press, 1988.

——. *Transcendance et intelligibilité*. Paris: Labor et Fides, 1982.

Lévy, B. *Le Logos et la lettre*. Paris: Verdier, 1988.

——. *Le Nom de l'homme*. Paris: Verdier, 1984.

Lévy, B.-H. *La Barbarie à visage humain*. Paris: Grasset, 1977.

——. *Éloge des intellectuels*. Paris: Grasset, 1987.

——. *L'Idéologie française*. Paris: Grasset, 1981.

——. *Le Testament de Dieu*. Paris: Grasset, 1979.

Lieberman, S. *Hellenism in Jewish Palestine*. New York: The Jewish Theological Seminary, 1962.

Lindon, J. *Jonas*. Paris: Éditions de Minuit, 1955.

Lipovetsky, G. *L'Empire de l'éphémère*. Paris: Gallimard, 1987.

——. *L'Ère du vide*. Paris: Gallimard, 1983.

Loraux, M. "Les bénéfices de l'autochtonie." In "La transmission." *Le Genre humain*, nos. 3–4 (1982).

——. "Blessures de virilité." In "Le masculin," *Le Genre humain*. Paris: Complexe, 1984.

——. "De l'amnistie et de son contraire." In *L'Usage de l'oubli*. Paris: Seuil, 1988.

——. *Les Enfants d'Athéna. Idées athéniennes sur la citoyenneté et la division des sexes*. Paris: La Découverte, 1984.

Lyotard, J.-F. *La Condition post-moderne*. Paris: Éditions de Minuit, 1979.

——. *Le Différend*. Paris: Éditions de Minuit, 1983.

——. *Économie libidinale*. Paris: Éditions de Minuit, 1974.

——. *Figure forclose, L'écrit du temps*. Paris: Éditions de Minuit, 1984.

——. *Heidegger et les Juifs*. Paris: Galilée, 1988.

Lyotard, J.-F., and J.-L. Thébaud. *Au juste*. Paris: C. Bougois, 1979.

McLuhan, M. *La Galaxie Gutenberg. La genèse de l'homme typographique*. Paris: Gallimard, 1977.

Maggiori, R. *De la convivance*. Paris: Fayard, 1985.

Maggiori, R., and C. Delacampagne. *Philosopher*. 3d ed. Paris: Fayard, 1984.

Maggiori, R., et al. *Lire Gramsci*. Paris: Éditions universitaires, 1973.

Maïmonide. *Le Guide des égarés*. 3 vols. Paris: Maisonneuve, 1959.

Malka, S. *Lire Lévinas*. Paris: Éditions du Cerf, 1984.

Malka, V., and André Néher. *Le Dur Bonheur d'être juif*. Paris: Le Centurion, 1978.

Malka, V., et al. *Le Judaïsme hier-demain*. Paris: Buchet-Chastel, 1977.

Mallarmé, S. *Le "Livre" de Mallarmé*. Edited by J. Scherer. Paris: Gallimard, 1957.

Mandel, A. *Un apprentissage hassidique*. Paris: Mazarine, 1982.

——. *Les Cent Portes*. Paris: Flammarion.

——. *Le Messie est en retard*. Paris: Desclée de Brouwer, 1988.

——. *Nous autres, juifs*. Paris: Hachette-Littérature, 1978.

——. *Le Périple*. Paris: Fayard, 1972.

——. *Le Petit Livre de la sagesse populaire juive*. Paris: Albin Michel, 1963.

——. *La Vie quotidienne des juifs hassidiques*. Paris: Hachette-Littérature, 1974.

——. *La Voie de hassidisme*. Paris: Calmann-Lévy, 1963.

Marcuse, H. *Culture et Société*. Paris: Éditions de Minuit, 1970.

——. *Éros et Civilisation*. Paris: Éditions de Minuit, 1963.

——. *L'Homme unidimensionnel*. Paris: Éditions de Minuit, 1968.

——. *L'Ontologie de Hegel*. Paris: Éditions de Minuit, 1972.

——. *Raison et Révolution*. Paris: Éditions de Minuit, 1968.

——. *Vers la libération*. Paris: Éditions de Minuit, 1969.

Marion, J.-L. *Dieu sans l'être*. Paris: Fayard, 1982.

——. *L'Idole et la distance*. Paris: Grasset, 1977.

Merleau-Ponty, M. *Phenomenology of Perception*. Translated by Colin Smith. London: Routledge and Kegan Paul, 1962.

——. *La Prose du monde*. Paris: Gallimard, 1969.

——. *Signes*. Paris: Gallimard, 1960.

——. *Le Visible et l'invisible*. Paris: Gallimard, 1964.

Meschonnic, H. *Les Cinq Rouleaux*. Paris: Gallimard, 1970.

——. *Critique du rythme*. Paris: Verdier, 1983.

——. *Jona*. Paris: Gallimard, 1985.

——. "Le Langage dans la Bible." In *La Bible au présent*. Paris: Gallimard, 1982.

——. *Modernité, modernité*. Paris: Verdier, 1988.

Meyer, M. *De la problématologie*. Paris: L.A.F., 1994.

Misrahi, R. *Les Actes de la joie; fonder, aimer, agir*. Paris: PUF, 1987.

——. *La Condition réflexive de l'homme juif*. Paris: Julliard, 1963.

———. *Construction d'un château*. Paris: Seuil, 1981.

———. *Le Désir et la Réflexion dans la philosophie de Spinoza*. Paris: Gordon and Breach, 1972.

———. *Éthique, politique et bonheur*. Paris: Seuil, 1983.

———. *Lumière, commencement, liberté*. Paris: Plon, 1969.

———. *Marx et la Question juive*. Paris: Gallimard, 1972.

———. *Spinoza*. Paris: Seghers, 1964.

———. "Spinoza." Presentation and translation of the correspondence. In *Oeuvres complètes*. Paris: Gallimard, 1954.

Mongin, O. "Comment juger?" In *Emmanuel Lévinas*. Paris: Les Cahiers de la nuit surveillée, 1984.

———. "Entrer dans le XXe siècle. La guerre et ses arrière-pensées." In *Franz Rosenzweig*. Paris: Les Cahiers de la nuit surveillée, 1982.

———. "Face à l'éclipse du récit." *Espirt*, nos. 8–9 (August–September 1986).

Mopsik, C. *La Cabale*. Paris: Éditions J. Grancher, 1988.

———. *Lettre sur la sainteté. Le Secret de la relation entre l'homme et la femme dans la Cabale, étude préliminaire, traduction et annotations*. Paris: Verdier, 1986.

———. *Le Palmier de Débora (de Rabbi Moïse Cordovero), introduction, traduction et annotations*. Paris: Verdier, 1985.

———. *Le Zohar, introduction, traduction et annotations*. 3 vols. Paris: Verdier, 1981, 1984, 1991.

———. *Le Zohar sur le livre de Ruth, introduction, traduction et annotations*. Paris: Verdier, 1987.

Morin, E. *La Connaissance de la connaissance*. Paris: Seuil, 1986.

———. *La Nature de la nature*. Paris: Seuil, 1977.

———. *Le Paradigme perdu: la nature humaine*. Paris: Seuil, 1973.

———. *Science avec conscience*. Paris: Fayard, 1982.

———. *La Vie de la vie*. Paris: Seuil, 1980.

Moses, S. *L'Ange de l'histoire. Rosenzweig, Benjamin et Scholem*. Paris: Seuil, 1992.

———. "La critique de la totalité dans la philosophie de Franz Rosenzweig." *Les Études philosophiques*, no. 3 (1976).

———. "Franz Rosenzweig, L'étoile de la Rédemption." *Le Débat*, no. 13 (June 1981).

———. "La pointe d'Enoch. L'art et l'idole selon les sources juives." In *Idoles*. Paris: Denoël, 1985.

———. "Politique et religion chez Franz Rosenzweig." In *Politique et religion*. Actes du XXe Colloque des intellectuels juifs de langue française. Paris: Gallimard, 1982.

———. "Révélation et dialogue chez Franz Rosenzweig." *Revue des sciences philosophiques et théologiques* 61 (1977).

———. *Système et révélation. La philosophie de Franz Rosenzweig*. Paris: Seuil, 1982.

Nancy, J.-L. *L'Expérience de la liberté*. Paris: Galilée, 1988.

———. *L'Oubli de la philosophie*. Paris: Galilée, 1986.

———. *Le Partage des voix*. Paris: Galilée, 1982.

Naouri, A. "La bouche de l'enfant." *Psychosomatique*, no. 15 (1988).

———. *L'Enfant porté*. Paris: Seuil, 1982.

———. *Parier sur l'enfant*. Paris: Seuil, 1988.

———. *Une place pour le père*. Paris: Seuil, 1985.

Néher, A. *Amos, contribution à l'étude du prophétisme*. Paris: Vrin, 1980.

———. *Clefs pour le judaïsme*. Paris: Seghers, 1977.

———. *L'Essence du prophétisme*. Paris: Calmann-Lévy, 1983.

———. *L'Exil de la parole. Du silence biblique au silence d'Auschwitz*. Paris: Seuil, 1970.

———. *L'Existence juive, solitude et affrontements*. Paris: Seuil, 1962.

———. *Ils ont refait leur âme*. Paris: Stock, 1979.

———. *Jérémie*. Paris: Stock, 1980.

———. *Moïse et la vocation juive*. Paris: Seuil, 1980.

———. *Notes sur Qohélét, l'Ecclésiaste*. Paris: Éditions de Minuit, 1951.

———. *Le Puits de l'exil, la théologie dialectique du Maharal de Prague*. Paris: Albin Michel, 1966.

———. *Regards sur la tradition*. Paris: Bibliophane, 1989.

Néher, A. E. Amado Lévy-Valensi, and J. Halpérin. *La Conscience juive*. Actes des Colloques d'intellectuels juifs de langue française. 4 vols. Paris: PUF, 1963–1972.

Néher, A., R. Aron, and V. Malka. *Le Judaïsme, hier-demain*. Paris: Buchet-Chastel, 1977.

Néher, A., A. Epstein, and E. Sebban. *Étincelles*. Paris: Albin Michel, 1970.

Néher, A., and V. Malka. *Le Dur Bonheur d'être juif*. Paris: Le Centurion, 1978.

Néher, A., and Renée Néher. *Histoire biblique du peuple d'Israël*. Paris: Maisonneuve, 1982.

Ouaknin, J. *Être juif*. Paris: Bibliophane, 1989.

Patočka, J. *La Crise du sens*. Vol. 1, *Comte, Masaryk, Husserl*. Vol. 2, *Masaryk et l'action*. Brussels: Ouisa, 1985, 1986.

———. *Essais hérétiques sur la philosophie de l'Histoire*. Paris: Verdier, 1981.

———. *Le Monde naturel comme problème philosophique*. The Hague: Nijhoff, 1976.

———. *Le Monde naturel et le mouvement de l'existence humaine*. Dordrecht, Boston, London: Kluwer Academic Publishers.

———. *Platon et l'Europe*. Paris: Verdier, 1973.

———. *Qu'est-ce que la phénoménologie?* Paris: Millon, 1989.

Petitdemange, G. "Adorno, la dissonance." *Exercices de la patience*, nos. 3–4 (1982).

———. "L'écriture du désastre." *Exercices de la patience*, no. 2 (1981).

———. "E. Lévinas et la politique." *Projets* (1978).

———. "E. Lévinas ou la question d'autrui." *Études* (1972).

———. "Éthique et transcendance: sur les chemins d'Emmanuel Lévinas." *Recherches de sciences religieuses* 64, no. 1 (1976).

———. "Hegel et Rosenzweig, la différence se faisant." *Les Cahiers de la nuit surveillée*, no. 1 (1982).

———. "Introduction à la théologie athée de Franz Rosenzweig." *Recherches de science religieuse* 74, no. 4 (1986).

———. *Liberté et sacrifice. Essai politique.* Paris: Millon, 1990.

———. "Philosophie et violence." In *Lévinas, autrement que savoir.* Paris: Osiris, 1988.

———. "L'un ou l'autre, la querelle de l'ontologie Heidegger-Lévinas." *Les Cahiers de la nuit surveillée,* no. 3 (1984).

Piekarz, M. *Braslav Hassidism.* Mossad Bialik, 1972.

Popper, K. *Conjectures et réfutations.* Paris: Payot, 1985.

———. *La Découverte de la logique scientifique.* Paris: Payot, 1973.

———. *La Société ouverte et ses ennemis.* Vol. 1, *L'ascendant de Platon.* Vol. 2, *Hegel et Marx.* Paris: Seuil, 1979.

Potok, C. *L'Élu.* Paris: Calmann-Lévy, 1987.

Rachline, F. *De Zéro à epsilon. Vers une nouvelle théorie de l'économie.* Paris: First, 1991.

Raphaël, F. "L'idéologie de la 'nouvelle droite.'" In *La Bible au présent.* Paris: Gallimard, 1982.

———. "Les Juifs en France: interrogations et exigences politiques." In *Politique et religion.* Paris: Gallimard, 1981.

Ratsbi, I. *The Extraordinary Letters of the Torah.* Jerusalem, 1978.

Renaut, A. *L'Ère de l'individu.* Paris: Gallimard, 1989.

———. *Le Système du droit.* Paris: PUF, 1986.

Richir, M. *Au-delà du renversement copernicien. La question de la phénoménologie et son fondement.* The Hague: Nijhoff, 1976.

———. *Phénomènes, temps et être. Ontologie et phénoménologie.* Paris: Millon, 1987.

———. *Phénoménologie et Institution symbolique.* Paris: Millon, 1988.

Ricoeur, P. *A l'école de la phénoménologie.* Paris: Vrin, 1986.

———. *Le Conflit des interprétations.* Paris: Seuil, 1969.

———. *De l'interprétation. Essai sur Freud.* Paris: Seuil, 1965.

———. *Du texte à l'action. Essai d'herméneutique II.* Paris: Seuil, 1986.

———. "L'identité narrative." *Espirit,* nos. 7–8 (1988). Issue devoted to P. Ricoeur.

———. *Lectures II. La contrée des philosophes.* Paris: Seuil, 1992.

———. *Les Métamophoses de la raison herméneutique.* Conference proceedings. Under the direction of Jean Greisch and Richard Kearney. Paris: Le Cerf, 1991.

———. *La Métaphore vive.* Paris: Seuil, 1975.

———. *Soi-même comme un autre.* Paris: Seuil, 1990.

———. *Temps et Récit.* 3 vols. Paris: Seuil, 1983, 1984, 1985.

———. *"Tempts et récit" de Paul Ricoeur en débat.* Conference proceedings. Paris: Le Cerf, 1990.

Rolland, J. "Penser au-delà." *Exercices de la patience,* no. 1 (1980).

———. "Pour une approche de la question du neutre." *Exercices de la patience,* no. 2 (1981).

———. *Présentation et annotation de* De l'évasion *d'E. Lévinas.* Paris: Fata Morgana, 1982.

Rolland, J., et al. *La Vérité nomade. Introduction à Emmanuel Lévinas*. Paris: La Découverte, 1984.

Rosalato, G. *Éléments de l'interprétation*. Paris: Gallimard, 1985.

———. *Essais sur le symbolique*. Paris: Gallimard, 1969.

———. *La Relation d'inconnu*. Paris: Gallimard, 1978.

———. *Le Sacrifice*. Paris: PUF, 1987.

Rosenzweig, F. *L'Étoile de la rédemption*. Paris: Seuil, 1982.

Rosset, C. *L'Anti-nature*. Paris: PUF, 1973.

———. *La Force majeur*. Paris: Minuit, 1983.

———. *Logique du pire*. Paris: PUF, 1971.

———. *L'Objet singulier*. Paris: Éditions de Minuit, 1979.

———. *Le Philosophe et les Sortilèges*. Paris: Éditions de Minuit, 1985.

———. *Le Principe de cruauté*. Paris: Éditions de Minuit, 1988.

———. *Le Réel et son double*. Paris: Gallimard, 1976.

———. *Le Réel. Traité de l'idiotie*. Paris: Éditions de Minuit, 1977.

Roviello, A. M. *Sens commun et modernité chez Hannah Arendt*. Brussels: Ousia, 1987.

Safran, A. *La Cabale*. Paris: Payot, 1983.

Sarte, J.-P. *L'Être et le Néant*. Paris: Gallimard, 1945.

———. *L'Existentialisme est un humanisme*. Paris: Nagel, 1970.

Saussure, F. *Cours de linguistique générale*. Paris: Payot, 1980.

Scholem, G. *Du frankisme au jacobinisme. La vie de Moses Dobruska alias Franz Thomas von Schonfeld alias Julius Frey*. Paris: Seuil, 1981.

———. *Les Grands Courants de la mystique juive*. Translated by M. Davy. Paris: Payot, 1950.

———. *La Kabbale et sa symbolique*. Paris: Payot, 1980.

———. *Le Messianisme juif. Essais sur la spiritualité du judïsme*. Translated by B. Dupuy. Paris: Calmann-Lévy, 1974.

———. *Le Nom et les Symboles de Dieu dans la mystique juive*. Paris: Éditions du Cerf, 1983.

———. *Les Origines de la Cabale*. Paris: Aubier-Montaigne, 1966.

———. *Sabbataï Tsevi. Le Messie mystique*. Paris: Verdier, 1983

Schopenhauer, A. *Le Monde comme volonté et comme représentation*. Translated by A. Burdeau. Paris: PUF, 1989.

Sibony, D. *L'Amour inconscient. Au-delà du principe de séduction*. Paris: Grasset, 1983.

———. *L'Autre incastrable*. Paris: Seuil, 1978.

———. *Avec Shakespeare*. Paris: Grasset, 1988.

———. *Du vécu et de l'invivable: psychopathologie du quotidien*. Paris: Albin Michel, 1991.

———. *Écrits sur le racisme*. Paris: C. Bourgois, 1988.

———. *Entre dire et faire. Penser la technique*. Paris: Grasset, 1989.

———. *Le Féminin et la séduction*. Paris: Le Livre de poche, 1987.

———. *Le Groupe inconscient. Le lien et la peur*. Paris: C. Bourgois, 1980.

———. *La Haine du désir*. Paris: C. Bourgois, 1978.

———. *Jouissance du dire. Nouveaux essais sur une transmission d'inconscient*. Paris: Grasset, 1985.

———. *La Juive. Une transmission d'inconscient*. Paris: Grasset, 1983.

———. *Le Nom et le Corps*. Paris: Seuil, 1974.

———. *Perversions*. Paris: Grasset, 1987.

———. *Le Peuple psy*. Paris: Balland, 1993.

———. *Les Trois Monothéismes*. Paris: Seuil, 1992.

Soloweichik, Y. D. *L'Homme de la Halakha*. Jerusalem: W.Z.O., 1979.

Starobinski, J. *Les Mots sous les mots*. Paris: Gallimard, 1971.

Steiner, G. *Martin Heidegger*. Paris: Albin Michel, 1981.

———. *Le Sens du sens*. Paris: Vrin, 1988.

Stengers, I., et al. *La Nouvelle Alliance*. Paris: Gallimard, 1979.

Straus, E. *Du sens des sens*. Paris: Millon, 1989.

Taylor, M. C. *Errance. Lecture de Jacques Derrida*. Paris: Éditions du Cerf, 1985.

Todorov, T. *Mikhaïl Bakhtine, le principe dialogique*. Paris: Seuil, 1981.

Tollet, D. *Histoire des juifs de Pologne de XVIe siècle à nos jours*. Paris: PUF, 1992.

Tomatis, A. *L'Oreille et le langage*. New ed. Paris: Seuil, 1991.

———. *Pourquoi Mozart?* Paris: Fixot, 1991.

Trigano, S. *La Demeure oubliée*. Paris: Lieu Commun, 1984.

———. "Le Livre au coeur de l'être." Preface to *L'Epître des sept voiles* by Aboulafia. Paris: Éditions de l'Éclat, 1985.

———. *La Nouvelle Question juive*. Paris: Gallimard, 1979.

———. *Le Récit de la disparue*. Paris: Gallimard, 1977.

Vattimo, G. *Les Aventures de la différence*. Paris: Éditions de Minuit, 1985.

Viderman, S. *Le Céleste et le Sublunaire*. Paris: PUF, 1977.

———. *La Construction de l'espace analytique*. Paris: Denoël, 1970.

———. *Le Disséminaire*. Paris: PUF, 1987.

Vigée, C. *L'Extase et l'errance*. Paris: Grasset, 1982.

———. *La Faille du regard*. Paris: Flammarion, 1988.

———. *Pâque de la parole*. Paris: Flammarion, 1983.

———. *Le Parfum et la Cendre*. Paris: Grasset, 1984.

Wahl, J. *Études kierkegaardiennes*. Paris: Vrin, 1974.

Wahlens, A. de. *Une philosophie de l'ambiguïté*. Louvain: Nauwelaerts, 1971.

———. *La Philosophie de Martin Heidegger*. Louvain: Nauwelaerts, 1971.

Weil, G. *Initiation à la Massora*. Leiden: E. J. Brill, 1964.

Weil, G. E., P. Rivière, and M. Serfaty. *Concordance de la Cantilation de Pentateuque et des cinq Mégillot*. Paris: Éditions du C.N.R.S., 1978.

Wiesel, E. *Célébration biblique*. Paris: Seuil, 1975.

———. *Célébration hassidique*. Paris: Seuil, 1972.

———. *Contre la mélancolie*. Paris: Seuil, 1982.

———. *Un juif aujourd'hui*. Paris: Seuil, 1977.

———. *La Nuit*. Paris: Éditions de Minuit, 1958.

———. *Paroles d'étranger*. Paris: Seuil, 1984.

Weiss, J. *Studies in Braslav Hassidism*. Mossad Bialik, 1974.

Yerushalmi, Y. H. *Zakhor. Histoire juive et mémoire*. Paris: La Découverte, 1984.

Zagdanski, S. *L'Impureté de Dieu*. Paris: Éd. du Félin, 1991.

Zarader, M. *La Dette impensée. Heidegger et l'héritage hébraïque.* Paris: Seuil, 1990.

———. *Heidegger et les paroles de l'origine.* Paris: Vrin, 1986.

Works in Hebrew

Commentaries on the Torah

Abravanel al ha-Torah, 3 vols.

Ba'al ha-Turim, by Yaacov ben Asher, Feldhoeim, 1971, 1 vol.

Emek davar, R. Zvi, Naftali, Berlin, 5 vols.

Gur Aryeh, Maharal of Prague, commentary on Rashi, 5 vols.

Hirsh, Shimshon Rafael, in English and in German, 5 vols.; in Hebrew, 3 vols.

Kedushai Levi, R. L. Isaac of Berdichev, 1 vol.

Leibowitz, Nehama, *Bereshit-Shemot* (commentaries), Jerusalem.

Mekhilta of Rabbi Ishmael.

Midrash ha-Gadol, M. Kook, 5 vols.

Midrash Rabbah, Levi-Epstein ed., 5 vols.

Nahmanides, Introduction to the Pentateuch, M. Kook, 1959.

Noah Elimelekh, Mossad harav Kook, 1978, 2 vols.

Peri Tsaddik, Rabbi Zadok ha-Kohen.

Rabbenu Behayeh, M. Kook, 1967, 2 vols.

Rambam al ha-Torah, M. Kook, 1960, 2 vols.

Sefat Emet, R. Alter Migur, 5 vols.

Shem Mishmuel, Rabbi of Sokhochov, 8 vols.

Sifrei, *Bamidbar* and *Devarim*, Horowitz ed., Jerusalem, Wahrman Books, 1966.

Torah Kohanim.

Torah Shlemah, Menahem Kacher, rabbinical anthology, 32 vols.

Torah Temimah, R.B.L., Epstein, 5 vols.

Tzafnat Paneah, R. Yossef Rosen, edited by R. M. Kacher, 6 vols.

Babylonian Talmud

Albeck, M. Kook, 1952.

Kakati, Hekhal Shlomo ed., Jerusalem, 1977, 12 vols.

Mishnah, usual eds.

Talmud Babli, Vilna ed., 1880, 20 vols.; in German, translated by L. Golschmidt, Berlin, 1925, 9 vols.; in English directed by I. Epstein, Soncino, 1948, 34 vols.; Steinsaltz ed.: several tractates (1967–1984), publication in process of completion.

Commentaries on the Talmud

Ben Ish Hai, *Ben Jehoyada*, 3 vols.

Ein Ya'akov, Vilna ed., 1894, 3 vols.

Gaon of Vilna, commentary on the Talmudic *Haggadot*.

Maharal of Prague, commentary on the Talmudic *Haggadot*.

Maharsha, in the usual eds.

Meiri, complete ed., 12 vols.

Rashi, in the usual eds.

Tosafot, in the usual eds.

Works of Halakhah
Maimonides, *Yad Hahazakah, Mishneh Torah*, M. Kook, 1954, 20 vols.
Mekor Hayyim, 5 vols.
Sedei Hemed, 10 vols.
Shulkhan Arukh, classical ed.
Tur Shulkhan Arukh, classical ed.

Works of the Cabala, of Hasidism, and of Jewish Thought
Ben Yissakhar, 1868.
Kol ha-Nevuah, Rabbi David Ha-Kohen, M. Kook, 1978.
Likkutei Amarim, *Tania*, 1 vol.
Likkutei Halakhot, R. Nahman of Bratslav, 3 vols.
Likkutei Moharan, R. N. of Bratslav, 3 vols.
Pardes Rimonim, by R. M. Cordovero, 2 vols.
Sefer ha-Bahir, M. Kook ed., 1964.
Sefer Yetzirah, 1 vol.
Sheni Luho ha-Berit, Amsterdam, 1698.
Shi'ur Komah, by R. M. Cordovero, 1 vol.
Tikkunei Zohar, M. Kook ed., 1 vol.; *Hassulam* ed., 2 vols., incomplete; with
   commentary by Gaon of Vilna, 1 vol.
Works of Rav Kook, *Orot Ha-Kodesh*, 3 vols.
Works of Rabi Zadok ha-Kohen, in particular: *Mahashavot Ha-Rutz*.
Zohar, M. Kook ed., 1964, 3 vols.

Concordances, Dictionaries, Encyclopedias
Mandelkern, S. *Veteris Testamenti hebraïcae atque Chaldaïcae Concordantiae.*
   Leipzig: Veit et comp., 1896.
Talmudic Concordance, Y. Kossofsky, 40 vols.
Zoharic Concordance, 4 vols. (*Otsar ha-Zohar*).
Dictionaries: Hebrew-French and French-Hebrew by M. Cohn, Larousse, 2
   vols.; Aramaic-English, M. Jastrow, Soncino, 1 vol.
Encyclopaedia Judaica (in English), Jerusalem, 1973, 16 vols.

Index

About the Author

Marc-Alain Ouaknin, an Associate Professor in the Department of Comparative Literature at the University of Bar-Ilan in Israel, is a rabbi and has a doctorate in philosophy. He teaches Talmudic philosophy and directs the Center of Jewish Research and Studies in Paris.